Criminal Appeals Handbook

3rd edition

Criminal Appeals Handbook

3rd edition

Farrhat Arshad KC
Barrister, Doughty Street Chambers

Kate O'Raghallaigh
Barrister, Doughty Street Chambers

Gregory Stewart
Solicitor and Higher Courts' Advocate,
GT Stewart Solicitors & Advocates

Bloomsbury Professional

LONDON • DUBLIN • EDINBURGH • NEW YORK • NEW DELHI • SYDNEY

BLOOMSBURY PROFESSIONAL

Bloomsbury Publishing Plc
50 Bedford Square, London, WC1B 3DP, UK
1385 Broadway, New York, 10018, USA

Bloomsbury Publishing Ireland Ltd
29 Earlsfort Terrace, Dublin 2, D02 AY28, Ireland

First published in Great Britain 2026

1

British Library Cataloguing-in-Publication Data

A catalogue record for this book is available from the British Library.

ISBN: PB: 978 1 52653 225 1
Epdf: 978 1 52653 227 5
Epub: 978 1 52653 226 8

Typeset by Evolution Design and Digital (Kent)
Printed and bound by TJ Books, Padstow, Cornwall

MIX
Paper | Supporting responsible forestry
FSC® C013056

Foreword

All provincial practitioners will recognise what we used to call 'the Milton Keynes effect'. As you travel rapidly past that city on the train to London, you read again your grounds of appeal and realise that what you thought brilliant 12 months ago, and what somehow got past the single judge, is actually virtually unarguable. The sinking feeling of alarm is mitigated only by the thought that it won't take all that long, and you can recover afterwards with a restoring lunch. The sensation will be familiar to London practitioners, although their discovery may take place on a bus.

The Court of Appeal Criminal Division is an unusual part of the justice system. It handles a very large number of cases and all of them matter. Many of its decisions attract a great deal of public comment and scrutiny. The advocates who present the cases on paper and orally may not appear there regularly and will often not have the practice of the court at their fingertips as they do when working in the Crown Court or the Magistrates' Court. They often do not have an instructing solicitor to liaise with the court and negotiate the procedural hurdles of lodging grounds, bundles of documents, authorities and skeleton arguments. They will often have to overcome obstacles in accessing their client to give advice and take instructions. All of this requires an awareness of how the Registrar and the Criminal Appeal Office operates.

Appearing in the Court of Appeal is alarming for the young advocate and the frisson of concern never quite disappears however often you have been there and however serious the cases you have done. I hope that this is not because the judges are alarming or concerning, but because the work is difficult and the outcomes are important. The cases are dealt with quite quickly, and the judges will have read the papers. Advocacy in these circumstances is inevitably a demanding job.

The best reassurance for the advocates heading their way on the early train past Milton Keynes is the knowledge that everything has been properly prepared according to the rules and that, even if they don't agree with the argument, the court cannot fault the way it is presented. This is where this book will be of particular value.

The authors have set out practical and accessible advice on all aspects of the work of the court. They have done this in a way which combines practical assistance and succinct but perceptive legal analysis. I am very grateful to them for this which will contribute to the smooth functioning of the court, and make working there more rewarding for practitioners. It is a work which will be of value to all whose work involves the Court of Appeal Criminal Division, whether they are appearing there for the first time or presiding over the court.

Lord Justice Edis
Vice-President of the Court of Appeal, Criminal Division

Preface

Appealing against a conviction or a sentence that was imposed in the Crown Court can be a daunting business. There is a striking contrast to be found between the ease with which an appeal can be brought against a decision of the Magistrates' Court and the difficulties and uncertainties involved in appealing from the Crown Court.

A defendant who wishes to appeal against a conviction or a sentence that was imposed in the Magistrates' Court simply must lodge a notice of appeal. They are then entitled to a complete re-hearing in the Crown Court. In contrast, appealing a conviction or sentence that was imposed in the Crown Court, which is always to the Court of Appeal, requires an application to be made for leave to the Court of Appeal. If leave is granted the appellant has the opportunity to persuade the Court to allow the appeal. That opportunity is a narrow one. It often consists of a short hearing before a Court that, having read the papers, may already have formed a preliminary view of the merits of the case.

This is a process that poses particular challenges for disgruntled defendants and their lawyers. Defendants who have acclimatised themselves to the pace and formality of the Crown Court find themselves having to adjust to new and very different proceedings; there is a new set of legal terms to grapple with, further delays, a process from which they seem to be excluded, and that may culminate in a hearing at which trials that may have lasted for weeks are considered in minutes, and matters that seemed so crucial at trial are barely mentioned.

Their lawyers must seek to persuade a Court in which the swift, sometimes brutal dispatch of business and a ruthless focus on essentials replaces the comparatively relaxed pace of life in the Crown Court. It requires a different approach and even a different set of skills in order to achieve the best result for their clients.

The aim of this book is to assist those who seek to challenge a conviction or sentence, or pre-trial order, which was imposed in the Crown Court, to obtain leave and go on and secure a successful outcome. The statistics are not promising but this book tries to help beat the odds by ensuring procedural errors are avoided and the paperwork is in an optimal state to do that. It is intended for defence lawyers but also for defendants and their families who want a better understanding of the appeal process. For those who choose to represent themselves we hope the book points them in the right direction, but it is not our intention to encourage anyone to do so. The need for effective legal representation is never more important than at the appeal stage. That effectiveness can only be increased when clients understand what they should expect of their lawyers and both lawyers and clients appreciate and can focus on the questions that will be of importance to the Court. The chapter on funding may assist those who need representation to get it.

As convictions and sentences that have been imposed by the Crown Court can only be appealed to the Court of Appeal, the focus of this book is largely on appealing to that Court. Chapter 1 provides a brief introduction to the Court, its judges, constitution, rules and administration. Chapter 2 considers the sources of law that it applies. Chapters 3 and 4 consider the tests for appeal, potential grounds and the powers of the Court in relation to conviction and sentence (including confiscation), respectively.

Chapters 5 to 8 then address the practicalities of appealing. Chapter 5 considers the important but often overlooked question of defence investigations, it can be the source of the new material that provides the basis for an appeal. We are greatly indebted to Emily Bolton and James Burley at Appeal for their invaluable contributions based on their acclaimed work exposing miscarriages of justice. Chapter 6 deals with the practicalities of preparing the case; applying for leave, renewal of such applications and extensions of time, whilst Chapter 7 considers preparation for hearings. Chapter 8 deals with applying for legal aid to cover legal advice or representation whilst touching on the other ways of obtaining legal assistance, through private instruction, innocence projects and charities.

One of the most important features of the appeals process is the Criminal Cases Review Commission, which has the power to refer cases back to the Court of Appeal that have previously been considered and refused. Chapter 9 focuses on applying to the Commission whilst Chapter 10 sets out the procedure for appealing from the Court of Appeal to the Supreme Court.

Although a decision of the Court of Appeal or, very occasionally, the Supreme Court, will conclude the domestic appeal process, it need not always exhaust the search for justice. If a defendant's rights have been violated, he may apply for the case to be heard by the European Court of Human Rights. Chapter 11 addresses when and how such an application can be made and what can be achieved by doing so. We have concluded with three chapters on subjects with which the defence practitioner will occasionally have to grapple. Chapter 12 deals with interlocutory appeals. Chapter 13 addresses the issue of responding to prosecution appeals against sentence (or 'Attorney General's references') and against acquittal. Chapter 14 deals with appeals against certain findings and orders made in the Crown Court against defendants who are found to be suffering from serious mental disorders. Chapter 15 is a new chapter addressing bespoke areas that merit special attention: women; children; and the victims of trafficking, now better known as modern slavery.

Since the last edition of this book in 2019, there has been an overhaul of the Practice Directions in 2023 and the Procedure Rules in 2025. The post McCook world has crystalised to deliver a cultural change in the expectations of the Court. Failure to grasp the new landscape can result in a fall at the first hurdle. The court will expect applicants and their lawyers to be fully informed in all relevant matters including tactical decisions at the trial. If representation has changed, then an early waiver will be requested. These reforms should weed out unmeritorious applications. Those cases often reflected an understandable desire to reverse what went before, without a legal basis for doing so even when the outcome was unexpected or seemingly unjust. However, in theory, the reforms should filter out those cases so that the Court's sparse resources can be focused on the meritorious ones.

In retaining the focus on appeals in relation to serious criminal offences we have deliberately omitted two topics. First, appeals from the Magistrates' Court. As already indicated, the process of appealing from the Magistrates' Court to the Crown Court is straightforward. Lawyers will find what they need to know in the general criminal practitioner's textbooks. Self-representing appellants should also be able to comply with the procedural requirements for an appeal, perhaps with some assistance from the staff at the Court where their case was dealt with in relation to the completion of the relevant forms and time limits for doing so – currently 15 business days. The second is that of judicial review of the decisions of the Magistrates' Court and judicial review of certain decisions of the Crown Court.[1] It is a topic of considerable scope and complexity. The law is covered briefly in the established practitioner's textbooks but more extensively in judicial review textbooks. We could not hope, in the limited space that might have been devoted to the topic in this book, to match the guidance that is to be found in such publications.

This book is not intended to be a comprehensive guide to the Court of Appeal and its wide array of powers. Rather, it is intended for those asked to act for defendants who are aggrieved by a wrong sentence or who have suffered a miscarriage of justice in the Crown Court. Parliament's purpose in creating the Court of Appeal was to ensure that when such injustices occurred in the Crown Court there should be a remedy. We seek to assist defendants and their representatives to make best use of the rights of appeal that Parliament has provided. All practitioners in the criminal courts will have had the experience of getting a bad result, either the loss of a trial that should have been won or a sentence far harsher than predicted. Very soon, someone will ask: 'what next?' By combining our experience, knowledge and ideas in this book, we hope to assist in arriving at the right answer.

Farrhat Arshad KC
Kate O'Raghallaigh
Gregory Stewart

February 2026

1 Decisions in relation to trial on indictment may only be appealed to the Court of Appeal by virtue of the Senior Courts Act 1981, s 29(3). However, some decisions including bail and incidental orders (*R (M) v Isleworth Crown Court* [2005] EWHC 363 (Admin)), such as custody time limits, production orders and decisions in relation to appeals from the Magistrates' Court fall outside the scope of that section and may be challenged by way of judicial review.

Acknowledgements

We are deeply grateful to Kiran Goss from Bloomsbury for her endless patience in guiding us in our work on this updated edition. This edition owes much to the foundational work by the previous authors: Daniel Jones, Joel Bennathan KC (now Mr Justice Bennathan) and Rebecca Trowler KC (now Her Honour Judge Trowler). We would also like to thank our families and friends for their forbearance and support during the writing of this book. Finally, we should thank our colleagues for their professional advice and support when the answers are not clear and, of course, our clients whose cases have produced the knowledge we now share; it is the importance of those outcomes that keep us going despite the odds.

Contents

Table of Statutes

All references are to paragraph numbers

Table of Statutory Instruments

All references are to paragraph numbers

Table of Cases

All references are to paragraph numbers

S

T

Part 1
The Law

Chapter 1

Introduction to the Court of Appeal

INTRODUCTION

1.1 The Court of Appeal (Criminal Division) ('the Court') sits in the gothic setting of the Royal Courts of Justice, London, in courtrooms of dark and intimidating antiquity. This should not mislead us into thinking that the Court is itself one of our ancient institutions. It was created in the 20th century, following years of campaigning by legal reformers and fierce opposition from successive governments and members of the judiciary.[1] Its core function then, as now, is to hear appeals from the Crown Court against conviction and sentence (including appeals against confiscation orders). However, Parliament has since loaded the Court with powers to hear appeals from a variety of other decisions of the Crown Court and Court Martial. Although the focus of this book is on appeals against conviction and sentence, the additional powers that are most significant for general criminal litigation are also considered.[2]

THE DEVELOPMENT OF THE COURT OF APPEAL

1.2 The roots of the jury trial can be traced back to the Middle Ages. But if the jury system was one of the historic strengths of the English system of justice, the absence of a system of appeal against decisions of the jury was one of its great weaknesses. Before 1907 those who wished to challenge a conviction or a sentence imposed in the Assize and Sessions Courts (the predecessors of today's Crown Court) had two potential avenues of redress, neither of them satisfactory.[3] The principal argument against the creation of a Criminal Court

1 See W Cornish and G Clarke *Law and Society in England 1750–1950* (London, Sweet & Maxwell, 1989) pp 619–623.

2 The prosecution's own rights of appeal, which are considered in Chapter 13; appeals against interlocutory rulings, which are considered in Chapter 12; appeals against restraint, receivership and foreign confiscation requests, which are considered in Chapter 4.

3 From 1848 onwards a convicted person could ask the trial judge to refer the case to the Court for Crown Cases Reserved, which was established by the Crown Cases Reserved Act 1848, but only if the correctness of the conviction rested on a point of law. If the trial judge declined to refer the case, the only alternative was to fall back on the ancient practice of petitioning the government to grant a royal pardon. In contrast all but one US state had a criminal appeals court by 1840 (M Grossberg and C Tomlins (eds) *The Cambridge History of Law in America*, Vol 2 (New York, Cambridge University Press, 2008).

of Appeal that was made in the nineteenth century (in which some 50 bills for the creation of a Court of Appeal were introduced to Parliament but failed to become law[4]) was that the role of the jury would be undermined if judges could, on appeal, overturn the jury's decisions.[5] However, opposition was also driven by the perceived need for finality in criminal litigation[6] and a refusal, amongst some, to accept that the existing system was the cause of significant injustices.[7]

1.3 When Parliament finally bowed to public pressure and passed the Criminal Appeal Act 1907, these concerns found expression in the requirements for leave (or 'permission' as it is referred to in civil cases) to appeal in certain cases and also in the limited grounds upon which the Court could quash a conviction. Although the 1907 Act was repealed, it set the mould in which subsequent legislation was cast.

1.4 The 1907 Act created the 'Criminal Court of Appeal', which had the power to determine appeals against conviction and sentence from cases that had been heard on indictment in the Assize and Sessions Courts. An appeal against conviction could be brought without the need for leave of the Court when it was based upon a question of law. However, the leave of the Court or the certificate of the trial judge was required when an appeal was brought on a question of fact alone.

1.5 The Court had the power to set aside a conviction if it was:

(a) unreasonable;

(b) did not accord with the evidence;

(c) was wrong in law.

1.6 Even if the Court found that any of these criteria were satisfied, it did not have to set aside the conviction if 'no substantial miscarriage of justice had occurred'.[8]

1.7 A number of reforms were introduced by the Criminal Appeal Acts 1964, 1966 and 1967. Most notably, the 1966 Act re-constituted the Court as a branch of the existing civil Court of Appeal, enabling all High Court judges

4 L Radzinowicz and R Hood *A History of English Law and its Administration from 1750*, Vol V (London, Stevens & Sons, 1986) p 758.
5 W Cornish and G Clarke (n 1), pp 619–623.
6 As Spencer noted in M Delmas-Marty and JR Spencer (eds) *European Criminal Procedures* (Cambridge University Press, 2002) at p 28: 'In England the Jury was introduced as a substitute for the Judgment of God pronounced through the ordeal, and like the Judgment of God it was not open to challenge on the ground that it has given an answer that was wrong'.
7 Radzinowicz and Hood (1986), p 763.
8 Criminal Appeal Act 1907, s 4(1).

and Lord Justices of Appeal to sit in both Courts. Thereafter, the Court was known as the Court of Appeal (Criminal Division).

1.8 These changes were consolidated by the Criminal Appeal Act 1968 (CAA 1968) which (much amended by later legislation) contains the powers of today's Court of Appeal in relation to appeals against conviction and sentence.

1.9 The Senior Courts Act 1981 contains the overarching framework that now governs the Court of Appeal (Criminal Division) in all its activities. The need for such a framework is a testament to the many other appeals from the decisions of the Crown Court with which, since 1968, Parliament has empowered the Court to determine.

1.10 The last major reforms of the Court's powers are contained in the Criminal Appeal Act 1995, which made a number of amendments to the 1968 Act, the most important of which were:

(a) The introduction of a new test for appeal against conviction. Whilst the original criteria from section 4(1) of the 1907 Act had been preserved in section 2(1) of the Criminal Appeal Act 1968, the Criminal Appeal Act 1995 amended section 2(1) by replacing that criteria with a single test: the Court has to ask whether the conviction is 'unsafe'.

(b) The removal of the automatic right of appeal against conviction in those cases where the appeal is based on a point of law. Thereafter, either leave to appeal from the Court of Appeal or a certification from the trial judge would be required for all criminal appeals.

(c) The creation of the Criminal Cases Review Commission ('the CCRC') (the role of which is considered in Chapter 9).

Appeals from cases which pre-date the coming into force of CAA 1995

1.11 The test of unsafety applies to appeals against all convictions, whether they took place before or after the commencement of CAA 1995.[9] However, the pre-1995 rules in relation to leave remain in force in respect of appeals against convictions that took place before 1 January 1996. If one appeals against such a historic conviction there will be no requirement for leave where the appeal involves a question of law only.[10]

9 By virtue of the Criminal Appeal Act 1995 (Commencement No 1 and Transitional Provisions) Order 1995 (SI 1995/3061).

10 See *DPP v Majewski* [1975] 3 All ER 296 for the meaning of 'a question of law'.

THE CURRENT STATUTORY REGIME

1.12 The jurisdiction of the Court is set out in section 53(2) of the Senior Courts Act 1981. It provides that the Criminal Division of the Court of Appeal shall exercise:

(a) all jurisdiction of the Court of Appeal under Parts I and II of the Criminal Appeal Act 1968;

(b) the jurisdiction of the Court of Appeal under section 13 of the Administration of Justice Act 1960 (appeals in cases of contempt of court) in relation to appeals from orders and decisions of the Crown Court;

(c) all other jurisdiction expressly conferred on that division by this or any other Act; and

(d) the jurisdiction to order the issue of writs of *venire de novo* (a rarely used remedy that can be used to remit a case to the Crown Court where the Court is satisfied that the proceedings were so irregular that they did not constitute a proper trial).

1.13 Part I of the CAA 1968 sets out the Court's powers when determining appeals against conviction or sentence from the Crown Court. Part II sets out its powers when determining applications for leave to appeal from that Court to the Supreme Court. Part I of the CAA 1995 similarly deals with the procedure for appeals against conviction or sentence whilst Part II deals with referrals from the CCRC.

PROCEDURAL RULES AND GUIDANCE

1.14 Although the Court is a creature of statute and its powers are limited to those which Parliament has provided it, it does have the power to regulate its own procedures. Therefore, the statutory provisions relating to the conduct of appeals are supplemented by detailed procedural rules and guidelines from the following sources:

(a) The Criminal Procedure Rules 2025 (CrimPR)[11] – Part 1 contains the rules that apply to all criminal proceedings. Parts 34 to 44 contain the rules which apply to appeals to the Court of Appeal.

11 The Criminal Procedure Rules are set out in statutory instruments that are promulgated under the Courts Act 2003, s 69. The Criminal Procedure Rules Committee, which is chaired by the Lord Chief Justice, is responsible for drawing them up. Unless otherwise stated, references to 'CrimPR' are to the 2025 Rules, last amended in October 2025.

(b) The Criminal Practice Directions 2023 ('CPD')[12] – Part 10 of the CPD is specifically concerned with Appeals to the Court of Appeal Against Conviction and Sentence. The CPD are updated periodically.

(c) The 'Guide to Commencing Proceedings in the Court of Appeal (Criminal Division)' ('the Guide') is regularly updated. It is prepared by Court of Appeal lawyers under the direction of the Registrar. Guidance notes are produced by the Court for appellants, lawyers and others with an interest in the appeal process.[13]

(d) The case law of the Court – The Lord Chief Justice or Vice President of the Criminal Division occasionally use particular cases to provide guidance on what the Court expects from the parties. These individual decisions are often incorporated into the Practice Direction when it is updated.

THE JUDGES OF THE COURT OF APPEAL

1.15 The Court of Appeal is presided over by the Lord Chief Justice who is appointed by the Lord Chancellor. They may appoint another judge, such as Vice President of the Criminal Division, to assist them.[14]

1.16 The other permanent judges of the Court are a small number of holders, or former holders, of certain high judicial offices, and a larger number of 'ordinary' judges who on appointment to the Court of Appeal are known as Lord or Lady Justices of Appeal.[15] In addition, the Lord Chief Justice may ask High Court judges (referred to in the legislation as 'puisne judges') or judges who sit in the Crown Court ('circuit judges') to sit in the Court of Appeal.[16]

1.17 When a judge is sitting in the Court of Appeal, he or she should be addressed as 'my Lord' or 'my Lady'.

The composition of the Court

1.18 The Court is constituted, for the purposes of exercising any of its powers, when it sits as an uneven number of judges, not less than three.[17] In practice, it usually sits as a Court of three judges, presided over by a Lord or

12 The Lord Chief Justice has the power, under the Courts Act 2003, s 74 and the Constitutional Reform Act 2005, Sch 2, Pt 1 to make directions as to the practice and procedure of the criminal courts.

13 They can be found at: https://www.judiciary.uk/courts-and-tribunals/court-of-appeal-home/the-court-of-appeal-criminal-division/.

14 Senior Courts Act 1981, s 3.

15 Senior Courts Act 1981, s 2.

16 Senior Courts Act 1981, s 9.

17 Senior Courts Act 1981, s 55(2).

Lady Justice of Appeal. A court of five judges will occasionally sit on important cases when the Lord Chief Justice deems it appropriate. There may never be more than one circuit judge sitting in any one court.

1.19 A Court of two judges may be constituted by two High Court judges or a High Court judge and a Circuit judge.[18] It may only hear the following appeals:

(a) an appeal against sentence;

(b) a renewed application for leave to appeal against conviction or sentence where the single judge has already refused leave.

The 'single judge'

1.20 An application for leave to appeal against conviction or sentence is generally considered by a single judge, in practice this will be a High Court judge. The single judge may determine other applications (for example, an application for bail) that are made along with or following the application for leave. Alternatively, they may refer applications on to the full Court for its determination. Although their decisions are usually made on paper, they may choose to hold oral hearings.

THE REGISTRAR OF CRIMINAL APPEALS AND THE CRIMINAL APPEALS OFFICE

1.21 The role of the Registrar of Criminal Appeals ('the Registrar') is to assist the Court in the effective management of cases. It is both an administrative and a quasi-judicial role in that they have a number of case management powers, some of which are considered in Chapters 6 and 7 of this book.

1.22 The Registrar is assisted by the lawyers and administrative staff at the Criminal Appeals Office. Cases will be assigned to a lawyer and caseworker who will then take responsibility for preparing the case and communicating with the parties.

1.23 Their work is undertaken in the name of 'the Registrar', and it is the 'the Registrar' to whom correspondence with the Court should be addressed. However, it should be assumed that routine casework is undertaken without the Registrar's personal involvement.[19]

18 Senior Courts Act 1981, s 55(6).
19 Senior Courts Act 1981, s 31A(2)(b).

WHERE AND WHEN THE COURT SITS

1.24 The Court may sit anywhere in England and Wales, but it is based in the Royal Courts of Justice in the Strand (sitting usually in Courts 4 to 9) along with the Registrar and the Criminal Appeal Office.

1.25 It sits at the following times of year:[20]

(a) the Michaelmas sittings, which begin on 1 October and end on 21 December;

(b) the Hilary sittings, which begin on 11 January and end on the Wednesday before Easter Sunday;

(c) the Easter sittings, which begin on the second Tuesday after Easter Sunday and end on the Friday before the spring holiday; and

(d) the Trinity sittings, which begin on the second Tuesday after the spring holiday and end on 31 July.

COMMUNICATING WITH THE COURT

1.26 Correspondence to the Court should be addressed to:

The Registrar of Criminal Appeals
The Royal Courts of Justice
Strand
London
WC2A 2LL
DX 44451 Strand
Email: generaloffice@criminalappealoffice.justice.gov.uk

1.27 All correspondence to the Court should contain the case reference number which is to be found on all correspondence from the Court.

1.28 In practice, most correspondence will be considered and replied to by the lawyer or the caseworker who has been assigned to the case. The lawyer may pass on correspondence to the Registrar if the nature of the issues requires greater consideration. If the case is being prepared for hearing and a presiding judge has already been assigned, the lawyer may pass correspondence on to the judge's clerk.

20 Civil Procedure Practice Direction 2F.

SUMMARY OF KEY POINTS

- The Court of Appeal (Criminal Division) hears all appeals against conviction and sentence from the Crown Court. It also has power to hear a number of other types of appeal from decisions of the Crown Court and the Court Martial.
- The Court was created by statute. Its powers and jurisdiction are therefore defined by statute. Its overarching framework is contained in the Senior Courts Act 1981.
- Its powers in relation to appeals against conviction or sentence are to be found in the Criminal Appeal Act 1968 as amended by subsequent legislation, most notably the Criminal Appeal Act 1995. However, appeals against decisions that were made before 1 January 1995 take place under the provisions that were then in force.
- It has the power to regulate its own procedures. The legislation is supplemented by procedural rules and guidelines that are to be found in the relevant Criminal Procedural Rules, the relevant parts of the CPD, decisions of the Court itself and the Court's written guidance for advocates.
- It is based in the Royal Courts of Justice (sitting usually in Courts 4 to 9) where the Registrar of Criminal Appeals and the Criminal Appeal Office are also based. Occasionally, it sits outside London.
- Communication with the Court should be through written correspondence addressed to 'The Registrar' and should contain the Court's own case reference number.

Chapter 2

Applying the law: recent developments

INTRODUCTION

2.1 The Court of Appeal interprets and applies law from the following sources:

(a) Acts of Parliament;

(b) Statutory Instruments;

(c) decisions of the Superior Courts;

(d) the European Convention on Human Rights and decisions of the European Court of Human Rights;

(e) where appropriate and relevant, international law.

2.2 The overriding requirement to apply statutes remains a constant feature of our criminal law. However, in the last 25 years a once crystal-clear hierarchy of norms has become clouded as the Human Rights Act 1998 and developments in international law and related conventions have added complexity to the business of interpreting domestic criminal law. It has also been a period in which the Court of Appeal has returned on several occasions to the question of when it is entitled to depart from its own previous decisions. The focus of this chapter is upon these developments.

STARE DECISIS[1] AND THE COURT OF APPEAL

2.3 The Court of Appeal must follow the decisions of the Supreme Court and those of its predecessor, the Judicial Committee of the House of Lords.[2] The judges who sit in the Supreme Court also sit in the Judicial Committee of the Privy Council which hears appeals from a number of Commonwealth

1 The doctrine of *stare decisis* is an abbreviation of the maxim '*stare decisis et non quieta movere*', which translates as 'to stand by things decided and not disturb settled points'.

2 The Supreme Court was created by the Constitutional Reform Act 2005. It came into existence on 1 October 2009.

countries. Its decisions are not strictly binding on the Court of Appeal but will carry great weight and are likely to be followed unless there is very good reason to depart from them.

2.4 As a general rule the Court of Appeal is bound to follow its own decisions. However, there are exceptions to that rule. It is the scope of those exceptions that needs to be considered.

2.5 In *Young v Bristol Airplane Co Ltd*[3] the Court of Appeal (Civil Division) held that the Court of Appeal was bound to follow a previous decision of the Court unless one of the following exceptions applied:

(a) there is a conflict between two Court of Appeal authorities and the Court must decide which to follow;

(b) the decision of the Court of Appeal cannot stand with a decision of the Supreme Court;

(c) the decision was *per incuriam* (taken without consideration of relevant statutory provision or binding case law (*Morelle Ltd v Wakeling*[4])).

2.6 The rule of *stare decisis* is less strictly applied in the Criminal Division of the Court of Appeal, dealing as it must with questions involving the liberty of the subject.[5] It has been established that the Criminal Division of the Court of Appeal has a residual discretion to decline to follow a previous decision for reasons that lie outside the categories identified in *Young v Bristol Airplane*. The scope of that discretion has been considered in three cases in which the Court was presided over by successive Lord Chief Justices (*R v Simpson*,[6] *R v Rowe*[7] and *R v Magro*[8]). These cases indicate differing approaches to the scope of the discretion. However, the following principles emerge:

(a) It is only in very rare cases that the Court will decline to follow a previous decision of the Court of Appeal.

(b) If it is considering doing so it will usually sit as a Court of five judges rather than the usual two or three. Such a Court will usually be presided over by the Lord Chief Justice.

3 [1944] KB 718.
4 [1955] 2 QB 379.
5 *R v Taylor* [1950] 2 KB 368, 34 Cr App R 138; *R v Gould* [1968] 2 QB 65, 52 Cr App R 152. In *DPP v Patterson* [2017] EWHC 2820, the Admin Court held that the test as to dishonesty set out in *R v Ghosh* [1982] QB 1053 no longer represented the law in light of the decision in *Ivey v Genting Casinos (UK) Ltd* [2017] UKSC 67 and that it was clear from *Gould* that the Court of Appeal might depart from *Ghosh* without the matter returning to the Supreme Court.
6 [2003] EWCA Crim 1499.
7 [2007] EWCA Crim 635.
8 [2010] EWCA Crim 1575.

(c) If the effect of refusing to follow a previous decision would be to render the appellant guilty of a crime of which he or she would not otherwise be guilty, the Court will be bound to follow the decision in question.

(d) If failing to follow the previous decision has the effect of exposing the appellant to some lesser disadvantage, which may be a powerful factor against departing from the decision.

(e) If the previous decision can be said to be *per incuriam*, very broadly understood (for example, if the matter in issue was not properly argued or if all the relevant authorities were not drawn to the Court's attention), the Court may in those circumstances decide not to follow that decision.

(f) However, if the previous decision was reached following full argument on the point and careful consideration of all the relevant authorities and statutory provisions, the Court may regard itself as being bound to follow that decision.

JUDGMENTS OF THE EUROPEAN COURT OF HUMAN RIGHTS

2.7 The European Convention on Human Rights ('the Convention') is a Convention between European states which was incorporated by the Human Rights Act 1998 (HRA 1998) into domestic law. The effect of the HRA 1998 is to require the Courts to:

(a) interpret legislation in so far as possible to give effect to the Convention. However, Parliament remains the ultimate source of law. Therefore, if the Court is unable to interpret a statute so as to render it compatible with the Convention, it must make a declaration of incompatibility that will require Parliament to consider amending the legislation;

(b) interpret statutory instruments in accordance with the requirements of the Convention or refuse to apply them if they cannot be interpreted in a way that is compatible with the Convention;

(c) develop the common law so as to give effect to the Convention.

2.8 The European Court of Human Rights (ECtHR) determines cases brought against a state that is a signatory to the Convention. The HRA 1998 requires that in determining the scope of Convention rights the domestic courts must 'take account' of any relevant judgment of the ECtHR.[9]

2.9 This requirement is interpreted by the domestic courts as meaning that they should give great weight to the judgments of the ECtHR and strive to

9 Human Rights Act 1998, s 2(1)(a).

follow them. However, they do not regard themselves as bound to follow the ECtHR. If, after careful consideration, the domestic courts reach a different conclusion as to what the Convention requires, the courts should not follow the jurisprudence of the ECtHR.[10]

2.10 The case law[11] suggests that when the Court of Appeal is contemplating disagreeing with the ECtHR it will sit as a Court of five judges presided over by the Lord Chief Justice or the Vice President. Faced with a conflict of approach between the Supreme Court and the ECtHR, the Court of Appeal is bound by the doctrine of precedent to follow the Supreme Court.

2.11 Whether the ECtHR provides a useful avenue of redress, when an appeal against conviction or sentence is refused is considered in Chapter 11, below.

EUROPEAN UNION LAW AND INTERNATIONAL LAW

2.12 The UK's direct application of EU criminal law ceased with the passage of and subsequent amendments to the European Union (Withdrawal) Act 2018 (EU(W)A 2018). Pursuant to section 5 of that Act, the principles of sovereignty of EU law and the general principles of EU law are no longer part of domestic law. The Trade and Cooperation Agreement (TCA) now governs cooperation between the UK and EU and covers information exchange and mutual legal assistance in criminal matters.

UK criminal law includes 'retained EU law' and domestic law. 'Retained EU law' is a concept created by the EU(W)A 2018. That Act took a 'snapshot' of EU law as it applied to the UK on 31 December 2020 and provided for it to continue to apply in domestic law. The Retained EU Law (Revocation and Reform) Act 2023 made provision for specific secondary legislation and EU-derived laws to be revoked (Schedule 1) and provided that the UK's domestic enactments now override incompatible retained EU law.

2.13 International law consists of customary international law (general international practice which is accepted as law) and international treaties. Whilst the UK was a member of the European Union, its domestic criminal law was shaped by the principles and instruments of EU law.

2.14 An important example of the role that both EU and international law have played in the criminal law lies in the protection of victims of human trafficking. The UK's international obligations in relation to victims of trafficking derives from the *Council of Europe Convention on Action against*

10 *R v Horncastle* [2009] UKSC 14.
11 *R v Horncastle* [2009] EWCA Crim 964; *R v McLoughlin* [2014] EWCA Crim 188.

Trafficking in Human Beings 2005 and Directive 2011/36, implemented in England and Wales by the Modern Slavery Act 2015. Section 45 of the Act now provides a defence for individuals who have committed certain offences under compulsion attributable to slavery or relevant exploitation.

2.15 Although international law may, in some circumstances, be a source of rights, it is a well-recognised principle that criminal offences may now only be created by Parliament. Moreover, an unincorporated treaty does not form part of the law of the United Kingdom.[12]

SUMMARY OF KEY POINTS

- The Court of Appeal (Criminal Division) is bound to follow the decisions of the Supreme Court and its predecessor, the Judicial Committee of the House of Lords.
- It is generally bound to follow previous decisions of the Court of Appeal. However, there are certain exceptions that would allow it to depart from such a decision.
- In interpreting the requirements of the European Convention on Human Rights, it must have regard to the decisions of the European Court of Human Rights. However, it is not bound by them.
- As things stand, the Court may, where appropriate, take into account international law when interpreting the requirements of our criminal law, even when it has not been incorporated into domestic law by statute.
- Upon exit from the EU, EU law ceased to apply to the UK save to the extent that it has been incorporated into domestic law, or its application is preserved by the exit Treaty and subsequent domestic statutes.

12 *R (SC) v Secretary of State for Work and Pensions* [2021] UKSC 26 at [74]–[96] (per Lord Reed PSC).

Chapter 3

Appeals against conviction

INTRODUCTION

3.1 To succeed in an appeal against conviction, the applicant has to meet a single test: whether the conviction is unsafe.

THE MEANING OF 'UNSAFE'

3.2 Section 2(1) of CAA 1968, as amended by CAA 1995, provides that:

> 'Subject to the provisions of this Act, the Court of Appeal –
>
> (a) shall allow an appeal against conviction if they think that the conviction is unsafe; and
>
> (b) shall dismiss such an appeal in any other case.'

3.3 The meaning of the term 'unsafe' was considered by Lord Bingham CJ, as he then was, in the judgment of the Court in *R v Criminal Cases Review Commission, ex p Pearson*[1] at para 10:

> 'The expression "unsafe" in section 2(1)(a) of the 1968 Act does not lend itself to precise definition. In some cases unsafety will be obvious, as (for example) where it appears that someone other than the appellant committed the crime and the appellant did not, or where the appellant has been convicted of an act that was not in law a crime, or where a conviction is shown to be vitiated by serious unfairness in the conduct of the trial or significant legal misdirection, or where the jury verdict, in the context of other verdicts, defies any rational explanation. Cases however arise in which unsafety is much less obvious: cases in which the court, although by no means persuaded of an appellant's innocence, is subject to some lurking doubt or uneasiness whether an injustice has been done (*R v Cooper* [1969] 1 QB 267 at 271). If, on consideration of all the facts and circumstances of the case before it,

1 [2000] 1 Cr App R 141.

the court entertains real doubts whether the appellant was guilty of the offence of which he has been convicted, the court will consider the conviction unsafe. In these less obvious cases the ultimate decision of the Court of Appeal will very much depend on its assessment of all the facts and circumstances.'

3.4 An unsafe conviction, then, can be considered a wrongful conviction. Although Lord Bingham was careful not to seek to provide a comprehensive definition of the factors that might lead the Court to regard a conviction as unsafe, the passage outlines some of the key features of the test.

Error or new evidence giving rise to doubt as to guilt

3.5 Is a conviction unsafe only when there are grounds to doubt the guilt of the convicted person, or does it involve wider questions of fairness and procedural regularity in the trial process? As Lord Bingham's speech from *Pearson* indicates, the Courts have come to embrace the broad understanding of the test; a conviction may be unsafe even where there is no doubt as to guilt, where the conviction has been obtained following a trial that was unfair.

3.6 However, it is only in rare cases that the Court will be prepared to find a conviction unsafe in the absence of any real doubt as to guilt. In most appeals, the Court's approach is to consider whether, had the error or irregularity not occurred, 'the only proper and reasonable verdict [would] be one of guilty.' (*R v Davis, Rowe and Johnson*[2]). If the Court concludes that the verdict would still have been one of guilty, it is likely to find that the conviction is safe.

3.7 This approach has at times involved the Court placing itself in the position of the jury and asking how the matter, which is the subject of the appeal, may have led to it returning a different verdict. In another series of cases, however, the Court has made clear that it is they who decide which convictions are, or are not, safe.

3.8 In relation to grounds of appeal concerning a failure of disclosure, the Court would consider whether the material which was withheld could have affected the jury's verdict, but was entitled to do so in the light of all the facts now known to the Court – *R v Craven*.[3] Even if the disclosure failures were 'deplorable' the conviction may be upheld if the material did not significantly add to the position before the jury – *R v Simmons*.[4]

2 [2001] 1 Cr App R 8 at 132.
3 [2001] 2 Cr App R 12.
4 [2018] EWCA Crim 2534.

The jury impact test

3.9 The correctness of the 'jury impact' approach was considered in appeals that turned on the admission of fresh evidence. In *Stafford v DPP*,[5] the House of Lords held that when fresh evidence was received by the Court, the Court itself had to assess the impact of that evidence on the safety of the conviction and not what effect it might have had upon the jury.

3.10 In *R v Pendleton*,[6] the majority of the House of Lords found that whilst the fundamental question of whether the conviction was unsafe was for the Court itself, the Court might be at a disadvantage in relating that evidence to the evidence that the jury had heard. Therefore, in all but the clearest cases, it would be wise for the Court to consider whether the evidence might reasonably have affected the verdict of the jury.

3.11 In *Dial v State of Trinidad and Tobago*,[7] the Privy Council retreated from *Pendleton*, instead emphasising that, 'The primary question is for the Court itself and is not what effect the fresh evidence would have on the mind of the jury.'[8] In the Board's view, it was only in 'difficult cases' that it might be helpful for the Court to test its view by applying the jury impact test.[9] In the subsequent case law, differently constituted Courts emphasised either the potential jury impact of fresh evidence or the Court's own task of assessing for itself the potential impact of the evidence (see *R v Noye*[10]). In *Maharaj v The State*,[11] in setting out its approach to fresh evidence cases, the Board stated that the admission of fresh evidence, 'does not automatically trigger the jury impact test and the Board consider that the occasions when it does so are likely to be few and far between.'[12] Whilst there has been an increasing retreat from *Pendleton*, it ought to be remembered, however, that *Pendleton* was a decision of the (then) House of Lords, and thus binding on the Court of Appeal.

3.12 Although the two approaches will generally produce the same result there may be some benefit to the defence to frame arguments in terms of the potential jury impact of the error or new evidence that is the subject of the grounds of appeal. It may be cited so long as it is couched in the terms that were recognised as correct in *Pendleton* and the later case law. However it is done, it remains crucial to address the strength of the prosecution evidence untouched by any legal flaw, failure in disclosure or whatever other ground is

5 [1974] AC 878.
6 [2001] UKHL 66.
7 [2005] 1 WLR 1660, PC.
8 At para 19 of the judgment.
9 Ibid.
10 [2011] EWCA Crim 650.
11 [2021] UKPC 27.
12 At para 68.

advanced. By whichever intellectual route the Court assesses what is 'unsafe', an appeal in which they form the impression that a convicted applicant was manifestly guilty is almost certain to fail.

'Unsafe' and 'unfair'

3.13 Article 6(1) of the European Convention on Human Rights, provides the right to a fair trial, with Article 6(3) providing a number of specific fair criminal trial guarantees. After the Human Rights Act brought the Convention into domestic force, an unfair trial was an unlawful trial and a conviction following such a trial is unsafe. This logic was not immediately recognised by the Court of Appeal in *R v Davis, Rowe and Johnson*[13] which, at para 135 stressed that an unfair trial and an unsafe conviction were two distinct concepts. However, without eliding the two tests, the Court has since made it clear that a trial that is unfair will almost certainly also be unsafe.

3.14 In *R v Togher*,[14] Lord Woolf CJ said: 'we consider that if a defendant has been denied a fair trial it will almost be inevitable that the conviction will be regarded as unsafe.'

3.15 This principle was confirmed in subsequent cases such as *R v Forbes*[15] and the Privy Council case of *R v Randall*,[16] in which Lord Bingham made clear that in the absence of a fair trial a conviction was likely to be unsafe even in the face of strong evidence of guilt:

> 'There will come a point where the departure from good practice is so gross, or persistent, or prejudicial, or irremediable that an appellate Court will have no choice but to condemn the trial as unfair and quash the conviction as unsafe, however strong the grounds for believing the defendant to be guilty.'

3.16 This jurisprudence is consistent with the law in relation to abuse of process, which recognises that a prosecution may give rise to abuse of process if either a fair trial was not possible (category 1 abuse) or it would not be fair to try the defendant (category 2 abuse) (*R v Horseferry Road Magistrates' Court, ex p Bennett*[17]). The refusal of the trial judge to stay a case as an abuse of process may itself be the subject of appeal. In *Hamilton v POL*,[18] the appeals arising from the Post Office Horizon accounting system, the court considered both categories of abuse and set out key principles that applied. It was not

13 See fn 2, above.
14 [2001] 1 Cr App R 33, para 30.
15 [2001] 1 Cr App R 31.
16 [2002] UKPC 19.
17 [1993] 3 All ER 138 (HL).
18 [2021] EWCA Crim 577.

necessary for an appellant alleging category 2 abuse to prove misconduct going beyond that which established category 1 abuse. In relation to category 2 abuse, the failures were so egregious as to make the prosecution of any of the Horizon cases an affront to the conscience of the court.[19]

3.17 However, it is not every breach of the right to a fair trial that will render a conviction unsafe. It will only be if the trial itself could be said to be unfair that the conviction would be considered unsafe (*R v Togher*[20]). To take an obvious example, a trial that was so delayed as to lead to a violation of the Article 6 right to a trial 'within a reasonable time' will very rarely be the basis of a successful appeal if it was fair in all other regards, see *AG's Ref (No 2 of 2001)*.[21]

3.18 This is not to say that individual breaches of Article 6, particularly Article 6(3), cannot form the basis of successful grounds as long as the appellant has been able to show that had these breaches not taken place there was a real chance that he or she would not have been convicted or that the unfairness was so profound as to amount to an abuse of process.

Procedural irregularity

3.19 When the Court can be satisfied that a procedural irregularity in the trial process materially disadvantaged a defendant such that in the absence of the defect the jury may have had a doubt as to their guilt, then the usual approach of considering whether there are real grounds to doubt the appellant's guilt can be applied without difficulty. An example of this approach in action can be found in relation to the judge's decision to allow an amendment to the indictment in *R v O'Connor*,[22] where the applicant would be expected to explain how the amendment was unfair and how it disadvantaged him or her in the conduct of the case. In *R v Boateng*[23] the conviction was held to be unsafe where the statement of offence alleged the wrong subsection, and the wrong details were set out in the particulars.

3.20 In such cases, it will be important to be able to explain whether the procedural flaw was raised at trial and if not, why not. The Court will wish to know that the defence did not make a deliberate tactical decision not to raise the point, in the belief that this would give the defendant some advantage at trial, only to switch tactics on appeal; if the Court does form such a view, it will be much harder for any appeal to succeed.

19 At paras 127–138.
20 See fn 15, above.
21 [2004] 2 AC 72.
22 [1997] Crim LR 516 (CA).
23 [2016] 2 Cr App R 5.

3.21 If the defendant has suffered no clear disadvantage, will procedural irregularity lead to the conviction being quashed? The approach of the Courts is to ask whether it was the intention of Parliament that the failure to follow the procedure in question should render the proceedings a nullity. If so, then it is likely that the conviction will be unsafe. An example of this principle at work can be found in *R v Clarke and McDaid*[24] in which the House of Lords held that the failure to sign an indictment rendered the trial process a nullity because Parliament had provided in sections 1 and 2 of the Administration of Justice (Miscellaneous Provisions) Act 1933 that an indictment must be signed to be valid and a trial could only take place on the basis of a valid indictment.[25]

3.22 A further example is to be found in relation to misjoinder. When charges wrongly joined are therefore in breach of rule 9 of the Indictment Rules (*R v Smith (Brian Peter)*[26]), the misjoined charge will be quashed. However, this misjoinder will not render the proceedings a nullity and the remaining charges will be unaffected, unless prejudice is caused to the defence. In *R v Lalchan*,[27] where there had been a failure to obtain the consent of the Attorney-General before prosecution, the prosecution sought to argue that the trend of modern authority was to treat a procedural failure of this kind as not entirely invalidating the proceedings and that the focus should be on the fairness of the trial and on fairness to a defendant. The five judge Court of Appeal disagreed: the language of the section and the statutory context and purpose spoke strongly against dismissing the requirement as a mere technicality. It was the purpose of the provision that proceedings commenced without consent should be invalid.

'Lurking doubt'

3.23 Despite all that has been said above about the need to advance particular grounds, the Court may in rare circumstances be prepared to conclude that a conviction is unsafe, in the absence of either irregularity at trial or new evidence, if it nonetheless has some doubt or uneasiness about the verdict which makes the Court wonder if an injustice had been done.

3.24 This was recognised as a proper basis to quash a conviction in *R v Cooper*.[28] That this ground has survived the introduction of the new test of unsafety was indicated by Lord Bingham in *Pearson*, although in *R v Pope*[29]

24 [2008] UKHL 8.
25 However, following the Coroners and Justice Act 2009, s 116, it is no longer the case that an indictment must be signed in order for it to be valid.
26 [1997] 1 Cr App R 390.
27 [2022] EWCA Crim 736.
28 [1969] 1 QB 267 (CA) at 271.
29 [2012] EWCA Crim 2241.

the Court indicated that it would only be in the most exceptional circumstances that a conviction would be found to be unsafe on this ground alone.

Conclusion: 'unsafe' as a flexible test

3.25 The above comments are illustrations of how the Court has approached the question of unsafety in particular circumstances. They should not be regarded as immutable doctrines. The Court has repeatedly emphasised that there is a single statutory test of unsafety and has shown considerable flexibility in its application.

3.26 The Court does not always elaborate on the basis upon which it has concluded that the conviction is unsafe. This is often so when the Court finds that the conviction is unsafe because of the cumulative effect of a number of errors that are detailed in a number of distinct grounds.

3.27 When the Court's basis for finding a conviction to be unsafe is set out, the Court may approach the issue of fairness and jury impact in a number of different ways. For example, the closer that the error complained of goes to a core feature of a fair trial, the more likely it is that the Court will be prepared to find that the conviction was unsafe without extensive enquiry as to what the verdict might have been if the error had not been made. So, when the judge fails to direct the jury on the balance and burden of proof, it has been held only when the case was overwhelming that the conviction would be regarded as safe (*Davis, Rowe and Johnson*[30]).

3.28 This does not make it easy for lawyers who are asked to advise on appeal against conviction. Given that an unsafe conviction is a wrongful conviction, it may be helpful to consider, in each case, why is it that the conviction must be regarded as wrongful. This is likely to provide the best guide to the way in which the Court will approach the case.

THE COURT'S APPROACH TO COMMON ISSUES

Appeal following a guilty plea

3.29 The fact that a defendant has pleaded guilty does not act as a bar to any appeal against a conviction from the Crown Court to the Court of Appeal.[31] However, the guilty plea is likely to be regarded by the Court as a very significant factor in favour of the safety of the conviction. In *R v Tredget*[32] the

30 See fn 2, above.

31 The position is different in appeals from the Magistrates Court to the Crown Court sitting in its appellate jurisdiction.

32 [2022] 2 Cr App R 1.

Court stated that the focus of the Court's attention was on the single question of whether the conviction is unsafe even after a guilty plea but that a guilty plea was a major, and normally a dominant, part of the facts and circumstances of the case. The Court went on to set out the three categories of case where, notwithstanding the admission of guilt, an appellant is entitled to submit that their conviction is unsafe:

(1) Those cases where a guilty plea is vitiated:

(a) an equivocal or unintended plea was entered;

(b) where the appellant was delusional when the plea was entered – *R v Swain*;[33]

(c) where the plea of guilty was compelled by an erroneous ruling of law – see para 20 of the judgment in *R v Asiedu*.[34] But a distinction must be drawn between the ruling rendering a defence more difficult or even hopeless rather than unarguable. Only in the latter cases, stated the Court, would an appeal be allowed;[35]

(d) where improper pressure is applied, including, but not limited to, by the judge – *R v Nightingale*.[36] In *R v Inkster*[37] the judge incorrectly advised the unrepresented defendant he did not have a defence in law, following which the defendant changed his pleas to guilty. The Court held the pleas to be a nullity as the incorrect advice, 'went to the heart of his plea, and therefore it was not a free plea, nor a true acknowledgment of guilt';

(e) where incorrect legal advice had been given. Here, either it must be shown that the advice went to the heart of the plea so that the plea would not be a free plea but a nullity – *R v Saik*,[38] or even where it was not so fundamental as to render the plea a nullity, its effect was to deprive the defendant of a defence which would probably have succeeded such that a clear injustice had been done – *R v Boal*.[39] See *R v PK*[40] and *R v Elmi*[41] as to 'clear injustice'.

33 [1986] Crim LR 480.

34 [2015] 2 Cr App R 8.

35 See para 155 of judgment in *Tredget*. See also *R v Chalkley and Jeffries* [1998] 2 Cr App R 79.

36 [2013] 2 Cr App R 7.

37 [2020] EWCA Crim 796.

38 [2004] EWCA Crim 2936. See also *R v Carrasco* [2024] EWCA Crim 499, where the appellant had been given incorrect legal advice as to the length of sentence that would make him liable to deportation. The Court did not consider that the advice had deprived the appellant of a defence available in law and on the material available it was not accepted that there was any proper basis for considering that the guilty plea was anything other than a true acknowledgment of guilt.

39 [1992] 95 Cr App R 272. For later examples of such cases see paras 158–159 of *Tredget*.

40 [2017] EWCA Crim 486.

41 [2023] 1 Cr App R 7.

(2) When there is a legal obstacle to his being tried of the offence – *R v Togher*.[42] *Togher* approved the broad approach in *R v Mullen*[43] '… for a conviction to be safe, it must be lawful; and if it results from a trial which should never have taken place, it can hardly be regarded as safe.'

(3) 'A small residual third category'[44] is where it is established that the appellant did not commit the offence, in other words that the admission made by the plea is a false one – *R v Verney*;[45] *R v Foster*;[46] *R v Jones (Noel)*.[47] However, in a case of a free and informed plea of guilty, unaffected by vitiating factors, it will normally be possible to treat the conviction as unsafe only if it is established that the appellant had not committed the offence, not that they may not have committed the offence.[48] The test applied by the Court in *R v Lee*[49] and *R v Brady*[50] was incorrect.

Trial rulings

3.30 There is a high threshold to cross when challenging the decision of a judge in relation to a ruling made at trial. It is not sufficient that the Court may not have reached the same decision. In *R v McCann*[51] it was said that:

> 'To reverse the judge's ruling it is not enough that the members of this Court would have exercised their discretion differently. We must be clearly satisfied that the judge was wrong; but our powers to review the exercise of his discretion is not limited to cases in which he has erred in principle or there is shown to have been no material on which he could properly have arrived at his decision. The Court must, if necessary, examine anew the relevant facts and circumstances to exercise a discretion by way of review if it thinks that the judge's ruling may have resulted in injustice to the appellants. See *Evans v Bartlam* [1937] AC 473.'

3.31 The Court will not readily interfere with a ruling but will where it is based on an error of principle, is *Wednesbury* unreasonable,[52] perverse[53]

42 [2001] 1 Cr App R 33.
43 [1999] 2 Cr App R 143.
44 See para 162 of *Tredget*.
45 (1909) 2 Cr App R 107.
46 (1984) 79 Cr App R 61.
47 [2019] EWCA Crim 1059.
48 At para 171 of *Tredget*.
49 (1984) 79 Cr App R 108, 113.
50 [2004] EWCA Crim 2230.
51 (1991) 92 Cr App R 239.
52 See para 17 of *R v Oladeji* [2010] EWCA Crim 222.
53 *R v Al Badi* [2007] EWCA Crim 2974.

or 'plainly wrong',[54] where there was no material on which the judge could have arrived at their conclusion or where the judge failed to take into account relevant factors in reaching their decision. Where decisions are particularly intertwined with other evidence at the trial the Court of Appeal gives a wider area of discretion to the trial judge. In *R v Hanson*[55] in relation to rulings on bad character, the Court held:

> 'If a judge has directed himself or herself correctly, this Court will be very slow to interfere with a ruling either as to admissibility or as to the consequences of noncompliance with the regulations for the giving of notice of intention to rely on bad character evidence. It will not interfere unless the judge's judgment as to the capacity of prior events to establish propensity is plainly wrong, or discretion has been exercised unreasonably in the *Wednesbury* sense.'

The judge's conduct

3.32 As always, the key test is whether the judge's conduct is such as to render the conviction unsafe. Appeals may succeed if the judge has made clear his or her preference for the prosecution case (see *R v Bryant*[56]), has undermined the advocate in the eyes of the jury, or has interrupted so much as to prevent the defence from being able to properly advance its case (see *R v Lashley*,[57] another successful appeal from the same trial judge as in *Bryant*).

3.33 In relation to the handling of witnesses, matters such as the imposition of time-limits on cross-examination or judicial questioning of witnesses may make the conviction unsafe but must be looked at in the context of the trial as a whole – *R v Bhatt*.[58] The relevant principles that apply when the ground for complaint is that the judge unfairly entered the arena are set out in *R v Mustafa*,[59] where it was held that the judge had not 'remained aloof from the fray' as required by the adversarial system.[60] Where the prosecution case was a strong one, 'it was all the more important … for the judge to be scrupulous in the fair treatment of the defence, and in ensuring the appearance (at the very least) of his own neutrality.' – *R v Tarik Hill*. [61]

54 *R v Hanson* [2005] 2 Cr App R 21.
55 [2005] 2 Cr App R 21, para 15.
56 [2005] EWCA Crim 2079.
57 [2005] EWCA Crim 2016.
58 [2022] EWCA Crim 926.
59 [2020] EWCA Crim 1723.
60 The 'core principle' identified in *Michel v The Queen* [2009] UKPC 41.
61 [2021] EWCA Crim 587.

Defective summing up

Judge commenting on the evidence

3.34 The judge is entitled to comment on the facts. It is the role of the judge to provide guidance on factual as well as legal issues. However, these comments should not jeopardise the jury's own consideration of the evidence by being clearly partisan. The judge should direct the members of the jury that they were the judges of fact and should only take into account views expressed by the judge to the extent that they agreed with their own. If this direction is provided, it will be regarded by the Court as an important factor in considering whether any comments made by the judge might have improperly influenced the jury. However, in a case in which the judge's comments were particularly extreme or damaging, the conviction will not be made safe by the parrot-like recitation that 'it is matter for you, the jury'; see Lord Bingham in *R v Bentley*,[62] citing with approval the judgment of Lloyd LJ in *Gilbey*.[63]

3.35 In *Mears v The Queen*,[64] the Board held that it was not necessary to show a usurpation of the jury's function. Comments which fall short of such a usurpation may nevertheless, 'be so weighted against the defendant at trial as to leave the jury little real choice other than to comply …'. It went on to say that, 'if the system is trial by jury then the decision must be that of the jury and not of the judge using the jury as something akin to a vehicle for his own views.'[65] *R v Hewson*[66] is a recent example of a conviction being quashed despite the legal directions being correct, as the summing up was so unbalanced as to render the conviction unsafe.

Summing up inadequate

3.36 A summing-up must accurately direct the jury as to the issues of fact which it must determine, and fairly state and analyse the case for both sides. Whether a summing-up which fails to achieve this basic requirement renders the conviction unsafe depends on the circumstances of the individual case – *R v Yousefi*.[67] In all but the simplest of cases it is likely that a failure to properly direct the jury as to the issues and evidence will render the conviction unsafe.

62 [2001] 1 Cr App R 21.
63 (unreported) 26 January 1990.
64 [1993] 97 Cr App R 239.
65 At pages 243–244.
66 [2023] EWCA Crim 1657. Available on https://caselaw.nationalarchives.gov.uk/.
67 [2020] EWCA Crim 791.

Summing up on a different basis to that advanced at trial

3.37 There is no bar to the judge summing up the prosecution case on a different basis to that which it was put by the prosecution at trial. However, the judge must proceed with caution. There is an obvious danger that the fairness of the trial will be prejudiced where the judge introduces lines of argument to which the defence have had no opportunity to respond (*R v Falconer-Atlee*[68]).

Leaving alternative verdicts to the jury

3.38 Whether to leave alternative, lesser counts to the jury is a matter that the judge should raise with counsel but is ultimately a matter for the judge. It should generally be done where it obviously arises on the evidence. In *R v Coutts*[69] the House of Lords held that, save in exceptional circumstances, an appellate court should quash a conviction as constituting a serious miscarriage of justice where a judge has erred in failing to leave any lesser alternative verdict which there is evidence to support. The decision in *Coutts* was 'explained' and, arguably, narrowed by the Court of Appeal in *R v Foster.*[70]

Getting the law wrong

3.39 As discussed above at 3.27, a failure to properly direct the jury on the balance and burden of proof will be regarded as highly likely to render a conviction unsafe. Other failures in directing the jury on the law, such as to correctly identify the elements of the offence or the defence relied upon may provide powerful grounds of appeal. A failure to give a proper good character direction will often lead to the conclusion that the conviction is unsafe. However, it should never be assumed that such errors will automatically lead the Court to conclude that the conviction is unsafe. If the judge has not provided the correct wording in a particular passage, the Court will look to the summing up as a whole to see whether it provided the jury with the appropriate guidance. Even in those cases where it failed to do so, the Court is likely to consider whether, in the circumstances of the case, there is a real risk that it led the jury to adopt the wrong approach.

3.40 Where a judge had put forward a number of general propositions about memory which the Court determined was 'guidance that was tantamount to directions on the issue of memory, which naturally tended to support the prosecution and was not firmly grounded in any expertise or established

68 (1974) 58 Cr App R 348.
69 [2006] UKHL 39.
70 [2007] EWCA Crim 2869.

principle or authority', the convictions were deemed to be unsafe and were quashed – *R v LMS*.[71]

The significance of 'specimen directions'

3.41 The Court of Appeal has made it clear that the specimen directions are not blueprints that must be slavishly followed (*R v Millard*[72]). In the foreword to the July 2024 edition of the Crown Court Compendium, the Lady Chief Justice emphasised both the benefit of the example directions set out there and the need for judges to craft bespoke directions:

> 'Given the increasing complexity and technicality of the law, the benefit afforded by the Compendium is not just helpful, but verging on a necessity. The Compendium strikes a careful balance between offering guidance and examples to save the judge from having to reinvent the wheel, without removing judicial independence and undermining the need to ensure that directions are bespoke to the individual requirements of each case. It is important to remember that the Compendium is only a guide. Legal directions always have to be crafted so as to be tailormade to the issues and evidence in each case. The text and the example directions provide a starting point, not the end result. So, whilst there is nothing wrong with parties, or even the judge, referring in terms to the Compendium, the Compendium is not a template to be followed slavishly. Rather, it should assist the judge who is addressing a legal point or crafting a summing up; the process still requires independent judicial thought in the context of the specific issues that arise.'

3.42 It is clear from this that a failure to follow the example directions that are contained in the Compendium will not itself render a direction defective. A direction will be defective only to the extent that it fails to clearly and accurately set out the relevant law as the jury should apply it taking into account the evidence in the particular case (*R v Keene*[73]).

Grounds in relation to the jury

Jury selection

3.43 Irregularities in the selection of the jury may give rise to an appeal. In certain circumstances the failure to follow the correct procedure for jury selection may render the trial a nullity, leading to the issue of the writ of *venire*

71 [2024] EWCA Crim 96.
72 [2003] EWCA Crim 3629.
73 [2010] EWCA Crim 2514, para 20.

de novo – *R v Tarrant*[74] where the judge had 'wrongly interfered' with the composition of the jury panel. See 3.92–3.93 below, on retrials and *venire de novo*.

Allegations of jury misconduct

3.44 It has been known for a convicted person, their family or lawyers to be contacted by former jurors who express disquiet at what took place in the jury room. If this occurs, those taking a statement from the former juror are in danger of committing an offence if they pose questions whose answers would breach section 8 of the Contempt of Court Act 1981, which prohibits the disclosure of a jury's deliberations. The Courts are not subject to that section and can authorise enquiries; see *R v Thompson*.[75] However, evidence in relation to jury deliberations is inadmissible unless the juror's approach involves a complete repudiation of his or her oath to try the case on the evidence, or involves extraneous material being introduced into jury deliberations.[76] It is therefore only in one of these two circumstances that jury deliberations can form a ground of appeal.

3.45 The sensible course for any lawyer coming into possession of complaints about the jury's deliberations from former jurors is to swiftly contact the Registrar to seek guidance and to draft grounds of appeal in reliance on what they have already, then allow the Court to control any further investigations.

3.46 If grounds are drafted based on a former juror's account, the Court may ask the Criminal Cases Review Commission to undertake enquires by tracing the whole jury and taking statements from them. It should not be assumed that these enquiries will be made as a matter of course. In *R v Baybasin*[77] the Lord Chief Justice stated that where a complaint is first raised after verdict, the Court will assume that any genuine problem would have been raised before, and will therefore not order enquiries to be made in the absence of any other 'strong and compelling evidence'. The evidence of jury irregularity relied upon must be credible and fulfil the fresh evidence considerations set out in the CAA 1968, section 23(2), before the Court will order the CCRC to investigate – *R v Cashman.*[78]

3.47 Even after an investigation, the Court may be wary of relying on the allegations made by former jurors when those matters were not raised at trial.

74 [1998] Crim LR 342.
75 [2010] EWCA Crim 1623.
76 *R v Mirza* [2004] 1 AC 1118.
77 [2013] EWCA Crim 2357.
78 [2025] 2 Cr App R 9.

Usually, the Court will proceed on the basis that a complaint made by a juror after a trial is simply a protest against a verdict with which he disagreed (see *R v Lewis*[79]). Similarly, a juror who assented to a verdict but then swiftly said he or she harboured doubts was found to have no basis to allow an appeal; second thoughts after conviction were not, said the Court, relevant, see *R v Ul Hamid and Khan*.[80] Where a juror alleged that the unanimous verdict was not in fact unanimous, the failure to speak out at the time the verdict was delivered was fatal to the appeal – *R v Haji*.[81] All this said, the reservations expressed by the Court are never in absolute terms. If a former juror is able to produce a powerful account such as casts doubt on the safety of the verdict, and if he or she has a credible explanation for not raising the matter during the trial, such later complaints can be the foundation for an appeal.

Possible jury bias

3.48 Allegations of jury bias will often not require investigation into what occurred in the jury room. That is because the Court's starting point is to consider the appearance of potential bias. *R v Saad Essa*[82] sets out the Court's approach to allegations of potential racial bias.

3.49 The Court will consider whether 'the fair minded and informed observer having considered the facts would conclude that there was a real possibility that the jury were biased' (*Porter v Magill; Weeks v Magill*[83]).

Adverse publicity

3.50 The Court takes the view that jurors know their duty and will be robust in disregarding what they have read or viewed in the media; see the trial direction of Hughes J, as he then was, later cited with approval by the Court in *R v Abu Hamza*.[84] The cases where appeals founded on adverse publicity have met with any success have almost all been where the publicity was during the trial and was focused on the facts of the case itself or had a direct and obvious link, such as *R v McCann*[85] and *R v Taylor*.[86] The question was the impact of the publicity on the safety of the conviction: whether the content affected the jury's fair appreciation of the evidence – *R v Warren*.[87]

79 [2013] EWCA Crim 776.
80 [2016] 2 Cr App R 29.
81 [2024] EWCA Crim 955.
82 [2023] EWCA Crim 608.
83 [2001] UKHL 67.
84 [2006] EWCA Crim 2918.
85 (1991) 92 Cr App R 239.
86 (1994) 98 Cr App R 361.
87 [2021] EWCA Crim 413, at para 95.

Fresh evidence

3.51 The Court has the power to receive fresh evidence after a conviction where it is 'necessary or expedient in the interests of justice' to do so. The considerations that the Court must have regard to are set out in section 23(2)(a)–(d) of CAA 1968 and are:

(a) whether the evidence appears to be capable of belief;

(b) whether it appears that the evidence may afford any ground for allowing the appeal;

(c) whether the evidence would have been admissible at trial; and

(d) whether there is a reasonable explanation for the failure to adduce that evidence at trial.

3.52 The Court has emphasised that the application of these considerations is highly case and fact specific but that all four need to be addressed in any application (see *R v Erskine*[88]). In the same case, Lord Judge CJ said at para 39: 'the considerations listed in (2)(a)–(d) are neither exhaustive nor conclusive, but they require specific attention'.

3.53 Whilst it was affirmed in *R v Hanratty*[89] that the considerations set out in section 23(2)(a)–(d) are not tests to be met but rather matters to which the Court must have regard, they are frequently, often by the Court itself, referred to as 'criteria' that must be met.[90] Appellants and those representing them should draw the Court's attention to the statutory language. It is possible for the Court to receive the fresh evidence even when all four matters are not satisfied – *R v Sales*.[91]

3.54 The consideration that often causes the most difficulty on a fresh evidence application is (d) – whether there is a reasonable explanation for the failure to adduce that evidence at trial. The Court's reluctance to receive 'fresh evidence' where it was available but not deployed at trial arises primarily from the 'one trial principle' and a fear of tactical decisions made in order to keep matters in reserve for appeal.

3.55 The Court has been willing to receive fresh evidence even where there is no reasonable explanation for the failure to adduce it at the proper time – *R v Cairns*,[92] where the Court was of the view that the fresh evidence should be

88 [2009] EWCA Crim 1425.

89 [2002] 2 Cr App R 30, see paras 86–105.

90 Recent examples are *R v Lahrar* [2022] EWCA Crim 1342; *R v Gaiziunas* [2024] EWCA Crim 246.

91 [2000] 2 Cr App R 431, at page 437D–E.

92 [2000] Crim LR 473.

received in light of the three other considerations and because, 'if tendered at the proper time could well have had a significant effect.' By contrast, in *R v H*,[93] Lord Justice Judge, as he then was, said at para 82: 'It follows that this court will only permit an appellant to present a factual case inconsistent with his instructions and sworn testimony at the trial at which he was convicted in the most exceptional circumstances'. One such exceptional case is *R v Soloman*[94] where the defence to charges of rape and buggery at trial was one of no sexual activity but fresh evidence which had been held back by the appellant for tactical reasons (later found by the police) undermined lack of consent. Following referral by the CCRC, the Court quashed the convictions for rape and buggery and substituted those of indecent assault. The Court saw this as permitting, 'the record to be put straight.'

3.56 The Court is willing to consider fresh evidence appeals despite lengthy delays. Recent examples are *R v Firkins*,[95] where the fresh evidence went to the reliability and credibility of the main prosecution witness, and *R v Peterkin and Mehmet*,[96] where the fresh evidence concerned the corruption of police officer witnesses, and the convictions of the deceased appellants were quashed. The test that the Court has to apply in determining whether a conviction is unsafe in the light of fresh evidence is considered above at 3.9–3.12. The procedures for doing so are considered in at 6.29.

Errors of defence lawyers

3.57 Allegations that the defendant's trial lawyers committed serious errors in the conduct of the defence case can provide a perfectly sound basis for an appeal, but there are three important things to bear in mind. First, the trial lawyers have to be given the chance to explain how they conducted the case. Second, the Court will require clear evidence of an error before this ground succeeds, and thirdly (as always), the Court must determine whether the errors make the conviction unsafe. 'An applicant or appellant who wishes to rely on the incompetence of his or her lawyers needs not only to show incompetence, but the potential consequences of that incompetence on the fairness of the trial' – *R v MT*.[97]

3.58 There is no one method for seeking the views of trial lawyers, as long as it is done fully and fairly, but when an appeal relies on any criticism of trial lawyers, it is crucial to ask focused questions that fully explore the issue that

93 [2002] EWCA Crim 730.
94 [2007] EWCA Crim 2633.
95 [2023] EWCA Crim 1491.
96 [2024] EWCA Crim 309.
97 [2023] EWCA Crim 558.

is being advanced on appeal, see *R v Grant-Murray*.[98] The applicant will have to waive privilege, and the trial lawyers need to be given a clear indication of what questions are being asked of them and what criticisms are being made. There is in all cases where fresh representatives bring an appeal, a duty to check that the facts are correct – *R v McCook*.[99] The practicalities of obtaining a waiver and communicating with previous representatives are considered at 6.13–6.14.

3.59 If the reply by the trial team conflicts with the applicant's account of what took place, the Court is likely to prefer the lawyers' recollections unless there are contemporaneous records that contradict them. So, obtaining as many of the trial notes and papers as possible is always a good idea.

3.60 Historically, the Court made clear that the decisions of trial lawyers made in good faith after proper consideration of the competing arguments and, where appropriate, after consultation with the defendant, would not make a verdict unsafe even though the Court disagreed with that decision. On the other hand, if a decision was taken in defiance of, or without, proper instruction, or when 'all promptings of reason and common sense pointed the other way', that may render a conviction unsafe (see *R v Clinton*[100]).

3.61 In more recent cases based on the failings of trial lawyers, the Court has moved away from any test of incompetence and instead focused on the single statutory test of safety – see *R v Day*.[101] In *Teeluck and John v State of Trinidad and Tobago*[102] the Board stated that the focus of the appellate court ought to be upon the impact which counsel's errors had had on the safety of the conviction.

3.62 However, *Day* has not altered the Court's traditionally cautious approach to criticism of former representatives. It tends to be robust in finding that trial lawyers who take decisions in the heat of a trial are not to be criticised unless those decisions were very clearly flawed. It is wary of applying the benefit of hindsight to difficult forensic decisions.

3.63 The final requirement is that the failings of the trial lawyers have the effect of making the conviction unsafe. These would have to be major and significant events in the case, for example not calling powerful alibi evidence, not advising the defendant properly about the advantages of giving evidence –

98 [2017] EWCA Crim 1228.
99 [2016] 2 Cr App R 30.
100 (1993) 97 Cr App R 320.
101 [2003] EWCA Crim 1060.
102 [2005] 2 Cr App R 25.

Sankar v Trinidad and Tobago;[103] failing to ask for a good character direction – *Sealey v Trinidad and Tobago*,[104] or a spectacularly ill-advised closing speech – *R v Simpson*.[105] Without such a connection, there can be very serious problems with the trial lawyers but no successful appeal will result.

3.64 In a spectacular example of this principle in action, the Court found that two murder convictions were safe even though trial counsel was under investigation for serious sexual offences and the supply of class A drugs and was also made bankrupt whilst simultaneously conducting two trials in different parts of the country. In rejecting the appeal, the Court reviewed not only the manner in which the advocate conducted the trials but also the strength of the evidence (which in the case of both appellants was overwhelming) (*R v Bolivar; R v Lee*[106]). While this may be very unlikely to occur, the appellate courts have suggested the possibility of representation being so disastrous that the subsequent conviction should be overturned regardless of safety, as the effect had been to deprive the convicted person of any sort of due process, see *Boodram v The State*.[107] However, see *R v Brooker*[108] for an example of the Court finding serious failings in counsel's conduct but nevertheless upholding the conviction.

Changes in the law

3.65 Changes in the law since conviction may provide grounds of appeal but only if this change has given rise to substantial injustice (*R v R (Amer)*[109]). This has been applied very robustly indeed; when the Supreme Court changed the *mens rea* for a joint enterprise in *R v Jogee*,[110] the Court of Appeal applied the 'substantial injustice' test in such robust terms in *R v Johnson*[111] as to lead to minuscule number of subsequent successful appeals. If the appeal is effectively based on a change of law and nothing else, but the conviction was properly returned at the time, after a fair trial, it was unlikely that a substantial injustice had occurred – *R v Cottrell; R v Fletcher*.[112] It is not always obvious whether a legal ruling amounts to a change of law rather than a restatement of existing principles – see *R v Tierney*.[113]

103 [1995] 1 WLR 194.
104 [2002] UKPC 52.
105 [2001] EWCA Crim 468.
106 [2003] EWCA Crim 1167.
107 [2002] 1 Cr App R 103.
108 [2024] EWCA Crim 103.
109 [2006] EWCA Crim 1974.
110 [2016] UKSC 8.
111 [2016] EWCA Crim 1613.
112 [2008] 1 Cr App R 7, para 46.
113 [2009] EWCA Crim 2220.

Categories not closed

3.66 As made clear at the start of this chapter, there is but one test: whether the conviction under appeal is 'unsafe'. If an event occurs at trial that proffers a basis for arguing it rendered the conviction unsafe, no lawyer should be put off initiating an appeal just because there seems to be little precedent.

THE COURT'S POWERS

3.67 The Court may either allow or dismiss an appeal. If it allows the appeal, it must quash the conviction. Unless it orders a re-trial the effect of the conviction being quashed is to require the Crown Court to record a judgment and verdict of acquittal.

3.68 If the Court quashes a conviction, it is not required to make any further order. However, it may:

(a) substitute the conviction with a conviction for an alternative offence upon which he could have been convicted in the Crown Court; or

(b) order that a re-trial take place; or

(c) re-sentence the appellant in respect of related convictions for which the sentence was not quashed.

3.69 Although CAA 1968 does not expressly frame these as alternatives, it would be difficult to see how they could be fairly combined.

Substituting a conviction

3.70 Where a defendant was convicted of a particular count but might, on the same evidence, have been convicted on an alternative count, the Court of Appeal has the power to substitute the conviction of one offence for a conviction of another.[114]

3.71 In *R v Graham*[115] in relation to conviction after trial the Court held that the power could only be exercised when the following criteria were met:

(a) the jury could, on the indictment, have found the appellant guilty of some other offence, because the allegation in the count under appeal expressly or impliedly included an allegation of the other offence; and

114 CAA 1968, s 3 in respect of offences for which he was convicted by a jury, s 3A in respect of offences to which the appellant had originally pleaded guilty.

115 (1997) 1 Cr App R 302.

(b) the jury must also have been satisfied of the facts that proved the appellant guilty of this other offence.

3.72 In relation to the first matter, the question was not whether the jury could have convicted of the alternative offence on the *facts* but whether they could have done so on the *indictment.*

In *R v MC*[116] the Court held that the offence 'on the indictment', namely an offence contrary to section 14 of the Sexual Offences Act 1956, could not be said to expressly or impliedly amount to or include an allegation of an offence under section 9 of the Sexual Offences Act 2003.

In *Graham* the Court stated that the fact the jury did not have a proper direction as to the other offence was a highly relevant consideration, as was the question whether there were reasonable grounds for concluding that the conduct of the defence would have been materially affected if the appellant had been charged with the other offence.[117]

3.73

Under the CAA 1968, section 3A, where there has been a guilty plea, the Court may substitute a plea of guilty to another offence, if:

(a) the appellant could have been found guilty of or pleaded guilty to that other offence; and

(b) the earlier plea of guilty indicates an admission of facts that would prove them guilty of the other offence.

3.74 The Court must impose a sentence for the new count, but that sentence cannot be so long as to increase the overall length of sentence above that which was imposed in the Crown Court.

Re-trials

The circumstances in which a re-trial can be ordered

3.75 The test for whether to order a re-trial is whether it is in the interests of justice to do so.[118] This involves consideration of a number of factors – *R v Maxwell (Paul).*[119] The following are commonly considered by the Court:

(a) how much of the original sentence the appellant has already served;

(b) the seriousness of the offence;

116 [2012] EWCA Crim 213.
117 At page 313B–C of *Graham*.
118 CAA 1968, s 7(1).
119 [2011] 1 WLR 1837.

(c) the time that has elapsed since the commission of the offence and any particular difficulties that the passage of time may cause the parties in now conducting the case;

(d) whether the appeal was allowed as a result of errors in the original trial which can be easily remedied at a re-trial (for example, errors in the legal directions that were provided to the jury) or whether difficulties in the original trial are likely to be present in any future trial (for example, abuse of process caused by delay, inherent weakness in the prosecution's case);

(e) whether there is fresh evidence and its effect;

(f) whether it is an appeal from a first or second trial, and

(g) personal circumstances of the appellant (for example, age or poor health).

3.76 The type of convictions that may be subject to a re-trial are set out in section 7(2):

> '(2) A person shall not under this section be ordered to be retried for any offence other than –
>
> (a) the offence of which he was convicted at the original trial and in respect of which his appeal is allowed as mentioned in subsection (1) above;
>
> (b) an offence of which he could have been convicted at the original trial on an indictment for the first-mentioned offence; or
>
> (c) an offence charged in an alternative count of the indictment in respect of which the jury were discharged from giving a verdict in consequence of convicting him of the first-mentioned offence.'

Whilst section 7 prevents the replacement of a less serious charge by a more serious charge on a re-trial, it does not prohibit the addition of other defendants or other charges if such additions are a result of further evidence coming to light since the original trial, and as long as the proposed amendment does not amount to a manipulation of the process or an abuse of process by the prosecution – *R v Feeley*.[120]

The procedure for making an order for re-trial

3.77 Whether to order a re-trial is a matter for the Court. There is no statutory requirement for an application for a re-trial to have been made before the Court

120 [2012] 2 Cr App R 13.

makes an order. However, it will usually only make it upon application of the prosecution. Therefore, the Court will expect the advocate who is appearing on behalf of the prosecution to have been provided instructions on this point prior to the appeal hearing. The defence advocate should be prepared to make submissions on the matter at the conclusion of the hearing.

3.78 If prosecuting counsel does not have instructions, the Court may put the matter back in order for him to do so. If it puts the case back to a future date for a final hearing to formally pronounce judgment and determine whether to allow a re-trial, it may consider whether to grant bail in the interim.

3.79 Once the decision of the Court to quash the conviction is formally recorded in the Crown Court as an acquittal, the Court of Appeal has no power to order a re-trial. Even if the application for a re-trial is made before this takes place, if by the time that the Court comes to consider the application the verdict of acquittal has been entered, the Court has no power to grant the prosecution application (*R v Blackwood*[121]).

The procedure once an order for re-trial is made

3.80 Once a re-trial is ordered the defendant must be arraigned on a new indictment that has been preferred by direction of the Court of Appeal, in the Crown Court. Arraignment must take place within two months of the order having been made.[122]

3.81 If it does not take place within two months, it may only take place if the prosecution applies to the Court of Appeal for leave for arraignment to take place and the Court is satisfied both that:

(a) 'The prosecution has acted with all due expedition'; and

(b) 'That there is good and sufficient cause for a re-trial' in spite of the lapse of time since the order for a re-trial was made.[123]

3.82 The Court may list the matter for legal argument. If it is not satisfied that both conditions are made out, the Court will direct that an order for acquittal be recorded by the Crown Court. 'Due expedition' means reasonable speed in relation to securing arraignment. Simply to overlook the deadline – a mandatory order of the Court of Appeal – was unacceptable and could not be categorised as anything approaching reasonable speed on the part of the prosecution – *R v Al-Jaryan*.[124]

121 [2012] EWCA Crim 390.
122 CAA 1968, s 8(2). See E.3 of the Guide.
123 CAA 1968, s 8(1B)(b).
124 [2021] 1 Cr App R 25, at para 30.

3.83 In *R v Layden*,[125] the Supreme Court considered the effect of the failure to re-arraign within two months. It reversed the Court of Appeal's decision that the failure invalidated the Crown Court proceedings but held that the failure may provide a ground of appeal against conviction.

3.84 When it makes an order for a re-trial, the Court has power to grant bail or order that the defendant be remanded in custody.[126] In practice, the Court of Appeal will often direct that any bail application should be made to the relevant Crown Court. Once an indictment is preferred in the Crown Court, any applications in relation to bail must be made to the Crown Court itself. The position during the period between an order being made and an indictment being preferred is unclear. However, there is dicta in *R v X*[127] to suggest that the Crown Court does have the power to deal with bail after an order for re-trial was made.

Powers of the Crown Court

3.85 Once the Crown Court is seized of the matter it has the power to amend the indictment. However, when considering the fairness of any application to amend, the Crown Court must take into account that the purpose of the order made by the Court of Appeal is to allow the defendant to be retried for the offences that they originally faced, not tried for new matters – see *Feely* above and *R v Booker*.[128]

3.86 The key limitation upon the power of the Crown Court is that a sentence that is passed in respect of a conviction that was secured following a re-trial may not be of 'greater severity' than the sentence that was originally imposed by the Crown Court.[129]

What was meant by 'greater severity' was comprehensively considered by the Court in *R v AB*.[130] The Court held that a longer sentence was not necessarily of greater severity where the circumstances had materially changed between the two sentencing exercises. It was necessary to look at any reduction for guilty plea (*R v Skanes*[131]), the effect of the principle of totality, the original judge's sentencing remarks, the overall impact of the sentence, including the release provisions that applied, and the punitive effect of non-custodial orders which were not imposed at the original trial but it was necessary or appropriate to

125 [2025] UKSC 12.
126 Section 8(2).
127 [2010] EWCA Crim 2367.
128 [2011] EWCA Crim 7.
129 By virtue of CAA 1968, Sch 2, para 2(1).
130 [2022] 1 Cr App R (S) 13.
131 [2006] EWCA Crim 2309.

impose after the re-trial.[132] The step by step approach is set out at para 35 of the judgment.

3.87 The court before which the offender is convicted on re-trial may pass any sentence passed on the original conviction even if by the date of the re-trial the offender has ceased to be of an age at which such a sentence could otherwise be passed.[133]

3.88 A sentence of imprisonment that is imposed following a re-trial takes effect as if it was imposed on the date of the original sentence. However, time spent on bail following an order for re-trial and time in custody before trial that would not have been counted towards the original sentence is to be deducted from this period.[134] Sections 240ZA and 240A of the CJA 2003 and section 325 of the Sentencing Act 2020 (crediting periods of remand in custody or certain types of bail) apply to any sentence imposed on re-trial as if it had been imposed on the original conviction.[135]

3.89 Legal aid to cover the re-trial is not granted by the Court of Appeal. Instead, an application must be made to the Legal Aid Agency.

Re-sentencing

3.90 If the appellant was convicted of two or more offences on an indictment, the Court may re-sentence him in respect of those remaining offences.[136] The power is often exercised to reduce the remaining sentences to take account in the reduction in the total level of criminality following the quashing of a conviction. But the Court may impose harsher sentences for the remaining offences than were originally imposed, including for an offence for which no separate penalty was originally imposed (*R v Dolan*[137]).

3.91 However, the Court may not impose a sentence that would have the effect of rendering the overall length of sentence longer than the overall length of sentence which was originally imposed in the Crown Court.[138]

132 At para 35 of judgment.
133 CAA 1968, Sch 2, para 2(2).
134 CAA 1968, Sch 2, para 2(3).
135 CAA 1968, Sch 2, para 2(4).
136 CAA 1968, s 4.
137 (1976) 62 Cr App R 36.
138 CAA 1968, s 4(3).

Re-trial and venire de novo

3.92 In a case in which the Court finds that there was never a valid conviction, because the proceedings were so irregular so as not to constitute a proper trial, it may make an order for *venire de novo*. The effect of this is to set aside the original conviction and order a new trial. If the Court makes such a finding, any re-trial is free of the procedural constraints in respect of re-trials under section 7 of CAA 1968. It is open to the Court to simply set aside the conviction without ordering a new trial – *R v Booth, Wood and* Molland.[139] An application for an order to issue a writ of *venire de novo* cannot be made as a free-standing application, outside of an appeal against conviction, and is subject to the leave provisions and time limits – *R v Stromberg*.[140]

3.93 A writ of *venire* may be issued where the proceedings were not properly commenced, or the verdict was not returned by a properly constituted jury. It may also be available in respect of other fundamental procedural errors that render the trial a nullity. The effect of issuing a writ of *venire de novo* is to return the proceedings to the stage they had reached immediately prior to the error causing them to be a nullity.

SUMMARY OF KEY POINTS

- In determining appeals against conviction, the Court applies the single statutory test of whether the conviction is 'unsafe'.
- A conviction that was obtained following a trial that was fundamentally unfair will usually be considered unsafe regardless of the strength of the evidence. However, not every unfairness that occurs during trial will render a conviction unsafe. In most instances the Court will consider the impact that the error or other unfairness may have had on the verdict of the jury.
- In relation to appeals that turn on fresh evidence, the Court has emphasised that the jury impact test may assist the Court, but it was ultimately for the Court itself to assess the potential impact of the evidence in question.
- The Court may be prepared to allow an appeal on the basis of its 'lurking doubt', in the absence of other grounds, in the most exceptional of circumstances.
- There are a limited number of circumstances in which a conviction may be appealed following a guilty plea. They include when the plea was entered following incorrect legal advice that went to the heart of the decision to plead guilty.

139 [1999] 1 Cr App 457.
140 [2018] 2 Cr App R 5.

- A procedural error may form the basis for grounds of appeal. However, unless the error was of such a serious nature that it rendered the proceedings a nullity, it will usually be necessary to show that it caused serious prejudice to the defence in the conduct of the trial.
- A wrongful trial ruling may provide grounds of appeal. However, the ruling must have been clearly wrong or unreasonable, not merely a ruling that the Court would not itself have made.
- The failure of the defence representative may give rise to grounds of appeal. But they must be given the opportunity to answer any criticism, and the Court will distinguish between genuine error and criticism of tactical decisions made with the benefit of hindsight. Any proven or admitted failure must have had the effect of rendering the conviction unsafe.
- If fresh evidence is relied on, the considerations of section 23 CAA 1968 must be addressed though not all need be met.
- If the Court allows the appeal and quashes the conviction it may, in certain circumstances, substitute a conviction for another offence or re-sentence the defendant for any offences that remain on the indictment or order a re-trial.
- If a re-trial is ordered, arraignment must take place within two months. Any application to extend this time must be made to the Court of Appeal.
- If the defendant is convicted following a re-trial, any sentence imposed may not be more severe than the sentence that was originally imposed.

Chapter 4

Appeals against sentence

INTRODUCTION

4.1 Under sections 9 and 10 of the Criminal Appeal Act 1968, a defendant may appeal to the Court of Appeal against any sentence that was imposed by the Crown Court on indictment and, in certain circumstances, against sentences imposed by the Crown Court, following a conviction in the Magistrates' Court. The rules regulating the bringing of an appeal against sentence are to be found in the Criminal Procedure Rules 2025, Parts 36 and 39 (and Part 42 in relation to confiscation orders) and in the Criminal Practice Directions 2023, Part 10. Regard should also be had to the 'Guide to Proceedings in the Court of Appeal, Criminal Division'[1] published by the Court of Appeal.

4.2 The right of appeal against sentence is subject to leave being granted by the Court of Appeal[2] or otherwise a certificate being issued by the sentencing judge stating that the case is fit for appeal.[3]

By section 11 of the Criminal Appeal Act 1968 (CAA 1968) the Court of Appeal has the following powers when determining appeals against sentence:

> '(3) On an appeal against sentence the Court of Appeal, if they consider that the appellant should be sentenced differently for an offence for which he was dealt with by the court below may –
>
> (a) quash any sentence or order which is the subject of the appeal; and
>
> (b) in place of it pass such sentence or make such order as they think appropriate for the case and as the court below had power to pass or make when dealing with him for the offence;

1 'The Guide', which is regularly updated by lawyers in the Criminal Appeal Office, was last updated in March 2026. The most up to date version of the Guide can be accessed from https://www.judiciary.uk/courts-and-tribunals/court-of-appeal-home/the-court-of-appeal-criminal-division/.

2 Section 11(1) Criminal Appeal Act 1968.

3 Section 11(1A) Criminal Appeal Act 1968.

but the Court shall so exercise their powers under this subsection that, taking the case as a whole, the appellant is not more severely dealt with on appeal than he was dealt with by the court below.'

4.3 The injunction upon the Court not to impose a more severe sentence than that which was originally imposed is clear and unequivocal. The Court cannot even impose a sentence that would be mandatory for a sentencing Court to impose (*R v Reynolds*[4]). However, whether a sentence is 'more severe' than the sentence that was the subject of appeal is not always clear. A life sentence cannot be imposed in place of a determinate sentence (*R v Whittaker*[5]). However, in *R v Bennett*,[6] the Court held that a hospital order with a restriction with an indefinite period in place of a determinate sentence, was not more severe than a determinate sentence.

4.4 In order to understand how the Court employs its powers it is necessary to turn from the statute to the body of principles that it has developed. The grounds upon which the Court may be prepared to allow an appeal against sentence overlap and the terms are not always used consistently. The precise classification of grounds is less important than ensuring that the grounds clearly and succinctly identify why the sentence is wrong, by applying the underlying principles to the facts of the case.

4.5 This chapter therefore considers the types of orders that can be appealed as sentences and then sets out the principles to be applied to such appeals. There are distinct principles and powers in relation to appeals against confiscation orders. Therefore, confiscation orders are considered separately in the latter part of the chapter. However, because of the wide range of orders which may be appealed as appeals against sentence, the principles that the Court has developed in relation to appeals against confiscation orders may well also be applicable to other sentence appeals.

APPEAL AGAINST SENTENCE ON INDICTMENT AND FOR CASES SENT FROM THE MAGISTRATES' COURT

4.6 The Court may hear appeals against sentences imposed in the Crown Court following a conviction on indictment. It may also hear appeals against sentence for summary offences that had been sent to the Crown Court for trial under section 41 of the Criminal Justice Act 1988 (power of Crown Court to deal with summary offence where person committed for either way offence) or under paragraph 6 of Schedule 3 to the Crime and Disorder Act 1998 (power

4 [2007] EWCA Crim 538.
5 [1967] Crim LR 431.
6 (1968) 52 Cr App R 514.

of Crown Court to deal with summary offence where person sent for trial for indictable-only offence).[7]

4.7 In addition, pursuant to section 10 of CAA 1968 the Court may also hear appeals against sentence for other offences sent from the Magistrates' Court in various circumstances.

What counts as a sentence?

4.8 Section 50 of CAA 1968 provides:

> '(1) In this Act "sentence", in relation to an offence, includes any order made by a court when dealing with an offender including, in particular –
>
> (a) a hospital order under Part III of the Mental Health Act 1983, with or without a restriction order;
>
> (b) an interim hospital order under that Part;
>
> (bb) a hospital direction and a limitation direction under that Part;
>
> (c) a recommendation for deportation;
>
> (ca) a confiscation order under Part 2 of the Proceeds of Crime Act 2002 (but not a determination under section 10A of that Act);
>
> (cb) an order which varies a confiscation order made under Part 2 of the Proceeds of Crime Act 2002 if the varying order is made under section 21, 22 or 29 of that Act (but not otherwise);
>
> (d) a confiscation order under the Drug Trafficking Act 1994 other than one made by the High Court;
>
> (e) a confiscation order under Part VI of the Criminal Justice Act 1988;
>
> (f) an order varying a confiscation order of a kind which is included by virtue of paragraph (d) or (e) above;
>
> (g) an order made by the Crown Court varying a confiscation order which was made by the High Court by virtue of section 19 of the Act of 1994; and
>
> (h) a declaration of relevance within the meaning of section 23 of the Football Spectators Act 1989; and
>
> (i) an order under section 129(2) of the Licensing Act 2003 (forfeiture or suspension of personal licence).

7 CAA 1968, s 9(b).

> (1A) [Section 82 of the Sentencing Act 2020] (under which a conviction of an offence for which … an order for a conditional or absolute discharge is made is deemed not to be a conviction except for certain purposes) shall not prevent an appeal under this Act, whether against conviction or otherwise.'

4.9 Since the list at section 50 is not exhaustive, the Court has had to consider whether a number of other orders are sentences.

Costs

4.10 Section 50(3) specifically provides that an order for recovery of defence costs under sections 23 and 24 of the Legal Aid Sentencing and Punishment Act 2012 is not a sentence within the meaning of section 9. However, an order that the defendant pay towards the costs of the prosecution is a sentence within the meaning of the section and may therefore be appealed (*R v Hayden*[8]).

Criminal Behaviour Orders

4.11 The making of a Criminal Behaviour Order following conviction is a sentence within the meaning of section 50 as is a subsequent decision of the Crown Court to vary or refuse an application to vary the order (*R v Preston Crown Court, ex p Langley*[9]).

Making and varying of Sexual Harm Prevention Orders

4.12 The making of a Sexual Harm Prevention Order (preceded by the Sexual Offences Prevention Order or 'SOPO') and also a subsequent decision of the Crown Court in relation to varying such an order is a sentence within the meaning of section 50 (*R v Hoath*; *R v Standage*,[10] approved in *R v Aldridge; R v Eaton*[11]).

Restraining orders

4.13 A restraining order that is made following conviction is clearly within the scope of section 50. However, by virtue of section 5A(5) of the Protection

8 (1974) 60 Cr App R 304.
9 [2008] EWHC 2623 (Admin).
10 [2011] EWCA Crim 274.
11 [2012] EWCA Crim 1456.

from Harassment Act 1997, so too is a restraining order that is made following an acquittal.

Financial reporting orders

4.14 Financial reporting orders are sentences for the purposes of section 50 (*R v Geraghty*[12]).

Appeals in relation to sentences fixed by law

4.15 A defendant who is the subject of a mandatory life sentence may appeal against the minimum term that he must serve.

Appeals by parents and guardians

4.16 Parents and guardians may appeal against:

(a) an order that they pay a fine, costs or compensation that has been imposed on a child or young person (section 380(6) of the Sentencing) Act 2020);

(b) an order, under section 377(2) of the Sentencing Act 2020 (binding over of parent or guardian).

A single right of appeal – more than one sentence

4.17 There is a single right of appeal against sentence (*R v Pinfold*[13]). A defendant cannot appeal against a particular aspect of their sentence and then separately appeal against another,[14] unless the case is referred back to the Court by the Criminal Cases Review Commission.

4.18 The significant exception to this relates to orders that are made on different dates as separate sentencing exercises. This occurs mainly in relation to confiscation orders, which may be made weeks or months after the original sentence was imposed. It will also apply to appeals against refusals to vary orders that were made on an earlier occasion. The 28-day time limit will run from the date when the order that is subject to appeal is made.

12 [2017] 1 Cr App R (S) 10.
13 (1988) 87 Cr App R 15.
14 *R v Geraghty* [2016] EWCA Crim 1523.

THE PRINCIPLES: GENERAL

What are the grounds of appeal?

4.19 The grounds upon which the Court has been prepared to allow appeals against sentence are numerous and overlapping. The terminology with which the Court describes sentencing grounds is not always consistently used. The most well-known terms are 'manifestly excessive or wrong in principle'. Although it may be said that the two terms themselves overlap (see *R v Ball*[15]), their meaning is sufficiently clear and broad to capture the variety of grounds that may be advanced. The Court will regard a sentence as manifestly excessive if it is improperly severe as a result, for example, of the judge having failed to apply the relevant guidelines, given too much weight to an aggravating feature or too little weight to a guilty plea or some piece of mitigation. A sentence may be wrong in principle if it was wrong for some other reason: if, for example, it was unlawful, or passed following a procedural failure, breach of legitimate expectation or some other important sentencing principle.

4.20 It may be helpful, therefore, for the grounds of appeal to state whether the sentence is challenged on the basis that it is manifestly excessive or wrong in principle. However, it is far more important that the grounds should go on to state clearly and succinctly exactly why it is said that the sentence is wrong. An appeal against sentence will not fail because the grounds have been misclassified. However, leave to appeal is often refused because the nature of the challenge is simply unclear.

Manifestly excessive

4.21 The term 'manifestly excessive' tends to induce a high degree of caution in the minds of many advocates. If this caution is based on a correct understanding of the term, then it is justified. It is intended to exclude those sentences in which different judges might disagree. The Court often states that the test is not whether they would have passed the same sentence but whether it is outside the range that could properly be imposed for the offence.

4.22 However, it is sometimes understood that the term 'manifestly excessive' means very or significantly excessive. It does not. If a sentence can be shown to be clearly outside that range, whether by a substantial or limited period, it is manifestly excessive.

4.23 It is right that the Court does not 'tinker' with sentences, but if a custodial sentence is manifestly excessive by months or even, in the case of

15 (1951) 35 Cr App R 164.

shorter sentences, by weeks, then a reduction in sentence by months or weeks will hardly be considered 'tinkering' by the person who has to serve it or by a fair-minded tribunal.

4.24 Whether a sentence is manifestly excessive will depend on the facts of each case. However, the following general principles apply:

The Court will consider whether the total sentence is wrong

4.25 When a defendant is sentenced for a number of offences, the Court of Appeal is generally concerned with the correctness of the overarching sentence (the total length of the sentences imposed in a single sentencing exercise) that was imposed (*R v Razaq*[16]). So, if it can be shown that an individual sentence was excessive but the overarching sentence was correct, an application for leave is likely to be refused.

Failure to follow the guidelines

4.26 The sentencing court is bound by the injunction of section 59 of the Sentencing Act 2020 (SA 2020) which provides:

> 'Every court –
>
> (a) must, in sentencing an offender, follow any sentencing guidelines which are relevant to the offender's case, and
>
> (b) must, in exercising any other function relating to the sentencing of offenders, follow any sentencing guidelines which are relevant to the exercise of the function,
>
> unless the court is satisfied that it would be contrary to the interests of justice to do so.'

4.27 The effect of this is that if the Crown Court fails to follow the applicable guideline without giving good reason for doing so, or, if it applies them incorrectly, this may provide a ground for appeal (*R v Mahendran*[17]). However, the sentencing judge is free to apply the guidelines in a flexible manner in order to achieve a just result:

> 'we have lost count of the number of times when this court has emphasised that these provisions are not intended to be applied inflexibly. Indeed, in our judgment, an inflexible approach would be inconsistent with the terms of the statutory framework … even when

16 [2011] EWCA Crim 1518.
17 [2011] EWCA Crim 608.

> the approach to the sentencing decision is laid down in an apparently detailed and on the face of it intentionally comprehensive scheme, the sentencing judge must achieve a just result.' (*R v Height and Anderson*[18])

4.28 The existence of a specific guideline will supersede previous Court of Appeal case law. However, section 59 of SA 2020 has not diminished the weight to be attached to decisions of the Court of Appeal. Therefore, the sentencing Court should take into account any significant sentencing guidance that is contained in authorities of the Court of Appeal that post-date the relevant guideline.

> 'The "interests of justice" consideration which now, and we assume always has and always will underpin the work of the Sentencing Guidelines Council (now the Sentencing Council), undoubtedly involves consideration of the subsequent thinking of this court and of the legislature on sentencing issues which may impact on every original definitive guidance. Just as the guidelines are not tramlines – an observation made time and time again – nor are they ring-fenced.' (*R v Thornley*[19])

4.29 The role of the Court of Appeal is to interpret the guidelines and provide practical illustrations of their operation, including examples where departure from them might be appropriate (*Dyer*[20]).

4.30 A distinction should be drawn between authorities that have an impact upon the guidelines and those cases which merely apply the guidelines to the facts of the case. Advocates should recall the injunction of the Court in *Erskine*[21] about the citation of cases which are merely fact specific. In *Thelwall*,[22] the Court of Appeal made it plain that the sentencing system now proceeds on the basis of guidelines, not case law, and so the citation of appellate decisions which were simply illustrations of the operation of a sentencing guideline on particular facts was unlikely to be of assistance. The only exception to that principle was where the Court had said something to clarify the terms of the guideline.

Procedural unfairness

4.31 A failure to follow the proper procedures, such as not obtaining a pre-sentence report, may provide grounds of appeal. However, the general

18 [2008] EWCA Crim 2500 at para 29.
19 [2011] EWCA Crim 153.
20 [2014] 2 Cr App R (S) 11 (61).
21 [2010] EWCA Crim 1425.
22 [2016] EWCA Crim 1755.

approach of the Court is to decline to interfere with a sentence where, had the correct procedures been followed, the sentence that would have been imposed would have been essentially the same.

Post-sentence developments

4.32 The Court is not confined to considering only the material to which the sentencing judge had access. It may, in its discretion, consider material that was not before the Court or events that have occurred since the sentence took place. The appellant's conduct following sentence will often play an important part in the sentencing process. If leave is granted, the Court may ask for a report from the prison on the appellant's progress on their sentence. The Court can order its own probation report in cases where it is of the view that it may be assisted by one, even if there was no probation report in the lower court.

4.33 In *Rogers*[23] the Court of Appeal emphasised the limitations on the use of new material in appeals against sentence. The material the Court will hear without an application under the Criminal Appeal Act 1968, section 23 for the court to admit 'fresh evidence' will include updated pre-sentence and prison reports on conduct in prison after sentence. However, it will not include fresh psychiatric or psychological evidence in support of an argument that a finding of dangerousness ought not to have been made or a hospital order should have been made. If an appellant seeks to introduce material of that type, the Court will apply the provisions of section 23.

Disparity in sentence

4.34 An unjustified disparity in sentence between co-defendants may give rise to grounds of appeal but only if 'right thinking members of the public with knowledge of the relevant facts and circumstances, learning of this sentence would consider that something had gone wrong with the administration of justice' (*R v Fawcett*[24]).

Unlawful sentences and the slip rule

4.35 When the Crown Court passes a sentence that is unlawful, in the sense that the Court does not have the power to impose it, the sentence may be appealed. However, consideration should first be given to returning to the Crown Court under the slip rule and asking the sentencing judge to correct the error. Section 385 of the Sentencing Act 2020 provides that a sentence that was

23 [2016] 2 Cr App R (S) 36 (370).
24 (1983) 5 Cr App R (S) 158.

imposed by the Crown Court can be 'varied or rescinded' up to 56 days from the date when the sentence was imposed.

4.36 It is only if the judge refuses, wrongly, to correct the error or the matter is not listed within the time limit for correction that an appeal to the Court of Appeal should be lodged.

4.37 In a case where there are other grounds of appeal, it may be tempting to bypass the Crown Court entirely and have all matters dealt with on appeal. However, the time limit for appeal runs from the date of any variation,[25] so nothing is lost by attempting to resolve such matters that can be resolved in the Crown Court.

Failure to credit time spent on a qualifying curfew

4.38 The court must specify the number of days on which a defendant has been subject to a qualifying curfew in relation to the sentence, to count towards time served.[26] The parties should attend court 'fully armed with the necessary information'[27] as to how many days a defendant has spent subject to a qualifying curfew.

4.39 Where a judge imposes a determinate sentence and days subject to curfew and/or time on extradition remand are to count as time served, the judge's direction is not part of the sentence. So long as the judge makes it clear that the court order will be subject to correction if an administrative error is discovered, the correction can take place. A hearing may be required if there is disagreement as to the existence or the extent of any error. That will not be subject to the statutory period of 56 days pursuant to section 385 of the Sentencing Act 2020, since there will be no alteration of the sentence: *R v Sesay (Yousif)*[28] at [11]. If the judge fails, without good reason, to state the period on curfew that should be counted to towards the sentence or if the period was miscalculated, the approach outlined by the Court in *R v Gordon*[29] should be followed.

4.40 Whenever a life sentence is imposed, the effect of section 322(2)(b) (for mandatory life sentences) and section 323(2)(c) (for discretionary life sentences) of the Sentencing Act 2020 is that the following periods must be deducted from the minimum term to be served that would otherwise be set:

25 Sentencing Act 2020, s 385(6).
26 Sentencing Act 2020, s 25; Criminal Justice Act 2003, s 240A.
27 *R v Sesay (Yousif)* [2024] EWCA Crim 483 at [13].
28 Ibid.
29 [2007] EWCA Crim 165.

(i) the number of days for which the offender was remanded in custody in respect of the offence for which the life sentence is imposed or a related offence;

(ii) the credit period for any period which the offender spent on bail subject to a qualifying curfew with an electronic monitoring requirement; and

(iii) any period which the offender spent in custody awaiting extradition for the offence in respect of which the life sentence is imposed.

The result of that calculation will be the minimum term, which itself is part of the sentence of the court. Thus, if an error is made in any part of the calculation it cannot be corrected administratively, being part of the sentence, but can only be varied by the Crown Court pursuant to section 385 of the Sentencing Act 2020 (within 56 days of the sentence being imposed) or by the Court of Appeal (Criminal Division) on appeal: *R v Sesay (Yousif)*.

RIGHTS OF APPEAL: CONFISCATION ORDERS AND OTHER ORDERS UNDER THE ASSET RECOVERY LEGISLATION

4.41 Section 50 of CAA 1968 provides that an appeal against a confiscation order, whether under the Proceeds of Crime Act 2002 (POCA 2002) or the Drug Trafficking Act 1994 (except when the order has been made by a High Court judge) or the Criminal Justice Act 1988, is an appeal against sentence. However, there are a number of other orders that a Crown Court can make under this legislation, only some of which attract a right of appeal against sentence.

4.42 A refusal to vary a confiscation order under section 23 of POCA 2002 is not a sentence and there is no appeal to the Court of Appeal. Therefore, the only way such an order can be challenged is by way of judicial review. However, as section 50 provides, decisions in relation to a reconsideration of benefit and available amount (POCA 2002, sections 21 and 22) and variations of orders made whilst the defendant was considered an absconder (section 29 under POCA 2002), are considered sentences.

4.43 In contrast, any variation or refusal to vary a confiscation order under the Drug Trafficking Act 1994 (except when the confiscation order has been made by a High Court judge), or the Criminal Justice Act 1988 is a sentence within the meaning of section 50.

4.44 Appeals against restraint or receivership orders under POCA are not appeals against sentence. However, they attract their own rights of appeal.[30]

30 The rights of appeal in relation to receivership orders are to be found at POCA 2002, s 65.

PRINCIPLES: CONFISCATION

Grounds of appeal

4.45 There are no prescribed grounds of appeal against confiscation orders. Common grounds of appeal are that the judge erred in fact or law. The Court is often cautious about interfering with errors of fact, unless they are clear and significant. It normally accords considerable respect to factual findings of the Crown Court judge who heard the case, particularly if their judgment depends to a significant extent on assessment of live evidence that the judge heard in either the course of the confiscation hearing or the preceding trial.

The slip rule

4.46 Section 385 of the Sentencing Act 2020 applies to confiscations orders (by analogy with the decision of *R v Bukhari*[31] in relation to section 155 of the PCCSA 2000).

Fresh evidence

4.47 The statutory rules in relation to fresh evidence apply to confiscation proceedings (*R v Stroud*[32]). A party seeking to adduce fresh evidence must therefore meet the requirements of section 23 of CAA 1968. Much of the case law on fresh evidence in appeals against conviction is applicable to appeals against a confiscation order.

Appeals against confiscation orders made by consent

4.48 In *R v Mackle*,[33] the Supreme Court held that a confiscation order that had been made with the consent of the defendant but following clearly erroneous legal advice, may be appealed. This overturned the decision of the Court of Appeal in *R v Hirani*[34] in which the Court found that, in the absence of exceptional circumstances, a defendant was bound by an order to which he consented, even if that consent was based on an entirely incorrect understanding of what he was consenting to, following bad legal advice.

4.49 *Mackle* did not provide any guidance as to how the Court of Appeal should now approach appeals based upon allegations of consent being given

31 [2008] EWCA Crim 2915.
32 [2004] EWCA Crim 1048.
33 [2014] UKSC 5.
34 [2008] EWCA Crim 1463.

as a result of flawed legal advice. However, it is likely that the Court will approach them in a similar manner to appeals against conviction in which it is argued that a guilty plea was tendered following bad legal advice.

Extension of time to appeal against a confiscation order following a change in the law

4.50 Following the judgment of the Supreme Court in *R v Waya*,[35] in which the Court held that the First Protocol of the Convention required the Crown Court to ensure that any confiscation order represents a proportionate interference with the defendant's property, a number of applications for extension of time within which to appeal against sentence were made by applicants whose confiscation order had been made some time ago and had not appealed because the law, prior to *Waya*, provided no grounds upon which to do so.

4.51 In *Bestel v R*,[36] the Court held that the principle of finality that decisions made under the law as it was then understood should not be disturbed unless this would cause substantial injustice, should be followed in confiscation cases.

POWERS OF THE COURT: CONFISCATION

4.52 The Court has the power under section 11(3) Criminal Appeal Act 1968 to impose an alternative sentence to that which was subject to appeal. However, it also has the power, under section 11(3A) to quash a confiscation order and then to remit the case to the Crown Court with a direction that a new confiscation hearing take place. When it does so, the Court of Appeal must give directions to the Crown Court as to the conduct of the new hearing. The Crown Court must not impose a confiscation order that is more severe than that which was subject to appeal.

PROSECUTION RIGHTS OF APPEAL IN CONFISCATION CASES

4.53 The prosecution enjoys rights of appeal against the terms of a confiscation order or the refusal to make a confiscation order under POCA 2002 only. Section 31 of POCA 2002 provides:

35 [2012] UKSC 51.
36 [2013] EWCA Crim 1305.

4.54 *Appeals against sentence*

'(1) If the Crown Court makes a confiscation order the prosecutor may appeal to the Court of Appeal in respect of the order.

(2) If the Crown Court decides not to make a confiscation order the prosecutor may appeal to the Court of Appeal against the decision.

(3) Subsections (1) and (2) do not apply to an order or decision made by virtue of section 10A, 19, 20, 27 or 28.'

4.54 As subsection (3) provides, the prosecution enjoys none of the rights of appeal against variations of a confiscation order that are enjoyed by the defence.

SUMMARY OF KEY POINTS

- The only statutory test on an appeal against sentence is whether 'the appellant should be sentenced differently for an offence'.
- The Court had recognised a number of grounds of appeal against sentence, the most well-established of which are that a sentence is 'manifestly excessive' or 'wrong in principle'. Between them, these terms cover most of the types of arguments that can be advanced. However, for the applicant, the classification of grounds is less important than ensuring that the grounds clearly identify the way in which it is said that the sentence in question is flawed.
- In determining whether a sentence is manifestly excessive, the Court will consider whether the sentence, as a whole, is excessive.
- The Court may be prepared to find that a failure to follow the sentencing guidelines renders a sentence manifestly excessive. However, it has reiterated that guidelines are not a straightjacket and may be interpreted in a flexible manner.
- The unjustified disparity in sentence between co-defendants may give rise to grounds of appeal but only if 'right thinking members of the public with knowledge of the relevant facts and circumstances, learning of this sentence would consider that something had gone wrong with the administration of justice'.
- A failure to follow the proper procedures may provide grounds of appeal. However, the general approach of the Court is to decline to interfere with a sentence where, had the correct procedures been followed the sentence that would have been imposed would have been essentially the same.
- An unlawful sentence may be corrected on appeal. However, consideration should first be given to whether the unlawful element of the sentence can be corrected by returning to the Crown Court under the slip rule.

- If the Court allows an appeal, it may quash the sentence and replace it with any sentence that the Crown Court had the power to impose. However, this new sentence must not be more severe than the sentence that was appealed.
- Confiscation orders may be appealed as well as decisions in relation to the variations of confiscation orders but not variations under section 23 of POCA 2002.
- When appeal is based on alleged errors of fact, the Court may be reluctant to interfere with the findings of the Crown Court judge save in the clearest circumstances.
- A confiscation order that has been made with the consent of the defendant may be appealed if it can be shown that, as a result of bad legal advice or some other reason, the defendant did not understand the order he was agreeing to.
- If the Court allows an appeal against a order it may simply quash the order, impose a new order or remit the case to the Crown Court for a new confiscation hearing to take place.
- The prosecution may also appeal against a confiscation order or a refusal to make a confiscation order but only when proceedings are under POCA 2002.

Part 2
The Appeal Process

Chapter 5

Defence investigations

INTRODUCTION

5.1 Post-conviction defence investigations can play a vital role in correcting miscarriages of justice. By engaging in active factual investigation – as opposed to merely reviewing trial papers – defence representatives can obtain fresh evidence that demonstrates that a conviction is unsafe or that a sentence was wrong. Whilst the Criminal Cases Review Commission (CCRC) has statutory powers and resources which enable it to undertake such investigations, the CCRC's mishandling of the case of Andrew Malkinson,[1] as detailed in the Henley Report,[2] highlights why it cannot always be depended upon to unearth such fresh evidence.

5.2 When investigating a crime, the police have a duty to pursue all reasonable lines of enquiry and to obtain evidence which points away from, as well as towards, the suspect.[3] This includes material the police investigator believes may be in the hands of third parties. If that is the case then the investigator should inform the disclosure officer who, in turn, should ask the party to retain it and this should be recorded and notified to the prosecutor.[4] As recent history has highlighted, especially when resources are scarce, it should not be assumed that has been done.[5] The failure of disclosure and the collapse of several high-profile trials over the years led to the House of Commons'

1 *R v Andrew Malkinson* [2023] EWCA Crim 954.

2 Chris Henley KC, 'Independent review by Chris Henley KC of the CCRC's handling of the Andrew Malkinson case', published on 18 July 2024 (https://cloud-platform-e218f50a4812967ba1215eaecede923f.s3.amazonaws.com/uploads/sites/5/2024/07/Integrated-Report-Response-Redacted-Copy.pdf).

3 Criminal Procedure and Investigations Act 1996 (CPIA), s 23; Para 3.5 CPIA Code of Conduct; Para 17 Attorney General's Guidelines on Disclosure.

4 Para 3.6 CPIA Code of Conduct.

5 A critical report by HM Inspectorate of Constabulary led the police and prosecution to issue joint guidance in July 2017 in an effort to improve the process: 'Making it Fair – A Joint Inspection of the Disclosure of Unused Material in Volume Crown Court Cases' (www.justiceinspectorates.gov.uk/hmicfrs/publications/making-it-fair-disclosure-of-unused-material-in-crown-court-cases).

Justice Committee looking into serious failings in disclosure by police and prosecutors.[6]

It is often the case that by the time a defendant is charged the police will be firmly committed to a particular view of the case and it is inevitable that resources will be focused on obtaining evidence that will help secure a conviction in accordance with that particular view. Every day we all generate huge amounts of electronic data on our phones and social media. Police usually seize any electronic devices found on the suspect, as well as from their home and sometimes their workplace. Often that is used to bolster the prosecution case by adducing potentially harmful messages, pictures and social contacts, which are then used to build associations with co-defendants and cell siting of where the defendant was. Less often is that material considered for prosecution witnesses who may not be telling the truth or who may have misremembered events. In cases where the parties are known to each other or the prosecution witnesses have an ulterior motive in making the accusations, this material may be either highly relevant to the defence or may help to undermine the prosecution case. The potential problems with seizure and disclosure have been recognised by the Attorney-General, who published an important review of how disclosure should operate in practice to take account of these concerns.[7]

5.3 In an age of austerity when police do not have the budget to do everything they should it is all the more important that defence lawyers appreciate that they are not solely dependent on the efforts of the police investigators. They can actively pursue other avenues themselves to obtain potentially relevant information. Indeed, some of these avenues may not be open to the police as witnesses may be reluctant to speak to them or the police may be unaware of information that the defendant has access to.

If this was not considered properly pre-trial then it becomes indispensable after conviction because, at that point, most prosecution investigations will cease entirely. It will only be those who act on behalf of the potential appellant who have an interest in continuing to work on the case. Such defence investigations may uncover evidence to start an appeal or they may reveal material that triggers further prosecution disclosure or persuades the CCRC to commence their own investigation using their extensive powers (see Chapter 9).

6 Case of Liam Allen, who was acquitted in December 2017 (https://publications.parliament.uk/pa/cm201719/cmselect/cmjust/859/859.pdf).

7 See Disclosure in the Digital Age: Independent Review of Disclosure and Fraud Offences at https://assets.publishing.service.gov.uk/media/67e279b64fed20c7f559f558/Disclosure_in_the_Digital_Age_-_Independent_Review_Report_CP1285_WEB_0.1.pdf.

WHAT ARE DEFENCE INVESTIGATIONS AND WHO MAY CARRY THEM OUT?

5.4 Defence investigations are attempts to obtain relevant material in a way that maximises the chances of it being admitted as fresh evidence by the Court of Appeal under section 23 of the Criminal Appeal Act 1968 (CAA 1968).

5.5 Most appeal cases will benefit from new material that supports the appellant's case, and this includes appeals against sentence. For example, in the most straightforward appeal against sentence it may be possible to obtain medical evidence that was never before the Crown Court or a compelling character witness who was never asked to give a statement. Fresh material can be especially relevant for young appellants. The Sentencing Council guidelines require the sentencing judge to actively consider relevant material about the defendant's background and take that information into account when considering mitigating factors and take specific account of welfare considerations. These include any difficulties the defendant faced as a child and any issues that might impact upon culpability due to their lack of maturity.[8] Often educational assessments, psychological reports or social services records will not have been obtained prior to the original sentence. These should have been considered by the original defence team in order to provide the sentencing judge with a full picture of the young person's circumstances and the difficulties they may have faced and contributed to their offending. These investigations can throw up mental health issues or show that the defendant had been subject to coercive and controlling behaviour. It may show that the defendant was a victim of forced labour or trafficking;[9] it may reveal that they were a refugee who had a defence to a false document offence.[10] Sometimes insufficient efforts will have been made given the increasing rush to plead guilty and maximise credit, to identify these underlying issues which can go to sentence and, in some cases, the question of whether they should have pleaded guilty in the first place (see Chapter 15 Special Cases). However, whether the Court will be prepared to admit this material as fresh evidence is a different matter (see Chapter 3).

5.6 It is best that investigations are carried out under the direction of the defence lawyers. Investigation carried out by a solicitor is much more likely to result in evidence that will be admitted by the Court of Appeal. As officers of the Senior Courts, they are subject to the discipline of their professional body should they mislead the Court or attempt to conceal the true picture, which

8 Overarching Principles of Sentencing Children and Young People: www.sentencingcouncil.org.uk/overarching-guides/crown-court/item/sentencing-children-and-young-people.

9 Modern Slavery Act 2015, s 45.

10 Immigration and Asylum Act 1999, s 31.

may make the Court more likely to attach weight to the material that they uncover. However, evidence obtained by non-lawyers should also be admitted as long as it was obtained in a proper manner. Many private investigators are former police officers who are experienced in producing relevant witness statements that can be independently corroborated. However, former police officers may not be the right people to use in certain investigations, especially with regards to witnesses who have a negative experience of the police. The Legal Aid Agency may be more likely to agree to fund private investigator work as it saves public money given it is billed at a lower hourly rate and paid as a disbursement rather than the slightly higher hourly rate that can be claimed by the solicitor.[11] This is an important factor in investigative work that can be time-consuming and open-ended. Of course, you will need to agree the scope of the work in advance and obtain prior approval from the Legal Aid Agency (or your private client) for the anticipated work (see Chapter 8).

THE ETHICS OF DEFENCE INVESTIGATION

5.7 Obtaining evidence in a manner that protects its integrity maximises the chance of it being admitted by the Court of Appeal. Being aware of potential ethical pitfalls is particularly important in appeal cases. Interviewing witnesses who gave evidence for the Crown at trial is a matter that often gives rise to particular concern. An unwillingness to speak to them often stems from a fear that the defence team could be accused of influencing the witness to change their evidence, particularly if the witness previously gave statements that are inconsistent with what they are now saying.[12] There is a general principle of evidence that 'there is no property in a witness' as a witness to a relevant fact (if competent), will be usually compellable to give evidence.[13] However, it has been found, that in a criminal matter, where the witness has given evidence for the prosecution they are not compellable by the defence.[14] Therefore, the defence should be cautious about approaching former prosecution witnesses and should alert the prosecution to an intention to do so and invite them to raise any objections. They should also give them the opportunity to be present at any proposed attendance on the witness to ensure there is no undue pressure on the witness to co-operate.

11 Currently Enquiry Agents guidance hourly rate is £25.60 outside London and £18.40 in London (https://assets.publishing.service.gov.uk/government/uploads/system/uploads/attachment_data/file/791497/Guidance_on_the_Remuneration_of_Expert_Witnesses_April2019.pdf).

12 M Hannibal and L Mountford *Criminal Litigation Handbook 2013/14* (Oxford, Oxford University Press, 2013) para 1.11.6, and for a recent refusal by the Court of Appeal to accept retraction evidence see *R v SB* [2019] EWCA Crim 565.

13 *See Harmony Shipping Co SA v Davis* [1979] 3 All ER 177.

14 *Kelly* (1985) The Times, 27 July 1985.

5.8 These and other concerns can be minimised by following best practices and the relevant ethical rules that can be found in the solicitor's Code of Conduct.[15] The Law Society has published guidance to assist defence solicitors when dealing with defence witness notices, which has some application generally.[16] In particular, the investigator should:

(a) create a careful file note of the meeting or significant conversation with a witness that lays out exactly what was said by all parties;

(b) never misrepresent who they are, who they work for and why they are asking questions;[17]

(c) take care not to pressurise a witness in any way and remember that it is the witness's prerogative to refuse to be interviewed;[18]

(d) never take advantage of an unrepresented third party;[19]

(e) never interview a represented person without the consent of their legal representative; and

(f) never give legal advice where there is a conflict of interest.[20]

5.9 Defendants themselves should not be involved in questioning potential witnesses nor should their family or friends, or any other potential defence

15 See https://www.sra.org.uk/solicitors/standards-regulations/code-conduct-solicitors/.

16 Law Society Practice Notes: Defence Witness Notices, 21 December 2015. See https://www.lawsociety.org.uk/topics/criminal-justice/defence-witness-notices.

17 The people you are interviewing or asking for records from may ask you questions in return about what you are up to. This is part of the natural give and take of conversation and does not mean they are unwilling to talk to you. This does not mean you have to explain things that are confidential to the defendant or things that, strategically, you would rather not have in the public realm. You can simply explain that you are investigating for an appeal on behalf of a defendant, and that you want to hear everyone's side of the story.

18 This includes thinking carefully about who is the best person to do the interview, with reference to matters such as age, gender, race, etc. The suspicion that a witness's feeling of being intimidated stems from prejudice does not obviate the fact that they felt intimidated. Achieving Best Evidence (ABE) techniques and Special Measures can be employed when appropriate with vulnerable witnesses.

19 A lawyer has a duty to represent their client to the best of their ability, but they also have a duty not to take advantage of those who do not have legal representation in order to do so (Solicitors Regulation Authority Code of Conduct, Chapter 11, Outcome 11.1). One way of dealing with this situation may be to ensure that the potential witness has independent legal assistance before formalising what they have to say in a s 9 witness statement. Another is to discuss the interview with the SRA Ethics Helpline team.

20 See the Solicitors Regulatory Authority Code of Conduct, Chapter 3, Outcome 3.5. If someone else wants to confess to the crime, or confess to previous perjury in the case, the defendant's lawyer cannot advise them of the legal implications of doing this. It is necessary to get the information from them about what they would tell the Court (because that is your duty to your client), but the defendant's lawyer cannot advise them of the risks they face. They should obtain independent legal representative before they make any formal statement. Again, the SRA Ethics helpline can be a helpful resource here.

witnesses. The case of *R v Calvert*[21] provides a recent example of where the Court of Appeal cited 'the possibility of undue influence upon' a witness by the appellant's family when declining to admit fresh evidence.

THE TECHNIQUES OF INVESTIGATION

Funding for an investigation

5.10 Where leave has not been applied for and the purpose of the investigation is to put the defence in a position to make an application for leave to appeal, or to make an application to the Criminal Cases Review Commission, funding can be requested from the Legal Aid Authority under the Advice and Assistance scheme. (See Chapter 8 for consideration of funding applications under the scheme.) If leave is granted the Court may grant a representation order to allow the appellant's solicitors to undertake particular tasks. (See Chapters 6 and 8 at 6.46 and 8.9–8.10.)

Conducting the investigation strategically

5.11 Planning an investigation involves:

(a) knowing what evidence was before the jury and what evidence was available to both the prosecution and the defence at trial;

(b) prioritising the leads to follow first (given the limited resources available);

(c) working from the outside of the circle to the centre when approaching a sensitive issue or witness, so that as much information as possible is obtained before any evidence is removed from reach (such as a witness refusing to talk or a document being destroyed).

What you already know

5.12 It is always helpful to start by establishing what material is already in the hands of the defence. This will involve speaking to the defendant, their family and certainly their previous lawyers.[22] It is also important to gather as complete a case file as possible.

5.13 The following material should normally be sought:

21 [2025] EWCA Crim 345, para 60.

22 The Court of Appeal has held that speaking with previous legal representatives 'will henceforth be necessary … to ensure that facts are correct, unless there are in exceptional circumstances good and compelling reasons not to do so.' *R v McCook* [2014] EWCA Crim 734, para 11. See Chapter 6 for further discussion of the case.

(a) records of arrest and pre-trial detention (especially as to defendant's state of mind and the circumstances of admissions);

(b) the defendant's proof of evidence, comments on prosecution witnesses and defence case statement (and any character evidence);

(c) the defence solicitor's police station attendance notes;

(d) defence witness statements whether relied on or not and reasons why not called;

(e) police statements, plus material the police relied on in writing their statements reports (such as contemporaneous notes from notebooks and logs especially first descriptions which they have a duty to record);

(f) witness statements taken by the police, including contemporaneous handwritten notes;

(g) news media reports (often available through internet search engines);

(h) recordings of transcribed statements especially Achieving Best Evidence (ABE) recordings;

(i) other recorded evidence such as CCTV, copies of computer hard drives, mobile phone downloads, and any 999 calls;

(j) expert reports plus any material experts relied on in reaching their conclusions for both prosecution and the defence (and whether relied upon);

(k) the non-sensitive unused material schedule (MG6C), unused material provided to the trial team by the CPS and defence section 8 CPIA applications;

(l) trial solicitors' working file including notes, correspondence and billing (the latter is useful for working out when/whether material was actually read though the previous solicitor is not obliged to produce internal documents that do not relate to advice provided);[23]

(m) trial exhibits/material that went before the jury especially admissions;

(n) trial transcripts (access limited – see below);

(o) defence trial advocate's notebooks; solicitor or solicitor's clerk's notebooks;

(p) any previous grounds of appeal;

(q) any previous applications to Criminal Cases Review Commission (CCRC) and any statement of reasons from the CCRC;

23 The Law Society has published a Practice Note: Who owns the file? 16 January 2019.

(r) HMPPS prisoner records from the Branston Prison Registry;[24]

(s) prison and probation files, including OASYS reports and the most recent parole dossier from the National Offender Management Service (NOMS), which may contain historical documents that may have been destroyed by others; and

(t) prison healthcare records and medical records from the client's General Practitioner.

Whereas in older cases a request for case papers will generally result in many boxes of papers arriving at your doorstep, things have improved with the introduction of the Crown Court Digital Case System (CCDCS), as now the previous solicitor can simply add you to the Digital Case bundle which will give you access to the prosecution material, though you will still need to obtain the defence papers (as most defence lawyers do not save documents to the Defence Section for fear that they are disclosed inadvertently). As more solicitors work digitally, their files can increasingly be supplied in an electronic format. It is important to remember that only those prosecution documents which were put before the court will be on the CCDCS. Unused material and documents such as unused expert reports and the proof of evidence of the defendant are not uploaded to the CCDCS. When requesting a case file, it is advisable to request these be added to the CCDCS and for any other documents which were not uploaded. In addition, where the defendant had co-defendants, there may be both an 'individual' and a 'joindered' CCDCS file, so you should ensure you are added to both of these if you are representing both defendants; although a lot of the documents will be the same, there are often different documents on each of them.

5.14 Building an electronic file makes it easier and quicker to create a chronology of what happened, and who knew what and when, as well as an index of appeal issues, with each item linked back to the relevant pages of the file. A similar tagging of witness statements and police interviews is also helpful. There is increasingly sophisticated case analysis software to help with this task. Widely available optical character recognition software should be applied to case documents so that their text is searchable.

5.15 In older cases the trial lawyers may no longer be in possession of the case file, as they may have determined that their obligation to keep the file has expired.[25] In these circumstances it may be necessary to reconstruct the trial solicitor's files from individual sources such as the Court, the CPS, the police, the CCRC, the defendant and their supporters. Sometimes the parole dossier may be all that is left as a source of relevant material.

24 Obtainable from the Data Access and Compliance Unit (at the Branson Registry).

25 See https://www.lawsociety.org.uk/contact-or-visit-us/helplines/practice-advice-service/q-and-as/how-long-should-i-retain-my-closed-files-in-storage.

5.16 A complete trial transcript is an invaluable guide to what occurred at trial but the cost of ordering one from the relevant transcription company can be prohibitively high. Generally, legal aid funding under advice and assistance (see Chapter 8) can be obtained for specific, arguably necessary transcripts, such as the summing up, mitigation and sentencing hearings, or the evidence of specific witnesses, but the LAA will not grant funding for transcripts of whole proceedings. You will also need to obtain the authorisation from the resident judge at the Crown Court where it was tried (see 8.41). Time is of the essence in ordering transcripts: the current Crown Court Record Retention and Disposition Schedule[26] specifies that the digital audio recordings of trials only need to be retained for seven years.

Seeking additional material from the prosecution

5.17 Following conviction the prosecution's statutory duty to disclose relevant material ends.[27] However, as clarified by the Supreme Court in *R (on the application of Nunn) v Chief Constable of Suffolk Constabulary*,[28] there is a continuing common law duty of disclosure when material 'comes to light after the conclusion of the proceedings, which may cast doubt upon the safety of the conviction'. This duty is reflected in paragraph 140 of the Attorney General's Guidelines on Disclosure (2024).

5.18 In *Nunn*, the Supreme Court held 'there is no continuing right to indefinite re-investigation of cases following conviction.' However, the Court also ruled that the police and prosecutors should co-operate with post-conviction defence investigation '[i]f there appears to be a real prospect that further enquiry will uncover something which may affect the safety of the conviction', adding that: 'It is in nobody's interests to resist all enquiry unless and until the CCRC directs it.'

5.19 Attempts to obtain new material from the prosecution can start with written requests to the investigating police force, the Crown Prosecution Service or the relevant prosecuting authority which should:

(a) specify as clearly as possible what material is sought;

(b) explain why it is sought with reference to any potential grounds of appeal and/or its potential impact on the safety of the conviction;

(c) state why you believe that they have the material in question; and

(d) ask for full reasons to be given for any refusal to provide disclosure.

26 See https://assets.publishing.service.gov.uk/media/5f3fc97bd3bf7f67ad325013/crown-court-rrds.docx.

27 Criminal Procedure and Investigations Act 1996, s 7A.

28 [2014] UKSC 37.

5.20 If the prosecutor refuses to provide further material, the Court of Appeal may order its disclosure, but it will only consider doing so after an application for leave has been lodged with the Court (see Chapter 6). Therefore, at the CCRC stage, or until an application for leave is made, the only remedy is an application for judicial review of the police or prosecutor's refusal to disclose. This should start with a detailed pre-action letter setting out why the police or prosecution should exercise their discretion to provide access to the material in question.

Seeking new material

Subject Access Requests under the Data Protection Act 2018

5.21 Material which contains or constitutes personal information about a particular person may be obtained through a 'Subject Access Request' (SAR) made to a 'competent authority'[29] under section 45(1) of the Data Protection Act 2018 (DPA 2018).[30] Such requests may be made to the agency that holds the information with the written authorisation of the person to whom the data relates, enabling the request to be made on their behalf by their lawyer.

5.22 Under section 45(4) DPA 2018, access to personal data may be restricted, either wholly or partially, in order to:

(a) avoid obstructing an official or legal inquiry, investigation or procedure;

(b) avoid prejudicing the prevention, detection, investigation or prosecution of criminal offences or the execution of criminal penalties;

(c) protect public security;

(d) protect the rights and freedoms of others.

Any such a restriction to the right of access to personal data must be a necessary and proportionate measure, having regard to fundamental rights and legitimate interests of the individual, and only to the extent that, and for so long as, is necessary.[31] That restriction might arguably apply on appeal cases when the information sought is still relevant to other active investigations or prosecutions.

5.23 If the request is made by someone other than the subject, then a signed authorisation form will also be required which entitles the person making the

29 Data Protection Act 2018, Sch 7 sets out a list of competent authorities, which includes ministerial government departments, courts, police forces, the parole board, and prisons (including those which are privately run). See https://www.legislation.gov.uk/ukpga/2018/12/contents.

30 An SAR, is a request made for records that relate to the person making the request, or their representative.

31 Data Protection Act 2018, s 45(4); which mirrors the test for restricting a Convention right.

request to obtain the documents they are requesting on behalf of the subject. This is so, even where the application form specifically states that the data subject must sign the form themselves. Where a person is in prison or detained, it is not necessary to comply with the requirement to provide identification documents, although this is stated on the majority of application forms. In this situation, it may assist if you can confirm the client's location via email with the National Offender Management Service (NOMS) prisoner location service and then send a PDF of this email along with the SAR.[32]

A difficulty sometimes arises where a client has previously been imprisoned but has been transferred to hospital under section 47 or section 49 of the Mental Health Act (MHA), as the NOMS prisoner location service records will state that the person has been released from prison. If this is the case, generally it is best to explain this situation to the Data Controller and see what other proof may be acceptable to them – for example, email confirmation from the detained person's treating clinician stating that they have been transferred to hospital under section 47 or section 49 MHA.

5.24 It is important to include the requestor's name and contact details, the data subject's full names and any relevant information that will help the agency concerned to locate the material that is sought. The information should be provided without undue delay and, in any event, within one month of them either receiving the full request (with all necessary information) or them obtaining the data which is requested.[33] Where an organisation fails to comply with this deadline, ultimately you can report them to the Information Commissioner's Office.

5.25 Since the DPA 2018 came into force, SARs should no longer involve the payment of any administration fee. As a result, many organisations are struggling to comply with the guidelines as the number of requests has increased considerably. There is an exception to this, whereby a reasonable fee may be charged if the data subject has made 'manifestly unfounded or excessive requests'.[34] There is no example or definition of 'manifestly unfounded or excessive'. An excessive request may be one that merely repeats the substance of previous requests. For example, if you have already requested a client's prison healthcare records and require an update, you should request the records from the last date of the previous records onwards, rather than requesting all records, in order to avoid a request being viewed as excessive. The Information Commissioner's Office website provides a useful guide to making SARs and has examples of pro-forma request letters that can be followed. A large number of agencies and organisations, including the Metropolitan Police, have their

32 Prisoner Location Service (NOMS): https://www.gov.uk/find-prisoner.

33 Data Protection Act 2018, ss 45(3) and 54.

34 Data Protection Act 2018, s 53.

own SAR application form available online, but it is not compulsory to use such forms.

If a client has been in prison for a long time, they may no longer be registered with a General Practitioner. If so, their medical records will have been sent to Primary Care Support England (PCSE), which is an NHS department responsible for storing residual medical records. These records can be obtained directly from PCSE by completing the application form available the PCSE website.

Requests under the Freedom of Information Act 2000

5.26 Applications for data held by public authorities that does not fall under section 7 of the Data Protection Act 1998 can be made under section 1 of the Freedom of Information Act 2000 (FOIA 2000). Again, a clear and detailed guide to making such applications is to be found on the Information Commissioner's website.

5.27 Such applications can be a useful means of obtaining information that is important for understanding the evidence in the case, for example, how those with a role in the case are trained to do their jobs and the procedures that are followed by particular institutions. However, freedom of information requests cannot generally be used to bypass the requirements of disclosure in criminal proceedings and obtain material that is held by the prosecution in relation to the case. Material held for the purpose of a criminal investigation or prosecution is exempt from the requirements of section 1 to the extent that the information holder does not regard it as being in the public interest to disclose it.[35]

Under section 32 of FOIA 2000, information held only by virtue of being contained in documents created or held for the purpose of court, inquiry or arbitration proceedings is exempt from disclosure under section 1, regardless of the public interest in disclosure. However, defence investigators can instead seek access to court records under the provisions contained within Part 5 of the Criminal Procedure Rules 2025.

Records collection generally

5.28

(a) It is important to follow up on requests sent out. A request may have to be sent several times as many organisations are dealing with large increases in the numbers of requests.

35 Freedom of Information Act 2000, s 30.

(b) If the investigator believes that a record exists, but the relevant agency states they cannot find it, or that it has been destroyed, it can be helpful to ask for a sworn statement from a representative of the agency or company attesting to what searches have been made, or to their personal knowledge of the destruction of that particular document.

(c) It is always necessary (and beneficial) to be polite and courteous to the record-holders.

(d) Although it is important to be specific about what records are sought, it is helpful to try to draft a request in such a way as to catch other potentially relevant documents that may be in the possession of the record holder. In the case of SARs, this can be done by requesting 'any and all personal data held, including but not limited to that which is contained within or constituted by …' before going on to list specific documents being sought.

(e) The investigator should personally search any archived files if permitted to do so.

(f) The investigator should think outside the box ('where else would copies of that missing record end up?').

(g) Good records should be kept of all requests made, including follow-ups to the original request. This will become particularly relevant when submitting an application for an extension of time for leave to appeal as it will be necessary to justify any delay in making the application, which is often contributed to by delays in obtaining documents.

Visiting and recording the crime scene and other significant locations

5.29 Visiting the crime scene or another location that is significant to the case is something that the defence should consider as part of their preparation for trial. However, it is often overlooked. When investigating a case for a potential appeal one should not assume that site visits have been done or that they could not now assist in any appeal. Even if site visits have already taken place, a fresh pair of eyes may notice something that has previously been missed. If a site visit is to take place, the following should be borne in mind:

(a) It is useful to take cameras with the capacity to shoot both stills and moving footage. One film of a location can then be shot with a voiceover by the film-maker describing what can be seen and its relevance. A second film should be taken without the voiceover, so the ambient sound can be recorded. Stills of the same areas should also be taken.

(b) Measurements should be taken where possible, using a tape measure or a rolling measuring wheel. This should be done after any film and stills have been taken.

(c) If access to private property is required to make the recording, the owner should be asked, unless of course the owner or occupier is a complainant, in which case filming will have to be restricted to what can be seen from the street at a time when the complainant is not likely to be disturbed or upset. The relevant privacy, trespass, harassment or data protection laws should be consulted and followed if it appears that filming may give rise to legal issues.

(d) Since the relevant events took place, features of the scene may have changed significantly due to factors such as the passage of time or seasonal changes.

Conducting interviews with potential witnesses

5.30 In addition to the ethical considerations already discussed, the following guidelines will help the investigator obtain useful evidence from potential witnesses:

(a) Where possible, and provided it does not put the investigator at risk, the investigator should seek to conduct the interview at the witness's own home where they are likely to be more relaxed, less pressed for time and where there is a possibility of meeting other potential witnesses. The investigator will be more likely to obtain information by knocking on the door at a time when the witness may be expected to be home rather than phoning or writing to ask for an appointment.

(b) The investigator should be courteous and respectful at all times and dress appropriately for the meeting.

(c) The investigator should prepare for the interview by reviewing all relevant materials in order to understand what the witness has already said, and drawing up an interview plan, including a set of questions. It may be useful for the investigator to take the materials with them, but care needs to be taken not to distract or influence the witness. The witness may be more at ease if the investigator is not working from notes but rather engaging in direct conversation, so memorising the interview plan as much as possible can be helpful.

(d) The investigator should be prepared to explain their role, the status of the case and what may happen next. The investigator should be careful not to misrepresent their role nor make any assurances to the witness that cannot be kept.

(e) If questioned about their view of the case, the investigator should stay non-committal, objective and open.

(f) The questions asked of the witness should generally be open-ended.

(g) Close attention should be paid to what is said and the witness should be asked to clarify what they have said, if necessary. Notes should be taken to the extent that is possible without making the witness feel uncomfortable. A record should be typed up as soon as possible afterwards. Witnesses may be distrustful of recording equipment so it should only be used in very particular circumstances and only with the witness's consent.

(h) Pregnant pauses should be allowed to develop as often an uncomfortable silence is filled by the interviewee saying what is on their mind.

(i) The contact details of the interviewee should be confirmed, and they should be informed that the defence team may wish to contact them again.

(j) Notes should be reviewed for coherence. It is important that anyone who reads the notes can understand what was said.

(k) If the decision is made to take a statement from a witness, it should be done using the format required for admission of the statement under section 9 of the Criminal Justice Act 1967, which allows for the statement to be admitted before the Court without the witness needing to appear. It is preferable to handwrite out such a statement during the first interview than to arrange to send a typed version.

CO-OPERATING WITH OTHER INVESTIGATORY BODIES

Investigation by the Criminal Cases Review Commission

5.31 The CCRC can deploy powers to carry out investigations that are unavailable to the defence representatives on appeal. Under sections 17 and 18A of the Criminal Appeal Act 1995 (CAA 1995), the CCRC has powers to compel disclosure of documents from public and private bodies that the appellant may not be able to access via *Nunn* requests or the other methods outlined above. This includes sensitive material (eg material relating to police informants). Under section 19 of the CAA 1995, the CCRC can appoint an external police force to assist in in investigating a case, including by interviewing witnesses under caution.

However, the CCRC has limited capacity to substantially investigate cases and, as mentioned above, has recently come under criticism for the quality of its reviews. Accordingly, it is advisable that appeal representatives undertake as much investigation as it properly can in advance of an approach to the CCRC. The fruits of such investigation, including fresh evidence and new leads, may then assist in persuading the CCRC to make use of its statutory investigative powers.

5.32 An application to the CCRC which can provide material, give an account of the steps that have already been undertaken, and provide the CCRC with the responses to any defence enquiry can greatly assist the speed and success of any investigation that the CCRC itself decides to carry out and may assist in persuading the CCRC that such an investigation is necessary.

5.33 For full consideration of applications to the CCRC, see Chapter 9.

Journalistic investigations

5.34 Historically, print and broadcast journalists have done much of the heavy lifting when it comes to righting miscarriages of justice. They can play a vital role in uncovering evidence which the applicant's lawyers can later use in court.

5.35 However, it is necessary to exercise caution when co-operating with or seeking to enlist the help of journalists. Whilst the primary duty of a lawyer is to their client subject to their duty to the Court, the journalist's own overriding duty is to tell the truth as they see it. The interests of a defendant and a journalist's desire to expose the truth may coincide, but they may clash.

5.36 Therefore, in those cases where it is believed that co-operating with a journalist may lead to the uncovering of new evidence or may simply raise the profile of a case, it is important to consider the risks and benefits of doing so and ensure that the terms of the relationship are clear at the outset. An investigating lawyer should also be clear about how this work can be performed while remaining in line with the SRA Principles and Code of Conduct. Additionally, the lawyer must make sure to comply with the obligation to keep confidential material disclosed during the trial process but not aired in open court, as set out in section 17 of the Criminal Procedure and Investigations Act 1996.

SUMMARY OF KEY POINTS

- Defence investigations can uncover vital material for an appeal against conviction or sentence.
- Investigations do not have to be carried out by the defendant's lawyers. However, they should be carried out under their direction.
- Following clear ethical guidelines when conducting any investigation will assist in any application to have evidence that has been obtained considered by the Court of Appeal.
- Investigations should be carefully planned. It is first necessary to establish what material the defence already have and what material the prosecution may already have that might be disclosed, before considering whether further material should be sought.

- Disclosure requests may be made to the prosecution and police and, if not complied with, orders for disclosure may be sought from the Court of Appeal when leave has been granted, or judicial review commenced where it has not. However, strong, well-evidenced arguments will likely be needed to overcome prosecution and police objections that their disclosure duties are limited following a conviction.
- Material may be sought from public authorities pursuant to the principles in *Nunn* and the Attorney General's guidelines, the Data Protection Act 2018 and the Freedom of Information Act 2000.
- Interviewing witnesses, including those who gave evidence for the prosecution in the Crown Court, can be of vital importance but should be done with care, following clear ethical principles.
- Site visits should not be overlooked. It should not be assumed that they took place before trial or, even if they did, that another site visit would not yield further information.
- Informing the Criminal Cases Review Commission of the work that has been undertaken in any defence investigation and providing the Commission with any material obtained may help to persuade the Commission to conduct their own investigation and may assist them in doing so.

Chapter 6

Applying for leave to appeal

INTRODUCTION

6.1 There are two ways to appeal a conviction or sentence in the Crown Court to the Court of Appeal: either an application to the Crown Court judge for a certificate to appeal, or an application to the Court of Appeal for leave to appeal. As it is rare for a Crown Court judge to grant a certificate to appeal, it is far more likely that the application will be direct to the Court of Appeal.

The application to the Court of Appeal is usually decided on the papers by a High Court judge (the 'single judge'). If the application is refused it may then be renewed orally by asking for a hearing before the Full Court.[1] In some cases the Registrar may bypass the single judge and refer the application to the Court for a full hearing (see 6.54 below).

Before considering an application to the Court of Appeal, the advocate should first consider whether the 'slip rule' can be used to avoid having to trouble the Court at all. This is likely to arise in sentencing cases where a legal or factual error was made by the judge or the parties that should be brought to the sentencing judge's attention. As the time limit is short (56 days) and it needs to be dealt with by the same judge, this should be done quickly and, if necessary, can be dealt with in the defendant's absence in some circumstances.[2]

6.2 This chapter will focus on the usual route of applying for leave to appeal to the Court of Appeal, as well as renewing that application and withdrawing it ('abandonment').

6.3 The preparation and advocacy at the actual hearing before the full Court is considered separately in Chapter 7.

6.4 **Note on terminology and the procedural rules:** anyone applying for leave to appeal is referred to as the 'applicant' until leave is granted, when they become the 'appellant'. As with other areas of criminal litigation, the

1 Time limit is within ten business days of the SJ refusal, CrimPR 36.5(2)(b).
2 Sentencing Act 2020, s 385; *R v Warren* [2017] EWCA Crim 226.

relevant procedures on appeals are set out in detail in procedural rules, which should be closely followed. These are found in the relevant 'divisions' of the Criminal Practice Directions 2023 (CPD)[3] and the Criminal Procedure Rules (CrimPR).[4]

Chapter 10 of the CPD deals with Appeals to the Court of Appeal (Criminal Division) and Parts 36 and 39 of the CrimPR apply to Appeals Generally and Appeals against Conviction and Sentence. Links to the latest iterations of these can be found on the Court of Appeal, Criminal Division website.[5]

The CPD requires that parties comply with the guidance set down by the Registrar in the 'Guide to proceedings in the Court of Appeal, Criminal Division' ('The Guide').[6]

Following these rules will help applicants and their lawyers navigate through the process of a criminal appeal. It will also enhance the chances of a favourable outcome. Ignoring them could seriously damage the applicant's prospects and may result in criticism by the court and even wasted costs.

ADVICE ON APPEAL

The trial lawyer's duty to advise promptly on appeal

6.5 The duty of lawyers to provide advice on appeal is set out in the Guide at A1:

> 'Provision for advice and assistance on appeal is included in the Crown Court representation order. Immediately following the conclusion of the case, legal representatives should give oral advice to their client as to the prospects of a successful appeal (whether against conviction or sentence or both). If there are reasonable grounds, grounds of appeal should be drafted, signed and sent to instructing solicitors as soon as possible and in sufficient time for the application to be lodged within the time limits. On receipt solicitors should send a copy of the documents received from the advocate to their client.'

6.6 Advocates should not settle or sign grounds of appeal unless they consider that they are properly arguable. Grounds must be carefully drafted and properly set out and particularised pursuant to CrimPR 39.3 (CPD 10.4.1).[7]

3 The latest version at the time of writing is CPD 2023, fourth amendment November 2025.
4 The latest version at the time of writing is 2025.
5 See https://www.judiciary.uk/courts-and-tribunals/court-of-appeal-home/the-court-of-appeal-criminal-division/.
6 Produced by the Registrar of the Court of Appeal. The latest version at the time of writing is March 2026.
7 B3.3 of the Guide.

As the opinion of the defendant is generally irrelevant as to whether there is a legal point to be argued, the lawyers may proceed with an appeal which has merit even when the defendant cannot be contacted because they have absconded[8] or have been removed from the jurisdiction. In appeal cases it is law and ethics that determine what is the right advice, not the views of the client.[9]

The defendant's right to seek a second opinion

6.7 A defendant should consider carefully the advice that they are given, but they are not bound to accept it. They may ask their solicitor to instruct a new advocate to advise on appeal (although whether to do so will be a matter for the solicitor). Alternatively, they may wish to seek assistance from new solicitors. There is a limited amount of publicly funded advice available. This is dependent on whether there is a good reason to provide the advice and whether the defendant has passed a very restrictive means test. Even if they do, many criminal lawyers refuse to take on these cases as they are very poorly paid (see Chapter 8).

Such advice needs to be given promptly because the time limits for lodging an appeal are very short. It can take a considerable amount of time for a new defence team to get up to speed with the case afresh so they may not be able to lodge an appeal in time even if the preliminary advice is positive. This will add another hurdle as it means an application will be required for an extension of time. This has become slightly less of a problem with the introduction of the Digital Case System in the Crown Court (CCDCS), which has made it easier to access the prosecution case papers and some defence documents online by being invited on to the Digital Case.

Time limits, extensions and the need for expedition

6.8 An application for leave to appeal must be lodged no later than 28 days after the decision which is being appealed.[10] It is a common mistake to assume that the time limit to appeal against a conviction runs from the date of sentence. In fact, the period for appeal runs from the date of the ruling or verdict being appealed. For conviction it starts at the date of the verdict, sentence runs from the date of sentence and a confiscation appeal runs from the date on which the confiscation order was made.

6.9 The court may grant an extension of time in which to appeal, either before or after the 28 days have expired.[11] It will usually only do so if it decides

8 See Ch 7 which deals with the rules for representatives when a client absconds.

9 *R v Okedare* [2014] EWCA Crim 228.

10 CAA 1968, s 18(2).

11 CAA 1968, s 18(3).

that there is merit in the application for leave itself. Indeed, the CrimPR now ask that the application for an extension is made at the time '*when serving that notice or making that application*'. This allows the Court to consider the extension and the substantive application together.[12] Even then, it is not bound to grant the extension but must take an overall view of what justice requires.[13] It should be noted that the Court requires an explanation for what has occurred in the whole period of time from the date of conviction and/or sentence to the instruction of representatives to the submission of the Form NG – *R v Dacres*.[14] The longer the delay, the higher the hurdle to overcome in establishing 'injustice' were the extension not to be granted.[15]

6.10 The fact that the court does generally consider the merits of the application for leave to appeal when deciding whether to grant an extension should never lead the applicant or their lawyers to be complacent about time limits. If nothing else, it is more difficult for the court to consider an application in a sympathetic light if the applicant or their legal advisors appear to have done little or nothing for a significant period of time, than one in which they have clearly worked hard to ensure that the application is lodged as soon as possible. The longer the period that has elapsed since the 28-day period has expired, the greater the need to show why there has been a justifiable delay.[16]

6.11 When new lawyers are instructed to advise on appeal, unavoidable delays may well arise from the need to consider transcripts from the trial and contact previous lawyers before advising on the merits. The court will be more sympathetic to such delays if it can see that the delay was due to serious attempts being made to ensure the factual basis for the appeal was correct and that any new evidence or legal points were fully aired with the previous team. The court will want the fullest picture of what decisions were taken at the trial and what advice was provided and that the new team have fully complied with their *McCook* duties (see 6.13 and 6.14 below).[17] However, the court has made it clear that time limits will be taken seriously:

> 'Time limits are set for good reason and in the interests of justice. They must be strictly observed unless there are good and exceptional reasons for their not being so observed. As was made clear by Lord Taylor CJ in *R v Burley* – an unreported decision referred to in *Williams* [2010] EWCA Crim 3289 at paragraph 5 – the interests of justice as a whole require the strict observance of time limits.'[18]

12 CrimPR 36.4, the Guide, para B.4.1.
13 *R v Thorsby* [2015] EWCA Crim 1.
14 [2024] EWCA Crim 447.
15 Ibid at paras [25]–[32].
16 *R v Wilson* [2016] EWCA Crim 65.
17 *R v McGill* [2017] EWCA Crim 1228.
18 *R v Roberts* [2016] EWCA Crim 71 at para 39.

The Practice Direction makes it clear that any late amendments will face an even higher hurdle.[19]

Obtaining transcripts for the purpose of advising on appeal

6.12 It will often be necessary for the advocate to have access to transcripts from the original trial to advise on whether there are arguable grounds to appeal. A quote for the relevant transcript will be needed to get prior authority from the Legal Aid Agency (LAA) (or to agree the disbursement with a privately paying client). This quote can be obtained from the transcription company for the court where the case was heard. The application form includes guidance with a list of the relevant transcription companies.[20] It is necessary to get permission from the judge who heard the case (or the resident judge) to authorise release of the transcript. This is done by completing a Form EX107 setting out what transcripts you need and why you want them, as well as specifying when you need them.[21]

It is also possible to listen to the recording of the proceedings (provided the hearing was in public and no reporting restrictions apply). Following a period of time when judges were seemingly reluctant to allow access to recordings, the Court produced guidance in *R v Lake*[22] reiterating that, if the procedure set out in the CrimPR was followed and good and sufficient reason given for the request, access to the recordings should be provided.[23] This is now reflected in the CrimPR.[24]

The funding for transcripts is considered in detail in Chapter 8, but in general terms, the cost of transcripts must be met by the LAA or the client prior to an application for leave, as the Registrar will not obtain transcripts unless and until an application for leave is lodged.

Contacting trial lawyers – due diligence

McCook – the new regime

6.13 Anyone considering an appeal against conviction or sentence should note that there has been a significant change of culture in recent times. Having become dismayed by the volume of appeals from new legal teams raising novel points along with potential criticisms of decisions taken at trial, the Court has

19 CPD 10 Appeals.
20 See https://assets.publishing.service.gov.uk/media/686cdd6afe1a249e937cbdce/EX107_0725.pdf.
21 Form EX107 has a declaration that you agree to pay the costs of the transcript.
22 [2023] EWCA Crim 710.
23 At paras [72]–[75] of the judgment.
24 CrimPR 5.5(1).

made it clear that the new lawyers have a heavy burden to overcome to satisfy themselves that the proposed grounds are properly arguable and based on a sound history of the previous advice received and the instructions given.[25]

The new team should advise the applicant that the Registrar will expect a waiver of privilege (on previous advice received – not current advice being given) so the court can investigate what instructions or advice was provided at trial and any tactical decisions that were taken. The Guide sets out the duty to take steps to obtain objective and independent evidence to substantiate the factual basis for fresh grounds[26] and warns that, 'failure to lodge a signed waiver may mean that the single judge and/or the Court will not have sufficient information to determine whether the grounds of appeal are arguable. Grounds of appeal may be dismissed on that basis.'[27]

6.14 This guidance is also set out in the updated CPD.[28] These directions are essential reading for any fresh team of lawyers, as failure to comply could easily lead to a wasted costs order and/or a loss of time direction. Part 10.4.4 of the CPD sets out what is required of fresh representatives and should be considered in detail. In summary, fresh representatives must:

(a) confirm within the grounds of appeal that the duties set out in *McCook* have been complied with;

(b) if privileged information is within the grounds of appeal, or fresh evidence is relied upon, then a signed waiver of privilege must also be lodged with the grounds of appeal – following the guidance in *R v Singh (Kunwar)* (Practice Note);[29]

(c) if trial representatives fail to respond to inquiries within a reasonable time, fresh representatives should instead seek other objective independent evidence to substantiate the factual basis for the grounds as far as they are able. A statement confirming that the trial representatives have failed to respond to their *McCook* inquiries must be lodged with the grounds of appeal;

(d) fresh representatives must consider obtaining other objective independent evidence if the information provided by the trial representatives contradicts the appellant's instructions.

25 *R v Davis and Thabagu* [2013] EWCA Crim 2424; *R v Achogbuo* [2014] EWCA Crim 567; *R v McCook* [2016] 2 Cr App R 30.

26 At B.7.2.

27 At B.7.3.

28 CPD 10 Appeals, section 10.4.

29 [2017] 2 Cr App R 15.

TRIAL JUDGE'S CERTIFICATE

Whether to apply for a trial judge's certificate

6.15 The alternative to applying for leave is to apply to the judge who conducted the trial or imposed the sentence (depending on the nature of the decision being appealed) for a certificate that the conviction or sentence is fit for appeal.[30]

6.16 A certificate can only be granted in very exceptional circumstances[31] and it will only arise when the appeal involves a point of law:

(a) The procedure is governed by section 1(2)(b) of CAA 1968 and Part 39.4 CrimPR.

(b) An oral application may be made immediately after the relevant decision[32] or a written application must be made 'not more than 10 business days' after the conviction/sentence occurred[33] providing the same information (with the necessary adaptations) as an appeal notice.[34]

(c) If the judge decides to issue the certificate they must do so within 28 days of the decision. This statutory time limit may not be extended, unless it relates to insanity or unfitness to stand trial.[35]

(d) The certificate is issued by the Crown Court officer sending it to the Registrar – Part 36.8(5) CrimPR.

(e) The refusal to grant a certificate may not be appealed.

(f) If the certificate is granted, the Crown Court may also grant bail pending appeal – Senior Courts Act 1981, section 81(1)(f) but this power must be exercised within 28 days of the matter appealed against. Bail can only be granted by the judge who presided over the matter being appealed – SCA 1981, section 81(1C).[36]

(g) If the certificate is granted there is no requirement to lodge grounds. However, a Form NG must still be lodged with the Court of Appeal.

30 CAA 1968, s 1(2)(b) in respect of conviction; CAA 1968, s 11(1A) in respect of sentence.
31 *R v Kalis* [2003] EWCA Crim 1080.
32 CrimPR 39.4(1)(a).
33 CrimPR 39.4(1)(b).
34 CrimPR 39.4(2).
35 CAA 1968, s 16A(2)(b).
36 Paras 6.38–6.42 below deal with bail where the leave application is to the Court of Appeal.

THE GROUNDS OF APPEAL

Who may draft grounds of appeal?

6.17 The grounds may be drafted by the applicant, or their solicitor or advocate. The Registrar will not accept grounds drafted by a third party unless they are expressly adopted by the applicant (except in exceptional cases, where the applicant lacks the capacity to do so).

The form and content of the grounds

6.18 The purpose of the grounds is to convince the High Court judge who will consider them ('the single judge') to grant leave to appeal. They should therefore be drafted with care so as to ensure that they are as clear, concise and persuasive as possible. Detailed rules for both the notice and the grounds are set out in the CPD (10.4) and in the CrimPR themselves (Parts 39.2 and 39.3). These should be consulted to ensure the notice and grounds are in the prescribed form. A summary is set out below.[37]

6.19 The grounds must be lodged with the relevant appeal notice (with separate Form NGs for conviction/sentence/confiscation), and they must be signed and dated. The CPD and the Criminal Procedure Rules provide detailed advice on the expected content of both the appeal notice (if there is no prescribed Form NG) and the grounds; including the precise requirements that they should be concise, drafted on A4-size portrait format (in not less than 12-point type with 1.5 spacing), must identify each ground of appeal on which the appellant relies,[38] identify the transcript required[39] and must include in the appeal notice electronic links to relevant documents/digital evidence,[40] identifying with particularity the sections of any such material the court needs to consider as well as where and how that is to be found[41] and include an electronic copy of each authority relied upon in a single document.[42]

6.20 CrimPR 39.3(2) prescribes how the grounds should be set out:

(a) include in no more than the first two pages a summary of the grounds that makes what then follows easy to understand;

(b) in each ground of appeal identify the event or decision to which that ground relates;

37 For sample grounds see App A.
38 CrimPR 39.3(1)(b).
39 CrimPR 39.3(1)(c).
40 CrimPR 39.3(1)(f).
41 CPD 10 Appeal at 10.4.1 c.
42 CrimPR 39.3(1)(g).

(c) in each ground of appeal summarise the facts relevant to that ground, but only to the extent necessary to make clear what is in issue;

(d) concisely outline each argument in support of each ground;

(e) number each ground consecutively, if there is more than one;

(f) identify any relevant authority and—

  (i) state the proposition of law that the authority demonstrates, and

  (ii) identify the parts of the authority that support that proposition; and

(g) where the Criminal Cases Review Commission refers a case to the court, explain how each ground of appeal relates (if it does) to the reasons for the reference.

Defective grounds will be returned by the CAO for revision within a directed period. Failure to revise might lead to the court refusing leave.[43]

FRESH AND AMENDED GROUNDS PROCEDURE

6.21 Where the previous lawyers submitted grounds that were rejected by the single judge and the new lawyers want to put in fresh grounds, CrimPR 36.14(5) provides that an application to vary must be made. However, the CPD is not so limited. CPD 10.4.5 provides that 'where the appellant wants to rely on a ground of appeal that is not identified by the appeal notice, an application is required.' It refers back to rule 36.14(5) with no reference to that referring to the post single judge position. The safer course may therefore be to apply to vary even pre-single judge.

6.22 The principles to be applied were extensively discussed in *R v James* (per Hallett LJ, VP):[44]

> '(i) As a general rule, all the Grounds of Appeal an applicant wishes to advance should be lodged with the Notice of Appeal/Application; subject to their being perfected on receipt of transcripts from the Registrar.
>
> (ii) The filter mechanism provided by section 31 of the CAA 1968 (consideration of the application for leave by the single judge) is an important stage in the process and should not be "bypassed" solely on the basis that lawyers instructed post-conviction would have done or argued things differently from the trial lawyers. Fresh Grounds advanced by fresh counsel must be particularly cogent.

43 CPD 10.4.2.
44 [2018] EWCA Crim 285.

(iii) Once an application for leave has been considered by a single Judge, if the applicant wishes to advance fresh Grounds that have not in substance been considered by the single judge, they require the leave of the court. Applications to advance fresh Grounds must be accompanied by an application to "vary" the notice of appeal. If there is any doubt as to whether a Ground is 'fresh', an application to vary should be made.

(iv) The advocate should address in writing the relevant factors which the full Court is likely to consider in determining whether to allow variation of the notice of appeal and an extension of time for the renewal if required.

(v) In deciding whether to vary the Grounds of Appeal, the full Court will take into account the following (non-exhaustive) list of issues:

   (a) The extent of the delay in advancing the new ground/s;

   (b) The reason for the delay in advancing the new ground/s;

   (c) Whether the issues / facts giving rise to the new Grounds were known to the applicant's representative at the time he or she advised the applicant regarding any available Grounds of Appeal;

   (d) The overriding objective (CrimPR 1.1) namely acquitting the innocent and convicting the guilty and dealing with the case efficiently and expeditiously;

   (e) The interests of justice.

(vi) The application to vary would not require "exceptional leave" (by demonstrating substantial injustice) but the hurdle for the applicant is a high one. Counsel should remind themselves of the provisions of the PD. 39C.2 namely that "Advocates should not settle grounds unless they consider that they are properly arguable. Grounds should be carefully drafted." They should also bear very much in mind their duty to the court.

(vii) Advocates should also remind themselves of the rules relating to time limits. Leave will not be given to renew out of time unless the applicant can persuade the court that very good reasons exist. If the application to renew out of time is accompanied by an application to vary the Grounds the hurdle is higher.

(viii) For pragmatic reasons we suggest the application to vary should be considered by the full Court and not on the papers. An applicant would have a right to require a review of a decision not to vary if it were made by the Registrar or single Judge and a full Court hearing would in any event be required.

(ix) Assuming that the applicant will have received advice and assistance on appeal from his trial advocate, who will have advised that no grounds exist on which to challenge the safety of the conviction or settled the original Grounds of Appeal in the notice of appeal, fresh counsel should in every case be required to comply with the duty of due diligence as explained in *McCook* [2014] EWCA Crim 734. Waiver will almost certainly be required.

(x) Once the trial lawyers have responded, "fresh counsel" should again consider with great care their duty to the court and whether the "fresh grounds" should be advanced as properly arguable and particularly cogent.

(xi) The Registrar should obtain, in advance of the full Court hearing, transcripts relevant to the new Grounds and (where required) a Respondents' Notice relating to the new Grounds.

(xii) The CrimPR Committee may wish to consider formulating rules for the lodging of a Notice of Application to vary a notice of appeal.

(xiii) On any renewal the full Court when refusing an application to vary the notice of appeal has the power to make a loss of time order or order for costs in line with *R v Gray and Others*. By analogy with *R v Kirk* [2015] EWCA Crim 1764 (where the Court refused an extension of time) the Court has the power to order costs of obtaining the Respondent's Notice and or transcripts.'

The above procedure should be carefully followed and clients advised accordingly of the possible consequences.

PARTICULAR ISSUES

Appeals against conviction (evidence)

6.23 In an appeal against conviction, it is important to identify the particular error at trial or fresh evidence that is relied upon. However, it is just as important to identify how this makes the conviction 'unsafe'. Whilst this should not involve a lengthy description of the evidence, it is helpful to set out the context in which the error is said to be significant. A common reason for refusing leave is the single judge's assessment that the evidence was so strong that the error, or new evidence, would have made no difference to the jury's decision. When the prosecution case appears to be strong, the grounds should anticipate this objection: was the case truly overwhelming? If not, why not? If it was overwhelming, could the new evidence itself have created a doubt where none otherwise existed?

Appeal against sentence (general)

6.24 The grounds should set out the offence, the relevant sentencing powers of the Crown Court including the maximum sentence that was available for the offence, whether the plea was guilty or not guilty, details of previous convictions and any other order made by the judge when passing sentence. The applicable Sentencing Guideline and the category in which the respective parties submitted the offence should fall into should also be referred to. In a case involving several sentences it may be useful to include a table setting out this information in relation to each offence and specifying whether it was a concurrent or consecutive sentence.

Appeal against sentence (assistance provided to the police)

6.25 When a ground of appeal is that insufficient weight was given for assistance that the applicant had provided to the police, special considerations apply. As these cases involve sensitive information that may be damaging to the applicant (or others), should it become public, there is a particular procedure to be followed.[45] The grounds of appeal and Form NG should be lodged with the Court of Appeal in the usual way. They should make no mention of the fact that information had been given to the sentencing judge in the form of a 'text' about assistance that the applicant had provided to the police. This means that if the only ground of appeal is the failure of the Crown Court to make a proper reduction in sentence for such assistance, the grounds will be a very short, bland document. A separate note should then be lodged with the grounds, marked for the attention of the Registrar. It should alert the Registrar to the existence of the text and might also include any arguments in relation to the text that the applicant wishes the court to consider. The Registrar will ensure that the text is obtained and provided to the single judge and if leave granted to the full Court with the necessary steps taken to prevent publicity. If the representatives wish to make oral submissions in relation to any confidential material, an application to list the case anonymously or in camera must be made to the Registrar in advance of the appeal hearing in order to ensure the appropriate recording equipment is in place and the case is listed correctly.[46] The principles that apply to such reductions were comprehensively considered in *R v Royle*.[47]

NEW ARGUMENTS

6.26 If the appeal is based on a legal argument that was not raised in the Crown Court, the court will want to know why it was not raised. If it is

45 The Guide B.3.2.
46 The Guide B.3.2.2.
47 [2023] EWCA Crim 1311.

necessary to apologise for failing to spot a legal point, then apologising in the written grounds is more likely to disarm any criticism than having that concession extracted by judicial cross examination at the full hearing.

Failure to object to things said in the summing up

6.27 If the appeal concerns the judge's summing up the Court will want to know:

(a) Did the judge give the advocate the opportunity to address them, before the summing up, on any matters about which the applicant now complains? If so, did the advocate raise the point that is now raised on appeal? If not, why not?

(b) Did the advocate seek to address the judge at the conclusion of the summing up in relation to the matter? If not, why not?

Criticism of previous lawyers

6.28 This is subject to detailed guidance which must be followed (see 6.13). The client needs to be advised at an early stage that waiver of privilege will be expected so the previous lawyers can respond fully, and the court will be able to look at the instructions given at the time of the trial and the advice provided. Any indication that the matter should have been pursued then or was deliberately avoided for tactical reasons will be likely to be fatal to the appeal – but see the exceptions set out in Chapter 3.

FRESH EVIDENCE

6.29 In *R v Singh (Kunwar)* Practice Note[48] the Court made recommendations for the assistance of the parties and the judges where applications for leave to appeal were based on fresh evidence. At the leave stage the single judge should actively consider the reason why the evidence was not sought at the trial stage. This will involve asking whether there has been a waiver of privilege and, if not, why. A Respondent's Notice will be required, and the single judge should direct one if none has been filed. Having considered the response of the trial representatives, the single judge should consider whether admission of the fresh evidence is potentially arguable. If it is not, then leave should be refused, but if it is potentially arguable, the single judge should normally not grant the applications for leave and any extension of time but should refer them to the full court. The single judge should refer the application for directions. The parties should then seek to agree those directions and submit them to

48 [2017] 2 Cr App R 15.

the Registrar for approval by the court. Only if agreement cannot be reached should it be necessary for there to be an oral hearing in relation to them.[49]

In any appeal based on fresh evidence, the following steps need to have been taken:[50]

(a) The section 23(2) CAA 1968 considerations (as discussed in Chapter 3) need to be addressed.

(b) If the applicant seeks to call evidence by way of live witnesses, Form W must be completed for each proposed witness.[51] In practice the court may well hear and decide the appeal without actually hearing any witnesses. Nonetheless, that is a decision for the court to take, and the lawyers preparing the appeal need to offer the court the option of hearing the evidence.

(c) The court has the power to order the attendance of a witness.[52] This includes witnesses who would not be compellable to give evidence at trial, such as previous lawyers and jurors.[53] If such an order is required, the Form W should make that clear. The granting of such an order does not mean that the court will hear the evidence. That will be decided by the full court at the hearing.

(d) The statements of the witnesses (in section 9 form) or the documents that constitute the fresh evidence, should all be attached.

(e) There must be a '*Gogana*' statement[54] from the applicant's solicitor in section 9 form (or affidavit) setting out why the evidence was not available at trial and how it came to light. The Guide points out, 'This will implicitly require fresh representatives to comply with *McCook*'.[55]

(f) Applications for any of the following orders should be made in accordance with the relevant Parts of the Criminal Procedure Rules.[56]

    (i) written witness statements (Part 16 CrimPR);

    (ii) measures to assist a witness or defendant to give evidence (Part 18 CrimPR);

    (iii) expert evidence (Part 19 CrimPR);

    (iv) hearsay evidence (Part 20 CrimPR);

49 *R v Kunwar Singh*, at paras [47]–[51].

50 The Guide B.8.

51 See https://www.gov.uk/government/publications/notice-of-application-for-a-witness-order-andor-permission-to-call-a-witness.

52 CAA 1968, s 23(1)(b).

53 CAA 1968, s 23(3).

54 *R v Gogana* (1999) *Times*, 12 July. See App B.

55 The Guide B.8.2.

56 Part 39.7(1) CrimPR.

(v) evidence of bad character (Part 21 CrimPR);

(vi) evidence of a complainant's previous sexual behaviour (Part 22 CrimPR).

If these issues are raised in the grounds, then they should be addressed in the Respondent's Notice (RN) or if raised in the Respondent's Notice then the applicant has 10 business days to respond. The court and the Registrar have powers to make directions without a hearing.[57]

The court can also make orders for the production of exhibits, documents or other material (Part 39.7(3) CrimPR); or the attendance of witnesses before the court, or an examiner on behalf of the court, provided the correct procedure is followed (Part 39.7(4)–(7) CrimPR).

CHANGE IN LAW APPEALS

6.30 Where the application is lodged in time (see 6.8) the test is whether the conviction is 'unsafe'. Where the application is made out of time then 'exceptional leave' will be required. This will only be granted if the applicant will suffer 'substantial injustice' due to the change in the law.[58]

Applying for extension of time within which to appeal

6.31 For those applications that are lodged after the end of the 28-day period there is a box to be ticked in the Form NG indicating that an application for an extension is being made. In addition to ticking the box it is essential that the reasons for delay should also be clearly explained either in the grounds or as a separate document.

6.32 In a case involving significant delay, particularly where that delay has been brought about by the time that it took fresh solicitors to prepare the appeal, the application should be accompanied by a chronology of the work that has been done in the lead up to lodging the application, with particular reference to the timing of instructions and actions taken. (See 6.8–6.11 above, for consideration of time limits, extensions and the need for due diligence.) The 'substantial injustice' test may prevent leave being granted even where the appeal is unopposed or had substantial merit.[59]

57 Part 39.7(2) CrimPR.

58 *R v Johnson* [2016] EWCA 1613; see Ch 3. The Guide B.3.3.

59 *R v Ordu* [2017] EWCA Crim 4 (where, it should be noted, the conviction was spent). See Ch 3.

CITATION OF AUTHORITIES

6.33 In *R v Erskine*[60] the court emphasised that the only authorities that should be cited are those which are strictly necessary to advance the case. Lord Judge CJ said at para 75:

> 'If it is not necessary to refer to a previous decision of the court, it is necessary not to refer to it.'

6.34 In appeals against conviction, the court emphasised that the authorities relied on, should be those which establish a particular proposition, and not those which do 'no more than illustrate or restate an established proposition.' (*Erskine*, para 78)

6.35 The Court was particularly concerned about unhelpful citation of authorities in sentencing cases:

> 'Advocates must expect to be required to justify the citation of any authority. In particular where a definitive Sentencing Guidelines Council guideline is available there will rarely be any advantage in citing an authority reached before the issue of the guideline, and authorities after its issue which do not refer to it will rarely be of assistance. In any event, where the authority does no more than uphold a sentence imposed at the Crown Court, the advocate must be ready to explain how it can assist the court to decide that a sentence is manifestly excessive or wrong in principle.' (*Erskine*, para 80)

6.36 The Guide provides that advocates must comply with the provisions in CPD 10.8.9–10.9.12 (skeleton arguments and citation of authorities) and are expected to provide only the essential authorities to determine the issue(s).[61] This reflects the position in the Practice Direction.[62] The Court publishes a list of frequently cited authorities which practitioners do not need to supply within their bundles. If any of these authorities are relied on, practitioners need only cite the case and the relevant paragraph number(s).[63] While it is important to follow this guidance it is also important that it should not cause such anxiety that an authority that is genuinely significant is not drawn to the court's attention. The golden rule must be that the advocate is able to justify reference to a particular authority in the light of the approach that *Erskine* requires. The definitive citation rules are summarised in the Practice Direction.[64]

60 *R v Erskine* [2009] EWCA Crim 1425.
61 The Guide B.3.6.
62 See CPD 10.8.9–10.8.15.
63 The Guide B.3.6.
64 CPD 10.8.4, 10.8.11 and 10.8.12.

OTHER DOCUMENTS TO BE LODGED IN SUPPORT OF THE APPLICATION

6.37 It is always worth considering what other documents might be needed for the court to understand the grounds. Examples would include the written directions to the jury if they were being criticised, or a witness statement that was admitted in evidence by way of a hearsay ruling that is a ground of appeal. If there was relevant CCTV or other footage it should be supplied with a summary if it would assist. In appeals based on new material that relies on the applicant being a victim of trafficking, the Criminal Appeal Office will want the relevant material including the National Referral Mechanism (NRM) assessment and accompanying evidence to be lodged with the Form NG.

It makes sense to copy and attach such documents to avoid any delay caused by the Registrar later having to obtain them.

OTHER APPLICATIONS WHICH MAY BE MADE ALONG WITH THE APPLICATION FOR LEAVE

Applications for bail

6.38 The single judge does have the power to grant bail pending appeal. However, the court has held that bail pending appeal should only be granted in 'exceptional circumstances' in which the court concludes that it is necessary in order to 'do justice in the case'.[65]

6.39 Bail cannot be applied for until an application for leave is lodged.[66] If a bail application is included with the application for leave, then usually the single judge will consider it when they decide whether to grant leave.

6.40 The application for bail should be made with Form B and served on the Registrar and the prosecution.[67] The rules for bail applications are at Part 39.8 CrimPR. If bail is granted with pre-conditions before release, such as a surety, the specific steps are outlined at Part 39.9.

6.41 If the issue of bail is urgent because of the shortness of the sentence or ill-health of the applicant, an e-mail should be sent to the Registrar making this clear.[68] In extreme cases the Registrar may ask the single judge to consider bail before the application for leave is considered. However, the court only

65 *R v Watton* (1979) 68 Cr App R 293.
66 *R v Suggett* (1985) 81 Cr App R 243.
67 The Guide B.9.2.
68 The Guide B.9.3.

grants bail in exceptional circumstances, so it is very unlikely to do so without consideration of the strength of the application for leave itself.

6.42 The granting of bail should not create an expectation that the applicant will not be returned to prison should the appeal fail.[69]

Request for an expedited hearing

6.43 As well as applying for bail or in cases where bail is unlikely to be granted the applicant can ask for an expedited hearing. There is no form to be submitted but a note attached to the application should make clear the reasons for urgency. The Registrar can refer the case to the full court immediately for a rolled-up hearing of leave and, if granted, the appeal.

Requests for transcripts

6.44 Once an application for leave is lodged, the Registrar will obtain a copy of the summing up to verdict (in an appeal against conviction), sentencing remarks (in an appeal on sentence) and prosecution opening facts (in a sentence following a guilty plea).[70]

6.45 If an advocate considers any further transcript essential to the issues they must identify these and provide a note of dates and times.[71] If the Registrar and the advocate are unable to agree the extent of the transcript to be obtained, the Registrar may refer that matter to a judge or the full Court.[72] If an applicant is paying privately for legal representation, an order for the summing up to verdict and other relevant transcripts should be obtained by the applicant's representative.[73] Where the judge has provided a written ruling or sentencing remarks these should be hyperlinked within the grounds of appeal so that the Registrar can consider whether this avoids the necessity to obtain a transcript.[74]

Applications for funding

6.46 The Form NG contains a box to apply for a representation order. It will be granted if leave to appeal is granted.[75] A representation order can be

69 *R v Kalia* (1974) 60 Cr App R 200.
70 The Guide B.5.1.
71 The Guide B.5.1.
72 The Guide B.5.3.
73 The Guide B.5.5.
74 The Guide B.5.6.
75 Legal Aid in the Court of Appeal is non-means tested – see Ch 8.

retrospective to the date the application was lodged[76] but cannot include work undertaken before the application was lodged.[77] Usually, it will be only be granted for an 'advocate alone' which will not cover the instructing solicitor. If the appeal requires work by the solicitor and they have a criminal legal aid contract,[78] an application can be made by the advocate to the Registrar to extend the representation order.[79] This can be done by letter and it will help if the advocate provides a supporting note confirming the work that needs to be done. An application for a solicitor's representation order can be made at any stage once an application has been lodged. There is no prescribed form, but the advocate should submit a note to the Registrar which outlines the work that is to be done by the solicitor and why that work cannot be undertaken by the advocate. Although the application could be for a general representation order for solicitors to assist with the preparation of the application/appeal, the Registrar is more likely to grant a representation order for a limited and specified purpose.[80] If the Registrar does not grant the application to extend the order they will usually refer it to the single judge or the full court.

6.47 If the Crown Court representation order was for a junior and a leading junior or KC, the Court of Appeal will normally grant a representation order for a single advocate only on the basis that two advocates will not be needed for the presentation of the appeal.[81] If a representation order for two advocates and/or solicitors is required, the advocate must apply to the Registrar or single judge and provide written justification in accordance with the Criminal Legal Aid (Determinations by a Court and Choice of Representative) Regulations 2013.[82] There is no prescribed form and a note will be sufficient.[83] See Chapter 8 for a detailed consideration of funding.

Disclosure of third-party material

6.48 If third-party material is needed for the appeal the applicant must provide a clear and compelling explanation why the material was not obtained in the Crown Court. The principles and procedure are set out in *R v Niwar Doski*.[84] The full court, the single judge and Registrar can order a third party to

76 Regulation 8(2).
77 See *R v Tredget* [2022] EWCA Crim 1894.
78 See D.4.6 of the Guide – if they do not have a LAA standard crime contract, they may apply to the LAA for an individual case contract (ICC) by virtue of which the solicitor is employed on behalf of the LAA to represent an appellant in a given case.
79 The Guide B.8.5.
80 See the Guide at D.4.4, D.4.5 and D.4.6.
81 The revised Form NG asks that a copy of the Crown Court representation order is attached if possible.
82 SI 2013/614.
83 The Guide D.4.4.
84 [2011] EWCA Crim 987.

produce documents or other material, but they will only do so in exceptional cases: 'It should not be assumed that the court will be prepared to embark on this exercise without very good reason'.[85]

6.49 An application for third-party material should contain:

(a) completed Form W;

(b) details of the material sought;

(c) its relevance to the appeal;

(d) details of the party against whom any order for production of the material is to be made; and

(e) details of any refusal of the party to provide the material on a voluntary basis.

6.50 The application should be served on the party in question (and anyone the material relates to) so that they can raise any objections.[86] If there are objections, the court may direct that there is a hearing so that the parties who are directly concerned can be heard, before deciding to make the order.

Request for an oral leave hearing

6.51 It is possible to apply for an oral leave hearing to argue the grounds before the single judge, but exceptional reasons must be demonstrated.[87] This is rare given that the applicant will have a right to an oral hearing if they renew the refused application (on the papers).

LODGING THE GROUNDS – DIRECT LODGEMENT

6.52 The form NG, signed grounds of appeal and any accompanying documents must be lodged directly with the Registrar.[88] There are separate Form NGs for conviction, sentence and confiscation that should be completed separately for each. They should be sent by secure email to the Criminal Appeal Office.

6.53 When an application for leave is received by the Registrar, the Criminal Appeal Office's lawyer will:

85 At para 13 of *Doski*.

86 *R (on the application of TB) v The Combined Courts at Stafford* [2006] EWHC 1645 (Admin).

87 The Guide C.2.1, which sets out the procedure that applies in such hearings.

88 CrimPR 39.2; The Guide B.2.1.

(a) check that the application for leave is in valid form and if it is not, contact the advocate to rectify the defects;

(b) if the application is out of time, check an application for extension of time has also been made;

(c) contact the Crown Court to ensure that all relevant exhibits are retained until the conclusion of any appeal;

(d) obtain the transcripts and any other documents that are necessary for the single judge to determine the application;

(e) if relevant, check there is a waiver of legal privilege and contact previous lawyers for their comments on matters raised in the application;

(f) if appropriate, ask the prosecution for their views, before the case is sent to the single judge.[89] If the prosecutor wishes to make observations on the appeal, they will serve a Respondent's Notice (see 6.58).

6.54 The Registrar has the power to refer a case directly to the full court to deal with leave and any appeal as a rolled-up hearing. There are a number of reasons why this might be done: if the case concerns fresh evidence; if co-defendants have already been given leave to argue the point; if the need for a hearing is urgent or the question of law is particularly complicated; or if the Registrar is of the view that the application may be considered vexatious. However, this latter is unusual.

STEPS BEFORE THE CASE IS SENT TO THE SINGLE JUDGE

Perfecting the grounds

6.55 Before the case is considered by the single judge the Registrar will send the relevant transcripts from the trial to the applicant or their lawyers, if represented. This is so that the grounds can be reviewed or 'perfected'. The 'perfected' grounds should be a new document. It will replace the original grounds, should contain references to the page and paragraph number of the relevant passages in the transcripts and hyperlinks to the relevant page.[90]

6.56 The applicant will be given 14 days to perfect the grounds, or they will need to apply for more time.[91] The advocate should include a list of any relevant case law with the perfected grounds along with copies of any authorities (see 6.19).[92]

89 Part 39 CrimPR specifies when a prosecution response is required.
90 The Guide, B.6.1.
91 The Guide B.6.3.
92 CrimPR 39.3(1)(g) and see The Guide at B.3.5.

6.57 The Registrar may direct that the transcripts must be returned unmarked so a copy should be made and kept for any future hearings.

Responses from trial lawyers and the respondent

6.58 The applicant will be given the opportunity to respond to the observations from the trial lawyers to any additional questions asked by the Registrar. This can be made by amending the grounds or in a separate document. It may be unnecessary to add anything if it is already covered in the grounds.

6.59 The Registrar may serve an appeal notice on any party directly affected by the appeal and must do so if the Criminal Cases Review Commission refers a conviction, verdict, finding or sentence to the court. The party may respond but they *must* do so if the Court or Registrar directs, or they want to make representations to the Court. They will have ten business days to respond (or 20 in the case of a referral by the CCRC).[93]

6.60 The Registrar will *always direct* a Respondent's Notice in all conviction and sentence applications involving a fatality and also in attempted murder cases.[94]

Other examples of when the Registrar *might* direct a Respondent's Notice include:[95]

- where an assertion is made in the grounds of some irregularity that happened during the trial that cannot be fully reflected in the transcript;
- the grounds are legally complex, or the facts of the case are complicated and a Respondent's Notice might assist;
- there is a complaint about the prosecution and their conduct of the trial;
- Derogatory remarks are made about the credibility of a victim;
- there is fresh evidence not produced at trial;
- one of the grounds of appeal is that there were inconsistent verdicts;
- the grounds raise a juror irregularity or other conduct which might require investigation by the police;
- the grounds have not been considered by a single judge and there is an application to vary the notice of appeal before the full Court pursuant to *R v James and Ors*;[96]

93 Part 39.6(1)–(4) CrimPR.
94 The Guide B.10.5.
95 The Guide B.10.6.
96 [2018] EWCA Crim 285.

- the grounds raise points of general public importance which require a co-ordinated approach from the prosecution.

The prosecution will always be *invited* to lodge a Respondent's Notice in the following conviction cases[97]:

(i) all applications involving rape, attempted rape or a serious sexual offence;

(ii) all applications where the CPS Complex Casework Unit dealt with the case, or the case was high profile;

(iii) all applications where the offence was perverting the course of justice, misconduct in public office and any conspiracy.

6.61 The respondent should serve their Respondent's Notice (Form RN) on the applicant.[98] However, they sometimes fail to. It is therefore worth contacting either the CPS Appeals Unit or prosecuting counsel directly in order to check if one has been completed.

6.62 The applicant should respond urgently to any new points in the Form RN as the papers will go to the single judge as soon as the Form RN is received and should ask the Court staff to confirm that any applicant response to the RN has made its way to the single judge.

DECISION OF THE SINGLE JUDGE

6.63 Once the perfected grounds, the trial lawyers' comments and the Form RN are received, the papers will be sent to the single judge who may:

(a) grant leave on some or all of the grounds that are arguable;

(b) refuse leave on all grounds; or

(c) refer the case to the full Court.

6.64 Other applications, including representation and any extensions of time, will also be considered. The reasons for the decisions will be set out in the Form SJ, which will be sent to the applicant. If the judge refuses leave, they will also initial the 'loss of time box' if they believe the application is hopeless (see 6.71 and 6.73).

6.65 If leave is granted, then a representation order will be granted to the advocate to appear at the hearing to argue any grounds that have been given leave.

97 The Guide B.10.6.
98 Part 39.6(3)–(6) CrimPR; the Guide B.10.2.

6.66 Waiting for the decision of the single judge can be frustrating because, once the papers have been sent to the judge, the Criminal Appeal Office cannot tell the applicant precisely how long it will take the judge to consider them. Often 'the papers are with the judge' is the only indication that will be given.

RENEWING AN APPLICATION FOR LEAVE

6.67 The applicant can renew the application for leave on any of the grounds that have been refused. The application must be lodged within ten business days of receipt of the Form SJ.[99] This is done by completing the SJ Renewal Form that is on the reverse side of the Form SJ and sending it to the court. The ten business day period will only be extended in exceptional circumstances. Any application for extension will be referred to the full court with the renewal application.

6.68 If all of the grounds were refused, the application to renew will be heard by the full court. If leave has been granted on some grounds, the renewed application for leave for the remaining grounds can be argued at the full appeal hearing. However, when leave is partially granted the applicant will have to remember to complete the renewal form for any refused grounds that they want to re-argue at the appeal hearing.

6.69 The decision to renew is often difficult. It is not made any easier by the fact that legal aid will have come to an end. The advocate and their solicitor will need to reflect on the reasoning of the single judge when reviewing the strength of the grounds. On the one hand, the advocate should not have drafted grounds unless they thought that they were arguable, on the other a High Court judge has said the case is not arguable. In *R v Tamiz and Tamiz*[100] the Court warned against applications being renewed automatically. Consideration should be given to what the single judge has said in refusing grounds and to what answers there are to the points made by the single judge.[101]

6.70 The applicant will need to be advised on the risk of a 'loss of time' order (see below) and whether the advocate is prepared to act *pro bono* or, if not, the cost of renewing privately. The advocate will note the advice in the Guide that they should never act simply because they are instructed to do so, but only if there are reasonably arguable grounds (see 6.6). Having said that if the grounds are properly arguable the advocate should stand by them. Many appeals are allowed despite refusal of leave by the single judge. Indeed, some appeals have been allowed even when the single judge has initialled the loss of time box. If the advocate does act pro bono on the renewal and leave is granted

99 Crim PR 36.5(2)(b).
100 [2024] EWCA Crim 200.
101 At paras 104 and 105 of judgment.

by the court, then usually a retrospective representation order will be granted to cover the hearing (see Chapter 8).

The risk of loss of time served and costs

6.71 The biggest risk for the applicant is that the court will direct that some of the time served whilst appealing should not count towards sentence.[102] The court should only do this if it thinks the application lacks any merit. Guidance as to the approach that should be taken is set out in *R v Gray*.[103]

6.72 The initials of the single judge in the loss of time box on the Form SJ is an indication to the full court that it should consider making an order for loss of time. That creates a higher risk of a 'loss of time' order being made. Even if the box is not initialled there is still a risk. An order can be made even when the applicant's advocate advised that there were arguable grounds of appeal.[104] The full court is becoming increasingly active in considering loss of time orders.

6.73 In the end, the decision to renew must be the applicant's, but they will rely heavily on the advice they receive and whether the advocate will agree to act *pro bono*. Even if a loss of time direction cannot be made because the applicant has been released from detention the single judge should additionally consider whether to indicate that an adverse costs direction should be considered by the full court.[105]

Renewing when considering taking the case to the European Court of Human Rights

6.74 Where the applicant wants to take a point to the European Court of Human Rights they should consider renewing the application.[106] Otherwise there is a danger that, by not renewing, it could later be said that the domestic remedies had not been exhausted, which can be a bar to the European Court considering the application. Where compatibility with a Convention right arises, the Registrar will give notice to any party potentially affected.[107]

Renewing other applications

6.75 On renewing an application for leave, the applicant can also renew other applications, including bail. These applications are renewed on the same

102 CAA 1968, s 29(1); the Guide C.5.1.
103 [2014] EWCA Crim 2372.
104 *R v Hart* [2006] EWCA Crim 3239.
105 The Guide C.4.2; *R v Terence Nolan* [2017] EWCA Crim 2449.
106 See the discussion in Ch 11.
107 Part 36.12(2) CrimPR.

SJ Renewal Form to renew the leave application. They need to be made within ten business days of receipt of the SJ decision. They will be considered by the full court at the renewal hearing.

ABANDONING AN APPLICATION FOR LEAVE

6.76 Any application will be considered by the court unless it is abandoned by the applicant. The decision to abandon is made by lodging a Form A with the court prior to the hearing. The Form A needs to be signed by the applicant or their lawyer. Abandonment can be made at the hearing, but only with the leave of the court.[108] The main reasons to abandon are to avoid the risk of a loss of time or costs order.

6.77 Abandonment is treated as being a final determination of the full Court – CrimPR 36.13(4)(c). Once an appeal is abandoned no new appeal against the same decision may therefore be brought, unless the case is referred to the court by the Criminal Cases Review Commission. Abandonment cannot be withdrawn. Therefore, by abandoning a case the appellant is effectively signing away his appeal rights.

Abandonment as a nullity

6.78 Abandonment may only be challenged on the basis that an apparent abandonment is a nullity. An applicant who wants to reinstate an application or appeal after abandonment must apply in writing to the Registrar with reasons – CrimPR 36.13(5). Abandonment will be a nullity when the Court concludes that the mind of the applicant did not go along with the act of abandonment (*R v Medway*[109] and *R v Zabotka*[110]). The clearest example of this would be where the applicant signed a notice of abandonment thinking that he was signing a different type of document.[111]

Bad legal advice giving rise to nullity

6.79 The court may accept that the abandonment was a nullity if it was based on bad legal advice (*R v L*[112]), but only if that advice was positively wrong, not if it was advice on a difficult point with which some might agree and others disagree (*R v Smith (Paul James)*).[113]

108 Part 36.13(2) CrimPR.
109 (1976) 62 Cr App R 85.
110 [2016] EWCA Crim 1771.
111 As happened in *R v Mohamed* [2010] EWCA Crim 2464.
112 [2013] EWCA Crim 1913.
113 [2013] EWCA Crim 2388.

Making an application for reinstatement

6.80 If the Court agrees the abandonment was a nullity it will reinstate the application. An application to reinstate an appeal or application for leave following abandonment is heard before the full court and the applicant must satisfy the court that it was a nullity.[114] The procedure is contained in CrimPR 36.13(5).

SKELETON ARGUMENTS

6.81 It may be useful to serve a skeleton prior to the hearing especially if there is a novel point to argue or it involves a complex sentence.[115] This is considered in more detail in Chapter 7. The CPD paras 10.8.3 to 10.8.6 set out detailed provisions as to skeleton arguments and their form. Skeletons should be no more than a numbered list of points that the advocate wants to cover for each ground using no more than one or two sentences. The document should define the issues,[116] be as succinct as possible,[117] and not normally exceed 15 pages.[118]

THE BUNDLE

6.82 Save where the summary is comprised of a single document, the CAO will prepare an 'index to the bundle' containing electronic links to the documents and material which the Registrar considers necessary to understand and determine the appeal. It is only in exceptional circumstances, that paper bundles may be provided.[119] On occasion the parties have been directed to prepare and lodge indexed bundles.[120] Where digital or paper bundles are prepared by the Criminal Appeal Office, a copy of the index will be provided to the appellant/advocate. If the advocate or appellant considers that there is additional material which it is necessary to include in the bundle, they must notify the Registrar of this in writing.[121] CPD 10.7.4 sets out detailed rules as to the form of bundles and is considered in more detail in Chapter 7.

114 *R v Medway* (1976) 62 Cr App R 85; *R v Zabotka* [2016] EWCA Crim 1771.
115 CPD 10 Appeal, para 10.8.2.
116 CPD 10.8.3(d).
117 CPD 10.8.3(b).
118 CPD 10.8.3(e).
119 CPD 10.7.1.
120 CPD 10.7.2. Where an appellant who is not privately represented is directed to lodge indexed bundles, a Representation Order may be granted by the Court or the Registrar for this purpose.
121 CPD 10.7.3.

THE HEARING

6.83 Preparation for the Hearing is considered in more detail in Chapter 7. Normal case management duties apply to appeals just as in any criminal matter.[122] The Registrar and the single judge have extensive statutory powers that apply to efficient management of the case and obtaining evidence.[123] If the Registrar refuses to make a procedural direction there is a right of appeal to the single judge.[124]

The judges hearing the appeal will have the papers prepared by the lawyers at the Criminal Appeal Office. These consist of a case summary which comes in two parts. Part 1 goes to the advocate (or unrepresented appellant). They can be shown to the lay and professional client, but they are not for wider circulation and should not be copied without permission. Part 1 consists of:

(i) a summary of the proceedings in the Crown Court including names of the representatives and any co-defendants;

(ii) a history of the proceedings in the Court of Appeal;

(iii) a summary of the case drafted by the lawyer in the Criminal Appeal Office based on the appeal documents,

(iv) the transcripts and trial statements or exhibits;

(v) the submissions, rulings, summing up and sentencing remarks.

The case summary is a matter for the lawyer drafting it, but an advocate can raise relevant matters to their attention as it is meant to be an objective document. This should be raised as soon as possible so that amendments can be made in good time.

Part 2 is for the court only and consists of:

(i) a summary of the grounds

(ii) in a sentence case, the antecedent history of the applicant or appellant and any pre-sentence report, medical report or other reports for sentencing.

The advocate should note that the court will have access to the source material so they can refer them to it.[125] Generally the hearings are to be conducted in public but the Court may order any hearing to be in private.[126] Where a hearing is about a public interest ruling, that hearing must be in private unless the court otherwise directs.[127] Reasonable notice of hearings should be given to

122 Part 36.2 CrimPR; the Guide introduction and at B.11.
123 CAA 1968, s 23(1)(a), s 31 and Parts 36.2 and 36.3 CrimPR.
124 CAA 1968, s 31A(4).
125 CPD 10 Appeal, para 10.6.7.
126 CrimPR 36.6(1).
127 CrimPR 36.6(2).

anyone affected by the judgment.[128] An appellant (but not an applicant) who is in custody, has a general right to attend the full hearing. That is unless the court directs that it is only a point of law or the appellant was found to lack capacity.[129] This attendance will generally be by way of a prison video link (PVL).[130] Therefore, it is important, especially in sentencing renewals, to confirm with the client in advance that they will waive this right to appear at the appeal hearing if the renewal is successful and the court wishes to proceed to a full appeal hearing immediately. This is generally good advice as a successful renewal is more likely to lead to a successful appeal with the same judges rather than taking the chance it will be adjourned and then heard by less receptive ones. It will also save time and costs, which will be well received. The advocate can expect to be asked if they have instructions to proceed.

The judgment

6.84 Unless the court made a specific direction, the draft judgment is provided to the lawyers about three working days before being handed down.[131] Any observations should be directed to the judge's clerk. It should not be circulated to the parties until two hours before being handed down.[132] Any breach of these directions may be treated as contempt.[133] The Court reiterated the importance of counsel and solicitors observing the embargo in *R v Counihan.*[134]

Miscellaneous appeals

6.85 The above outlines the general procedures in everyday appeals against conviction, sentence and confiscation. Chapters 12, 13 and 14 look at more specialist appeals and there is detailed guidance on the specific procedure or forms required for these miscellaneous appeals against interlocutory rulings, ancillary orders or costs in the Guide.[135]

SUMMARY OF KEY POINTS

- Appeals from the Crown Court against conviction or sentence require leave from the single judge or full court except in rare cases where it

128 CrimPR 36.7(1).
129 CrimPR 39.11.
130 CAA 1968, s 22(c) gives the court the power to direct PVL.
131 CPD 10.9.3.
132 CPD 10.9.7.
133 CPD 10.9.11.
134 [2024] EWCA Crim 747.
135 The Guide, section H.

might be appropriate to apply to the Crown Court for a certificate of fitness for appeal.

- Application for leave to appeal must be lodged within 28 days of the decision which is challenged.
- The court has the power to extend the time either before or after the 28 days expire. However, the application to extend must contain an explanation for the delay.
- The application must be made using the specified Form NG and in accordance with the requirements of Part 39.3 CrimPR.
- All other applications, including extension of time, bail and any application for a representation order should be lodged with the grounds.
- The application must be lodged at the Criminal Appeal Office unless it relates to a preparatory, 'terminatory' or similar trial ruling, in which case it is lodged at the Crown Court and also at the Court of Appeal.
- The Registrar's office will prepare the case in order to either send it to the single judge or refer it directly to the full court for consideration.
- If leave on any ground is refused by the single judge it may be renewed. The application for renewal must be lodged within ten business days of the decision.
- The court may consider exercising its power to make a loss of time order if an application for leave is renewed that the court regards as being 'wholly without merit'. If the single judge has indicated on the Form SJ that the court should consider this, then there is a strong chance that it will do so.
- If leave has been granted on some grounds, renewal needs to be made within ten business days on any remaining grounds that need to be re-argued at the final hearing.
- Other applications that were refused by the single judge may also be renewed before the court.

Chapter 7

Preparing for hearings in the Court of Appeal

INTRODUCTION

7.1 Every advocate who has appeared before the Court of Appeal will have had the experience of preparing the case thoroughly and arguing it passionately only to sit down and listen to the Court deliver a judgment that had clearly been written before the hearing commenced. It is tempting to ask what was the point in arguing it at all?

7.2 Before the hearing the Court will often have formed a preliminary view of the case. However, just as every advocate will have had the experience of failing to change the Court's collective mind, judges attest to occasions when the Court was convinced by effective oral advocacy.

7.3 If belief in one's ability to persuade is the first principle of advocacy in the Court of Appeal, the second is that the task of persuading the Court does not begin with the hearing itself. As the Court inevitably forms a preliminary view of the case, it is important to try to influence its thinking as early as possible by effective drafting, ensuring that important documents are lodged in good time and that the relevant authorities are drawn to the Court's attention.

7.4 This chapter covers the preparation for and presentation of the hearing. The topics covered apply to both appeals with leave and oral applications for leave to appeal. When different considerations apply to each type of hearing, this is made clear.

PREPARING FOR THE HEARING

Considering the Court bundle

7.5 The Registrar (in practice the lawyer at the Criminal Appeal Office who has been assigned to the case) is responsible for compiling the bundle of material that will be considered by the judges. It will be sent to the parties in advance of the hearing. It should be read with care. This is the case that the Court will read. In particular it is necessary to do the following:

Ensure that all the relevant documents are included

7.6 If either of the parties wish the Court to consider any document that is not in the bundle, they should write to the Criminal Appeal Office's assigned case lawyer, enclosing the document, stating its relevance and asking that it be included. Alternatively, try telephoning the lawyer (whose details and direct number are normally to be found in the correspondence) to discuss the contents of the judges' bundles.

Consider the case summary

7.7 Within the bundle will be the case summary that will have been prepared by the lawyer in the Criminal Appeal Office. It will contain what the writer considers to be the significant information about the facts of the case and its procedural history.

7.8 It should be considered carefully. It is vital that it is accurate and that it refers to the facts that are significant to the appeal. They are usually both accurate and comprehensive but if there is an amendment that should be made, the Registrar should be written to and asked to include it. Whether to make the amendment sought is a matter for the judgment of the summary writer. If it is decided not to include that matter in the case summary, the Court will be provided with the document that requested its inclusion.

7.9 Advocates can (unless the Registrar states otherwise) show the summary to their clients but it should not be copied or reproduced.

Check the time estimate that has been given to the case

7.10 The summary writer's view of the likely time estimate will be on the front page. It will be used to list the case. The Court will expect hearings to be concluded within the time estimate. Therefore, if it is thought that the time estimate is inadequate, the Registrar should be written to and told why; bear in mind, before doing so, that the hearing will be conducted by three experienced judges who will have already read into the case.

Skeleton arguments

7.11 The Criminal Practice Direction provides:[1]

1 CPD, Chapter 10.

'10.8.1 Advocates should always ensure that the Court, and any other party as appropriate, has a single document containing all of the points that are to be argued.

10.8.2 In cases of an appeal against conviction, advocates must serve a skeleton argument when the appeal notice does not sufficiently outline the grounds of the appeal, particularly in cases where a complex or novel point of law has been raised. In an appeal against sentence, it may be helpful for an advocate to serve a skeleton argument when a complex issue is raised.

10.8.3 Subject to any direction given by the court a skeleton argument must:

a. contain a numbered list of the points the advocate intends to argue, these should be grouped under each ground of appeal, and stated in no more than one or two sentences;

b. be as succinct as possible.

c. at the beginning of any document state the correct Criminal Appeal Office number and the date on which the document was served, and conclude with the advocates' names;

d. define the issues;

e. not normally exceed 15 pages (excluding front sheets and back sheets) and be concise;

f. be presented in A4 page size and portrait orientation, in not less than 12-point font and in 1.5 line spacing;

g. be set out in numbered paragraphs;

h. be cross-referenced to any relevant document in any bundle prepared for the court;

i. be self-contained;

j. not include extensive quotations from documents or authorities.'

Paragraphs 10.8.4 and 10.8.9 to 10.8.12 of the CPD set out how authorities should be referred to in the skeleton argument.

A chronology of relevant events will be necessary in most cases.[2]

7.12 It may well be helpful to draft a skeleton in a case that is to be presented in a different way before the Full Court to the way in which it was first presented in the grounds (for example, if particular grounds are not going to be advanced before the full Court, or more recent authorities relied on).

2 CPD, 10.8.6.

New grounds of appeal

7.13 The appellant must obtain leave to advance any new ground that was not in the application for leave. Whilst the advocate should not be afraid to pursue a powerful new ground, the Court has profoundly discouraged this course; see *R v James*[3] and Chapters 3 and 6 for more detail as to the procedure that must be followed.

Provision of authorities

7.14 Authorities will already have been provided with the Grounds of Appeal, as set out in Chapter 6. If, when preparing for the appeal, the advocate discovers a further authority these should be provided to the Court as soon as possible. Electronic copies must be provided and where there is more than one authority, they should be provided in a single electronic document.[4] They should, wherever possible, be provided in pdf format with optical character recognition and significant documents and all sections in bundles must be bookmarked. An index should be prepared and if practicable entries should be hyperlinked to the indexed document.[5] The Guide sets out detailed guidance on the preparation of bundles etc at section G (Annex 1).

7.15 In deciding what authorities (if any) to rely on, it is important to bear in mind what the Court said in *Erskine* about not placing unnecessary authorities before the Court and, in particular, not relying on sentencing cases that pre-date a sentencing guideline or guideline case, unless there is very good reason to do so. (See 6.33–6.36 for full details.)

LISTING THE HEARING

7.16 The Court of Appeal Listing Office is responsible for fixing a date for hearing, of which the parties are notified. It will consider applications for a hearing to be moved but will generally not move a case because the advocate has another case in a lower court. Appearances in the Court of Appeal must take precedence.[6]

3 [2018] EWCA Crim 285.
4 CPD, 10.8.13.
5 CPD, 10.8.14.
6 CPD, 10.3.2.

THE HEARING

Presence of the appellant/applicant

Hearings with leave

7.17 An appellant who is in custody has the right to be produced at their full hearing, unless they suffer from insanity or a disability.[7] This will almost always be by way of a video link, and the Court now has video conference facilities. There is no right to be present at a preparatory hearing, although production can be requested, and the Court may give leave.[8]

7.18 If the appellant does not wish to be produced, the appeal can take place in his absence. For this to take place the Registrar may require his consent to be in writing.

Renewed applications for leave

7.19 Applicants have no right to be present at renewed applications for leave. If an application for leave to appeal against conviction is successful then the full hearing will generally take place at a later date at which an appellant who is in custody will then be produced. However, if the application for leave to appear against sentence is successful, the Court will usually proceed to determine the appeal at the same hearing, in the absence of the appellant.[9] If this takes place, the Registrar will then write to the appellant informing them of the result of the hearing and of their right to have a further hearing at which they will be present but that the Court will only consider new submissions at such a hearing if the applicant presents new material 'with an important bearing on sentence' (*R v Spruce and Anwar*).[10]

7.20 In order to avoid this taking place, the applicant's solicitors should, in advance of the hearing, obtain their client's instructions on whether they would wish to be present at the full hearing. In any event, it is often the practice of the Court to produce the applicant from custody in cases where the effect of granting leave and allowing the appeal against sentence would be his immediate release.

When the appellant has absconded

7.21 If the appellant has absconded whilst in custody or on bail, the Court may dismiss the appeal, hear it in the absence of the appellant or adjourn the

7 Application can be made and leave given in such circumstances – CAA 1968, s 22.
8 CAA 1968, s 22.
9 As permitted by CAA 1968, s 22(3).
10 [2005] EWCA Crim 1090.

case pending their being returned to custody. In *R v Gooch*[11] the Court held that it was only in exceptional cases that the Court would hear the appeal. However, the principles that apply where an applicant or appellant has absconded were revisited in *R v Okedare*[12]. The following approach should now be taken:[13]

- applications from absconders should not be treated as ineffective per se;
- if there are grounds for believing an absconder has given authority to appeal, expressly or impliedly, or the case is one where the court might wish to intervene in the interests of justice, the court should proceed as normal. The application should be put before the single judge;
- the single judge may adjourn the application for more information, grant/refuse leave or refer the application to the full court as usual;
- if the single judge is satisfied there is no authority to pursue an application for leave and the application is not one the court would wish to entertain, they have the power to treat the application as ineffective and time will continue to run;
- the Court would expect orders declaring an application ineffective and orders staying applications brought on behalf of absconders to be the exception rather than the norm at the single judge stage;
- it remained the professional responsibility of the lawyer to highlight the fact that their client had absconded, for the benefit of the Criminal Appeal Office and the single judge. The lawyer must provide a full account of the circumstances of the absconding (with updates if necessary) coupled with an explanation for the basis for the assertion of authority and/or any reason why the court would wish to entertain the application;
- where the single judge has given leave, it remained for the full court to decide whether it was prepared to hear the appeal on the merits. If it was not so satisfied, the appeal could be stayed;
- where leave was refused, given the potential adverse consequences to an applicant who renews, a lawyer should consider their duties to the client and to the court very carefully before advancing a renewed application that might have adverse consequences for the client, absent clear instructions from them. In these circumstances, the court may be unwilling to infer authority to renew from the mere fact of their having been instructed to represent the client at trial. However, again, the interests of justice may prevail and there may be cases where the court is prepared to entertain a renewal application notwithstanding any issue over authority;

11 *R v Gooch* [1998] 2 Cr App R 130 (CA), confirmed in *R v Okedare* [2014] EWCA Crim 228.
12 [2014] EWCA Crim 228.
13 At paras 31–40 of *Okedare*.

- the Court saw no reason to differentiate between applications for leave to appeal against conviction and applications for leave to appeal against sentence. Where a retrial was concerned, those acting for the appellant would be notified of the order for a retrial and if the appellant was still absent at the time of their re-arraignment, then they would be deemed to have waived their right to be re-arraigned and a not guilty plea entered.

When the appellant has died

7.22 Section 44A of CAA 1968 provides that an appeal can continue when an eligible person can be identified and approved by the Court to take over their case. The power to approve can be exercised by the single judge but upon refusal, the applicant is entitled to have the application determined by the Full Court.[14] The categories of eligible persons are:

(a) the widow or widower, or surviving civil partner, of the dead person;

(b) a person who is the personal representative (within the meaning of section 55(1)(xi) of the Administration of Estates Act 1925) of the dead person; or

(c) any other person appearing to the Court of Appeal to have, by reason of a family or similar relationship with the dead person, a substantial financial or other interest in the determination of a relevant appeal relating to them.

7.23 Except in the case of an appeal on a reference by the Criminal Cases Review Commission, an application for such approval may not be made after the end of the period of one year beginning with the date of death.

Whether the prosecution will be represented at the hearing

7.24 The prosecution will be represented in appeals against conviction. They may choose, or be asked by the Court, to appear in appeals against sentence. They may also choose, or be asked by the Court, to appear at a renewed application for leave.

Orders restricting public access or reporting of hearings

The public right to attend court hearings

7.25 The general rule is that the Court should hear appeals in public, but it may order that a hearing take place in private. The opposite approach applies

14 CAA 1968, 44A(6).

when the Court is hearing a Public Interest Immunity application which must be held in private, unless the Court decides to hold it in public.[15]

7.26 An order that a hearing take place in private may be made under the Court's inherent power.[16] An order may also be made under the following statutory powers:

(a) in any appeal against a review of sentence (section 390 of the Sentencing Act 2020 in relation to appeals pursuant to 387 or 388 of the Sentencing Act 2020);

(b) where a witness under the age of 18 is giving evidence (section 37 of the Children and Young Person's Act 1933) (note: such an order cannot apply to members of the press);

(c) where the Court hears evidence in relation to a sexual offence (section 25 of the Youth Justice and Criminal Evidence Act 1999) (with an exception for one nominated member of the press);

(d) where the trial court could sit in private (section 1 of the Domestic and Appellate Proceedings (Restriction of Publicity) Act 1968).

Reporting restrictions

7.27 The press are entitled to report, in full, the Court's proceedings unless it makes an order placing a restriction upon the reporting of a particular case. The usual power used is section 4(2) of the Contempt of Court Act 1981, which provides an order can be made where it appears to be necessary for avoiding a substantial risk of prejudice to the administration of justice. One of the following three automatic statutory reporting restrictions may apply:

(a) Section 1 of the Sexual Offences (Amendment) Act 1992 gives the victim of a sexual offence lifetime anonymity in respect of their identification. The types of offences covered by this section are set out in section 2 of the Act (as amended by subsequent legislation) and includes the majority of sexual offences.

(b) Section 11 of the Criminal Justice Act 1987 and section 37 of the Criminal Procedure and Investigations Act 1996 provide limitations to the facts that may be reported in an appeal in relation to a preparatory hearing.

(c) Section 71 of the Criminal Justice Act 2003 provides that reporting restrictions apply to prosecution appeals against a preparatory ruling;

15 CrimPR 36.6(2).
16 CrimPR 36.6(1).

(d) Sections 45 and 45A of the Youth Justice and Criminal Evidence Act 1999 provide the power to restrict publications of the proceedings.

7.28 Part 6 of the CrimPR sets out the proper approach to the making of reporting restrictions and also contains a list of all statutory powers to make such an order.

7.29 In all cases where a reporting restriction might be appropriate, for example one involving children,[17] the parties should check with the Clerk of the Court whether any restrictions are in place. Any application should be made at the commencement of the hearing.

Hearing appeals regarding public immunity applications

7.30 In *R v McDonald, Rafferty and O'Farrell*[18] the Court set out the principles that should govern appeals in which the conduct of a Public Interest Immunity hearing in the Crown Court is the subject of challenge.

Televised Court hearings

7.31 The general ban on filming and recording in court is contained within section 41 of the Criminal Justice Act 1925, and section 9 of the Contempt of Court Act 1981. The Court of Appeal (Recording and Broadcasting) Order 2013[19] was made pursuant to section 32 of the Crime and Courts Act 2013, which allowed the making of orders for filming in particular courts as an exception to the general ban on such broadcasts. Recording is only of the submissions of a legal representative; exchanges between a legal representative and the Court and the Court giving judgment.[20]

The procedure at the hearing

Appeals with leave

7.32 The case commences with the appellant being identified on the video link. The appellant's advocate will make submissions. The advocate for the respondent (if the respondent is represented) will then make submissions. There is a final reply from the appellant. The judges frequently adopt an interventionist approach and will not be slow to ask the advocate about a

17 Children and Young Persons Act 1933, s 39.
18 [2004] EWCA Crim 2614.
19 SI 2013/2786.
20 Article 6 of the Order.

particular point that concerns or interests them or to indicate that they think that an argument is a bad one. It is advisable to meet the Court's questions head on.

7.33 If there is evidence to be called, the appellant will generally be expected to call the witness and examine him and the respondent to cross-examine in the normal way. However, when, if at all, that evidence is to be called is a matter to be determined by the Court. Where there is more than one witness, the order may have been determined at the directions stage. If it has not been, or there has not been a directions hearing, the parties are expected to agree an order of witnesses and submit that to the Registrar.

7.34 Unless there is a clear indication, in advance of the hearing, that the Court does not wish to hear from a particular witness, or the prosecution agree the witness, the witness should be at Court and in a position to give evidence if called.

7.35 In most cases the Court gives judgment at the end of the hearing. In more complex cases it may give a reserved judgment, and the parties will be informed of the date of a further hearing for judgment to be pronounced.

Renewed applications for leave

7.36 The hearings follow the same procedure as full hearings. Successful renewed applications for leave to appeal against conviction usually result in the Court listing the case for a full hearing on another occasion at which the appellant (if in custody) can be produced and the prosecution can be represented. However, in fresh evidence cases, the Court may wish at a leave hearing to hear the fresh evidence *de bene esse* (meaning on a provisional basis without yet determining its admissibility) but then go on, if leave is granted, to consider the full appeal at the same hearing. It will only do so if the prosecution is represented at the hearing.

7.37 If a renewed application for leave to appeal against sentence is successful, the Court will generally proceed to determine the appeal at the same hearing.

SUGGESTIONS FOR ADVOCACY

7.38 When preparing:

(a) Re-read everything.

(b) Identify the strongest point (or points) and be prepared to argue it concisely but with conviction. Not to do so is to throw away the opportunity that is presented by oral advocacy.

(c) Search out the difficulties in the case. Every case has them. The Court will identify them and ask the advocate about them.

(d) Clearly tab up the significant parts of the transcript so that they can be found quickly in Court.

(e) If it is intended to rely on authorities that have not been lodged with the Court or that were lodged late (and may not have reached the judges), three additional copies should be brought to court (along with an explanation for not having provided them earlier).

7.39 In Court:

(a) When a judge sits in the Court of Appeal he or she is always addressed as My Lord or My Lady.

(b) The Court will expect an advocate to introduce his opponent.

(c) The advocate should set out at the outset whether the hearing is an appeal, leave having been granted by the single judge or the Full Court; is an application for leave that has been referred to the Full Court; or whether it is a renewed application for leave, the single judge having refused leave.

(d) The Court will not expect the advocate to tell it about the facts of the case. It should be assumed that the relevant facts are in the papers and that the judges will have read the papers.

(e) It should not be assumed that the Court will be bound by the views of the single judge. Although it is wise to carefully consider the reasons of the single judge for granting or refusing, it is unwise to place reliance on the fact that leave has been given in the submissions themselves.

(f) If there are apologies that may have to be offered (if an argument was missed at trial) or concessions that are going to have to be made (if the judge got the law right once, and the grounds rely on his getting it wrong at some other stage), it is often best to make them immediately. It is more attractive to hear an advocate face up to a problem, admit it and then go straight on to argue why nonetheless the appeal should be allowed, than to witness the Court having to cross examine them into an admission they should have made at once.

(g) When making an application for leave that is out of time, the advocate should not forget that the application to extend time must also be made. It is sometimes sensible to mention at the outset when the advocate proposes to deal with it (it usually makes sense to address it at the conclusion of the substantive arguments on the grounds, unless the Court wants it to be addressed immediately) so that the Court is aware that the advocate has not forgotten the need to do so.

(h) The Court's questions should not be ignored or met with obfuscation but should be answered as clearly and well as possible.

APPLICATIONS AT THE CONCLUSION OF THE CASE

Applying for leave to appeal to the Supreme Court

7.40 If the appeal is dismissed, the appellant has 28 days to apply to the Court of Appeal to:

(a) certify a point of law of general public importance; and

(b) grant leave to appeal on the point to the Supreme Court.[21]

7.41 The Court of Appeal rarely certifies a point of law and almost never grants permission to appeal.

7.42 If the Court of Appeal certifies a point and refuses leave to appeal, the appellant then has 28 days to apply to the Supreme Court for permission to appeal.[22] However, if the Court of Appeal refuses to certify a point of law the appellant cannot apply to the Supreme Court. This is frustrating for appellants and their lawyers who feel there is a good legal argument that deserves further consideration, but both the Court of Appeal and the ECtHR have held that section 33 of CAA 1968, which, in effect, allows the Court of Appeal Criminal Division to terminate any further domestic appeal, is compatible with Article 6 of the Convention.[23]

7.43 A certified point is in the form of a question which should be framed in a way that identifies a particular legal issue that arose in the appeal but also indicates its wider importance.

7.44 If the Court has given judgment on the day of the hearing, the application to certify and for leave to appeal can be made orally, immediately after the judgment. However, it can be useful to reflect and draft a question with some care.

21 CAA 1968, s 34(1) and CrimPR 43.2. Statute does not provide a deadline for applying to certify but as leave must be applied for within 28 days, the same deadline applies.

22 CAA 1968, s 34(1). As with the application to the Court of Appeal, the application must be made 'within 28 days'.

23 *R v Dunn* [2010] EWCA Crim 1823 and application 62793/10 (declaration of inadmissibility, by a majority).

Applying for certification when considering an application to the European Court of Human Rights

7.45 If the appellant wishes to take the case to the ECtHR, it is advisable to make the application to the Court for leave and certification or the appellant may later face a difficulty in satisfying the ECtHR that they have complied with the requirement to exhaust all domestic remedies. (See 11.6 and 11.7 for full discussion.)

Costs

7.46 Orders for costs are not routinely made in the Court of Appeal and the law governing such payments has been greatly restricted in recent years.

Costs against an unsuccessful appellant or applicant

7.47 The Court can award costs against an unsuccessful appellant or applicant, but only when satisfied it is just and reasonable.[24] CrimPR 45.6 sets out the procedure and requirements before a costs order is made on appeal proceedings.

Costs for unnecessary or improper expenses

7.48 If the Court is satisfied that a party's unreasonable or improper act or omission has put another party to expense, it may order that party to pay some or all of the other party's costs.[25] The Court may make such an order on the application of a party or on its own initiative. An application should be made in accordance with the requirements of rule 45.8 of the CrimPR in writing, as soon as practical after becoming aware of the grounds for doing so and in any event no later than the end of the case. A copy should be served on the Registrar and one on the other parties.

Wasted costs orders against representatives

7.49 'Wasted costs' are defined by section 19(1) of the Prosecution of Offences Act 1985 as any cost incurred 'as a result of an unnecessary or improper act or omission by, or on behalf of, another party to the proceedings'.

7.50 The Court may make a wasted costs order against a legal representative or 'other representative', defined in the Act as a person who is exercising a

24 Prosecution of Offences Act 1985, s 18(2).
25 Prosecution of Offences Act 1985, s 19(1).

right of audience or right to conduct litigation on behalf of any party to the proceedings[26]. 'Wasted costs' in that section is defined as:

(a) as a result of any improper, unreasonable, or negligent act or omission on the part of any representative or any employee of a representative; or

(b) which, in the light of any such act or omission occurring after they were incurred, the court considers it is unreasonable to expect that party to pay.

7.51 The guidance for making a wasted costs order is to be found at CrimPR 45.9. of the Costs Practice Direction. Further guidance is to be found in *Re P (A Barrister)*[27] and *Asif v Ditta and Another*.[28]

7.52 As an alternative to making a wasted costs order the Court may, when the appellant is funded by a representation order or costs are to be paid out of central funds, make adverse observations about the representative's conduct of the case, for use in a costs assessment.[29]

Costs against a third party

7.53 The Court may make an order for costs against a third party when the Court considers that there has been serious misconduct by that party.[30] Guidance on the use of that section is at CrimPR 45.10. It is noted that such orders can only be made either of the Court's own volition or on the application of a party to the case.

Applications for a representation order following successful applications for leave

7.54 In successful applications for leave to appeal, an application for a representation order may be requested at the conclusion of the hearing. It is a good idea to be specific, so if the preparation *and* presentation of the appeal was all unfunded, asking for 'a representation order for the preparation and presentation of the appeal' will avoid any danger of the Registrar later taking the view that only the work on the day of the hearing was covered by the order obtained.

26 Prosecution of Offences Act 1985, s 19A.
27 [2001] EWCA Crim 1728.
28 [2021] 2 Cr App R 21.
29 CrimPR 45.9(11). See 8.19.
30 Prosecution of Offences Act 1985, s 19B.

SUMMARY OF KEY POINTS

- It is important to carefully read the appeal bundle to ensure that:
  - o it contains all the documents that are important to the appeal;
  - o that the case summary is accurate and covers the points that are important to the appeal;
  - o that the time estimate that has been given for the hearing is accurate.
- Whether to lodge a skeleton argument is a matter for the advocate unless specifically directed by the Court, but the Court does not encourage advocates to provide skeleton arguments when the case is already fully set out in the appeal notice.
- Lists of any reported authorities and bundles of any unreported authorities should be lodged with the grounds or perfected grounds. The guidance in *Erskine* should be considered when determining what authorities to rely on.
- Leave of the Court will be needed in order to argue any ground that was not contained in the original grounds that were considered by the single judge.
- The appellant has a right to be present at all appeals with leave, normally by video link, but not at renewed applications for leave. If the Court, having given leave to appeal against sentence, goes on to allow the appeal at the same hearing at which the appellant has not been produced, the appellant will be written to asking if they wish to have a hearing at which they will be produced.
- When an appellant or applicant has absconded, the Court has a discretion as to whether to hear the case, adjourn or dismiss the appeal. Refusal to hear the appeal should not be used as punishment for the absconding.
- If the appellant dies before the hearing, the case may proceed if an approved person can be appointed to continue the case on his behalf.
- The prosecution will be represented at appeals against conviction. They may be represented at appeals against sentence or renewed applications for leave depending on whether the Court requests it or the prosecuting authority themselves decide to be represented.
- The Court's hearings are open to the public unless an order is made that a particular hearing be held in private. Certain reporting restrictions may automatically apply or be made by the Court depending on the nature of the case. In a case in which the parties believe that an order restricting public access of press reporting of the case should be made, it should be applied for at the commencement of the hearing.

7.54 *Preparing for hearings in the Court of Appeal*

- In straightforward appeals the Court will give judgment at the conclusion of the hearing. In complex cases judgment may be reserved to another date.
- At the conclusion the advocate should remember to make any necessary application for a representation order or to certify a point of law of general public importance for the Supreme Court.

Chapter 8

Public funding and pro bono assistance

INTRODUCTION

Two distinct types of funding

8.1 The chances of successfully appealing your conviction or sentence will be greatly enhanced if you can afford a lawyer. However, as the appeal process is long and tortuous, the cost can be beyond the budget of most people. Having said that, the impact of a conviction or sentence can be such that people do manage to find funds to instruct a lawyer, often with the help of their family. Whilst there is publicly funded advice ('legal aid') available to those who cannot afford a lawyer, the financial limits for this advice are set at such a low level for both income and capital that only those who are unemployed with no savings will qualify financially. This usually means that, in reality, only those in prison with no savings, or those who receive state benefits will be able to access legally aided advice. At the same time, the number of solicitors prepared to take on these cases on legal aid is in severe decline. That is because the payment rates are well below the local hourly rates that solicitors would charge for everyday private work. Currently, for a senior solicitor, the legal aid hourly rate would be less than a fifth of the corresponding private rate. This makes it increasingly financially unsustainable to offer this service.

There are two sources of legal aid. The first is the existing legal aid covering the criminal matter at the Magistrates' Court or Crown Court. That order will cover 'advice and assistance' on any appeal. The second is where a new solicitor is asked to advise, which is known as 'freestanding advice and assistance'. The statutory basis for all forms of legal aid is the Legal Aid, Sentencing and Punishment of Offenders Act 2012 (LASPO 2012).[1] The important details are found in the main three regulations for legally aided appeals work: the Criminal Legal Aid (General) Regulations 2013 (SI 2013/09), the 'General Regulations'; the Criminal Legal Aid (Remuneration) Regulations 2013 (SI 2013/435), the 'Remuneration Regulations';[2] and the Criminal Legal Aid (Financial

1 LASPO, ss 14–19 set out the statutory basis for legal aid in criminal proceedings including advice and assistance.

2 Remuneration Regulations, Reg 6 refers to Sch 3, which sets out what can be claimed and the fees for both advice and assistance and advocacy under a representation order.

Resources) Regulations 2013 (SI 2013/471), the 'Means Regulations'.[3] Any practitioner who wants to provide legally aided advice needs to be familiar with all of them. The General Regulations define the generic class of advice that cover both types of advice and assistance.[4]

Type 1 – Advice and Assistance under the Crown Court Representation Order

8.2 As already mentioned, the usual starting point is the client's existing legal aid which will usually be the Crown Court Representation Order. The client's lawyers (the solicitor assigned on the order and the instructed advocate) should provide a brief advice at the end of the Crown Court case. If that advice is positive, the Crown Court Representation Order will also cover preparing the grounds to lodge at the Court of Appeal.

Type 2 – Advice and Assistance under the Standard Criminal Contract (SCC)

8.3 It is not widely known, but those who qualify for legal aid can obtain a second opinion if they do not agree with the advice from their trial team. A new solicitor may be able to provide 'freestanding' advice and assistance, if they hold a Legal Aid contract to do criminal work (or a specialist Appeals and Reviews contract).[5] The relevant contract provisions are set out in two documents: the 'Standard Terms'; and the 'Specification' to the SCC. There is also important guidance produced by the Legal Aid Agency (LAA) which is found in the Criminal Bills Assessment Manual (CBAM).[6]

Any organisation that has a General Crime Contract can carry out work under the SCC. The rules for advice on appeal is covered in section 11 of the Specification headed 'Appeals and Reviews Class'. As these rules do not affect general criminal work, they are not widely known and only a small number of firms doing legal aid work will offer to provide 'freestanding' advice and assistance, on appeals. This is also because the work is seen as both complex and badly paid.

3 Means Regulations specify who qualifies financially for advice.

4 Criminal Legal Aid (General) Regulations 2013 (SI 2013/09) 'General Regulations', reg 2 provides that 'criminal legal aid' means 'advice, assistance and representation made available under s 13, 15 and 16 of the Act' (LASPO); General Regulations, reg 33(c) provides that 'advice and assistance' includes 'an appeal or potential appeal against the outcome of criminal proceedings'.

5 General Crime Contract which is generically referred to as the Standard Criminal Contract 2025 (SCC) with the Legal Aid Agency (LAA).

6 The contract documents can be found at: www.gov.uk/government/publications/standard-crime-contract-2025.

There is a widespread assumption that the original trial lawyers will have provided a full written advice addressing any concerns the client has raised at the end of the Crown Court case. The continued stagnation of legal aid fees for Crown Court work makes that assumption less reliable. Advocates and litigators are not actually paid anything extra to provide a negative advice. As a result, there is a financial deterrent to expend a lot of time considering anything but an obvious error by the judge or the jury. This is even more the case where the fixed fee for the Crown Court work is often very low. This means it can be difficult for aggrieved clients and their families to obtain a comprehensive post-conviction advice explaining precisely why they do not have an appeal. Often their only option is to pay privately. The potential for miscarriages of justice occurring are exacerbated by the publicly funded fees currently paid to both prosecutors and defence advocates, which are often well below a reasonable level for the work required; as a result there may be even greater need to check that the original lawyers got it right first time round at the trial.

Representation under the Court of Appeal Representation Order

8.4 If leave to appeal is granted, then the Court of Appeal will grant a Representation Order if it is requested on the Appeal Notice (Form NG). Representation in the Court of Appeal is not means tested. The funding regime under the Court of Appeal Representation Order is like that under the original Crown Court Representation Order. The same hourly rates are applied which depend on the grade of fee earner. The main difference is that the actual work done is claimed at the applicable hourly rate, unlike the Litigator Graduated Fee Scheme (LGFS) and the Advocates Graduated Fee Scheme (AGFS) where fixed fees have replaced hourly rates. The other difference is that the Representation Order usually covers the advocate who drafted the grounds but does not include the instructing solicitor. However, an application can be made to extend its scope to include a solicitor to do specific work and, if necessary, more than one advocate.[7] There is no standard application form, so this is done in writing, usually with a written advice from the instructed advocate. If permission to appeal is refused, there will be no Representation Order issued in the Court of Appeal, but the solicitor and the advocate can submit a claim for the work they did advising positively between the end of the Crown Court case and up to the refusal of permission by the single judge. That bill should be sent to the Costs' Officer at the Court of Appeal. The claim should be made within three months of the Single Judge's decision.[8]

7 The Court of Appeal can exercise the power in LASPO, s 19(1) to grant representation and the Criminal Legal Aid (Determination by a Court and Choice of Representative) Regulations 2013 (SI 2013/614) allow the Court of Appeal to grant representation of its own motion or on an application.

8 See 8.13 below for the rules on claiming.

Actual representation replaces advice and assistance

8.5 Once the Court of Appeal has issued a Representation Order, that order will replace the 'advice and assistance' under the original Crown Court Order. The LAA have made it clear that advice and assistance under the SCC cannot be used to supplement an 'advocate only' Order in the Court of Appeal.[9]

Pro bono assistance

8.6 There are also a small number of organisations who provide free assistance or representation for appeal work. The limited availability of legal aid means that these can be a vital backstop for those who seek to challenge their sentence or conviction. The assistance that they may provide is considered at the end of this chapter.

WORK UNDER A CROWN COURT AND COURT OF APPEAL REPRESENTATION ORDER

The funding rules

8.7 The funding rules for carrying out work on an appeal under either a Crown Court Representation Order or, once permission is granted, a Court of Appeal Representation Order, are very similar. Payment for the work is based on the same rates and both claims are assessed by a costs' assessor in the Criminal Appeal Office. Funding or related queries should be addressed to the Registrar, who is head of the Criminal Appeal Office.

As already discussed at 8.2 above, the usual starting point for advice on appeal is the Representation Order in the Crown Court. That order includes 'advice and assistance on any appeal'.[10] The scheme of funding work under Representation Orders is set out in LASPO (which refers to the grant of funding by the court as a 'determination').[11] The relevant rates of pay are set out in the Remuneration Regulations.[12]

To appreciate how legal aid works in the Crown Court it is important to bear in mind that most Crown Court work is paid by way of fixed fees. These are the LGFS for solicitors and the AGFS for advocates. The fixed fee is based on four factors: the type of offence; the outcome; the page count; and the number of days of trial. No additional fee is paid for a negative advice on appeal at

9 SCC, para 11.7.

10 Legal Aid, Sentencing and Punishment of Offenders Act 2012, s 42; 'representation' includes 'advice and assistance as to any appeal'.

11 LASPO, s 16.

12 Schedule 3 sets out the rules and rates for Court of Appeal work for both advocates and solicitors, Sch 4 sets out the rates for solicitors under the LAA contract and Sch 5 sets out the rates for experts under the LAA contract.

the end of the case as that work is included in the fixed fee. However, if the appeal advice is positive and grounds are lodged at the Court of Appeal, then an additional and separate claim can be made for the advice and grounds by both the solicitor and the advocate to the Criminal Appeal Office. The initial paper application for permission to appeal is usually determined on paper by the Single Judge (SJ). The paper decision will be received on a Form SJ. If the SJ refuses permission then the case is at an end and a claim for the fees for the work done on the positive advice is made by sending it to the Criminal Appeal Office Costs Office.[13]

If the SJ grants permission, or decides to refer the application to the Full Court, then a Representation Order will usually be granted but just for the advocate who drafted the grounds. The advocate will then be able to claim for the work preparing for the full hearing and attending the appeal. Whilst the Registrar usually limits representation to the advocate only, if specific litigation work needs to be done by the solicitor ('litigator'), an application should be made to the Registrar to extend the order to cover the solicitor for those specific tasks. It is rare for the Registrar to agree to extend the order 'generally' to cover a solicitor, but it can be done if a lot of litigation work is required.

What advice is covered?

Check the guide

8.8 The first place to look at what work will be allowed preparing an appeal is the 'Guide to Proceedings in the Court of Appeal, Criminal Division' ('The Guide').[14] This summarises the various rules and guidance contained in the Criminal Practice Directions (CPD), the Criminal Procedure Rules (CrimPR) and the Remuneration Regulations (see 8.1). The Guide is a good place to start when considering what work the Registrar will be likely to authorise and what work they will consider necessary and reasonable when their office assesses the claim. The Guide reminds the Crown Court advocate to provide basic advice as soon as the Crown Court case finishes. The Crown Court Order only covers advice and assistance drafting the grounds. It does not cover work related to the appeal itself, so if exceptional work needs to be done, such as instructing a new expert that requires a Representation Order, it is best to lodge provisional grounds with the Criminal Appeal Office and send a note to the Registrar setting out why a Representation Order should be granted to cover that additional work.[15]

13 The claim is made on the old ex post facto claim form – see COA Bill of Costs at Appendix C.
14 See Appendix A for March 2026 version. The best place to find all related guidance is: https://www.judiciary.uk/courts-and-tribunals/court-of-appeal-home/the-court-of-appeal-criminal-division/.
15 The Guide A.4.

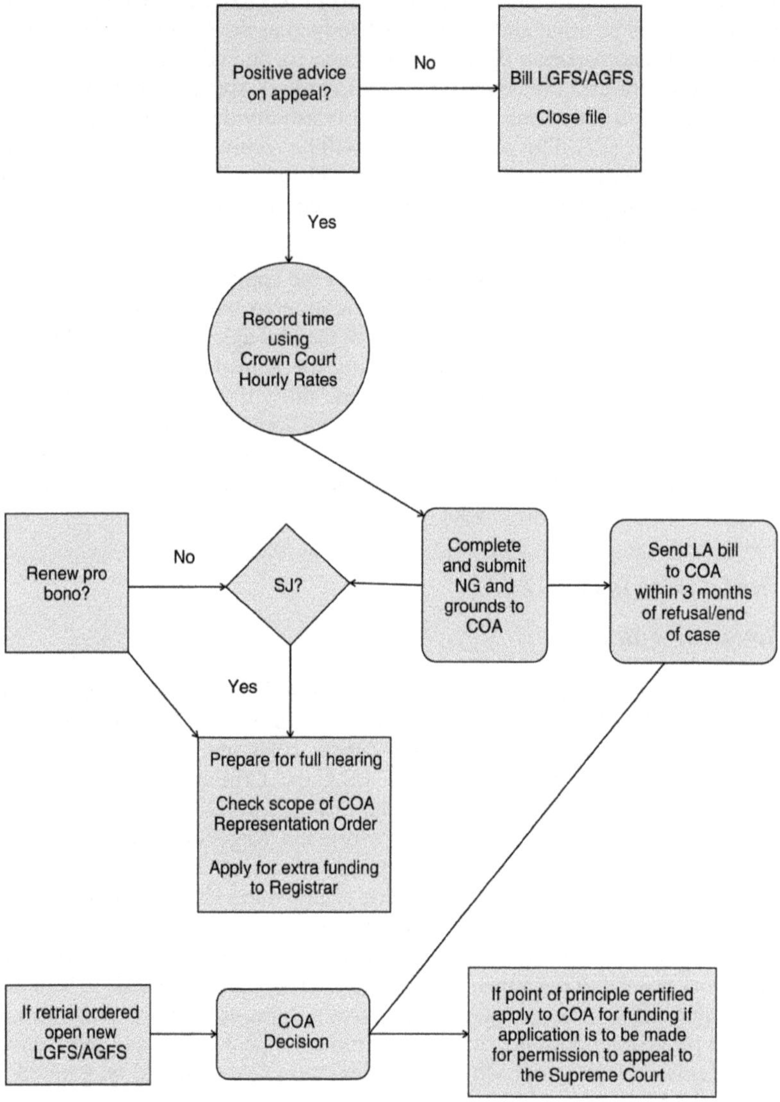

Figure 8.1 Flowchart for appeals under the Crown Court representation order

Extending the order

8.9 The Registrar will not usually extend the order to allow work by a solicitor unless they are persuaded that there is good reason to do so. This is because the Registrar will assume that the appeal involves discrete points of law which can be dealt with by the advocate without any further instructions from the solicitor. Such an approach ignores the reality that the solicitor is expected to update the client, liaise with the court and the advocate to ensure the appeal runs smoothly and the client is kept informed. Indeed, solicitors often receive complaints from clients or their families when they do not. They may even be asked by the Legal Ombudsman to explain a lack of communication with the client. In the consumer age there is an expectation that the solicitor will continue to assist with the case, and this is often *pro bono* as the Order will not cover this work. Sometimes the Criminal Appeal Office will ask the solicitor for updates whilst at the same time refusing to extend the Representation Order to allow them to claim for work. This may be an opportunity for the solicitor to apply for an extension, if there is a lot of contact from the Criminal Appeal Office. The solicitor should keep under review whether there is a need for specific work, such as instructing an expert or taking a witness statement, then they should write to the Registrar explaining why and include a full supporting note from the advocate. The Registrar may be more likely to agree to extend the order to allow an attendance on the appellant if they are vulnerable because of their age or a mental difficulty, or if new instructions are required. The 'Special Cases' discussed later in Chapter 15 will often involve issues that do require an extension for a litigator to do supporting work. If an extension is granted it will set out the limited purpose(s) for which the solicitor is assigned on the order. Usually, it will not cover attending the client in person or attending the appeal hearing, so if these steps are necessary, they should be applied for in writing in advance setting out why it is reasonable and necessary to carry out the work. The Registrar can extend the order at any time and often there will be more than one application to extend it. Therefore, it is important to check carefully what work is authorised and, apply for specific extensions.

No prior authority or payments on account

8.10 If there is any doubt about what is allowed, clarification can be obtained from the Criminal Appeal Office and an extension applied for. This must be done before the work is done. There is no set form of application. It just needs a letter or e-mail setting out the issues and explaining why the extension is required. It can be helpful to include a supporting note from the advocate setting out why the extension is needed. There is no mechanism for obtaining payments in advance for disbursements or for prior authority of specific amounts. So you should be careful to ensure that your terms and conditions of instruction reflect that, and you can only pay what is allowed on assessment though you may agree to make further submissions on any reduction to reassure the expert so they will take on the case.

Effect of refusal by single judge

Legal Aid ends

8.11 If the single judge refuses leave they will also refuse any application for a Representation Order. This means any further advice will have to be either privately funded or *pro bono*. The original Crown Court order does not cover renewal. This means that your '*right*' to renew your application at an oral hearing will be dependent on whether you can afford to pay an advocate to renew for you – or persuade them to act *pro bono*. If you cannot afford to pay for the renewal, the best approach is to ask the advocate who signed the grounds to explain why the SJ decision has altered their view on whether there were arguable grounds. The Guide reiterates that the advocate should not sign grounds unless they believed them to be reasonably arguable. It is worth asking the advocate why they have changed their view as often the SJ decision is quite short and succinct and does not engage fully with the individual grounds. If the advocate can be persuaded to renew *pro bono,* they have the comfort of knowing that if they succeed in getting leave from the Full Court, they will also get a retrospective Representation Order. The lack of legal aid for renewal to the Full Court is not a breach Article 6 of the ECHR.[16]

Depending on the comments of the Single Judge, and whether they have initialled the 'loss of time' box on the Form SJ, the advocate may be willing to renew the application *pro bono* before the Full Court. If the renewal of the application for leave is successful, the Full Court will usually grant a Representation Order even if the substantive appeal fails. That Order will cover the preparation and advocacy for the full renewal hearing, but it will not usually cover the work done by the solicitor unless it is specifically requested at the renewal hearing and the court agrees.

Post-SJ refusal advice

8.12 As the court can grant retrospective representation when they grant leave on a renewed application then it may be worthwhile asking the court to consider extending the Representation Order to cover not just the advocate but also the solicitor who worked on the renewal. As this will be unusual, it will require exceptional justification, but it is possible and should be considered in preparation for the renewal hearing. It is useful if the solicitor can provide a schedule of work done so that the advocate can fully argue it.[17]

CLAIMING FOR WORK DONE IN THE COURT OF APPEAL

Claims for solicitors and advocates

8.13 The rules for claiming fees for work done in the Court of Appeal are contained in the Remuneration Regulations.[18]

16 *R v Oates* [2002] EWCA Crim 1071.
17 CBAM, para 6.9.4; *Regina v Gibson (Ivano)* [1983] 1 WLR 1038.
18 Remuneration Regulations, reg 6 refers to the fees set out in Sch 3.

The Claim for Costs must be submitted within three months from the conclusion of the case.[19] The time limit may be extended by the Criminal Appeal Office if there is 'good reason', but any costs allowed may be reduced if there is not a good reason for the delay (and it is reasonable to reduce them). If the costs' assessor proposes to reduce the fees, they must give the solicitor or advocate the opportunity to make submissions, and they can appeal to the Costs Judge if they are unsatisfied by the reasons given for the reduction.[20]

The Claim 'must be in such a manner and form as the appropriate officer may direct' and sent to the costs team at the Criminal Appeal Office.[21] It should include a copy of the Representation Order and any receipts or vouchers for any disbursements.

All assessments are based on:

> 'All the relevant circumstances of the case including the nature, importance, complexity or difficulty of the work and;
>
> the time involved and allow a reasonable amount in respect of all work actually and reasonably done.'[22]

The solicitor and advocate should include a note justifying each item of work and the time spent with the claim. This should highlight any special circumstances of the case and provide as much information as possible to assist the costs' assessor with reference to the above test.

Solicitors' claims

8.14 The costs' assessor must take account of the 'class of work done'. The assessment will look at whether the work done was reasonable and the time spent.[23]

Solicitors' work in the Court of Appeal is broken down into five classes:

(i) preparation (which includes all the general work a solicitor will do on a case);

(ii) advocacy;

(iii) attending at court with the advocate;

(iv) travelling and waiting; and

(v) dealing with routine letters and telephone calls.[24]

19 Remuneration Regulations, Sch 3, paras 2 and 5.
20 Remuneration Regulations, reg 31.
21 SCC, para 5.25.
22 Remuneration Regulations, Sch 3, para 1(2); CBAM, the general principles in para 2.4 also would apply.
23 Remuneration Regulations, Sch 3, para 3(2).
24 Remuneration Regulations, Sch 3, para 3(1).

The claim should set out these classes of work in separate sections and record the date each item of work was done, the time taken and amount claimed.

The claim must specify the level of fee-earner and set out any work done for more than one indictment.[25] It must also set out why any enhancement is claimed (see 8.15).[26] If a claim is made under a retrospective Representation Order (see 8.11), the claim must confirm that none of the fees have been claimed under a defence costs order from Central Funds (this is unlikely as costs from Central Funds can no longer include legal fees in the Court of Appeal).[27]

The level of fee earner will be either:

(i) Grade A, is a senior solicitor (this is normally 10 years post qualification experience 'PQE' or eight years' specialist experience);

(ii) Grade B, is a non-senior solicitor or an experienced legal executive; or

(iii) Grade C, is a trainee or paralegal.

The rates that can be claimed are set out in the Remuneration Regulations.[28] As already discussed, these rates are well below the average private rate that would be charged and have remained almost unchanged since the mid-1990s. The assessor will look at the level of fee-earner for each item on the bill and firstly decide if that person was the right grade of fee-earner for that task. The use of Grade A fee earners will attract extra scrutiny, so it is important that the note, sent with the claim, makes it clear why using a Grade A solicitor was justified. The usual reasons are the complexity or seriousness of the case. A Grade A fee earner may be justified if the client is especially vulnerable. It may be worth pointing out that the fee-earner who dealt with the original case, and who knows the case history and the client, was able to work more quickly and therefore save costs overall which can be used to justify using a higher grade. You may be able to show that a more experienced fee-earner has accomplished a task quicker than a less experienced one would and that this has reduced the claim overall or that a less experienced one would have needed to do additional work getting up to speed with the case if a routine task was delegated to them. It is important to provide this information in the note with the Claim.

Enhancement of the standard rate for litigators

The relevant factors

8.15 Given the low hourly rates for solicitors and advocates, it is vital that 'enhanced' rates are claimed whenever possible.[29] If allowed, the hourly rate

25 Remuneration Regulations, Sch 3, para 2(3).
26 Remuneration Regulations, Sch 3, para 3(2); CBAM, para 3.1 applies to all assessments.
27 Prosecution of Offences Act 1985, s 16A.
28 Schedule 3, para 7.
29 Remuneration Regulations, Sch 3, paras 8(2).

will usually double as it will be enhanced by 100%. Usually, it will only apply to non-routine work as, by definition, the work must be exceptional (not routine). However, if there is an exceptional amount of travel or waiting because of the location of the client or the nature of the case, then it may be worth making a claim to enhance the lower rate for travel and waiting. Enhanced rates can be claimed for any of the 'specified offences'.[30]

To claim enhanced rates the solicitor must show:

(a) the work was done with exceptional competence, skill or expertise;

(b) the work was done with exceptional despatch; or

(c) the case involved exceptional complexity or other exceptional circumstances.

If made out, the appropriate uplift will depend on:

(i) the degree of responsibility accepted by the fee-earner;

(ii) the care, speed and economy with which the case was prepared; and

(iii) the novelty, weight and complexity of the case.

The usual uplift is up to 100% and for a solicitor based in London the appropriate uplift should be the full 100% taking account of the local Senior Courts' Costs Office (SCCO) rates.[31] If it is a very complex or serious fraud it can be up to 200%.[32] The test of 'exceptional' means 'unusual or out of the ordinary' for the *general type* of case, it does not mean exceptional for *that type* of case.[33] A claim for enhancement may be more likely to be allowed by the assessor if the solicitor (or advocate) focus on the particular tasks that meet the enhancement criteria rather than claiming a blanket enhancement across the entire Claim.

To maximise the chances of being successful in claiming an enhancement all actual work which can be shown to be reasonable and necessary should be clearly recorded. Exceptional 'competence, skill or expertise' may be shown by the standard of work carried out which can be indicated by a favourable outcome. Exceptional 'despatch' will require real urgency. This may be because of late service of papers or the need to consider a large volume of work in a short period of time which resulted in rearranging or cancelling other work or working unsociable hours. It will assist, if you can evidence the need to rearrange other work to accommodate the urgency of the task and point out any evening or weekend work with times and dates. The general factors that may

30 Remuneration Regulations. Sch 1, Part 7 provides a list of the specified offences A, B, C, D, G, I, J and K.

31 These are local guideline hourly rates for general litigation approved by the SCCO and they are much higher than the rates for publicly funded work.

32 CBAM 2018 (June) para 9.1.

33 *R v the Legal Aid Board, ex p RM Broudie* [1994] 138 SJ 94.

have made the original case exceptional are set out in CBAM. These include the character of the defendant (including any vulnerability); if the case was particularly weighty or complex; the type of case or degree of public interest; significant expert issues; difficulties with defence witnesses; or the exceptional length of trial.[34] They may not necessarily apply at the appeal level, as it may be based on a narrow legal issue. Enhancement submissions will need to focus on the appeal aspects to the work. The fact that the Registrar has agreed to assign a solicitor is a good starting point for submissions.

The bill will be assessed by a member of the costs' team at the Criminal Appeal Office who will not necessarily be aware of the details of the case so it is helpful to start the note carefully setting out the factors in the case that justify both the level of fee-earner who worked on the case and any grounds for enhancement. These should focus on the individual circumstances of the case and the client. If the time spent on a piece of work is longer than one would expect, the reason should be clearly explained in the note with the claim.

Advocate's claim

8.16 The advocate submits their claim on the same type of claim form as the litigator and the matters they are required to set out are much the same. The claim must:[35]

> 'A claim must—
>
> (a) summarise the items of work done by an advocate in respect of which fees are claimed according to the classes specified in paragraph 6(2);
>
> (b) state, where appropriate, the dates on which the items of work were done, the time taken, the sums claimed and whether the work was done for more than one assisted person; and
>
> (c) give particulars of any work done in relation to more than one indictment or a retrial.
>
> (5) The advocate must specify any special circumstances which the advocate considers should be drawn to the attention of the appropriate officer.'

The Remuneration Regulations set out the minimum prescribed fees and hourly rates that can be claimed and the applicable hourly rates, basic fees, refreshers and subsidiary fees. There are minimum and maximum amounts for subsidiary fees.[36]

34 CBAM, para 9.1.3.
35 Remuneration Regulations, Sch 3, para 5; see COA Claim Form at Appendix C.
36 Schedule 3, paras 9(1)–(3).

However, as with litigator fees above, the assessor can allow a higher rate for the advocate under Schedule 3, paragraph 9(4):

> 'Where it appears to the appropriate officer, taking into account all the relevant circumstances of the case, that owing to the exceptional circumstances of the case the amount payable by way of fees in accordance with the table following sub-paragraph (1) would not provide reasonable remuneration for some or all of the work the appropriate officer has allowed, the appropriate officer may allow such amounts as appear to the appropriate officer to be reasonable remuneration for the relevant work.'

The advocate can claim for a higher fee than the specified rate if the 'exceptional circumstances' mean that the set fees would not provide 'reasonable remuneration' for the work done.[37] The factors set out at 8.15 would equally apply to the advocate's claim. For serious and complex cases, the notional hourly rate for KCs is approximately £200 per hour, but the Senior Costs Judge recently allowed a notional hourly rate of £275 per hour for a KC in a costs appeal involving a murder case with a complicated background involving bad character evidence.[38]

Disbursements

8.17 As there is no mechanism for obtaining prior authority you will not be able to guarantee that disbursements will be allowed on assessment. Therefore, care should be taken to justify fully disbursements that are unusual or larger than usual. A common example is the distance travelled from the solicitor's office to attend a client. Make it clear why a video link attendance was not possible – or appropriate. The cost of Crown Court transcripts that were not obtained through the Registrar may also be disallowed unless reasonable.[39]

The guideline fees for experts are set out in Schedule 5 of the Remuneration Regulations. These rates can be increased if justified in exceptional circumstances. If the rate is higher than the guideline, it is often worth asking the prosecution what they have paid their respective expert as a comparison to justify a higher rate on an 'equality of arms' basis. It is helpful to get the expert to provide examples of similar cases where the higher rate was allowed on assessment or by the LAA in the Crown Court or on previous appeals by the Criminal Appeal Office. As already discussed, (see 8.10), it is good practice to ensure that your terms and conditions for instructing experts make it clear that you cannot guarantee payment of their fees in full and you will not be liable for any reduction. It should also make clear that fees for actual attendance at Court

37 Remuneration Regulations, Sch 3, para 9(4).
38 *R v Sherome Williams* [2025] EWHC 2412 (SCCO).
39 Remuneration Regulations, Sch 3, para 4.

are claimed from the Court direct as you will not have any means to pay these under public funding. However, the reality is that experts may be reluctant to accept instructions unless you offer to argue their fees on assessment. Any refusal to a pay fees or disbursements can be appealed to the Senior Courts Costs Office (SCCO) and if successful costs will be awarded (see 8.18 below).

Appealing the assessment

8.18 If the costs are not allowed in full, then further representations can be made within 21 days of the initial assessment. If those representations are not completely successful an appeal can be submitted to the Costs Judge at the SCCO.[40] Since Covid most of these appeals are conducted on the electronic platform and hearings can be attended using Microsoft Teams. You need to lodge a Form A[41] and pay a fee of £100 which is refunded if you are successful (even in part). If the appeal to the Costs Judge is successful, even in part, the judge will usually award the additional costs of preparing and attending the costs appeal as well as the previously disallowed amount.

Other costs orders

8.19 If the court makes an adverse observation about the conduct of the case by either the litigator or advocate, the Appropriate Officer may reduce the fees. If they intend to do so they must give the person affected an opportunity to make representations as to whether the fee should be reduced and the extent of any reduction.[42] The Practice Direction addresses this in detail.[43] The Court of Appeal can also order an unsuccessful applicant to pay the costs of another party and any legal aid costs. It should not be done as a penalty and exceptions apply.[44]

FUNDING UNDER THE 2025 STANDARD CRIMINAL CONTRACT (SCC)

What work can be done?

Consider the SCC and CBAM

8.20 This is the alternative type of legal aid. The SCC sets out the types of advice that can be provided by organisations who hold a contract with the LAA (and referred to as 'providers'). Any solicitor or advocate wanting to

40 Remuneration Regulations, Sch 3, para 11.
41 The Senior Courts Costs Office Guide 2023.
42 Remuneration Regulations, reg 26.
43 Criminal Practice Direction (Costs in Criminal Proceedings) 2015, para 4.3.
44 Criminal Practice Direction (Costs in Criminal Proceedings) 2015, para 3.3.

provide advice under this type of legal aid needs to understand the relevant sections of the SCC along with the LAA guidance in CBAM. CBAM sets out the LAA's approach to the work it will allow providers to do and how funding requests will be viewed. The rules and guidance go into detail as to what can and cannot be done. Remember that the guidance is just that and may be departed from if justified. The SCC Specification is structured into sections: 1–8 apply generally to all classes of criminal work; and sections 9–13 refer to specific areas of work. Appeals and Reviews are covered at section 11.[45] If there is a conflict between any terms, then the general sections take precedence over the specific ones.[46] CBAM also has general and specific sections.[47] If there is a conflict between the SCC and CBAM, then SCC takes precedence.[48]

Advantages of using the SCC

8.21 If a new team of lawyers are instructed after conviction they could, in theory, apply to transfer the Crown Court Representation Order and provide advice and assistance under that order. That would require an application to the Crown Court where the matter was heard.[49] Given the strict criteria for transfer it is unlikely to be successful unless there has been a complete breakdown in the relationship between the defendant and their trial lawyers. In any event the new team will be reluctant to have the order transferred to them before they can assess the merits because there is no additional payment for a negative advice under the LGFS and AGFS. Therefore, a better solution is to assess whether the work qualifies under the 'Appeals and Reviews' class of work in the SCC. This 'Appeal and Reviews' class of work covers both applications for leave to the Court of Appeal and requests to the Criminal Cases Review Commission (CCRC) to review the conviction or sentence. It is important to gather as much information from the prospective client at the outset to be able to assess whether the case passes the initial sufficient benefits test (SBT) and whether the client will pass the means test. Any organisation who wants to do this work would be well advised to design an initial enquiry form to capture the necessary information.

Disadvantages of using SCC – costs limits and audit compliance

8.22 There are separate costs limits for applications to the Court of Appeal and the CCRC.[50] Once these limits are reached any additional costs or

45 SCC, para 11 deals specifically with Appeals and Reviews.

46 SCC, para 1.4.

47 CBAM, sections 1–3 deal with general interpretation whilst section 12 deals specifically with 'Appeals and Reviews'.

48 CBAM, para 1.1.

49 The Legal Aid Manual, ch 7.

50 For Court of Appeal cases, it is currently £314.81 and for CCRC applications £524.69 – see Remuneration Regs, Sch 4, Pt 8.

disbursements will require a costs extension by the LAA. As the work up to the first extension is self-authorised by the provider, it is essential that there are clear file notes complying with both the SCC and the guidance in CBAM. Apart from the applications for extensions to the upper limit, none of the preliminary work on the file will be subject to any ongoing checks by the LAA unless the file is requested for an audit. A selection of the provider's files will be carefully examined by the LAA annually ('LAA audit'). On a LAA audit, the main pitfalls are incorrect or incomplete application forms (CRM1/2), a lack of adequate evidence of means, conflicting information (says single but may have a partner whose means need assessing) or inadequate file notes recording decisions. to check the costs limit was extended before the work was done. Payments made when the rules are not complied with or when the limits are exceeded will be recouped.[51] Contract audits can be appealed, and while many successfully are, it is time-consuming and unpaid work, so it is better to try to avoid them by having tight supervision from the start.

Therefore, as authority for the initial work is 'self-granted', it is vital that the supervising solicitor ensures that the rules have been complied with and the relevant LAA tests are met. The solicitor should ensure that the funding forms are fully completed, the client qualifies on means and the SBT is met. This becomes all the more important as the further extensions by the LAA assume that the provider has followed the contract to the letter at the self-authorisation stage. If the file is audited later and the funding forms have not been completed properly or the SBT or means test wrongly applied funding for the entire file can be recouped. If that happens the LAA will try to recoup any monies that have been claimed. If, in fact, it can be shown that the client did qualify for funding submissions can be made to reinstate the funding, but it is better to avoid this arising in the first place. Another issue on audits can be late prior authorities after the costs have been incurred. The LAA will recoup payments for any disbursements incurred without an existing prior authority even if they are subsequently authorised. This is a very penal approach which could be challenged as an unfair contract term, but to date there has not been any such challenge and, for now, this is the approach that the LAA can take. So again, it is best to avoid such a scenario arising.

This is a major disincentive to organisations taking on this work as it can result in large recoupments that are caused by clerical errors which cannot be corrected later.

Another disincentive is cashflow as there is no mechanism for applying for payments on account. Appeals cases can last for many years which can mean substantial costs are run up on a complex advice file. The provider may well have paid out substantial disbursements to external advocates or expert(s) but then have to wait a long time, sometimes years, before they can claim those back from the LAA. As already mentioned, unlike other areas of criminal

51 SCC, para 5.19.

work, there is no mechanism to apply for pre-authorised disbursements to be paid by the LAA in advance. As a result, many experts who are accustomed to receiving payment at the time of their invoice for other areas of criminal work, will expect the same payment terms for appeals work even though the provider cannot get the pre-authorised disbursement paid till the end of the case. This bureaucracy and the fact that there is no means to obtain payment of disbursements before the case concludes, are severe disincentives to taking on this type of work.

Who can advise under the SCC?

8.23 All organisations holding a current general crime contract or a specific 'appeals only' contract are authorised to provide advice and assistance on Appeals and Reviews. However, if there is an existing Representation Order the LAA will expect advice to be given under that order (see 8.6 above) by the existing litigator and advocate unless there has been a justifiable change of provider. In that case the new provider should carefully consider the advice the client has already received and whether fresh advice at the public's expense is justified.[52] If the solicitor who has provided advice under the original order is asked to readvise under the SCC they may do so but they should consider whether they should make an application to the Court of Appeal for a Representation Order.[53]

The general supervisor requirements in the SCC apply.[54] Where the organisation holds an 'appeals only' contract there is an additional supervisor requirement that the supervisor must have held a non-conditional practising certificate for three years or they must have undertaken a minimum of 350 hours' casework in Appeals and Reviews in the past 12 months (or, if part-time, 1050 hours in the past five years).[55] The supervisor is required to sign a declaration to confirm that. They can supervise a maximum of four designated fee-earners.[56] Any advocate instructed to provide an opinion must be independent to the instructing litigator unless they are undertaking the advocacy:

> 'An in-house advocate instructed by you to give an opinion must be from a different organisation from your instructing Solicitor unless undertaking advocacy on the same case. The use of such an advocate who must not be a partner in, or employed by, or a consultant to your organisation will ensure that any opinion obtained is independent and objective (in the same way that an external opinion would be).'[57]

52 SCC, paras 11.3–11.5.
53 SCC, para 11.7.
54 SCC, paras 2.1–2.31.
55 SCC, para 2.26.
56 SCC, para 2.30.
57 SCC, para 4.14.

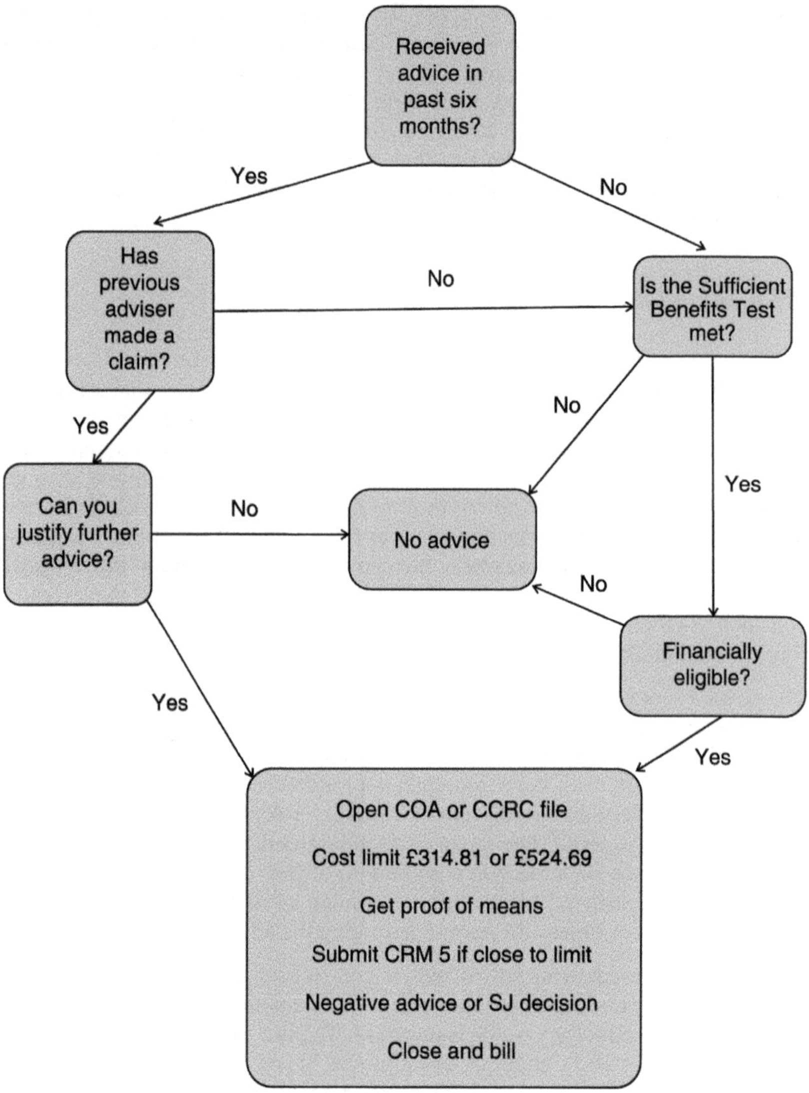

Figure 8.2 Flowchart for advice on appeal to COA or CCRC under SCC 2025 Appeals and Reviews Class

Bars to advising – previous advice and assistance

8.24 You cannot advise a client under this scheme if they have received advice from another provider (not counting the trial lawyer) within the past six months unless:

(a) there is a gap in time and circumstances have changed materially between the first and second occasions when the advice and assistance was sought;

(b) the client has reasonable cause to transfer from the first provider; or

(c) the first provider has confirmed that they will be making no claim for the payment for the advice and assistance.[58]

8.25 The six-month rule does not apply if the previous advice was given under a Representation Order.[59]

As that trial advice under the Representation Order was likely to be negative, the justification for fresh advice will need to be carefully considered. If they already have received a second opinion you will need to wait at least six months before providing fresh advice. After six months you may provide advice if the means test and the SBT are passed (see 8.32). The request will not pass the SBT if the previous advice dealt adequately with the matters the client is now raising. Providers will be expected to filter out these requests without opening an advice file. It will be easier for the case to pass the SBT if the client is in custody, so it relates to their liberty, or the conviction is having an ongoing impact on their life.[60]

PRE-CONDITIONS – FINANCIAL ELIGIBILITY (MEANS)

The Means Regulations

8.26 The first important matter to check is whether your client qualifies financially. The SCC adopts the financial eligibility rules in Part 2 of the Means Regulations.[61] The LAA will enforce them strictly when auditing any appeal files, so it is vital that the information on the file complies with the LAA requirements. They will look at the guidance in CBAM at Annex B: Financial Eligibility. If evidence is not satisfactory the LAA can issue a contract notice and recoup any costs and disbursements that have been paid. This may well include hefty disbursements to third parties that the provider will still be contractually liable for.

Deemed eligibility

8.27 There is 'deemed' financial eligibility if the individual (or their partner) is in receipt of the following benefits:

58 SCC, para 11.26.
59 CBAM, para 12.2.1.
60 CBAM, paras 12.2.2 and 12.2.3.
61 SCC, para 11.9.

(a) a 'qualifying benefit': income support; income-based jobseeker's allowance; guaranteed state pension credit; income-related employment and support allowance; and universal credit;[62] or

(b) they currently receive either:

  (i) any working tax credit payable under Part 1 of the 2002 Act claimed together with child tax credit payable under Part 1 of that Act; or

  (ii) any working tax credit payable under Part 1 of the 2002 Act with a disability element or severe disability element (or both).

  And in the case of (i) or (ii) the individual's total income from all sources for the year before signing the CRM1/2 is not more than £14,213, otherwise the full eligibility calculation must be carried out.

If relying on a qualifying benefit you must keep satisfactory evidence on the file.[63] It will passport them straight through to the sufficient benefit test (see 8.25).

Partner

8.28 If the client has a partner their resources need to be taken into account.

> '"Partner" means –
>
> (a) 'an individual's spouse or civil partner, from whom the individual is not separated due to a breakdown in the relationship which is likely to be permanent;
>
> (b) a person with whom the individual lives as a couple; or
>
> (c) a person with whom the individual ordinarily lives as a couple, from whom they are not separated due to a breakdown in the relationship that is likely to be permanent.'

This means that a client serving a custodial sentence may be separated from their partner physically but still in a relationship. You must not assume they are single because they are in prison.[64]

The financial resources of the individual's partner must be treated as the individual's financial resources unless:

(a) the individual's partner has a contrary interest in the matter in respect of which the individual is seeking advice and assistance; or

62 Means Regulations, Regs 14 and 2.
63 SCC, para 3.5.
64 CBAM, para 13.3.4.

(b) the Director of Legal Aid Casework considers that, in all the circumstances of the case, it would be inequitable or impractical to do so.[65]

Disposable income

8.29 For those who are not deemed eligible, their 'disposable' income cannot exceed £99, and 'disposable' capital must be no more than £1,000.[66]

The period of calculation is the seven days up to and including the date on which the CRM1 and CRM2 was signed.[67]

Although CBAM does not deal with specific evidence of means in the Appeals and Reviews chapter it does in the Prison Law chapter, which must also apply to appeals files. It warns providers not to assume that prisoners have no income (or capital). However, noting their prison income on the CRM1/2 will be sufficient and you are not required to provide further evidence of their prison income.[68]

To work out disposable income the following amounts can be deducted:

(a) income tax;

(b) National Insurance contributions;

(c) attendance allowance including constant attendance allowance in addition to a disability pension;

(d) disability living allowance and any payments out of the Social Fund;

(e) any back-to-work bonus treated as jobseeker's allowance;

(f) any direct payments under the Health and Social Care Act 2001 or section 17A of the Children Act 1989;

(g) any reasonable living expenses provided as an exception to a restraint order under section 41 of the Proceeds of Crime Act 2002; and

(h) any personal independent payment paid under Part 4 of the Welfare Reform Act 2012.[69]

If the individual has dependents, then there are fixed deductions of £48.50 for a partner and £77.78 for each child. There is also a list of deductions for maintenance.[70]

65 Means Regulations, reg 9.
66 Means Regulations, reg 8.
67 Means Regulations, reg 2.
68 CBAM, paras 13.2.2 and 13.2.5.
69 Means Regulations, reg 11.
70 Means Regulations, reg 12.

Disposable capital

8.30 To calculate 'disposable' capital deductions can be made:

(a) the value of the individual's (i) household furniture and effects; (ii) clothes; and (iii) tools and implements of the individual's trade; and

(b) any back-to-work bonus received payable by way of a jobseeker's allowance.

The value of any interest in land is the sale value less the amount of any mortgage debt or hereditable security secured on that land, to a maximum of £100,000. There is a capital disregard of the first £100,000 of the value of the property where the applicant resides.

Where the client lives with a partner or dependents there is a capital deduction of £335 for the first, £200 for the second and £100 for each of the rest.[71]

Usually, the proof of financial eligibility needs to be provided before any work is started unless it is impractical to do so. If it is not subsequently obtained, then any claim is limited to two hours work unless in exceptional circumstances it can be shown that the personal circumstances of the client make it impracticable to obtain the proof at any point during the matter. In that case a note can be made justifying it but generally it will be very risky to proceed without acceptable proof.[72]

Children

8.31 A child is a client who is under 18 at the date the application is signed.[73] The general rule in the SCC is that you should deal with the parent, guardian or other person responsible for the child.[74] However, you may accept instructions directly from a child where there is a good reason provided the child is old enough to give instructions and understand the nature of the advice and proceedings.[75] In that case the child must sign the form and you must decide 'whether it is just and equitable not to aggregate the Child's means with those of the person liable to maintain him or her'. There is a presumption that the means should be aggregated, but this can be rebutted if you decide it would not be equitable, and this is more likely to be the case where there is a conflict between the child and the person liable to maintain them. It should be easy to justify taking instructions direct from the child. The Law Society Guidance encourages solicitors to view the child as the client as the wishes or

71 Means Regulations, reg 13.
72 SCC, paras 3.5–3.7.
73 Means Regulations, reg 2.
74 SCC, para 4.20.
75 SCC, para 4.23.

views of the parent are often in conflict with those of the child. As children in criminal proceedings do not have an independent guardian to act for them there is a heavier burden on the solicitor to manage potential conflicts between the child and those who appear to be responsible for them. There will often be a potential conflict. Indeed, often the child will be in detention, which would make the Local Authority ultimately responsible in any event which is another factor that would justify not aggregating the means.

All work – the sufficient benefits test (merits)

8.32 This is the key test that must be satisfied in order to provide advice and assistance under the SCC:

> 'Advice and Assistance may only be provided on legal issues concerning English (or Welsh) law and where there is sufficient benefit to the Client, having regard to the circumstances of the matter, including the personal circumstances of the Client, to justify work or further work being carried out.'[76]

8.33 The same test applies to any application to any extension of funding under the scheme. As the provider is exercising a delegated function they are protected by the general principle that the assessor should only depart from that decision if it was 'manifestly unreasonable', which means no reasonably competent solicitor could have concluded that the SBT was met.[77] A clear file note should prevent any audit issues.[78]

8.34 It is a broad test, but it requires the issue to be a legal one which has a realistic prospect of success. You must consider the benefit to the client and the cost involved. Often the test comes down to whether a private paying client of moderate means would fund the step. This will be easier to justify if they are in custody or it has an impact on their everyday life. In a case in which trial lawyers have advised negatively, it is not sufficient that the client wishes to obtain a second opinion. The LAA will expect the new solicitors to show that there has been a change of circumstances or grounds for concluding that the advice may have been incorrect or incomplete. The LAA has indicated the minimum information they expect the provider to record on the file to show they have properly considered the SBT. This includes details of the offence(s), whether the client pleaded or was convicted, the name of their trial lawyers and any advice, the court and the date the case concluded, the date and length of sentence and, perhaps most importantly, why the client says the conviction is

76 SCC, paras 3.10 and 12.5; CBAM, para 13.4.
77 CBAM, para 2.4.5, CLA 56.
78 SCC, paras 12.6–12.7, else it will be refused.

unsafe or the sentence is wrong.[79] There is an assumption that previous advice was adequate unless rebutted so the LAA will require extra justification if previous advice was given and if it appears that the previous advice addressed the issues raised by the client the provider will have to point to an ongoing substantive issue or a material development since that advice.[80]

PRACTICAL ISSUES

Completing CRM 1 and CRM 2

8.35 The relevant application forms are currently known as CRM 1 and CRM 2. The general rule is that the client must be within the jurisdiction of England and Wales and sign the completed form in your presence.[81] A 'copy' of the completed application form must be kept on your file for audit purposes; if you work digitally it can be a scanned or electronic copy without keeping the wet ink copy.[82]

As most prospective clients will be serving prisoners it is unlikely that you will be able to invite them to your office to complete and sign the forms. Instead, you will want to send them the forms by post to complete. In that case you are allowed to send the forms to them as an exception to the general rule above. If this is the case, you will need to note this on the CRM2 form, by ticking to indicate that you have accepted a postal application and setting out the justification for this, as per the relevant sections of the SCC.[83] Alternatively you are allowed to claim the travel to visit them in order to complete the forms (see 8.37 below).

Once these forms have been completed the provider will need to check them for consistency. One area where particular care needs to be taken is whether there is a 'partner' whose income or capital needs to be taken into account (see 8.28 above). Prospective clients will often tick 'single' or 'separated' on the forms and at the same time supply other information that suggests they are married or in a long-term relationship. The fact that they may be separated due to the client's incarceration does not mean the partner's financial resources can be ignored unless that has brought about an end to the emotional relationship. The LAA will look at factors such as whether the partner was providing any regular financial support and/or visiting the client on a regular basis. Sharing the same address will be taken into consideration when a client is not in custody, but it may not mean they are in a subsisting relationship as they may be living together as separate households. If there is any contradictory information, it

79 CBAM, para 12.2.4.
80 CBAM, paras 12.2.5 and 12.2.7.
81 SCC, para 4.17.
82 SCC, para 4.18.
83 SCC, paras 11.11–11.12.

needs to be addressed before the file is opened and there should be a clear file note supporting your decision if you have exercised your discretion.

Filtering requests

8.36 You are required to filter requests for advice by checking whether the client has received negative advice already. If that advice appears to be sound, then you will not be able to accept the case.[84]

Outward travel or postal applications

8.37 Often clients will be unable to attend the solicitor's office as they will be in custody, so you can give advice and travel to a client before the forms are actually signed. Solicitors can also accept postal applications where there is good reason.[85] Telephone advice can also be provided to the client before signature. This work can be claimed provided the client completes the CRM 1 and CRM 2 and qualifies for advice. The reason must be noted on the file.[86] Unless you are visiting the prison or detention centre for some other reason that is already funded, generally it is safer for a solicitor to send the application forms to the client to complete and return. This is because prison visits are often cancelled or ineffective for reasons outside your control and if, as a result, the forms do not get signed you will be unable to claim for your time.

Is further advice justified?

8.38 Further advice can be justified if there appears to be new evidence or there is an issue with the conviction or sentence that was not addressed adequately in the previous advice. The LAA will want the file to show that there are substantive issues outstanding or there has been a material development.[87]

Applications to extend funding

8.39 The initial costs limits are modest.[88] If there is a substantive issue with either the sentence or the conviction you will need apply to extend the upper limit. This is best approached in stages. Each stage will set out the minimum work that needs to be done till the next stage is reached. The LAA will expect you to have carried out all the work authorised before reapplying. This can create practical problems if you do not carry out the anticipated work, but there

84 SCC, para 11.5.
85 SCC, para 4.25.
86 SCC, paras 11.11–11.15.
87 SCC, para 11.6; CBAM, para 12.2.7.
88 Currently for Court of Appeal cases £314.81 and for CCRC applications £524.69.

is other unanticipated work that needs to be carried out. There is no procedure for amending the extension once it is granted so you can either do the work and make a clear note for audit purposes or email the LAA for advice. If you can show it is reasonable to do the work it should be allowed on an audit assessment.[89] The solicitor must then apply for extensions using a CRM 5 eForm via the LAA portal. The application should set out a breakdown of the work using the correct rates specified in the Criminal Legal Aid (Remuneration) Regulations 2013.[90] The CRM 5 application will be considered by a specialist team at the LAA. Extensions cannot be obtained retrospectively.[91] The time spent making the application to extend can be claimed so it should be factored into the next stage of work as part of the CRM 5 application as it will be necessary to spend time drafting a further CRM 5 for any follow on application for a further extension.[92] Applications for extensions will set out the estimate of time for the litigator's work at the applicable hourly rates.[93] The application should show that the proposed work is reasonable and the SBT continues to be met.[94] The application will include any disbursements that will need to be authorised. The figures should not include VAT.[95] There is general guidance in CBAM on the disbursements that will be allowed under the SCC.[96]

It is important to note that it will be the actual costs that have been already incurred and not the previous limit extension that will be taken as the starting point for the new application. This means that any excess in your previous upper limit is lost when a new application is submitted. In certain exceptional circumstances, where it is necessary to urgently apply for further funding, the LAA may allow you to treat the remainder of the upper limit which has not yet been used as having already been incurred, but this is unusual and it should be assumed that this will usually not be allowed. A detailed note of any communication with the LAA regarding this should be kept on file.

The LAA assessor may return the CRM5 application with queries about the contents. A response with clarification can be sent back by e-mail. This response must be provided within five working days of the query.

Appeals against refusals

8.40 If an application for an extension is refused, submissions can be made to the crime finance team at the LAA. If these are unsuccessful then the

89 SCC, para 5.16.
90 SCC, para 5.15; CBAM, para 8.2.
91 SCC, para 5.13; CBAM, para 8.3.
92 CBAM, paras 3.3.4 and 7.1.11.
93 Remuneration Regulations Part 8, Sch 4. Routine items: London £4.04, national £3.98; preparation: London £52.15, national £49.22; travel and waiting £27.60.
94 CBAM, para 8.3.
95 SCC, para 5.15.
96 SCC, paras 5.35–5.44; CBAM para 7.

usual appeals procedure applies. Any request must be made within 28 days of the decision. The matter is referred to an Independent Costs Assessor (ICA). Submissions to the ICA should succinctly address the LAA's reasons for refusal and these are more likely to succeed if they contain specific references to relevant sections of the SCC and CBAM. The ICA should look at the issues completely afresh and they can confirm, increase or decrease the previous assessment. The solicitor and advocate can request an oral hearing if the issues are complex though most of appeals are dealt with on paper.[97] If you are still dissatisfied the only remedy would be judicial review. It should be noted that, when an application is made to the ICA it is not only the current application which can be reconsidered. The ICA has the power to reconsider the application for the extensions of the upper limit and increase or reduce the extension which has been appealed. If you are unhappy with the ICA decision you can apply for civil legal to challenge the decision by way of judicial review. If the client does not qualify for civil legal aid or it is refused, or you may agree to act under a Conditional Fee Agreement (CFA). The LAA will often reverse the ICA decision if they think the challenge has a good chance of success, so a detailed 'Letter Before Claim' can often work.

SPECIFIC APPLICATIONS FOR FUNDING

8.41 Common applications will include:

(a) Transcripts – These can be obtained for the relevant parts of the proceedings. In a sentence case this will be the Sentencing Remarks and possibly the prosecution opening and the defence mitigation. In a conviction case it will usually be the relevant parts of the summing up or the rulings in issue. If you may need evidential transcripts, you should consider whether the summary of the evidence in the Summing Up is sufficient without the actual transcript of the evidence.[98] In CCRC cases that have already been to the Single Judge or Full Court it is worth checking if there are any transcripts available from the Criminal Appeal Office. In CCRC cases you should obtain a transcript of the full Court of Appeal judgment to show that new issues are being raised on the application to the CCRC that were not previously raised in the Court of Appeal. The EX107 Form procedure must be followed for Crown Court transcripts.[99] This is a two-part process: the first is to get a quote by completing and sending the Form EX107 to the Crown Court via email, copying in the transcription company, and the second is to complete and

97 CBAM, para 4.4 but para 4.5 you can request an oral hearing.

98 CBAM, para 12.3.5.

99 For Court of Appeal transcripts, it is not necessary to request the permission of the court – this is automatically granted. The completed EX107 must simply be sent to the transcribers directly.

send the Form EX107 to the court.[100] There is a list of transcribers for the different Crown Courts set out in the EX107 guidance. The request must be approved by a judge, who will sign a section of the form to confirm their approval of a transcript being obtained. Once approved, the Court will send the completed EX107 to the defence team and to the transcription company, who will then provide a quote. The Form EX107 has a declaration that you agree to be responsible for the costs. However, there is a section of the form where you can indicate that you require a quote to be provided and approved by you before they will begin the transcription. Once a quote has been obtained you will need to apply to the LAA for an extension to cover the estimate provided. Often the actual cost will be less than that quoted, but if it is more you will need to apply for a further extension.

(b) Advocate's advice – if a realistic appeal point is identified an advocate will need to be instructed for an advice and, to draft the grounds. This will be an external advocate given the restrictions on advice by an in-house advocate (see 8.23 above). There are no actual specified hourly rates for advocates but currently the LAA will pay £92 per hour for a junior advocate and £126.50 for a senior advocate. The LAA will be reluctant to pay the higher rate unless you can show the case is 'exceptional' (applying the same factors discussed at 8.15 above). The fact that you intend to instruct a KC to advise on a case does not necessarily mean that the LAA will agree to grant the higher rate as it is often difficult to persuade the LAA that the higher rate is justified.[101] The request for funding should include a breakdown of the hours needed to advise and an advice from the advocate may be required outlining what they propose to do. For appeals against sentence this will usually involve four to six hours' reading and drafting, though this will be very case-dependent. There will inevitably be some duplication of work between the litigator and advocate as the litigator is not just a post box for the advocate.[102]

For more complex cases, especially CCRC applications involving expert issues, the number of hours could be 20–30 or more. These applications will be carefully scrutinised by the LAA and if not granted in full, further representations should be made and if they fail then you may need to draft an appeal to the ICA (see 8.18 above).

(c) Expert opinion – it is often necessary to instruct an expert. There is general guidance on what factors the LAA will look at when assessing

100 Guidance at: https://www.gov.uk/government/publications/order-a-transcript-of-court-or-tribunal-proceedings-form-ex107.

101 The current guidance the LAA employ appears to consider 'exceptional' as meaning for that type of case which is contrary to the guidance in Broudie that it should be compared to cases in general (see 8.15).

102 CBAM, para 8.4.

an application to pay their assistance.[103] The application may be stronger if supported by an advice from an advocate explaining the need for one. However, you should bear in mind that will lead to further costs so it may be better to apply without one in a straightforward case. The LAA may ask for at least two quotes in less straightforward cases, but often an expert you have used before for LAA work will be approved. The rates payable to experts are those set out in the regulations.[104] In exceptional cases the LAA may agree to increase these rates. If the expert is in a very specialist field and you cannot find a suitable one for LAA approved rates it can be useful to get the expert to provide details of other recent publicly funded cases they have done for either the prosecution or the defence where their higher rate was paid. There is a presumption that a further report will not be paid for so if you are unhappy with the first one, you will face resistance from the LAA to any application for a new one.[105]

(d) Travel – The LAA take a starting point that any return travel time over two hours will be disallowed unless justified. Good reason may be that your client has made several requests for advice from local providers without any response or that this is a complex matter and there are no solicitors with specialist criminal appeal experience who are closer to the client. Another good reason might be that you have significant knowledge of the case or the client. Generally, return travel over four hours will not be granted unless exceptional. The usual exception relied upon would be that your specific knowledge of the client or the case means it would not be cost-effective to instruct a firm closer to the prison or detention centre. That would be because it would take more preparation or attendance time for the new provider get up to speed than the additional amount of travel being asked for. Likewise, if your client is transferred to a different prison that is further away from your office it is possible to justify additional travel time being granted on this basis.

Criminal Cases Review Commission applications – special considerations

8.42 To make an application to the CCRC the applicant will have to have already unsuccessfully appealed the conviction or sentence. As that is a pre-requisite to making an application unless exceptional circumstance apply (see Chapter 9) the first question is to check whether an application for permission has already refused by the Single Judge or the Full Court, or a previous appeal has been refused after permission was granted. Unless

103 CBAM, para 7.2.

104 Criminal Legal Aid (Remuneration) Regulations 2013 (SI 2013/435) (updated version), Sch 5.

105 CBAM, para 7.2.8.

exceptional circumstances apply the advice will be on an out of time application for permission to the Court of Appeal not an application to the CCRC. In that case a file needs to be opened for that type of advice bearing in mind the guidance (see 8.24 and 8.25 above).

In a small number of cases the exceptional circumstances test might be met for an application direct to the CCRC bypassing the Court of Appeal; this may be because a lot of investigative work needs to be done which you will need the assistance of the CCRC and their extensive powers (see Chapter 9). These types of cases may include developments in forensic science, concerns about credibility of witnesses or police conduct, PII issues or undisclosed material which you would not have the resources or powers to pursue adequately.

Another issue that often arises at the outset which will affect funding is whether to renew an application for permission to the full Court when it was refused by the Single Judge. Usually that will be a better option as an application to the CCRC is the last resort which the client will still have if the full Court refuses permission. The SCC recognises these initial considerations apply.[106] If the CCRC is the correct option then your file opening note showing the SBT has been met should say why you think the CCRC referral criteria was met.

8.43 The LAA recognises that it is not easy to show that the referral criteria are met without some investigation of the history of the appeal. You will generally be able to open a file if the case potentially passes the referral test. A lawyer coming to the case afresh will be unable to decide immediately whether the case is likely to meet the referral criteria so you are allowed to provide 'initial case screening' to an eligible client who it appears may have an application. It is useful to have a detailed enquiry form for prospective clients to complete with questions covering the specific details you will need to consider. There is an example in the Annex. Often it will take longer and, as with all work in this area, file notes should clearly justify the time spent. In making an assessment 'the provider should initially take instructions and ascertain whether the case is both suitable to be heard by the Commission and whether the case meets the referral criteria applied by the Commission'. Often this work will give rise to difficult decisions as to whether the costs of further investigation are justified. The LAA expects the lawyer to make these decisions 'in light of the available information and using your professional judgement'.[107]

8.44 It may be necessary to obtain transcripts of the evidence. Before doing so you should check whether any have been obtained already by the Court of Appeal on a previous application. You should also consider whether the relevant evidence might be adequately summarised in the Summing Up (if

106 SCC, paras 11.20–11.24.
107 SCC, para 11.22.

available).[108] The LAA acknowledge the need to get the opinion of an advocate in these cases.[109] The reality is that these cases are often grave and complex. They can involve novel and complex areas of legal interpretation which may require advice from a leading advocate. The LAA will be reluctant to incur the costs of a leading advocate especially if a junior advocate has already advised. Therefore, the solicitor must decide whether to involve a KC from the start and ask them to justify the higher rate or instruct a junior advocate and see whether they feel the issues are within their competence. Often if the higher rate is refused the KC will agree to work for a lesser rate, though in principle if a case justifies the instruction of a KC the higher rate should be applied for and, if refused without good reason, the decision should be appealed to the ICA. Sometimes the ICA refuse these appeals on the basis that the higher rate is above that quoted in the general criminal regulations, but as the majority of general crime work is paid by the way of fixed fees the comparison is not helpful and should be challenged. The test is whether the case justifies a much more experienced advocate.

8.45 It may be necessary to obtain, expert evidence where there is an issue that is crucial to the safety of the conviction or sentence, although the LAA expects the defence lawyers to bear in mind that the CCRC can obtain or pay for expert reports.[110] It should be noted that if the CCRC obtain expert reports, these will not normally be disclosed to the applicant's lawyers during the CCRC's assessment and review process. This means that it is not possible to make representations to the CCRC on behalf of your client until the provisional statement of reasons is provided by the CCRC referencing any expert advice they have obtained. At that stage you may request sight of any expert opinion referred to in the CCRC's provisional conclusions so you can address the issues. They may agree to provide it though it is often preferable to instruct your own expert at an earlier stage, so you are in control of the material.

8.46 Once a case is referred back to the Court of Appeal by the CCRC the Registrar will grant a Representation Order to include an advocate and litigator. As soon as that is granted you should close and bill your advice and assistance file.

Claiming for work done under the advice and assistance scheme

8.47 You cannot advise under freestanding advice and assistance where there is a representation order in the proceedings and advice on appeal or sentence can be claimed under that representation order, except where the

108 CBAM, para 12.3.5–12.3.7.
109 SCC, para 11.25.
110 CBAM, para 12.3.3.

client has changed provider since the original proceedings.[111] However, this means you are allowed to advise and claim under freestanding advice and assistance for any *fresh* issue that arises subsequently. If that relates to an issue that you have not previously advised on regarding either a possible appeal to the Court of Appeal or a CCRC referral then an Appeals and Reviews matter can be opened as there is no other way to claim for this work under the original representation order. Of course, if it is a matter that you *should* have advised on originally, or it relates to an error or omission by you, you will need to consider whether a conflict of interest arises and whether the client should be advised to instruct a new team. If the point now raised was due to a questionable legal decision taken by the original external advocate, it may be possible to continue to act but with a new advocate instructed.

8.48 A claim should only be submitted when:[112]

(a) the matter has concluded;

(b) it is known that no further work will be undertaken for the client in the same matter;

(c) it is unclear whether further work will be undertaken and at least one month has elapsed since the last work was undertaken; or

(d) in the case of a claim for advice and assistance on an appeal against conviction or sentence, including an appeal by way of case stated or an application to vary a sentence, where a determination has been made by the relevant court as soon as the representation order has been issued.

Often in CCRC cases you will want to close and bill your file under condition (c) as soon as the application is acknowledged by the CCRC as it will be a long time before you will hear from them again. Once you have received their provisional reasons you can then re-open the file and start to record time again (see 8.49 below).

Further instructions after a matter ends or a claim has been submitted

8.49 Once you have closed and billed your file any subsequent advice and assistance in relation to the same matter will require a new application but will be subject to the previous upper limit. This can only be done if there are substantive issues outstanding from the first occasion or there has been a material development or change in the client's circumstances such that further advice is now required. The client must complete a further CRM 1 and CRM 2, and the means test and SBT must be passed. The same unique reference number

111 SCC, para 11.40.
112 SCC, para 11.42.

(UFN) must be used, and the second file should include a reference to the first and kept together for audit purposes.[113]

ALTERNATIVE SOURCES OF ADVICE AND ASSISTANCE

8.50 There are limitations to the type of work that the LAA may be willing to fund. Funding is rarely extended to complex cases or lengthy investigations. Moreover, the availability of funding does not guarantee that there will be competent lawyers who will be willing to undertake the work in question. Not only are the number of solicitors firms who undertake work in this area threatened by cuts to legal aid, but the limitations in the extent of funding may mean that competent firms who do have LAA contracts may feel that they cannot justify extensive work on complex cases for the limited funding that is available.

8.51 Whilst it is always open to a defendant with the means to pay for their legal representation, this is not an option for many of those who have been convicted of serious crimes, particularly when the conviction is followed by a substantial custodial sentence. It may, therefore, be necessary for the defendant to consider alternative means of advice or assistance.

Innocence projects

8.52 Innocence projects were first established in the USA. They are university-based projects in which students, under an academic supervisor and often also with the assistance of practising lawyers, investigate potential miscarriages with a view to obtaining evidence that is capable of proving the innocence of the convicted person. In the USA many of the projects have had success in obtaining the evidence that leads to the overturning of convictions.

8.53 The innocence projects that are based in England and Wales have been established more recently than many of their US counterparts and they have yet to achieve the success of which many US projects can boast. The first UK project was established at Bristol University in 2005 and there are now approximately 30 located at various universities.[114] Until 2014 many operated as affiliates to the Innocence Network UK, which was run by the founders of the Bristol University project and provided training and support for other projects. Despite this activity, the work of the UK innocence projects has yet

113 SCC, para 11.37–38.

114 Article by Lee Glendinning, *Guardian*, 3 September 2004. See: www.theguardian.com/uk/2004/sep/03/ukcrime.prisonsandprobation/print.

to lead to the overturning of a single conviction. Certain projects, particularly Bristol and Cardiff, have had successes in getting cases are referred back to the Court of Appeal by the CCRC as a result of evidence that they have uncovered. But in 2013 a lawyer from the CCRC remarked in a speech that the number of referrals that they had received from innocence projects was very low (17 in ten years from a total of five universities).[115]

8.54 There are a number of limitations to the innocence project model. The fact that they will usually only assist those who proclaim their total non-involvement with their alleged offence (precluding, for example, assistance being given to the defendant convicted of murder who claims to have suffered from provocation or diminished responsibility that would render them guilty of manslaughter) acts as a limit on the number of people that innocence projects can assist. However, it is the experience of lawyers that prisons are not short of prisoners who proclaim their innocence and seek to have their convictions overturned. It seems that there are limitations to what students, who lack legal training and can give neither full-time nor long-term commitment to a particular case can achieve.

8.55 They may be no substitute for qualified legal assistance, but innocence projects can supplement the work of lawyers, particularly in undertaking the investigative work for which funding may not be available. For those who seek to prove their innocence and cannot find a lawyer to take on their case, innocence projects may, for months or years, be their sole source of assistance.

The Centre for Criminal Appeals – Appeal

8.56 The Centre for Criminal Appeals, now known as Appeal, is a charitable organisation that was founded, on the model of American civil rights-era non-profit legal practices in order to assist those who wish to make an application to the CCRC and/or appeal a conviction in the Court of Appeal but lack the means to pay for their own representation. As a charity Appeal can raise private funds and have access to *pro bono* experts and advocates that will enable its lawyers to focus solely on appeals and overcome the limitations imposed by the public funding regime. The Centre takes on carefully selected cases which they believe will have strategic impact upon the criminal appeals system. Their model of work includes substantial hands-on investigative work to uncover new evidence, a methodology which is not generally achievable by legal aid funding. The Centre provides valuable advice and assistance,

115 Article by Jon Robbins, *Guardian*, 20 November 2013. See: www.theguardian.com/law/2013/nov/20/appeal-court-innocence-projects-dwaine-george.

particularly in those cases requiring significant investigation work and a long-term commitment by the legal team.[116]

Advocate (formerly known as the Bar Pro Bono Unit)

8.57 A number of advocates are prepared to provide advice and assistance in particular cases for free. The best chance of obtaining such assistance is through Advocate, which can obtain the details of a particular case and forward it to advocates who may have the experience and willingness to assist. However, it is not altogether clear that an advocate would have the willingness or the best professional expertise to undertake the type of extensive work for which funding would not be available under the advice and assistance scheme.

SUMMARY OF KEY POINTS

- The two regimes for public funding are: Representation Orders that are granted by the Crown Court; (and Representation Orders granted by the Court of Appeal); and funding for advice and assistance under the Standard Crime Contract. These sources of funding are mutually exclusive.
- Positive advice and assistance in lodging an appeal can be claimed by both the trial litigator and the advocate under the Crown Court Representation Order. No claim can be made for a negative advice.
- Funding for advice and assistance under the Standard Crime Contract will enable lawyers who did not represent the defendant at trial to provide advice and assistance (but not representation). It is subject to the criteria of means and merits. An application may not be made until six months have elapsed since the client was last advised under the scheme. The scheme also allows the original lawyers to look at a fresh issue that arises later provided they are not being criticised.
- Application for funding for advice and assistance is by way of CRM 1 and CRM 2. Each application for an extension of funds, including funding to cover the advice of an independent advocate, transcript, experts' reports or extensive work by defence solicitors, must be made through CRM 5.
- It will assist an application for extension of funding if it is supported by an advocate's advice that explains why the funding that is sought is necessary to the case.

116 See the Centre for Criminal Appeals Project website at https://appeal.org.uk/. It should be noted that lawyers from the Centre contributed to Chapter 5 of this book.

- The merits criteria must be satisfied in respect of each application for extension of funding. In order to meet the merits criteria, the application must provide some reason to show that the work could benefit the client. It is not sufficient simply to suggest that there should be a second opinion.
- For those cases which involve extensive work for which funding may not be granted, the defendant may wish to seek the assistance of an innocence project or Appeal.

Part 3

Applications from the Court of Appeal

Chapter 9

The Criminal Cases Review Commission

INTRODUCTION

9.1 The Court of Appeal will not allow a second application for leave to appeal conviction or sentence after a previous such appeal has been dismissed. The only route back to a second appeal to the Court of Appeal is by way of a reference back by the Criminal Cases Review Commission (CCRC).

9.2 In addition to its power to send cases back to the Court of Appeal, the CCRC can investigate convictions and has powers beyond those otherwise available to a convicted person and their lawyers. The CCRC can use those powers either when considering an application by a convicted person to refer a case to the Court of Appeal or, more rarely, when the Court of Appeal directs it to do so.

THE ESTABLISHMENT AND ROLE OF THE CRIMINAL CASES REVIEW COMMISSION

9.3 For many years, the only route back to the Court of Appeal, Criminal Division, for a second appeal was a reference by the Home Secretary. Such references were rare and the process by which applications were considered was slow and opaque. After a series of miscarriages of justice in the late 1980s and early 1990s,[1] a Royal Commission[2] recommended the power to refer possible miscarriages of justice be removed from the Home Secretary and placed in the hands of an independent body. Parliament enacted those

1 The late 1980s and early 1990s saw the exposure of a series of miscarriages of justice, related to wrongful convictions for terrorist crimes, which culminated with the 'Birmingham Six' appeal in 1991.

2 The Royal Commission on Criminal Justice, commonly referred to as the 'Runciman Commission', was established by the Home Secretary in March 1991 and reported in July 1993.

recommendations through the Criminal Appeal Act 1995 (CAA 1995), which established the CCRC as an independent, non-governmental body[3] with the following powers:

(a) to refer any sentence or conviction in the Crown Court to the Court of Appeal, if the CCRC is of the opinion that there is a real possibility that an appeal will be allowed;

(b) to refer, on the same basis, any sentence or conviction in the Magistrates Court to the Crown Court;

(c) to refer, on the same basis, any sentence or conviction by the Court Martial to the Court Martial Appeal Court;

(d) to conduct any investigation that the Court of Appeal may direct it to undertake in order to assist the Court in the determination of an appeal;

(e) to assist the Home Secretary by providing an opinion on whether to recommend the exercise of Her Majesty's prerogative of mercy in relation to a conviction.[4]

THE CCRC'S POWER TO REFER TO THE COURT OF APPEAL

9.4 The CCRC has a power to refer a conviction or sentence to the Court of Appeal where a person has been convicted of an offence on indictment in England, Wales or Northern Ireland – CAA 1995, section 9.[5] The power extends to a verdict of not guilty by reason of insanity and a finding that a person was under a disability when they did an act or made an omission.[6]

9.5 It may refer following an application or of its own motion where no application has been made.[7] A referral will be treated as an appeal, with leave, under CAA 1968 and must be heard by the Court.[8]

9.6 Although the CCRC only refers a small percentage of applications that it receives, there is a relatively high success rate once a matter is referred.[9]

3 CAA 1995, s 8 establishes its constitution.
4 CAA 1995, s 16(1). The CCRC has never been called upon to make a recommendation under this section.
5 CAA 1995, s 9.
6 CAA 1995, s 9(5), (6).
7 CAA 1995, s 14(1).
8 CAA 1995, s 9(2), (3).
9 Of the 27 CCRC referrals decided by the appeal courts in 2024/2025, 18 appeals were allowed, and nine dismissed (CCRC Annual Report and Accounts, 2024/2025, at p 26).

THE TEST FOR REFERRAL

9.7 Section 13 of CAA 1995 provides that no reference shall be made unless the CCRC considers that there is a 'real possibility' that:

(a) the conviction, verdict or finding under appeal would not be upheld because of an argument, or evidence, not raised in the proceedings which led to it (or on any appeal or application for leave against it); or

(b) in the case of a sentence, the sentence would not be upheld because of an argument on a point of law or information not raised in the proceedings which led to it (or any appeal or application for leave against it); and

(c) an appeal against the conviction, verdict, finding or sentence has been determined or leave to appeal has been refused.

9.8 However, section 13 gives the CCRC the power to refer even when (a) or (c) do not apply if there are 'exceptional circumstances' which justify making it; thus, there can be a reference back even where there is no new evidence or argument and/or when there has not been a previous appeal. The 'no new point' exception, however, only applies to an appeal against conviction, so for a sentence appeal there must be a new argument.

The discretion whether to refer

9.9 It is important to note that the CCRC has discretion not to refer even if the test under section 13 is satisfied. For example, if the conviction is likely to be quashed but only to be substituted by an alternative conviction, allowing the original conviction to stand may cause no real injustice to the applicant.[10] The appellate courts have been robust in protecting the CCRC's use of this discretion, no doubt fearing the opening of flood gates such as would drown the Court of Appeal in further cases, were the CCRC's 'gatekeeper' role undermined.

APPLYING TO THE CCRC FOR A REFERRAL

Who may apply?

9.10 An application does not have to be made by the defendant him or herself. This means that a family member with a substantial interest in the outcome of an appeal could make an application on behalf of someone who had died after conviction. However, when a defendant has died, the CCRC

10 *Smith (Duncan Wallace)* [2004] EWCA Crim 631, see para 29.

will only consider the application if an 'approved person'[11] (such as a family member) can be identified in whose name any application for leave might be made.

When to apply

9.11 Normally an application should be made to the CCRC only if:

(a) an appeal has been considered and refused by the Court of Appeal; or

(b) leave has been refused by the single judge (it need not have been renewed before the full Court); or

(c) an application for leave or an appeal with leave has been abandoned; and

(d) there is argument, evidence, or information in the terms of section 13(a) or (b) that was not considered by the Court of Appeal in that initial appeal.

9.12 What counts as 'new argument' is a matter to be considered in each case. However, a change in the law will not itself be regarded as giving rise to new argument that raises a real possibility of an appeal being allowed. Section 16C of CAA 1968[12] now provides that the Court may dismiss any reference[13] based solely on the change of law where, had the application for extension of time been made by the defendant, that application would have been refused. The Commission should now only refer cases involving a change in the law where the test of a change in the law giving rise to 'substantial injustice' (*R v Fletcher; R v Cottrell*,[14] *R v Jogee*[15] and *R v Johnson*[16]) may be said to be met. The CCRC has published guidance on this aspect of its discretion.[17]

9.13 There are no time limits for making an application, but this does not mean that the applicant should delay making it. There is no formal restriction on reapplying; in a number of recent successful referrals, application to the CCRC had to be made more than once.[18] However, applications which are substantially the same as those which have already been refused should clearly not be made.

11 CAA 1968, s 44A makes the nomination of an approved person following the death of a defendant a pre-condition for a valid appeal.

12 As inserted by the Criminal Justice and Immigration Act 2008, s 42.

13 Section 16C does not apply to sentence referrals.

14 [2007] EWCA Crim 2016.

15 [2016] 1 Cr App R 31.

16 [2017] 1 Cr App R 12.

17 CCRC Casework Policy – CW-POL-07 – 'The Discretion to Refer' (Version 2.0) (issued 9 May 2005).

18 *R v Victor Nealon* [2014] EWCA Crim 574; *R v Andrew Malkinson* [2023] EWCA Crim 954; *R v Lee Firkins and Robert Firkins* [2023] EWCA Crim 1491.

'Exceptional circumstances'

9.14 As indicated, the CCRC may, in exceptional circumstances, make a reference to the Court of Appeal even if there was no previous appeal. Whilst there is no statutory definition of 'exceptional circumstances', the CCRC's own guidance sets out a number of non-exhaustive situations in which exceptional circumstances may be made out.[19]

9.15 Among them are cases where there may be an arguable appeal, but this will depend on further investigations being carried out and third party material being obtained and considered. If the CCRC concludes that it is not possible for the applicant and their legal representatives to carry out this investigation but that it might be carried out by the CCRC, then this might give rise to exceptional circumstances. However, the Court has stressed that the mere existence of relevant third party material should not necessarily be regarded as giving rise to exceptional circumstances.[20]

Making the application

9.16 The CCRC's website contains guidance for the making of an application.[21] In addition, it has published individual 'Casework Policy' documents on various aspects of its work describing how it deals with common issues. These can be found in the 'About' section of the website.

9.17 It is advisable, although not necessary, that an application be made with the assistance of a lawyer. Funding may be available for legal representation under the 'Advice and Assistance' scheme (see Chapter 8 for details). While there have been a number of successful references back to the Court of Appeal by applicants in person, the involvement of a lawyer will (or at least, should) weed out the bad points, set out more clearly the good and thereby make the CCRC's task easier and increase the chances of a successful application.

9.18 The application should be made using the CCRC's application form. However, applications are likely to benefit from additional grounds which should set out the legal and factual issues that are relevant to the application, address the relevant statutory questions and include all material that may be of assistance to the CCRC in making its decision.

19 CCRC Casework Policy – CW-POL-06 – 'Exceptional Circumstances' (Version 3.0) (Issued 15 September 2025).

20 *R v Gerald* [1999] Crim LR 315.

21 See https://ccrc.gov.uk/the-application-process/.

Requesting an investigation

9.19 If an applicant wishes the CCRC to carry out an investigation, it is important to explain why the material sought is of importance to the application. It is also important to explain what steps the applicant and their lawyers have already taken to obtain the material sought and the outcome of any such enquiries.

THE DECISION-MAKING PROCESS

9.20 An initial screening takes place to ensure that the application is valid. Early steps are taken to secure potentially relevant material that is held by a public body. Certain cases will be given priority.[22] The case will then be allocated to a case review manager who will examine the issues raised in the application to see if there might be anything that could give grounds for referring the case. The CCRC is allowed to consider any representations and any matters that appear to be relevant.[23] Investigations are carried out when they are appropriate. Most are carried out by CCRC staff. However, investigators may be appointed to assist in carrying out enquiries. If necessary, the CCRC can, at any stage, ask the Court of Appeal to provide an opinion on a relevant matter of law.[24]

9.21 When the review is complete it is considered by either a single commissioner or a committee of three commissioners. A single commissioner may decide not to make a referral. However, only a committee of three commissioners can make a referral.[25] If they are of the view that a referral is justified then a final statement of reasons will be completed and sent to the applicant and the Court of Appeal. If it is decided not to refer, a provisional statement of reasons is drafted.

9.22 It is possible to ask for a face to face meeting to explain your issues with the provisional statement of reasons as this may be a much more effective way to expand on the application in the context of the provisional rejection. There is not a right to such a meeting, but it has been known for the CCRC to agree to a short video link meeting involving the lawyers. This was be attended by the case review manager and the commissioner. There will be an agreed time limit for submissions depending on the complexity of the case. It will usually be no more than one hour as the purpose is to provide an opportunity to

22 For example, if the applicant is serving a sentence that is soon to expire or is suffering from a potentially fatal illness.

23 CAA 1995, s 14(2).

24 CAA 1995, s 14(3).

25 CAA 1995, Sch 1, paras 6(2)(a) and 6(3).

explain how the provisional reasons fail to adequately address the issues raised in the application.

The provisional statement of reasons

9.23 The applicant and their lawyers will be sent a copy of the provisional statement of reasons and be given the opportunity to respond to any points made or to provide further information. The correspondence will usually indicate that any response must be received by a particular date. If more time is needed it should be requested with an explanation.

The final decision

9.24 The final decision will be contained in the 'Final Statement of Reasons' which will be provided to the applicant and their legal representative. The decision must be clear and fully reasoned in order that the applicant can understand how it has been reached. Fairness may require the disclosure of information that the Commission has considered when reaching its decision *(R v Secretary of State for the Home Department, ex p Hickey (No 2))*,[26] a decision made in respect of the Secretary of State's powers to refer pre-CCRC).

Likely timeframe for a decision

9.25 In 2024/25 the average time from allocation to a case review manager to decision (provisional statement of reasons) was 38.5 weeks for custody cases, and 51.5 weeks for liberty cases.[27] In 2023/2024, the figures were 31.4 weeks for custody cases and 42.1 weeks for at liberty cases.[28] The average time for a decision can be seen, therefore, to be increasing. The CCRC has ambitions to lower waiting times but for the present, an applicant would need to be advised that the average wait from application to decision is in the region of a year. However, the length of time can vary from weeks to many months depending on, amongst other things, whether the Commission needs to undertake any investigations.

26 [1995] 1 WLR 734 (DC).
27 The CCRC Annual Report and Accounts 2024/2025, KPI 2.
28 The CCRC Annual Report and Accounts 2023/2024, KPI 2.

CHALLENGING A REFUSAL TO MAKE A REFERENCE

9.26 A decision not to refer the case may be challenged by way of judicial review. As with any judicial review, the Court will not be concerned with whether the decision was right but only whether it was lawful, fair and reasonable (*Ex p Pearson*).[29] The Administrative Court has indicated that a high threshold will have to be crossed to persuade it that a decision of the Commission not to refer should be quashed (*Cleeland v CCRC*).[30] In *R v Charles*[31] the principles that apply to Judicial Review of the CCRC's decisions were reiterated.

9.27 Before Judicial Review proceedings are brought, attempts should first be made to persuade the CCRC to revisit the decision by making submissions in writing, pointing out errors in the decision, or matters not properly considered. Where that fails, it is necessary to write a letter before action to the CCRC setting out, in general terms, the basis of the challenge.[32] An application for Judicial Review must be filed 'promptly' and in any event no later than three months from the date of the decision under challenge.[33] The CCRC has published a Casework Policy document on Judicial Review of its decisions.[34]

THE PROCEDURE FOLLOWING A REFERENCE BEING MADE TO THE COURT OF APPEAL

9.28 The procedure, which is largely governed by section 14 of CAA 1995 and Part 39 of the CrimPR, can be summarised as follows:

(a) If the CCRC decides to make a reference to the Court of Appeal it must send that decision to every person who is likely be party to the appeal.[35]

(b) The decision is also passed to the Registrar of Criminal Appeals who must also serve notice of the decision on the appellant and 'any party directly affected by the appeal' (which obviously includes the Respondent).[36]

29 [2000] 1 Cr App R 141.
30 [2009] EWHC 474 (Admin), para 48.
31 [2017] 2 Cr App R 14, at para [47].
32 In compliance with the Judicial Review pre-action protocol.
33 Civil Procedure Rules, rule 54.5(1)(b).
34 CCRC Casework Policy, Judicial Review, CW-POL-13 (Version 2.0) (Issued 23 November 2021).
35 CAA 1995, s 14(4)(b).
36 Part 39.5 and 39.6 CrimPR.

(c) The Registrar is likely at this stage to grant representation orders for solicitors and counsel for the purpose of preparing the appeal.

(d) A Form NG should be served on the Registrar by the legal representatives of the appellant not more than 20 business days after the Registrar serves notice that the CCRC has referred a conviction to the Court of Appeal (application to extend that time can be made).[37] If the appellant does not serve an appeal notice the Court must treat that reference as the appeal notice.[38]

(e) Permission of the Court is required if the appellant seeks to advance grounds that are not related to the reasons given in the reference.[39] See *R v Winzar*[40] as to consideration of additional grounds where part of the CCRC reference has fallen away. The term 'related to', however, gives some latitude provided the grounds advanced are founded on one of the points on which the CCRC has sent the case back.

(f) Directions may be made for a particular case. However, the Court in *R v Siddall and Brooke*[41] suggested a timetable that parties should adhere to and indicated delay caused by a failure to adhere to the timetable may give rise to a risk of a wasted costs order being made.

AN OVERVIEW OF THE CCRC'S INVESTIGATORY POWERS

9.29 The CCRC's investigatory powers are largely contained in sections 17 to 25 of CAA 1995. The law in relation to those powers can be summarised as follows:

(a) The CCRC is authorised to obtain access to (and copy) all documents and material from public bodies if it believes it may assist the investigation. This includes communications data that has already been obtained and retained by a public body. The duty of the public body to comply with a request is not affected by any obligation of secrecy or other limitation on disclosure and therefore will often include material not disclosed or available to the defence at trial,[42] for example social services' files or other sensitive information.

(b) The power includes a power to direct that such material is preserved in an unaltered state until the CCRC further directs.[43] This may be important

37 Part 39. 2(1)(c) CrimPR.
38 CrimPR, r 39.5(2).
39 CAA 1995, s 14(4A), (4B); and see *Regina v Hallam* [2012] EWCA Crim 1158.
40 [2021] 1 Cr App R 16.
41 [2006] EWCA Crim 1353.
42 CAA 1995, s 17(4).
43 CAA 1995, s 17(2).

if there is a risk that efforts may be made to conceal or alter potentially relevant material.

(c) However, the person providing information to the CCRC may withhold consent for it to be disclosed to another party if an obligation of secrecy would otherwise have prevented disclosure to the CCRC and it is reasonable to do so.[44]

(d) Although the public body is required to provide such material to the CCRC as it requests, there is no formal sanction for any failure to do so, although the CCRC may seek a remedy by way of judicial review.

(e) In addition to carrying out its own investigations, the CCRC may require the appointment of an investigating officer to carry out inquiries on its behalf. Such a person may be from a public body or (more usually) from the police. The CCRC can direct that particular individuals are not appointed or that police officers should not be from the police force that carried out the original investigation.[45]

(f) With the two exceptions set out in (g) and (h) below, the CCRC is empowered only to obtain material from public bodies, not from private corporations. The meaning of 'public body' is narrowly defined.[46]

(g) As a 'relevant public body'[47] the CCRC may, in accordance with the provisions of the Investigatory Powers Act 2016 and its Codes of Practice, obtain communications data from private individuals and bodies. This includes postal, telephone and Internet Connections Records. The CCRC's powers and the process for obtaining such data is set out in its Casework Policy document.[48]

(h) If police officers are appointed to carry out an investigation, they may employ their powers under the Police and Criminal Evidence Act 1984 to obtain material from private individuals or bodies.

(i) It is a criminal offence under section 23 of CAA 1995 for present or former members or employees of the CCRC, or investigating officers appointed by the CCRC, to disclose information obtained in the course of the investigation save for one of the purposes contained in section 24 of CAA 1995.

(j) There is no obligation to disclose all material obtained in an investigation to an applicant or appellant. Indeed, there may be material which should

44 CAA 1995, s 25.

45 CAA 1995, s 19. *R v Hallam* [2012] EWCA Crim 1158 is an example of the successful use of s 19 to investigate a police investigation.

46 CAA 1995, s 22(1).

47 By virtue of the Investigatory Powers Act 2016, s 70.

48 CCRC Casework Policy – CW-POL-17 – 'Accessing Telecommunications Data' (Version 1.0) (Issued 15 July 2021).

not be disclosed. However, the CCRC should provide the applicant with sufficient disclosure to enable them to properly present their best case (*Ex p Hickey (No 2)*).[49] The CCRC's approach to disclosure is set out in its Casework Policy document 'Disclosure by the CCRC'.[50]

9.30 As can be seen from the powers listed above, the CCRC have far wider powers than those available to applicants and their lawyers. In many cases the CCRC have obtained social services records and/or material that would be withheld from any defendant as being subject to public interest immunity. While the CCRC guard their discretion to choose which enquiries they make, it is always worthwhile considering where fruitful material might be found when drafting an application.

CCRC INVESTIGATIONS AT THE DIRECTION OF THE COURT OF APPEAL

9.31 On any appeal against conviction the Court of Appeal may direct the CCRC to investigate and report to the Court on any matter, if it appears to the Court that:

(a) the matter is relevant to the determination of the case and ought, if possible, to be resolved before the case is determined;

(b) an investigation of the matter by the CCRC is likely to result in the Court being able to resolve it; and

(c) the matter cannot be resolved by the Court without an investigation by the CCRC.[51]

9.32 The Court may direct the CCRC to carry out such an investigation if any of the potential grounds turn on alleged irregularity in a jury's deliberations.[52] Serious failures by the prosecution in their duties of disclosure have also been the subject of investigations at the direction of the Court.[53] However, the only limits to the type of matter that the Court may ask the CCRC to investigate are those in (a) to (c) above.

9.33 The procedure for such investigations is governed by section 23A of CAA 1968 and section 15 of CAA 1995, which provide as follows:

49 [1995] 1 WLR 734 (DC).

50 CCRC Casework Policy – CW-POL-19 (Version 2.0) (Issued 31 March 2025).

51 CAA 1968, s 23A and CAA 1995, s 15(1).

52 *Regina v Shabir Ahmed* [2014] EWCA Crim 619; *Regina v Emma Mitchell* [2013] EWCA Crim 1072; *Regina v Ian Lewis* [2013] EWCA Crim 776.

53 For example, *R v Joof* [2012] EWCA Crim 1475.

(a) The Court may, at any time, either before leave[54] is considered or after it is granted, make such a direction. However, a direction may not be given by a single judge.[55]

(b) The copies of direction must also be made available to the appellant and respondent.[56]

(c) The investigation must be carried out 'in such manner as the CCRC sees fit'.[57]

(d) In doing so it may investigate any related matter that it believes to be relevant to the determination of the case by the Court, which ought to be and can be resolved by the Court.[58]

(e) The CCRC must keep the Court informed of the progress of the investigation[59] and must file a report either at the conclusion of the investigation or when directed to do so by the Court.[60] The report should detail the enquiries that were pursued[61] and should be accompanied by any statements and opinions received by the CCRC in the investigation.[62]

(f) The Court must notify the appellant and the respondent that the CCRC has reported and may make available to them the report of the CCRC and any statements, opinions and reports which accompanied it.[63]

TOO HIGH A TEST?

9.34 The CCRC has not been without its critics. Many lawyers who regularly advise would-be appellants and applicants argue that over the course of its existence the CCRC has grown more conservative and less willing to refer cases back to the Court of Appeal. Another common observation is that the outcome of a particular application may depend not just on the merits but on the quality and approach of the case review manager assigned to consider it, and on the Commissioner(s) who ultimately make the decision. Following recent travails, the CCRC now has a new Chair who has been asked to carry out a thorough review of the operation of the CCRC. It may well be that there is a cultural shift within the organisation following this review. In the meantime,

54 CAA 1968, s 23A(1)(aa).
55 CAA 1968, s 23A(1A).
56 CAA 1968, s 23A(3).
57 CAA 1995, s 15(1).
58 CAA 1995, s 15(2).
59 CAA 1995, s 15(3).
60 CAA 1995, s 15(4).
61 CAA 1995, s 15(5).
62 CAA 1995, s 15(6). However, by virtue of CAA 1995, s 15(7), the Commission need not include any reports that were made to the Commission by an investigating officer, pursuant to s 20(6).
63 CAA 1968, s 23A(4).

applicants and their representatives may need to be persistent in ensuring that the CCRC properly consider the grounds and evidence that are relied upon to show that there has been a miscarriage of justice.

SUMMARY OF KEY POINTS

- The CCRC has the power to refer appeals against sentence or conviction from the Crown Court to the Court of Appeal or from the Magistrates' Court to the Crown Court when it is of the view that there is a real possibility that the appeal will be allowed.
- It normally makes referrals following a failed or abandoned appeal if there is new evidence or arguments not originally advanced. However, it has discretion, in exceptional circumstances, to refer a conviction or sentence even when there was no initial appeal.
- The effect of a referral is that the case will be returned to the Court to be heard as an appeal with leave. However, the Court may dismiss such an appeal when the only ground for a referral is a change in the law.
- In determining whether to refer, the CCRC may carry out such investigations as it deems necessary.
- It must carry out an investigation when directed to do so by the Court of Appeal in relation to an appeal or an application for leave to appeal against sentence or conviction.
- In carrying out these investigations it has extensive powers to obtain material in the hands of public bodies and, in accordance with the relevant provisions of the Regulation of Investigatory Powers Act 2000, communication data in the hands of private bodies or individuals.
- It may carry out investigations itself or appoint police officers or members of other public bodies to do so.

Chapter 10

Appealing to the Supreme Court

INTRODUCTION

10.1 On 1 October 2009, the Supreme Court was established by the Constitutional Reform Act 2005 (CRA 2005). Its jurisdiction corresponds to that of the Appellate Committee of the House of Lords, which it replaced as the final court of appeal.[1]

10.2 The Supreme Court rarely grants leave to appeal from the Court of Appeal (Criminal Division). The effect of this is that when leave is granted the appellant's lawyers may be faced with a procedure that is entirely new to them. Supreme Court procedure has its own terminology and imposes upon the parties a number of exacting procedural requirements. However, there are a number of reasons why case preparation should not be as daunting as it might at first appear:

(a) Section 33 of the Criminal Appeal Act 1968 sets out the decisions of the Court of Appeal which may and may not be appealed to the Supreme Court.

(b) Rules relevant to the procedure for appealing to the Supreme Court are set out in the Criminal Procedure Rules Part 43.

(c) The Supreme Court also has its own Rules and Practice Directions (PD) which are clear and detailed. Practice Directions 1–11 and 13 governing civil proceedings apply to criminal proceedings in the Supreme Court subject to any modifications or additional provisions made by Practice Direction 12, which applies only to criminal proceedings.

(d) The staff of the Registry, which is headed by the Registrar of the Supreme Court, are usually helpful and tend to have more time to devote to a particular case than the staff in lower courts.

(e) A representation order for a leading advocate is routinely granted, even if there was none in the Court of Appeal. Earlier instruction of an experienced leading advocate should assist.

1 CRA 2005, s 40, Sch 9.

(f) The mystery that always surrounded appeals to the House of Lords has not attached itself to the Supreme Court because from the outset its proceedings have been broadcast. An appellant or his lawyers who want to know what to expect can turn on and see the judges who are likely to hear their case at work on another.[2]

10.3 **Note on terminology:** The right of appeal to the Supreme Court exists by virtue of section 33 of CAA 1968 which speaks of 'leave' to appeal. The Court's own Rules and Practice Directions, which apply also to civil appeals, use the term 'permission' to appeal. This chapter follows the statute and uses the term 'leave'.

THE TYPES OF CASES FOR WHICH LEAVE IS GIVEN

10.4 The test set for granting leave to appeal to the Supreme Court is that a point of law of general public importance is involved in the decision and it appears to the Court of Appeal or the Supreme Court (as the case may be) that the point is one which ought to be considered by the Supreme Court.[3]

10.5 The Supreme Court does hear a number of appeals that arise out of criminal litigation, but the number of appeals from the Court of Appeal Criminal Division is very low.

10.6 The reason for this low number is not hard to discern. The job of the Court of Appeal is to develop and clarify the criminal law. It is presided over by the Lord Chief Justice, the head of the judiciary, who can and does identify those cases that involve important questions of law and may allocate them to a Court of seven judges. There will be a limited number of cases that then justify further consideration.

10.7 Leave to appeal from the Court of Appeal appears to be given not simply to those cases which involve issues of particular importance but to those cases which involve genuinely difficult points of law and raise wide questions of principle which justify the sustained consideration and analysis that the Supreme Court provides.

10.8 Application for leave should seek to awaken the interest of the justices in the point of public importance which the Court of Appeal has certified, indicating why the point is sufficiently rich in its implications and calls for a depth of analysis that justifies consideration by the Supreme Court.

2 Hearings may be viewed by accessing the website of the Supreme Court or Sky Supreme Court Live.

3 CAA 1968, s 33.

APPLYING FOR LEAVE

10.9 Before an application for leave to appeal can be made to the Supreme Court, an application for leave and for a certificate of a point of law of public importance must already have been made to the Court of Appeal within 28 days of the relevant decision (or 14 days where the appeal is against the decision on an appeal by the Attorney-General against sentence).[4] The application for leave to appeal will usually be refused. However, it can only be made again before the Supreme Court if the Court of Appeal has certified a point of law of public importance (see Practice Direction 12, paragraph 12.8).

10.10 The applicant has 28 days from the refusal of leave by the Court of Appeal to apply to the Supreme Court for leave.[5] The procedure for making such an application is contained in the Court's Practice Direction 3.

10.11 The Supreme Court does not provide legal aid. Application for public funding must be made in England and Wales to the Legal Aid Agency, in Scotland to the Scottish Legal Aid Board, and in Northern Ireland to the Legal Services Agency.

A litigant can apply for waiver of the Court's fees under the 'help with fees' scheme described in the Court's Practice Direction 2. A litigant who receives public funding or legal aid does not need to apply for help with fees as the Court fees will be funded.

A party to whom a public funding or legal aid certificate has been issued must as soon as possible thereafter upload a copy via the portal. Any emergency certificate and subsequent amendments and the authority for leading counsel must also be uploaded.

An appellant who has applied for public funding should notify the Court by logging on to the portal. This will enable the appellant to explain the progress of the application for funding. This will in turn enable the Registry to grant extensions of time as appropriate (see Practice Direction 2, Rule 6(3), paragraphs 2.10 and 2.13; Practice Direction 3, paragraph 3.14; and Practice Direction 4, paragraph 4.23).

If granted, public funding will usually cover only solicitors and junior advocate at the leave stage and will be extended to cover the instruction of a leading advocate if leave is granted.

10.12 The application is considered by a panel of Supreme Court justices. They may decide to hold an oral hearing but decisions are generally made on the papers.

4 CAA 1968, s 34; para 43.2 CrimPR.
5 Supreme Court Rules 2024 (SI 2024/949), r 13(1).

PREPARING THE CASE FOLLOWING LEAVE

10.13 Once leave has been granted it is necessary to get to grips with the process of preparing the case for hearing. There is no substitute for acquainting oneself with the relevant practice directions that apply at each stage of the case.

10.14 However, the drafting is an exercise in advocacy as much as in rule compliance. Therefore, the leading advocate should be involved at each stage.

The form and content of Supreme Court documents

10.15 The Supreme Court has now moved to a system under which the vast majority of the documents filed are to be provided in electronic form only via the Court's case management portal. The only exception to this is the key document bundle, which is required for the appeal hearing and which must be made available both in electronic form and as hard copy. The Court has published Guidance called 'Electronic papers' on the Guidance section of the website. This gives litigants the up-to-date requirements for the presentation of documents for proceedings before the Court (see Practice Direction 5, paragraph 5.1).

The portal is the external facing online website established and operated by the Supreme Court. It enables the parties and their legal representatives to file applications, appeals and other documents with the Registry, to serve those documents on other parties involved in the appeal and to communicate with the Registry and with each other.

The portal was brought into operation on 2 December 2024 when the Supreme Court Rules 2024 came into effect.

Parties can also use the portal to pay any fees that are due before the party can commence or participate in the appeal (as to fees see the Guidance on the Court's website). The portal enables them to track the progress of their appeal whenever they wish.

The following Practice Directions provide the guidance as to the form and contents of the significant documents and procedural issues:

- applications for leave to appeal: Practice Direction 3;
- documents for the appeal hearing: Practice Direction 5;
- procedural applications, documents and orders: Practice Direction 7;
- miscellaneous matters including death of a party: Practice Direction 8.

Timetable following the granting of leave by the Supreme Court

10.16 If leave is granted,[6] the steps required and timetable for preparation are set out in Parts 4 to 6 of the Practice Directions. Of particular note are the following requirements:

(a) The appellant must, within 14 days of the grant of leave, file a notice of intention to proceed.[7]

(b) In a case in which a declaration of incompatibility with the European Convention on Human Rights is sought, Form 1 or 3 must be completed and served and filed along with the notice.

(c) The statement of facts and issues and the appendix must be filed by the appellant within 112 days after the filing of the notice. If the appellant is unable to comply with the relevant time limit, an application for an extension of time must be made.[8]

(d) No later than **eight weeks** before the proposed date of the hearing, the appellants must upload their written case to the portal.[9]

(e) The case is the statement of a party's argument in the appeal. A case must be in electronic form and should not (without permission of the Court) exceed 50 pages. Cases in excess of 50 pages will not be accepted unless permission to file a longer case has been sought and obtained.[10]

(f) No later than **six weeks** before the proposed date of the hearing, the respondents must upload their case to the portal. This deadline also applies to interveners).[11]

10.17 Not later than 28 days before the date fixed for the hearing, the appellant must send enough hard copies of the key documents bundle to the Registry to provide one to each Justice sitting and an additional copy for the Registry, and upload to the portal a single electronic file containing the key documents bundle.[12] The parties will have been informed by the Registry of the number of copies required as part of the listing process.

The key documents bundle must contain the documents specified in PD 5.20 and 5.21. The hard copy of the key documents bundle must be presented in the manner set out in PD 5.22.

6 Separate rules apply when leave has been granted by a lower Court; see Supreme Court Rules 2024, rr 20 and 21.
7 Supreme Court Rules 2024, r 19.
8 Supreme Court Rules 2024, r 27 and PD 5.3 and 5.5.
9 PD 5.17.
10 PD 5.9.
11 PD 5.18.
12 Supreme Court Rules 2024, r 28.

The appellant must also prepare the main hearing bundle.[13] This is a single electronic file containing the documents set out in PD 5.23. The appellant must follow the electronic bundle guidelines when preparing the bundle.[14] The appellant must upload the main hearing bundle to the portal not later than 28 days before the date of the hearing.

HEARINGS

10.18 Cases are generally heard by a panel of five justices. In particular cases the Justices may sit as a larger panel. It is only in 'wholly exceptional circumstances'[15] that the Court would sit in private. Most hearings take place in public and are broadcast. Judgments are reserved.

PARTICULAR ISSUES

Bail

10.19 Bail is not determined by the Supreme Court but by the Court of Appeal.[16]

Attendance of the appellant

10.20 There is no right for an appellant to be present at the hearing. The effect of this is that whilst an appellant on bail can attend, and is usually required to do so in order to surrender,[17] an appellant who is in custody will not be produced unless the Court deems it necessary, in which case the Court may arrange to sit in the Royal Courts of Justice.[18]

Costs

10.21 The Court 'may make such orders as it considers just in respect of the costs of any appeal, application for leave to appeal, or other application to or proceeding before the Court'.[19] Litigants who are publicly funded in accordance with the terms of the Legal Aid, Sentencing and Punishment of

13 Supreme Court Rules 2024, r 29.
14 The Practice Direction contains a link to the guidelines at para 5.24.
15 PD 6.10.
16 CAA 1968, s 36.
17 PD 12.39.
18 PD 12.38.
19 Supreme Court Rules 2024, r 53(1); PD 13.1.

Offenders Act 2012 will usually have their costs assessed by the LAA in their jurisdiction. PD 13 should be consulted for further details.

Death of a party

10.22 If a party to an appeal dies before the hearing, immediate notice of the death must be given via the correspondence function on the portal. The appeal cannot proceed unless and until a new party has been appointed to represent the deceased person's interest. An application to substitute the new party must be filed with the prescribed fee within 42 days of the date of notice of death.[20]

SUMMARY OF KEY POINTS

- The Supreme Court is the highest court of the land having been established by the Constitutional Reform Act 2005 to replace the House of Lords.
- It hears appeals from the Court of Appeal (Criminal Division) although leave to appeal from that Court is rarely granted.
- An application for leave can only be made if the Court of Appeal has first certified a point of law of public importance. The applicant generally has 28 days to apply to the Supreme Court itself for leave. The time will be extended if application is made to the Court of Appeal for a representation order.
- That application must be made in accordance with the Rules of the Supreme Court.
- If leave is granted there is a particular procedure to be followed for the preparation of the case, which is clearly set out in the Supreme Court Rules and Practice Directions.
- All documents lodged must be in a form that is prescribed by the Rules and Practice Directions.
- A representation order to allow for the instruction of the leading advocate will usually be granted only if leave is granted.
- Bail may be granted by the Court of Appeal.
- Hearings take place in public and may be broadcast live.
- The appellant has no right to be present at the hearing. Therefore, appellants will not generally be produced from custody.
- The Supreme Court has the power to award costs on such terms as it considers just.

20 PD 8.3–8.4.

Chapter 11

Applications to the European Court of Human Rights

INTRODUCTION

11.1 Making an application to the European Court of Human Rights (ECtHR) is for those who are prepared to play a long game in order to keep alive their chances of achieving a favourable result.

11.2 It is not part of the appeal process. The ECtHR cannot quash a conviction or reduce a sentence. However, the impact of a finding by the ECtHR that a conviction or sentence was obtained in a manner that breached an applicant's rights under the European Convention on Human Rights (Convention) can have a profound impact on the appeal process. It may provide a reason for the Criminal Cases Review Commission (CCRC) to refer the case to the Court of Appeal.

11.3 However, the fact that the ECtHR has found that there has been a violation of Convention rights does not necessarily require the CCRC to make a reference (*Dowsett v Criminal Cases Review Commission*[1]). A violation of a Convention right, even of the right to a fair trial under Article 6, does not necessarily render a conviction unsafe (see Chapter 3). Moreover, the domestic courts are not bound to agree with the ECtHR on what Article 6 requires. For an interesting example of the UKSC expressing concerns as to whether a decision of the ECtHR had sufficiently appreciated particular aspects of the domestic process, see *R v Horncastle*.[2]

11.4 However, the Convention has proved to be a powerful force in shaping the criminal law in significant and often unpredictable ways. A ruling from the ECtHR may lead the CCRC and ultimately the Court of Appeal to consider familiar issues in a new light and so open up the possibility of a successful appeal.

1 [2007] EWHC 1923 (Admin).
2 [2009] UKSC 14.

WHETHER TO APPLY

11.5 Before embarking on litigation that may take years to conclude, a potential applicant should consider carefully what they want to gain from the process. Do they want the satisfaction of a finding that their rights were violated? If so, it is necessary to consider the case law of the ECtHR in order to determine the prospects of obtaining such a finding. Do they want to be paid compensation? If so, it is also important to consider the level of compensation that might be awarded (remembering that sometimes the ECtHR decides not to award compensation at all) in the event that the application succeeds. Do they want to challenge the conviction or sentence? If so, it is necessary to consider whether there is a real chance that a finding by the ECtHR that the applicant's rights were violated will lead the CCRC to refer the case to the Court of Appeal. This final point must be considered in the light of the time that it is likely to take for an application to be determined. A sentence of three years or less will almost certainly have been completed by the time that the ECtHR has begun to determine whether – if the claim is admissible – there has been a Convention violation or not.

APPLYING TO THE ECtHR

Exhaustion of domestic remedies

11.6 The ECtHR 'may only deal with the matter after all domestic remedies have been exhausted'.[3] However, the domestic remedies must be available and effective. The applicant does not need to exhaust domestic remedies that have no reasonable prospect of success.

11.7 Applying this approach to the criminal appeal process:

(a) The applicant must have lodged an application for leave to appeal to the Court of Appeal.

(b) If that application was refused by the single judge and not renewed before the full Court, the ECtHR may well find the applicant had not exhausted his remedies (*Reilly v UK*).[4]

(c) If a renewed application for leave was refused by the full Court, the domestic remedies will normally have been exhausted (although see (e), below).

(d) If the Court of Appeal heard and dismissed an appeal, it may be held that domestic remedies would only be exhausted once an application for

3 Convention, Art 35(1).
4 App No 53731/00 (Dec) 26 June 2003.

leave to appeal to the Supreme Court had been sought. In *Selvanayagam v UK*,[5] the ECtHR accepted that domestic remedies had been exhausted when the applicant presented the separate opinions of several advocates, that an appeal to the House of Lords (the predecessor of the Supreme Court) would not have succeeded. However, it may be better not to take a risk and, in a case in which an application to the ECtHR may be made, apply for leave to appeal to the Supreme Court, notwithstanding the unlikelihood of the application being granted.

(e) An application to the CCRC will not usually be regarded as giving rise to an available remedy but may do in unusual cases where it was highly likely that the CCRC would have referred the case to the Court of Appeal. Such a situation might arise where a number of references had been made in similar cases (see *Tucka v UK (No 1)*[6]).

Time limits for lodging an application

11.8 To appeal to the ECtHR, you must submit your application within four months of the final domestic decision. The four-month time limit came into effect on 1 February 2022 and applies only to cases where the final domestic decision was made on or after that date. There is no discretion for the Court to extend time and compliance with the time-limit is a precondition of admissibility. Thus, failure to meet this strict criterion will result in an application being declared inadmissible. A determination that an application is inadmissible is final and cannot be reversed.

The clock stops running when the application is physically received by the Court, with all the required supporting documents. It is therefore important when preparing the application to dispatch it by recorded delivery and to allow time for any potential delays and for the possibility that the Registry of the ECtHR will indicate that a further document is required.

Standing

11.9 Domestic rules on standing will not be decisive.[7] An individual or organisation may bring an action on behalf of another if they have clear written authority to act on their behalf. An application cannot be made on behalf of a deceased person.[8] However, if an applicant dies before the case is determined, the ECtHR usually permits a spouse or close relative to continue the proceedings on his behalf.

5 App No 57981/00 (Dec) 12 December 2002.
6 App No 34566/10 (Dec) 18 January 2011.
7 *Scozzari v Italy* (2002) 35 EHRR 12, paras 138–139.
8 *Dupin v Croatia*, App No 363868/03 (Dec) 7 July 2009.

Drafting the application

11.10 Rule 47 of the Rules of the ECtHR sets out the information that needs to be included with the application. A failure to comply with its requirements will add to the delays that are a pronounced feature of proceedings before the ECtHR. At worst, failure to comply with rule 47 will lead the Registry to refuse to register the application and, if a second, properly completed, application is then lodged too late, to declare the application inadmissible through being out of time.

11.11 All the documents that are required should be supplied as copies, not originals. The exception is the requirement for an original dated and signed authority from the applicant authorising his lawyer to act on his behalf in the ECtHR proceedings.

11.12 The application form is on the ECtHR website along with the technical requirements, such as page size, font size, spacing, and the like. Three sections of the form require careful drafting:

(a) the statement of the facts;

(b) the alleged violation(s) of the Convention and the relevant arguments;

(c) confirmation of the exhaustion of domestic remedies and that the final domestic decision was made not more than four months before the application was made.

11.13 The statement of facts needs to be concise. It must not mislead or omit crucial unhelpful facts, but it is perfectly proper to focus on matters that support the argument that there has been a violation of the applicant's Convention rights.

11.14 The '*alleged violations*' section of the application form allows several pages for submissions. An additional 20 pages can be appended. In drafting this section every lawyer will follow his own style and preferences. However, the following points should be borne in mind:

(a) The ECtHR is not concerned with whether the UK courts have complied with UK law, practice and precedent, but whether the outcome is such as to breach Convention rights. Therefore, although the domestic law must be accurately stated, it is best to focus on the practical effect of the events in the UK courts and to contrast those effects with the guarantees of the Convention as amplified and explained by decisions of the ECtHR.

(b) Each of the 47 member states of the Council of Europe has its own legal system, so the enforcement of human rights must be flexible in its application. The ECtHR is concerned with substance – not form. In an Article 6 argument, it is concerned with fairness not with technicalities.

(c) The judges of the Court will not necessarily speak English as their first language. To allow for this, submissions about violations of Convention rights are best drafted in clear and direct language. An application must deal with technical legal matters, but the excessive use of legalistic terms or national jargon or idioms may not help the application find favour further down the judicial line.

11.15 Once the application has been received, the Registry will send the applicant's lawyers a letter giving the application number and, of late, a set of printed bar codes. The number and the bar codes can then be used in all future correspondence.

11.16 Whilst the Court proclaims to endeavour to deal with cases within three years of them being brought, the reality is that many cases take far longer than that and it is only obviously important or prominent cases which will proceed more quickly. For example, at the time of writing, the most recent judgment of an Article 6 claim (criminal limb) against the United Kingdom was published three years and two months after lodging by the appellant (*Ezeoke v UK*[9]). The case concerned a defendant who was tried by a jury five times for the same offence between 2017 and 2020, including during the Covid pandemic. The ECtHR found a violation of Article 6(1) on account of the 'excessive length' of the criminal proceedings but declined to award any compensation by way of just satisfaction.

Progress of the application

11.17 Once they are received by the ECtHR applications may be allocated to a single judge, a committee of three judges or a Chamber.

11.18 The application will be allocated to a single judge if it appears on its face to be inadmissible.[10] The judge may declare it inadmissible from which there is no right of appeal. Alternatively, he may forward it to a committee of three judges or to a Chamber.

11.19 A committee has the power to declare a case inadmissible or may declare it admissible and go on to deliver judgment on the merits if the underlying question in the case is already the subject of well-established case law.[11]

9 App No (61280/21) 25 February 2025.
10 Convention, Art 27.
11 Convention, Art 28.

11.20 A Chamber is composed of seven judges, one of whom must be from the state against whom the application is brought.[12] If a Chamber does not, at the outset, conclude that the case is inadmissible, it will make a '*communication*' of the complaint to the government of the state which stands accused of violating the applicant's rights. This is an invitation to the government to answer a series of questions, both about the admissibility and the merits of the application. These will often be directly taken from the application and will directly address the matter in issue. For example, 'Was the [event at trial that is complained about] a violation of the Applicant's right to a fair trial under Article 6?'

11.21 The fact a communication is made is, of course, an encouraging sign. However, many cases in which a communication takes place are later declared inadmissible or no violation of the Convention is found.

11.22 The applicant has a right of reply to any response from the government. In this way, the case is argued on paper and the Chamber will often make final determinations of admissibility and merits on the papers without an oral hearing.

11.23 In a small number of cases the Chamber will decide to hold a hearing before determining a case. It will set a date for both sides to travel to the Court and present brief, time-limited, oral arguments, followed by questions from the Court. The Registry supplies full and helpful directions about what is required of the lawyers on these occasions.

11.24 It is the normal practice of the Chamber to make a final determination of admissibility and merits in the same judgment, having considered all the representations from the parties.

Referral to a Grand Chamber

11.25 If either party wishes to challenge a judgment they can apply, within three months of judgment being given, for referral to a Grand Chamber, which is composed of 17 judges.[13] A panel of five judges will decide whether to accept the referral. If it is accepted the case will be considered afresh by the Grand Chamber as a complete re-determination. The Grand Chamber almost always holds an oral hearing before reaching its determination. In addition, a Chamber that is hearing the application may transfer it to the Grand Chamber, as long as neither party objects.[14]

12 Convention, Art 29.
13 Convention, Art 43.
14 Convention, Art 30.

A 'friendly settlement' in criminal litigation

11.26 During the correspondence the Registry will offer the two parties the chance to discuss a 'friendly settlement'. Such a settlement involves an agreement by the government to pay compensation and, in some cases, to vary its policies or its actions towards an applicant to remove the event or conduct that is claimed to amount to a violation. This mechanism will almost never provide a means of resolving a claim arising out of a sentence or conviction, as the government can obviously not agree to ignore a judicial finding or order, such as a conviction or prison sentence.

11.27 An exception might arise in a case where an applicant has a good claim that the time taken for his trial is too long to comply with Article 6. In such cases, the UK government may sometimes offer to make a payment. It may be worth considering accepting such an offer as the chances of such a violation leading to a conviction being quashed may be slim.

Representation

11.28 There is no requirement that an application be submitted by a lawyer. However, if the application is communicated to the respondent government the ECtHR requires an applicant to be represented by an advocate who is qualified within one of the 47 signatory states. [15] There is no right to self-representation nor is there a right to be represented by a lawyer or another from outside the contracting territories. Any request for self-representation or representation from someone outside the contracting territories must be made in writing to the president of the ECtHR.[16]

Legal aid

11.29 The right to legal aid does not arise unless and until a communication is made to the government of the state which is accused of violating the applicant's Convention rights. At that point means forms may be sent out to the applicant to be completed and returned to the ECtHR. Legal aid is granted only if the ECtHR is satisfied that the applicant does not have the means to pay for all or part of his own representation.[17] Although legal aid is paid by the ECtHR, it asks the domestic legal aid authority to conduct an assessment of means based on the information the applicant provided. It is the practice of the ECtHR to only pay for work undertaken by one lawyer. Reasonable travel expenses will be reimbursed if the advocate is required to attend an oral hearing.

15 Rules of the Court, r 36(2), (3).

16 *Manoussos v Czech Republic*, App No 46488/99 (Dec) 7 September 2002.

17 Rules of the Court, r 101(b).

THE CONSEQUENCES OF A SUCCESSFUL OUTCOME

The judgment

11.30 For the applicant who wants to return to the domestic courts to appeal his conviction or sentence, the most important outcome is a ruling that contains a finding that his rights have been violated. It will need to be studied with care to determine whether it provides the basis for an application to the CCRC for a reference.

Compensation

11.31 Even if the ECtHR finds that there has been a violation of the applicant's Convention rights, it will not necessarily order financial compensation. The finding of breach is often considered to be a sufficient remedy. If it does decide to award compensation it may do so on the basis of pecuniary and non-pecuniary loss. However, an application for compensation may be made within two months of the application being declared admissible.

Costs

11.32 There is no provision for the applicant to pay costs to the responding government if the application is withdrawn or dismissed. However, a successful applicant may be awarded his costs, to be paid by the government. It is, therefore, a good idea to keep a record of the tasks completed by solicitors, senior and junior counsel, the hours worked, and the hourly rate charged. This should be submitted with the applicant's reply to the government's observations as there is no separate costs stage of proceedings. Although the ECtHR will seek submissions from the government on the applicant's costs, it will generally award what seems to the Court to be a reasonable amount for the work undertaken; often this will be less than claimed but is always better than nothing. Costs, if awarded, must be paid within three months of the judgment becoming final.

SUMMARY OF KEY POINTS

- An application to the ECtHR may only be made after domestic remedies have been exhausted.
- It must be received by the Registry within four months of the decision of the domestic courts that exhausted the domestic remedies.
- A finding by the ECtHR that the conviction or sentence gave rise to a breach of Convention rights may lead the Criminal Cases Review Commission to refer the case back to the Court of Appeal, but only if it

was capable of leading the Court of Appeal to conclude that a conviction was unsafe or the sentence wrong and should be reduced on appeal.

- The requirement to exhaust domestic remedies does not involve an obligation to pursue those remedies that have no realistic prospect of success. A failure to lodge an application for leave to appeal will be a failure to exhaust domestic remedies, so may a failure to renew an application for leave before the full Court. Whether an application for leave to appeal to the Supreme Court was required, following an unsuccessful appeal in the Court of Appeal, may depend on the facts of the case. The ECtHR would not normally find that the applicant should have made an application to the Criminal Cases Review Commission for a reference but may do in certain circumstances.
- The application should be made using the forms available on the ECtHR website. Where the applicant is represented, the dated and original signature of the applicant must be provided on the authority section of the application form, together with the original signature of the representative showing that he or she has agreed to act for the applicant. Copies of all the documents required by rule 47 must be included or the application may not be considered.
- The application will be allocated to a single judge, committee or Chamber, any one of whom may make a declaration of inadmissibility.
- Should the Court not take the view that the application is clearly inadmissible it will issue a communication to the relevant government. It will give the applicant the right of reply to any response from the government.
- Both the final determination of admissibility and the merits of the case are likely to be made on the basis of these documents in a single judgment.
- The Chamber occasionally conducts oral hearings before making its judgment.
- The Chamber can send the case to the Grand Chamber (of 17 judges) for a determination. Alternatively, an unsuccessful party can request a re-hearing before the Grand Chamber (a request that is considered by a panel of five judges).
- Legal aid may be available after a communication has been made to the government of the state that is accused of breaching the applicant's rights.
- A successful applicant may apply for costs and compensation, but the Court has no power to order costs to a responding government if the application is withdrawn or dismissed.

Part 4

Other Rights of Appeal

Chapter 12

Appeals against interlocutory rulings

INTRODUCTION

12.1 The right of appeal most commonly arises at the conclusion of the case. However, Parliament has created a number of exceptions in which appeals may be brought against interlocutory rulings. One of those exceptions, the right of the prosecution to appeal against certain rulings, is considered in Chapter 13.

12.2 Other exceptions include the following appeals:

(a) appeals against rulings made at preparatory hearings in serious or complex fraud cases;[1]

(b) appeals against rulings at preparatory hearings in complex, serious or lengthy cases;[2]

(c) appeals against a ruling that a case should be tried by a judge alone because of the risk of jury tampering;[3]

(d) appeals against a decision of the trial judge to discharge a jury and continue to try the case alone;[4]

(e) appeals against a ruling that certain counts on an indictment should be tried by judge alone, following a conviction by a jury on sample counts.[5]

12.3 The procedures in relation to each appeal are very similar. They follow, in truncated form, the procedures for appealing against conviction and sentence. They are all governed by Part 37 of the Criminal Procedure Rules as well as their own specific statutory provisions. However, with the exception of appeals against a decision of the judge to discharge a jury and try the case alone, those statutory provisions replicate or adopt the statutory scheme for

1 CJA 1987, s 9.
2 CPIA1996, s 35.
3 CJA 2003, s 44.
4 CJA 2003, s 46(3).
5 Domestic Violence, Crime and Victims Act 2004, s 17(1).

appeals from preparatory hearings in complex or lengthy fraud cases that were introduced in the Criminal Justice Act 1987 (CJA 1987).

APPEALS AGAINST RULINGS MADE AT PREPARATORY HEARINGS IN SERIOUS OR COMPLEX FRAUD CASES

12.4 If a judge has made a wrongful ruling at the beginning of a complex or lengthy case, it would be a waste of time and money for the case to proceed for weeks or months on an incorrect footing when the matter might be immediately appealed and the matter corrected so that the trial can proceed on a correct basis (*R v Hedworth*[6]).

12.5 Such was the thinking behind section 9 of CJA 1987 which established a right of appeal from a ruling of the judge made in serious or complex fraud cases.

The circumstances in which a ruling may be appealed

12.6 Section 7(1) of CJA 1987 provides that:

> 'Where it appears to a judge of the Crown Court that the evidence on an indictment reveals a case of fraud of such seriousness or complexity that substantial benefits are likely to accrue from a hearing (in this Act referred to as a "preparatory hearing") before the time when the jury are sworn, for the purpose of –
>
> (a) identifying issues which are likely to be material to the determinations and findings which are likely to be required during the trial,
>
> (b) if there is to be a jury, assisting their comprehension of those issues and expediting the proceedings before them,
>
> (c) determining an application to which section 45 of the Criminal Justice Act 2003 applies,
>
> (d) assisting the judge's management of the trial; or
>
> (e) considering questions as to the severance or joinder of charges,
>
> he may order that such a hearing shall be held.'

6 [1997] 1 Cr App R 421.

12.7 Section 9(11) of the Criminal Justice Act 1987 provides the right of appeal to the Court of Appeal in relation to the following rulings made by the judge, in the course of a preparatory hearing:

- any question as to the admissibility of evidence;[7]
- any other question of law relating to the case;[8] and
- any question as to the severance or joinder of charges.[9]

12.8 The Court of Appeal does not have jurisdiction to hear interlocutory appeals in respect of other rulings made in the course of a preparatory hearing.

12.9 In *R v H*[10] the House of Lords held that whilst it was open to a judge to determine disclosure applications at the preparatory hearing, rulings in relation to disclosure were not questions of law within the meaning of section 9(3) of CJA 1987 and could not, therefore, be subject to an interlocutory appeal. The Court has stressed the exceptional nature of interlocutory appeals – *R v I, P, O, I & G*[11] and *R v Lear & Lear*.[12]

Appealing a ruling

12.10 The procedure for appealing is as follows:

(a) Leave is needed from the trial judge or the Court of Appeal.[13] Application for leave from the trial judge must be made orally immediately after, or in writing within two business days, of the decision having been made.[14]

(b) Application for leave to the Court of Appeal must be made in writing not more than five business days either after the decision that is the subject of the appeal or after the Crown Court judge refuses to give leave.[15] This time limit may be extended on application to the Court, by the Court, single judge or Registrar. The Registrar should be asked to exercise his or her power to refer a case directly to the full Court due to its urgency, and the advocate should set out the reasons why.

(c) An application for leave to appeal is made on Form NG (Prep).

7 CJA 1987, s 9(3)(b).
8 CJA 1987, s 9(3)(c).
9 CJA 1987, s 9(3)(d).
10 [2007] UKHL 7.
11 [2010] 1 Cr App R 10.
12 [2018] EWCA Crim 69.
13 CJA 1987, s 9(11); CPIA 1996, s 35(1).
14 CrimPR 37.4.
15 CrimPR 37.2.

(d) The application must be served on the Crown Court, the Registrar and every party directly affected by the order or ruling against which the appellant wants to appeal.[16]

(e) It must be made in the terms prescribed in rule 37.3 of the Criminal Procedure Rules.

(f) If the application is opposed, a respondent's notice (Form RN) should be served within five business days of the appeal notice having been served.[17]

(g) It is considered by the single judge. If refused it may be renewed before the full court within five business days of refusal.[18]

(h) The judge may continue a preparatory hearing notwithstanding that leave to appeal has been granted, but the preparatory hearing cannot be concluded until after the appeal has been determined or abandoned.[19]

(i) The party in custody has the right to attend; this will often be a virtual attending by way of a video link.[20]

(j) The Court can confirm, vary, or reverse the decision that is the subject of the appeal.[21] A right of appeal lies from the Court of Appeal to the Supreme Court.[22]

(k) Funding for the proceedings will generally be covered by the existing Crown Court representation order.

Reporting restrictions on appeals from preparatory hearings

12.11 Section 11(1) of CJA 1987 restricts the reporting of an appeal from a preliminary ruling to those matters specified within that section, which contains lists of the basic information about the case. However, the Court of Appeal may make an order to remove or amend reporting restrictions.[23]

16 CrimPR 37.2.
17 CrimPR 37.5.
18 CrimPR 37.7.
19 CJA 1987, s 9(13); CPIA 1996, s 35(2).
20 CrimPR 37.8.
21 CJA 1987, s 9(14); CPIA 1996, s 13(3).
22 CAA 1968, s 33.
23 CJA 1987, s 11(5).

APPEALS UNDER SECTION 35 OF THE CRIMINAL PROCEDURE AND INVESTIGATIONS ACT 1996

12.12 Section 29 of the Criminal Procedure and Investigations Act 1996 ('CPIA 1996') provides that a preparatory hearing may be held where the judge determines that the case is likely to be of such length, seriousness or complexity that there will be significant benefits from holding a hearing in order to:

(a) identify issues that are likely to be material to the determinations and findings which are likely to be required during the trial;

(b) if there is to be a jury, assist their comprehension of those issues and expedite the proceedings before them;

(c) determine an application to which section 45 of the Criminal Justice Act 2003 ('CJA 2003') applies (where the prosecution have applied, under section 43 or 44 of CJA 2003 for the trial to take place without a jury);

(d) assist the judge's management of the trial;

(e) consider questions as to the severance or joinder of charges.

12.13 In addition, the judge must order a preparatory hearing in a terrorist case.[24]

12.14 The right of appeal exists against a ruling, made at the preparatory hearing, in relation to:[25]

(i) any question as to the admissibility of evidence;

(ii) any other question of law relating to the case;

(iii) any question as to the severance or joinder of charges.

12.15 In *R v I (C)*[26] the Court of Appeal confirmed that the principles established in *R v H*, that in order to be appealable questions of law did not need to relate to one of the statutory purposes of a preparatory hearing, (see 12.9 above) applied to appeals under section 35 of CPIA 1996.[27] The case also sets out when preparatory hearings should be held.

24 CPIA 1996, s 29(1C), (6).
25 CPIA 1996, s 35(1).
26 [2009] EWCA Crim 1793.
27 See para 19 of judgment.

12.16 In *R v Aine Davis*[28] the Court considered whether the Court had jurisdiction to hear an appeal following a ruling on an application for a stay for abuse of process. The Court advocated a two stage test:

> 'The first asks whether, in principle, an appeal lies under section 35(1) from a ruling made in a preparatory hearing on an application to stay proceedings on the ground of abuse of process. That question turns on whether the ruling appealed from is a ruling "on any [...] point of law relating to the case" within the meaning of section 31(3) CPIA 1996. If the answer is "No", the court should not embark on the task of considering the substance of the appeal. If, however, the answer is "Yes", a second stage of analysis arises: how should the appellate jurisdiction in section 35(3) be exercised? In particular, in what circumstances can and should this court intervene to reverse or vary the judge's ruling?'[29]

The procedure for appealing

12.17 The procedures for appealing a ruling under section 35 of CPIA 1996 are the same as for the appeals against rulings in serious or complex fraud cases set out in 12.10 and 12.11, above. The relevant references for appeals under section 35 are contained in the footnotes.

Reporting restrictions

12.18 Section 37(1) of CPIA 1996 mirrors section 11 of CJA 1987 in creating an automatic reporting restriction (which may be removed or varied by the Court of Appeal) that applies to appeals against rulings made under section 35 and restricts reporting to certain basic facts.

APPEALS AGAINST A RULING THAT A CASE SHOULD BE TRIED BY A JUDGE AND NOT A JURY WHEN THERE IS A RISK OF JURY TAMPERING

12.19 A judge may, following an application by the prosecution, order that a trial take place without a jury in a case where there is a risk of jury tampering.[30] If such an application is made, a preparatory hearing must be held at which the application may be determined.[31] The Court must be satisfied to the

28 [2023] EWCA Crim 1018.
29 At para 38 of the judgment.
30 CJA 2003, s 44.
31 CJA 2003, s 45(2).

criminal standard (section 44(3)–(5) of CJA 2003) that the following criteria is made out:

> '(4) The first condition is that there is evidence of a real and present danger that jury tampering would take place.
>
> (5) The second condition is that, notwithstanding any steps (including the provision of police protection) which might reasonably be taken to prevent jury tampering, the likelihood that it would take place would be so substantial as to make it necessary in the interests of justice for the trial to be conducted without a jury.'

The procedure

12.20 Section 45 of CJA 2003 amends the relevant provisions of CJA 1987 and CPIA 1996 so as to ensure that the procedure for preparatory hearings and subsequent appeals applies to the decision of the judge as to whether to order that a trial take place without a jury under section 44. Therefore, the procedure for appeals and powers of the Court and reporting restrictions as set out at 12.10 and 12.11, above apply to appeals against such an order.

APPEALS AGAINST A DECISION TO ORDER A TRIAL WITHOUT A JURY WHERE JURY TAMPERING HAS TAKEN PLACE

12.21 If, after a trial has commenced, the trial judge is satisfied of the following;

(a) that jury tampering has taken place, and

(b) that to continue the trial without a jury would be fair to the defendant or defendants,

the judge may discharge the jury and proceed to try the case alone – Criminal Justice Act 2003, section 46(3).

12.22 However, if the judge decides that it is necessary in the interests of justice for the trial to be terminated, he must instead terminate the trial.[32]

32 CJA 2003, s 46(4).

12.23 Before determining whether the above test is satisfied, the judge must inform the parties of his grounds for concern and allow them to make representations.[33]

12.24 An order under section 46(3) or (5) may be appealed to the Court of Appeal. The Court may confirm or revoke the order.[34]

12.25 As an order does not take place within the context of a preparatory hearing, the relevant powers of the Court of Appeal in relation to appeals from preparatory hearings do not apply to appeals against a decision under section 46(3) of CJA 2003. However, rule 37.1 of the Criminal Procedure Rules applies to appeals against a decision under section 46 of CJA 2003.

12.26 For this reason, what is said above about appeals from preparatory hearings applies also to appeals against decisions made under section 46, with the following exceptions:

(a) Leave may be given by the trial judge or the full court,[35] but because it may not be given by the single judge, there is no procedure for renewing the application for leave.

(b) The power of the Court is simply to confirm or revoke the order.[36]

(c) The right to appeal to the Supreme Court against the decision of the Court of Appeal arises under section 47(6), which inserts the right into section 33(1) of CAA 1968.

RULING THAT A JUDGE SHOULD TRY CERTAIN COUNTS ALONE FOLLOWING CONVICTION BY A JURY ON SAMPLE COUNTS

12.27 In a case involving multiple counts, the prosecution may apply to the Crown Court for an order that certain counts are to be tried by a judge alone in the absence of a jury – the Domestic Violence, Crime and Victims Act 2004, section 17(1). The judge can only make such an order if satisfied that the following three conditions are fulfilled:[37]

(i) the number of counts included in the indictment is likely to mean that a trial by jury involving all of those counts would be impracticable;

33 CJA 2003, s 46(2).
34 CJA 2003, s 47(1).
35 CJA 2003, s 47(2).
36 CJA 2003, s 47(4).
37 Domestic Violence, Crime and Victims Act 2004, s 17(2); the conditions are at s 17(3)–(5).

(ii) if an order under subsection (2) were made, each count or group of counts which would accordingly be tried with a jury can be regarded as a sample of counts which could accordingly be tried without a jury;

(iii) it is in the interests of justice for an order under subsection (2) to be made.

12.28 Such an order may only be made at a preparatory hearing[38] and may be appealed to the Court of Appeal. The Domestic Violence, Crime and Victims Act 2004 amends the relevant sections of CJA 1987 and CPIA 1996 so as to ensure that appeals from decisions under section 17 are subject to their statutory regime.[39] Therefore, the powers of the Court of Appeal and the procedure for appealing are as set out at 12.10, above.

SUMMARY OF KEY POINTS

- There are a number of situations in which an appeal against an interlocutory ruling may be brought.
- These appeal rights largely follow the procedures set down in relation to appeals against rulings at preparatory hearings that were established by CJA 1987 in relation to appeals against rulings in serious or complex fraud cases.
- The procedure for such appeals is contained in Part 37 of the CrimPR, which sets out a truncated version of the procedure for appealing against conviction or sentence.
- Applications should be made using adapted forms for appeals against conviction and sentence.
- There are restrictions on the reporting of such appeals, which can, on application, be removed or amended by the Court of Appeal.

38 Domestic Violence, Crime and Victims Act 2004, s 18(1).
39 Domestic Violence, Crime and Victims Act 2004, s 18(5).

Chapter 13

Responding to prosecution appeals

INTRODUCTION

13.1 This chapter sets out the circumstances in which the prosecution may appeal to the Court of Appeal against a decision of the lower court and then moves on to focus on responding to two common types of prosecution appeal:

(a) Appeals under section 58 of CJA 2003 against a trial judge's ruling (often misleadingly referred to as appeals against 'terminating rulings').

(b) Appeals against sentences known as 'Attorney-General's References'.

THE PROSECUTION'S RIGHTS OF APPEAL

13.2 The prosecution's rights of appeal are far more restricted than those of the defence. The principle of the finality of the jury's verdict is respected and there is no general right of appeal against an acquittal. However, Parliament has established the following rights of appeal by the prosecution:

1 Appeals against rulings

   (a) Appeals against interlocutory rulings: these are considered in Chapter 12.

   (b) Appeals against a ruling of the judge in relation to a trial on indictment, pursuant to section 58 of CJA 2003 (see 13.3–13.22 below).

   (c) Appeals against evidentiary rulings in relation to qualifying offences, pursuant to section 62 of CJA 2003. However, section 62 is yet to be brought into force. At the time of writing, it is understood there are no plans to do so.

   (d) A reference by the Attorney-General of a point of law to the Court of Appeal following an acquittal on indictment, pursuant to section 36(1) of the Criminal Justice Act 1972. The acquittal will be unaffected by the Court of Appeal's decision, but the judgment of the Court will be available for the benefit of future cases.

2 Appeals against acquittals

(a) Section 54 of CPIA 1996 gives the prosecution the right to appeal to the High Court against an acquittal when there has been a conviction for interference or intimidation of a witness or juror in the proceedings that lead to the acquittal and there is a real possibility that the acquittal would not have taken place but for the interference or intimidation.

(b) Under Part 10 of CJA 2003 the prosecution may apply to the Court of Appeal to quash an acquittal in England and Wales and order a re-trial, or for a ruling that a foreign acquittal should be no bar to the defendant being tried for the same offence. This is the exception to the double jeopardy rule and the application will only be granted where there is 'new or compelling evidence'.

3 Appeals against sentence

(a) The prosecution has a right to appeal against a refusal to make a confiscation order under the Proceeds of Crime Act 2002 (see 4.53–4.54).

(b) Under section 14A(5A) of the Football Spectators Act 1989 the prosecution has a right to appeal against the refusal to make a banning order.

(c) Under sections 35 and 36 of the Criminal Justice Act 1988 the Attorney-General may refer a sentence to the Court of Appeal on the basis that it is unduly lenient (see paras 13.23 onwards, below).

PROSECUTION APPEALS AGAINST RULINGS UNDER SECTION 58 OF CJA 2003

13.3 Section 58 of CJA 2003 gives the prosecution the right of appeal against a judge's ruling in relation to a trial on indictment, which ruling relates to one or more offences included in the indictment. This is often referred to as a right to appeal against a 'terminating' ruling but the Court of Appeal has deprecated the use of the term (*R v Arnold*;[1] *R v AYP*[2]). It is misleading because the prosecution can appeal against a ruling even when it will not necessarily result in the defendant's acquittal. If, for example, a judge was to exclude a significant part of the evidence, the prosecution could appeal even if there was still some evidence remaining such as might enable the case to continue past a later submission of 'no case to answer'.

1 [2008] EWCA Crim 1034.

2 [2024] EWCA Crim 952. See H.1.2 of the Guide, which warns against using those terms in an application to the Court.

13.4 That said, the defining feature of these appeals is that the prosecution may only seek leave to appeal, if it is prepared to accept that the defendant will be acquitted of the count that is the subject of the appeal if it fails. For this reason, it will most usually be deployed where the ruling either does terminate the case on that count, or where it comes close to doing so.

When an appeal under section 58 may be brought

13.5 Leave to appeal may only be sought if the following conditions are met:

(a) The appeal must be against a ruling.[3]

(b) The ruling must be made in relation to a trial on indictment.[4]

(c) That was made before the summing up starts – CJA 2003, section 58(13).

(d) It must not be a ruling to discharge the jury –CJA 2003, section 57(2)(a).

(e) There must be no other right of appeal available to the prosecution – CJA 2003, section 57(2)(b). It follows that where an appeal may be brought under the regime for appeals against interlocutory rulings it must be brought under those provisions.

(f) The prosecution must have given notice of intention to appeal after the ruling was given or have applied for an adjournment in order to consider whether to appeal – CJA 2003, section 58(4).

(g) The prosecution must have given a valid acquittal agreement at the time when the indication of intention to appeal is given – CJA 2003, section 58(8).

13.6 The Court of Appeal has interpreted these preconditions strictly. If they are not met the appeal will be refused – *R v Arnold*.[5]

What is an acquittal agreement?

13.7 Section 58(8) of CJA 2003 requires the prosecution to give the undertaking that in the event of leave to appeal being refused or the appeal being abandoned, they will agree to the defendant being acquitted.[6] The significance

3 See s 74(1) for the broad definition given to ruling.

4 'Trial on indictment' has been held to include proceedings as to whether a defendant did the act or made the omission charged, pursuant to s 4A of the Criminal Procedure (Insanity) Act 1964 – *R v Ahmed (Nazir)* [2021] EWCA Crim 927.

5 [2008] EWCA Crim 1034.

6 CJA 2003, s 61(3).

of section 58(8) was considered in *R v T(N)*.[7] This was the judgment of a five-judge Court (led by the then Lord Chief Justice). The Court decided that the Court of Appeal has no jurisdiction to hear an appeal by the prosecution against a 'terminating ruling' made by a judge in the Crown Court on a trial on indictment unless the prosecution has complied with the requirement in section 58(8). The undertaking has to be given *at or before* the time that the prosecution notifies the Crown Court of its intention to appeal; a failure to give the undertaking at that time will be fatal to the appeal – *R v Arnold*.[8] 'At … that time' will be strictly interpreted – an acquittal agreement given 90 minutes after the prosecution notified the Crown Court of its intention to appeal, did not comply with section 58(8) and the Court of Appeal therefore did not have jurisdiction – *R v BJF*.[9]

13.8 If the defendant cannot be formally 'acquitted' because of the stage the case has reached, no such undertaking can be given and therefore the right of appeal does not arise. This has the effect of precluding an appeal under this section against a ruling made before arraignment – *R v Thompson*.[10] The acquittal guarantee must be given – *R v BJF*.[11]

The Court's power on appeal

13.9 Section 61 of the CJA 2003 sets out the Court's powers in relation to section 58 appeals:

> '(1) On an appeal under section 58, the Court of Appeal may confirm, reverse, or vary any ruling to which the appeal relates.
>
> (2) Subsections (3) to (5) apply where the appeal relates to a single ruling.
>
> (3) Where the Court of Appeal confirms the ruling, it must, in respect of the offence or each offence which is the subject of the appeal, order that the defendant in relation to that offence be acquitted of that offence.
>
> (4) Where the Court of Appeal reverses or varies the ruling, it must, in respect of the offence or each offence which is the subject of the appeal, do any of the following—
>
> (a) order that proceedings for that offence may be resumed in the Crown Court,

7 [2010] EWCA Crim 711.

8 See also *LSA* [2008] EWCA Crim 1034; *NT* [2010] EWCA Crim 711; *B* [2014] EWCA Crim 2078.

9 [2024] EWCA Crim 1670. See also *R v AWY* [2025] EWCA Crim 754, [2025] Crim LR 633.

10 [2006] EWCA Crim 2849.

11 [2024] EWCA Crim 1670.

(b) order that a fresh trial may take place in the Crown Court for that offence,

(c) order that the defendant in relation to that offence be acquitted of that offence.

(5) But the Court of Appeal may not make an order under subsection (4)(c) in respect of an offence unless it considers that the defendant could not receive a fair trial if an order were made under subsection (4)(a) or (b).

(6) Subsections (7) and (8) apply where the appeal relates to a ruling that there is no case to answer and one or more other rulings.

(7) Where the Court of Appeal confirms the ruling that there is no case to answer, it must, in respect of the offence or each offence which is the subject of the appeal, order that the defendant in relation to that offence be acquitted of that offence.

(8) Where the Court of Appeal reverses or varies the ruling that there is no case to answer, it must in respect of the offence or each offence which is the subject of the appeal, make any of the orders mentioned in subsection (4)(a) to (c) (but subject to subsection (5)).'

When can the Court reverse a ruling on appeal?

13.10 Section 67 of the CJA 2003 provides that the Court may not reverse a ruling on an appeal under this Part unless satisfied:

(a) that the ruling was wrong in law;

(b) that the ruling involved an error of law or principle; or

(c) that the ruling was a ruling that it was not reasonable for the judge to have made.

In *R v B*[12] Lord Judge CJ laid emphasis on the trial judge's experience and reputation and indicated that the decision had to be shown to be clearly wrong before the Court of Appeal would think it right to interfere. In *R v Qureshi*[13] the Court held that where the challenge was against a ruling of no case to answer the appeal could only succeed if the court was persuaded that the ruling was perverse: 'The well-known public law test in Associated Provincial Picture Houses Ltd v Wednesbury Corp [1948] 1 KB 223 applies.'[14] In *R v Ikram (Naveeda)*[15] the Court stated, 'The mere fact that a judge could reasonably

12 [2008] EWCA Crim 1144.
13 [2011] 2 Cr App R 25.
14 At para 18 of the judgment.
15 [2018] 2 Cr App R 6, at para 51 of the judgment.

have reached the opposite conclusion does not begin to provide a basis for a successful appeal.'

The procedure for appealing

13.11 The procedure for applications for leave, and subsequent appeals against rulings adverse to the prosecution, is to be found in Part 38 of the Criminal Procedure Rules. The General Rules found in Part 36 also apply. The statutory conditions precedent will be strictly interpreted – *R v Rowan.*[16]

13.12 The prosecution (appellant) must inform the Court that it intends to appeal or request an adjournment to consider whether to appeal.[17] CrimPR 38.2 provides that the appellant must either tell the Crown Court judge of any decision to appeal *immediately* after becoming aware of the ruling against which the appellant wants to appeal or, if the appellant wants time to decide whether to appeal, must ask the judge for time *immediately* after becoming aware of the ruling. The use of the word *immediately* correctly reflects the requirement of section 58(4) of the Act – *R v M.*[18] If the application for an adjournment is granted, it will be, as a general rule, until the next business day.[19] The Judge has discretion to adjourn for longer if there is a real reason for doing so – *R v H*[20] and see more recently *R v BJF.*[21]

13.13 The prosecution must give the undertaking in relation to an acquittal agreement at the time when it informs the Court of its intention to appeal. Once a decision has been taken, a notice and application to appeal[22] must be served on the Crown Court, Registrar and every defendant affected by the ruling no later than the next business day if the trial Judge expedites the appeal, or otherwise no later than five business days after telling the Crown Court judge of the decision to appeal.[23]

13.14 Permission to appeal is required and may be granted either by the trial judge or by the Court of Appeal.[24] Application for permission to the trial judge must be made orally immediately after the ruling is given or in writing at the expiry of the time given for consideration of whether to appeal. The trial judge

16 [2023] EWCA Crim 205.
17 CJA 2003, s 58(4).
18 [2012] EWCA Crim 792.
19 CrimPR 38.2(2).
20 [2008] EWCA Crim 483. at para 11 of judgment. See also the Guide at section H.1.2.
21 [2024] EWCA Crim 1670.
22 See CrimPR 38.8 for the relevant requirements of the notice.
23 CrimPR 38.3.
24 CJA 2003, s 57(4).

must hear representations from the defence and generally reach a decision on permission the same day that the application is made.[25]

13.15 Leave should be granted only where the trial judge considers there is a real prospect of success and not to speed up the hearing of the appeal.[26]

The respondent's notice

13.16 Once a notice of appeal has been lodged, the defendant, now the respondent, must within five days (or one day if the appeal is expedited) serve a respondent's notice including grounds of opposition, if it wishes to make any representations or if directed to do so by the Court.[27]

13.17 Defence representatives are usually covered by the Crown Court representation order if one is in force (such proceedings being considered incidental),[28] although the Registrar/Court can grant a representation order for two counsel or an application for a KC even if not covered by the Crown Court representation order, if the Regulations are satisfied.[29]

13.18 The requirements of the form and service of the respondent's notice are set out in CrimPR 38.7. The respondent's notice must:

> '(a) give the date on which the respondent was served with the appeal notice;
>
> (b) identify each ground of opposition on which the respondent relies, numbering them consecutively (if there is more than one), concisely outlining each argument in support and identifying the ground of appeal to which each relates;
>
> (c) summarise any relevant facts not already summarised in the appeal notice;
>
> (d) identify any relevant authorities;
>
> (e) include or attach any application for the following, with reasons –
>
> > (i) an extension of time within which to serve the respondent's notice,

25 CrimPR 38.5.
26 *JG* [2006] EWCA Crim 3276.
27 CrimPR 38.7.
28 Legal Aid, Sentencing and Punishment of Offenders Act 2012, s 16(3)(b) and Sch 3, para 5(3).
29 The Guide at H.1.2.

(ii) a direction to attend in person any hearing that the respondent could attend by live link, if the respondent is in custody;

(f) identify any other document or thing that the respondent thinks the court will need to decide the appeal.

(g) unless an authority identified under paragraph (5)(d) is published by the Registrar as one frequently cited, include or attach—

(i) an electronic copy of each authority so identified, or

(ii) if two or more such authorities not so published are identified, electronic copies of each together in a single electronic document.'

The Hearing

13.19 The defendant has the right to attend the appeal hearing, though the Registrar can direct that this occurs via a video link.[30] There is an automatic restriction on the reporting of appeals which may be lifted or varied by the Court.[31]

13.20 Where the ruling of no case to answer plus an additional ruling are appealed against, pursuant to section 58(7), the Court will need to examine the relationship of the other ruling to the no case ruling in deciding in which order to consider the rulings – *R v Ikram (Naveeda)*.[32]

13.21 Resisting an appeal will often involve persuading the Court to rely on the trial judge's experience and any advantages the trial judge had in hearing live evidence in the case. The Court of Appeal's powers in such an appeal are wider than simply to uphold or overturn a trial level ruling. Section 61 of CJA 2003 also permits the Court to vary a ruling. Where the ruling by the trial judge is difficult to defend in its precise terms the respondent may wish to argue that the overall merits of the ruling should lead the Court to uphold the ruling in modified terms.

13.22 Either party may appeal to the Supreme Court,[33] subject to the Court of Appeal certifying a point of law of general public importance and leave being granted either by the Court of Appeal or the Supreme Court.

30 CrimPR 38.11.
31 CJA 2003, s 71.
32 [2018] EWCA Crim 440.
33 Criminal Appeal Act 1968, s 33(1) as amended by the Criminal Justice Act 2003, s 68(1).

ATTORNEY-GENERAL'S SENTENCE REFERENCES

13.23 Section 36 of the Criminal Justice Act 1988 (CJA 1988) permits the Attorney-General to appeal against unduly lenient sentences in certain serious cases. The offences in relation to which the sentence may be appealed under section 36 include all indictable-only offences[34] and any other offence set out in the relevant statutory instrument made under the Act: the Criminal Justice Act 1988 (Reviews of Sentencing) Order 2006 (SI 2006/1116).

Grounds for an appeal

13.24 Section 36(1) makes it clear that the overarching basis upon which the Attorney-General can appeal is that the sentence passed was 'unduly lenient'. Section 36(2) goes on to specify that the test of undue leniency may be met where a sentencing judge has either erred in law as to his powers of sentencing or failed to pass one of the minimum sentences required by statute.

The procedure

13.25 The procedure is governed by Part 41 of the CrimPR. The general rules contained in Part 36 also apply.

Notification of an appeal and reply

13.26 Schedule 3 to CJA 1988 allows 28 days for the prosecution to lodge an application for leave to refer a sentencing case. The CrimPR impose requirements as to the form and content of the application.[35] In practice the prosecution will usually send out a standard letter with supporting documents within 28 days of the sentence being passed.

13.27 The Registrar will serve the application on the respondent who must make any representations not more than ten business days after the Attorney serves the application, or a direction to do so.[36] Most respondents will be keen to do so. The CrimPR impose requirements as to the form, content and service of the respondent's notice.[37] The respondent's notice must give the date on which the respondent was served with the application,[38] say if the respondent

34 CJA 1988, s 35.
35 CrimPR 41.2 and 41.3.
36 CrimPR 41.4(3)(b).
37 CrimPR 41.4. See The Guide to Proceedings at the Court of Appeal, Criminal Division at H.1.3 as to there not being a specific Form either to commence proceedings or to respond.
38 CrimPR 41.4(5)(a).

wants to make representations at the hearing of the application or reference,[39] and include any necessary applications to extend or attend the hearing.[40]

Application to vary

13.28 CrimPR 41.3(3) requires the grounds to be set out in the permission application – *R v Fathi*.[41] Where grounds later sought to be relied upon have not been set out in the permission application, the Attorney-General must apply to vary the application for permission, by serving notice on the Registrar and the defendant in accordance with the CrimPR[42] and can only do so at a hearing if the court gives permission – *R v Fathi*.[43] Good reason must be given as to why the new grounds were not originally included and why it would be right to allow them to be included at the later stage.

Funding for respondent's representation

13.29 Representation Orders are granted by the Registrar in order to enable the defendant to respond to an Attorney-General's Reference.[44]

Permission and full hearings

13.30 Attorney-General's References require leave from the Court, but the practice is to list the case and allow the Court to consider both leave and, if leave is given, to deal with the substantive appeal all in one hearing.

13.31 A respondent who is in custody has the right to attend at the substantive hearing though this may be by video link if the Registrar directs.[45] There is no right to be produced at any permission or other incidental hearings.

The Court's approach to Attorney-General's References

13.32 The Court must first decide whether the sentence was unduly lenient. In doing so, it has frequently made clear that sentencing judges are entitled to depart from sentencing guidelines provided there is a rational and justifiable

39 CrimPR 41.4(5)(b).
40 CrimPR 41.4(5)(c).
41 [2024] EWCA Crim 1434.
42 CrimPR 41.5.
43 At paras 34–35 of the judgment.
44 The Guide, H.1.3.
45 CrimPR 41.6.

basis to do so. Lord Phillips CJ emphasised in *Attorney-General's Reference (No 8 of 2007)*[46] that a judge who took such a decision should not waver from it for fear of a reference. The power to allow an appeal is for sentences that are *unduly* lenient, not just lenient. The test is a high one and is intended to capture those sentences which cause public concern and affect the confidence in the criminal justice system (*Attorney-General's Reference (Nos 3 and 5 of 1989)*).[47]

13.33 If the Court decides that the sentence was unduly lenient, it must then go on to consider whether and to what extent to reduce or vary the sentence. This is a matter that is within the discretion of the Court; there is no statutory guidance on the exercise of that discretion and the Court has been known to consider a wide range of factors.

13.34 In determining whether the sentence was unduly lenient, the Court considers the facts as they were before the sentencing judge. It is not open to the Attorney to assert that the judge proceeded on a wrong factual basis where the prosecution did not take the opportunity to correct it at trial – *Attorney-General's Reference (No 79 of 2009) (R v Haimes)*.[48] In considering whether the sentence was unduly lenient, the Court will not take account of new material not before the trial judge, as the Court's task was to decide whether the sentence imposed in the light of the material before the judge could properly be characterised as being unduly lenient – see *Attorney-General's Reference (No 19 of 2005)*.[49] This would be otherwise if the judge had wrongly rejected a request for further material.[50] Nor would it permit the Attorney to make a submission upon the reference as to a disputed *fact* that could have been taken in the court below but was not – *Attorney-General's Reference (KGS)*.[51]

13.35 The Court has, however, been prepared to look at new material in deciding whether to vary the sentence and in deciding what the new sentence should be (*Attorney-General's Reference (No 74 of 2010)*;[52] *Attorney-General's Reference (No 79 of 2015)*).[53] In both those cases, the new material in question consisted of probation reports but the Court's approach has wider application; in the event that the Court decides that a sentence was unduly lenient it will often consider material in relation to the progress of the respondent from the time when the sentence was passed in order to assist in determining whether to interfere with it.

46 [2007] EWCA Crim 922.
47 (1990) 90 Cr App R 358.
48 [2010] EWCA Crim 187.
49 [2006] EWCA Crim 785.
50 *Attorney-General's Reference (R v Valants and Martin)* [2021] EWCA Crim 1233.
51 [2024] 2 Cr App R (S) 9.
52 [2011] EWCA Crim 873.
53 [2016] EWCA Crim 448. See also *Attorney-General's Reference (R v Johnstone)* [2021] EWCA Crim 1683.

13.36 Difficulties have occurred where a defendant has been given reasons to expect a certain sentence, most commonly when a *Goodyear*[54] indication has been given. The fact that an indication was given does not necessarily mean that the Court will not interfere with the sentence, nor does the fact that the prosecution at the time raised no objection to the indicated sentence (see *Attorney-General's Refs (Nos 86 and 87 of 1999)*.[55] A concession by prosecuting counsel in the court below as to appropriate categorisation is not binding on the Attorney-General who is entitled to seek to depart from it, 'provided always that there is a proper and substantial justification for doing so' as such a concession is a matter of judgment or evaluation[56] but any such departure should be clearly and expressly flagged up in the text of the final reference itself and reasons given – *Attorney-General's Reference (R v Stewart)*.[57]

13.37 However, the prosecution's seeming consent may be a powerful reason not to increase a sentence, especially if the offender acted in reliance on the indication that was given – see *Attorney-General's References (Nos 25 and 26 of 2008)*.[58] In *R v Powell*,[59] where prosecution counsel had agreed to an erroneous categorisation under the aggravated burglary sentencing guideline, the court ruled that the sentence was unduly lenient, but it would not be just to permit the Attorney-General to go so far behind what was said to the sentencing judge as to raise the case to a higher category. In *Attorney-General's Reference (R v Susorovs)*,[60] whilst increasing the overall sentence, the Court imposed a lower sentence than it would otherwise have done, to reflect the unfairness in the way the proceedings had been conducted.

Discount for double jeopardy

13.38 Double jeopardy is the term used for the fear and distress that arises from being sentenced a second time. Traditionally, it was the case that following a finding of undue leniency, when considering what new sentence to impose, the Court would often make a discount from what would have been the correct sentence, had it been imposed at first instance, to take account of this – see *Attorney-General's References (Nos 14 and 15 of 2006) (French and Webster)*.[61]

54 *R v Goodyear* [2005] EWCA Crim 888.
55 [2001] 1 Cr App R (S) 141 (505).
56 See the distinction made between concessions as to fact and concessions as to judgment in *R v KGS* cited above at 13.34.
57 [2017] 1 Cr App R (S) 48.
58 [2008] EWCA Crim 2665.
59 [2018] 1 Cr App R (S).
60 [2017] 1 Cr App R (S) 15.
61 [2006] EWCA Crim 1335.

13.39 However, in *Attorney-General's Reference (No 45 of 2014) (R v Afzal)*[62] the Court of Appeal explained that cases in which the principle of double jeopardy is likely to arise are now rare, by reason of a number of factors: the changes in the sentencing regime, including greater clarity and uniformity in relation to sentencing for most offences as a result of sentencing guidelines, such that advocates can advise of the risk of a reference where a judge has departed from the guidelines without explanation or good reason; the rapid consideration by the Attorney General of sentences, leading to quick references to the court; and an approach to sentencing that has become more victim-oriented since 2006. See *Attorney-General's References R v Ferizi*,[63] and *R v Phelps*[64] for recent examples of the application of the double jeopardy principle.

13.40 Under section 36(3A) of CJA 1988 the Court should not make any allowance for double jeopardy when the reference relates to a minimum term for a life sentence under section 321 of the Sentencing Act 2020. This now applies both to mandatory and discretionary life sentences.[65]

Responding to the appellant's case

13.41 The respondent may seek to persuade the Court both that the sentence was not unduly lenient and that, even if it was, the Court should exercise its discretion not to increase the sentence. In cases where the correctness of the original sentence is difficult to justify, the focus of the submissions should often be on the latter point. In *R v Quartey*[66] the Court reminded itself of the discretion and refused to increase the sentence despite finding it unduly lenient.

13.42 In seeking to persuade the Court that the sentence is not unduly lenient, arguments that are commonly advanced include:

(a) the high threshold that must be passed for a sentence to be regarded as unduly lenient;

(b) the fact that the judge was experienced (if true) and the advantage that the judge had of having heard the evidence (if sentence was imposed after trial or *voire dire*);

62 [2014] EWCA Crim 1566.

63 [2016] EWCA Crim 2022.

64 [2017] EWCA Crim 2403.

65 Section 46(2) of the Criminal Justice and Immigration Act 2008 amended s 36A to omit 'in respect of an offence the sentence for which is fixed by law'. This came into force on 1 January 2020 by virtue of the Sentencing Act 2020 (Commencement No 1) Regulations 2020 (SI 2020/1236).

66 [2024] EWCA Crim 745.

(c) the particular facts of the case which justified the judge in departing from the guidelines or the usual sentencing practice.

13.43 In certain cases, the problem may be not that the judge passed an unjustifiable sentence but that he failed to justify it in his sentencing remarks. The respondent will seek to set out the facts of the case which justify the sentence that was imposed.

13.44 When seeking to persuade the Court not to increase sentence, the respondent will wish to focus on double jeopardy, any significant progress that the respondent has made in the completion of the sentence or any significant change of circumstances that has occurred since sentence was passed that would make it wrong to now increase it.

Appeal to the Supreme Court

13.45 Either party can refer a point of law involved in any sentence passed to the Supreme Court, subject to certification of a point of general public importance and permission.[67] The period for applying to the Court of Appeal for certification and permission is 14 days and a subsequent application for permission to the Supreme Court must be brought within 14 days after refusal of permission by the Court of Appeal.[68]

SUMMARY OF KEY POINTS

- Parliament has established a number of prosecution rights of appeal. The most commonly used are the right to appeal against rulings under section 58 of CJA 2003 and the Attorney-General's right to appeal against a sentence that is unduly lenient.
- The procedure for appealing under section 58 of CJA 2003 is governed by Part 38 of the CrimPR. Attorney-General's References are governed by Part 41. Part 36 applies to both.
- There are a number of preconditions on the right to appeal against a ruling, including a requirement that the prosecution provides an agreement that it will seek the acquittal of the defendant if the appeal fails.
- Such an undertaking must be given at the time an indication of an intention to appeal is given.
- Leave to appeal under section 58 may be given by the trial judge or the Court of Appeal.

67 CJA 1988, s 36(5) and (6).
68 CJA 1988, Sch 3, para 4.

- In respect of an Attorney-General's Reference, leave must be granted by the Court of Appeal. However, it is the normal practice of the Court to hold a single permission/appeal hearing.
- In these appeals the defendant becomes the respondent who must, if he wishes to be heard, serve and lodge a respondent's notice.
- In both types of appeal either party has the right to appeal/refer a point of law to the Supreme Court.

Chapter 14

Appeals in relation to defendants suffering from a mental disorder

INTRODUCTION

14.1 As a matter of principle, once a defendant is found to be suffering from either a disability that makes them unfit to be tried or from insanity, the case is no longer a criminal case.

The law in this area is dated and ripe for review. The Law Commission have published papers on unfitness to plead and the law of insanity and automatism.[1] Appeals against findings of a disability or insanity are covered in this chapter. These are appeals where the mental incapacity was raised at the time of trial. This type of appeal is in contrast to those where the incapacity was not identified at the time of trial. Whilst those appeals are covered by Chapters 3 and 6, they include common issues for appeal lawyers that can arise in murder appeal cases where a partial defence may be available that reduces culpability from murder to involuntary manslaughter.[2] Those cases often involve fresh expert evidence. They may feature criticism of the previous lawyers and an application to admit fresh evidence (see especially 6.28 and 6.29). Likewise, in any case where the appeal lawyer identifies the issue of non-insane automatism as a potential defence (that should have been considered at the original trial), the same considerations will apply. Before dealing with findings of unfitness it is worth briefly considering cases where the lawyers failed to identify or argue that the client was unfit.

CONVICTION AND SENTENCING CASES – WHERE INCAPACITY WAS OVERLOOKED OR MISDIAGNOSED

14.2 Where a defendant is clearly unfit it may be necessary to revisit recent 'convictions' where the fitness issue was not raised. This is especially important

1 See the Law Commission website for details.

2 Partial defences are available to murder under s 2 Homicide Act 1957 for offences before 4 October 2010 and since under s 52; s 54 and 55 Coroners and Justice Act 2009 (diminished responsibility and loss of control); and under s 4 Homicide Act 1957 as part of a suicide pact or under s .1 Infanticide Act 1938.

given the pressure on lawyers to enter quick guilty pleas. The recent case of *R v Ismael*[3] demonstrates how badly things can go wrong and the Court of Appeal did not hesitate to set aside the guilty pleas and quash the convictions.

In sentencing cases, similar issues can arise where the court should have considered a hospital order or a 'hybrid' order.[4] The Court will extend the usual time limit (28 days for an appeal or 14 days for a renewal) in a case where they agree that a Hospital Order should be imposed. That extension may be many years later. In one such case the Court was persuaded to extend time 33 years' later where expert evidence showed that the condition of the appellant was, in fact, treatable and would have been at the time so a section 37 and section 41 Hospital Order should now be made.[5]

The court summarised the powers to review:[6]

> 'In *R v Cleland* [2020] EWCA 906; [2021] 1 Cr App R(S) 21, the court at [48] confirmed that:
>
> > "... following the admission of fresh evidence as to the offender's mental health at the time of sentence, the court has the power to substitute the sentence which it considers is (and, as the evidence now shows, always was) appropriate."
>
> The court went on to say at [49], that if fresh evidence shows the offender's mental state at the time of sentence:
>
> > "... was otherwise than the judge believed it to be, the court has power to quash the original sentence if it considers that the appellant 'should be sentenced differently', and to impose such sentence as it considers appropriate."
>
> The court also confirmed at [55], that in circumstances such as these this court, when deciding whether an offender should now be sentenced differently, is entitled to take into account the extent to which punishment has already been imposed.'

In deciding the appropriate disposal under the Mental Health Act 1983, the Court will focus on:

> 'The evidence about the different release and post-release regimes is of particular importance in this case. This is always a key issue when deciding whether to make a section 31/41 Order or a hybrid order under section 45A of the 1983 Act, which ensures that any release is under the control of the Parole Board. There is no general rule about which regime is preferable. It all depends on the individual case, and

3 [2024] EWCA Crim 301.

4 See *R v Vowles* [2015] EWCA Crim 45; *R v Edwards* [2018] EWCA Crim 595.

5 *R v Miller* [2021] EWCA Crim 1955.

6 See *R v Miller* [2021] EWCA Crim 1955.

> public safety is a principal concern. The outcome is not dictated by the opinion of the medical experts but is informed by their evidence, and by the risk posed by the defendant.'[7]

In making that assessment the Court will not be concerned with any subsequent tribunal decisions and attempts to introduce this as fresh evidence will be viewed as 'misconceived'; the court will only be interested in actual expert evidence.

APPEALING FINDINGS OF INCAPACITY

14.3 The following parts of this chapter are concerned with the reverse scenario; as we look at the way of appealing a trial finding of incapacity.

A finding that an incapable defendant committed the act with which they are charged does not amount to a conviction nor should a hospital or supervision order made against such a defendant be regarded as a sentence (*R v H*).[8] However, the procedures for dealing with those suffering from mental disorders who commit criminal acts closely follow criminal law procedures. Appeals are no exception. The Criminal Appeal Act 1968 (CCA 1968) establishes the following rights of appeal from decisions of the Crown Court, the procedures for which follow those for appeals against conviction or sentence:

(a) A finding of unfitness to be tried may be appealed under section 15 of CAA 1968.

(b) A defendant who has been found to be unfit to be tried did the act or made the omission with which he is charged may appeal under section 15 of CAA 1968.

(c) A verdict of not guilty by reason of insanity may be appealed under section 12 of CAA 1968.

(d) A hospital or supervision order that was imposed following a finding under (b) or (c), above may be appealed under section 16A of CAA 1968.

14.4 The test to be applied and the powers of disposal which the Court may exercise following a successful appeal differ for appeals under each of the above provisions (and are considered at 14.8–14.21 below). However, appeals under these provisions share a number of common features. The law in relation to who has the right to appeal, the availability of public funding and the procedures to be followed are the same for each and are considered first.

7 *Osmond v The King* [2025] EWCA Crim 835, para 30 Edis LJ.

8 [2003] UKHL 1.

Who may appeal?

14.5 These are defence, not prosecution appeals. Given the nature of the disabilities in question, the rights of appeal can be exercised by a defendant's lawyer without the need for the defendant's consent. In *R v Antoine (Pierre Harrison)*[9] the Court held that an advocate who had appeared in the Crown Court had the authority to settle grounds, lodge notice of appeal and present the appeal on behalf of a defendant who suffered from a mental disability such that he was incapable of giving instructions.

Funding

14.6 There is no statutory provision for the granting of representation orders in respect of any of these appeals. The successful appellant may apply for a defendant's costs order. Advocates who are instructed by the Court to represent a defendant who suffers from a mental disorder may claim costs from Central Funds (see *Antoine*, above).[10] The question has arisen recently whether advocates have a continued authority after the Single Judge has refused permission to renew on behalf of someone who is unfit to give instructions. The Court agreed that if the advocate thought renewal was justified, the authority to act continued post refusal. If they did renew and the appeal was unsuccessful then the Court still had power to award costs from Central Funds:[11]

> 'We think that the principles governing what may be described as "standard" applications for leave to appeal to this court should also apply to applications made under section 16A of the Criminal Appeal Act 1968, namely where the Crown Court has made a hospital order. The practice of this court in cases where section 11(1) applies (ie, in cases where leave is required in relation to proposed appeals against conviction and/or sentence) is not to award costs out of central fund in the normal or ordinary course. Some particular reason is required …'

The Court held that an order for the proportionate costs relating to the successful renewal should be made from Central Funds to the advocates but not the preparation related to the unsuccessful renewals.[12]

9 *R v Antoine (Pierre Harrison)* [1999] 2 Cr App R 225.

10 CrimPR 45.4.

11 *R v Grey* [2023] EWCA Crim 1285, at [3].

12 *R v Kurtaj* [2025] EWCA Crim 1163, where the Court found that a previous conviction when the defendant was possibly unfit should not have been admitted but the verdict was not unsafe.

The appeal process

14.7 The procedure for these appeals follows that for appeals against conviction or sentence. They are contained in the provisions of CAA 1968 that apply to each appeal. In addition, Parts 36 and 39 of the CPR apply to all of them. The main features of the process are:

(a) an application for certification of fitness to appeal may be made to the trial judge within 28 days of the decision which is the subject of challenge (but see 14.9 below in relation to when the 28-day period runs in appeals under section 15);

(b) an application for leave to the Court of Appeal must be made using Form NG within 28 days of the decision but may be extended on application. Leave may be granted by the single judge or the full Court;

(c) an application for leave that is refused may be renewed orally before the Court;

(d) the defendant who is in custody because of a finding of unfitness to stand trial or insanity does not have a right to be present at the hearing;

(e) an appeal or application for leave may be abandoned using Form A;

(f) under section 33 of CAA 1968 there is a right of appeal from the Court of Appeal to the Supreme Court, which involves the usual requirements of certification and leave.

Appeals against findings of unfitness to plead and findings that the accused made the act or omission charged

14.8 Sections 4 and 4A of the Criminal Procedure (Insanity) Act 1964 set out a two-stage procedure for those defendants who are believed to be unfit: the Crown Court must first determine whether an accused, who appears to be suffering from some mental illness or disorder, is fit to stand trial and, if found not to be fit, must go on to determine whether he did the acts of which he is accused.

14.9 Under section 15 of CAA 1968 an appeal may be brought against both of these findings. The procedural requirements contained in section 15 are as set out at 14.5–14.7 above. The 28-day period for lodging an appeal is calculated from the date of the decision against which leave is sought. However, the trial judge may only grant a certificate of fitness to appeal within 28 days of the finding that the accused did the act or made the omission charged.[13]

13 CAA 1968, s 15(2)(b).

14.10 The test for an appeal under section 15 is whether the finding that is the subject of the appeal is unsafe. If the Court allows an appeal against a finding of disability, it may order that a trial take place and may make orders that are necessary and expedient for custody or release on bail.[14]

14.11 The Court's powers to dispose of an appeal under section 15 are contained in section 16. If the Court allows an appeal against a finding that the defendant committed the act or made the omission in question, it must quash the order and direct that a verdict of acquittal be recorded.

14.12 The Court has no power to order a re-trial. However, where the Court finds that there has been a procedural irregularity such as to render the proceedings in the Crown Court a nullity, it may, instead of allowing the appeal, issue a writ of *venire de novo* (discussed more fully in Chapter 3) and order that the case be remitted for fresh proceedings to take place. It did so in *R v D (David Michael)*[15] when it transpired that one of the doctors upon whose opinion the finding of unfitness had been based was not qualified.

14.13 There is no appeal against a finding that the accused is fit to be tried. If such a finding is made and the accused goes on to be convicted, leave to appeal against conviction may be applied for in the usual way. If, in the course of that appeal, the Court is satisfied on the requisite evidence[16] that the convicted person was not fit but did carry out the acts or make the omission charged, then it may not quash the conviction but must substitute one of the orders under section 5 of the Criminal Procedure (Insanity) Act 1964 (see 14.18 below) for any sentence that had been imposed.

APPEALS AGAINST A VERDICT OF NOT GUILTY BY REASON OF INSANITY

14.14 Section 2 of the Trial of Lunatics Act 1883 allows a jury to return a special verdict of not guilty by reason of insanity. Appeal against such an order may be brought under section 12 of CAA 1968 and follows the procedures set out at 14.5–14.7, above. The test is whether the special verdict is 'unsafe'.[17] Given the greater awareness of mental health conditions these days, it may be worth considering whether the prosecution should be approached to see if they would object to the appeal in light of new expert opinion and agree to withdraw the original proceedings in light of a successful appeal. The CPS

14 CAA 1968, s 16(3)(a), (b).

15 [2001] EWCA Crim 911.

16 The written or oral evidence of two medical practitioners, one of whom must be duly approved (Criminal Procedure (Insanity) Act 1964, s 4(5), (6)).

17 CAA 1968, s 13.

guidance on dealing with offenders suffering from mental health conditions in such prosecutions may assist.[18]

14.15 The Court's powers to dispose of an appeal are contained in section 13 of CAA 1968. If the Court finds that the verdict of insanity was unsafe but that the proper verdict would have been guilty of the offence charged or any other offence for which the jury might have found the accused guilty, it may substitute a verdict of guilty of that offence for the verdict of not guilty by reason of insanity.

14.16 If the Court finds that the verdict of insanity is unsafe but that, on the evidence of appropriately qualified and approved practitioners,[19] the accused suffered from a disability within the meaning of sections 4 and 4A of the Criminal Procedure (Insanity) Act 1964 and that they made the act or omission charged, it may make an order under section 5 of the Criminal Procedure (Insanity) Act 1964.

14.17 In all other cases in which an appeal is allowed, the Court must substitute a verdict of acquittal.

Appeals against an order made under section 5 of the Criminal Procedure (Insanity) Act 1964

14.18 Following a verdict of insanity or a finding that the defendant did the act or omission with which he is charged, the Crown Court may make one of the following orders under section 5 of the Criminal Procedure (Insanity) Act 1964. Those orders are:

(a) a hospital order (with or without a restriction order);

(b) a supervision order; or

(c) an absolute discharge.

14.19 Under section 16A of CAA 1968[20] an appeal may be brought against such an order (although it is unlikely that a defendant would seek to appeal an order for an absolute discharge). The procedural requirements for such an appeal are as set out at 14.5–14.7, above. If it allows the appeal, the Court may vary the order or may quash it and substitute it with another order under section 5.

18 See https://www.cps.gov.uk/cps/news/new-guidance-prosecutors-mental-health-conditions-and-disorders.

19 See fn 15 above.

20 As inserted by the Domestic Violence, Crime and Victims Act 2004, s 25.

14.20 The test on appeal is simply whether the Court 'considers that the appellant should be dealt with differently to the way in which the Court below dealt with him'.[21]

14.21 If the Court of Appeal disposes of an appeal by making an interim hospital order or a supervision order, that order may be revoked or varied by the Crown Court. The Crown Court also has the power to revoke or vary an interim hospital order or a supervision order when an appeal against that order is still pending.[22]

SUMMARY OF KEY POINTS

- The law in this area is dated and ripe for reform.
- Cases cease to be criminal where there is a finding of insanity.
- Insanity may be overlooked at trial especially when there was a failure to obtain a proper expert assessment. In these cases, the Court of Appeal will intervene to correct the failure.
- Defendants with treatable mental impairments who would be better suited to a Mental Health Act 1983 disposal can ask the Court of Appeal to review determinate or life sentences – sometimes many years later.
- In making a hybrid order the court will balance public protection and the need for treatment. They will examine the most effective sentence that addresses risk and whether that can be achieved under a Mental Health Act 1983 supervision.
- Findings of unfitness can be appealed in a similar way to convictions.
- Likewise, Supervision or Hospital Orders following such findings can be appealed.
- Rights of appeal can be exercised without the defendant's consent.
- Costs for making these appeals can be claimed from central funds but will only be awarded if the application has been successful to some extent and it may be made proportionate to the relative success of the application.
- The test on any appeal is whether the finding is unsafe.
- If the appeal is against the finding of unfitness is successful, the court may order a trial and deal with issues of bail.

21 CAA 1968, s 16B(1).
22 CAA 1968, s 16B(2)–(5).

- If the appeal against the finding that they did the act or omission is successful, then it must quash the finding and enter an acquittal.
- There is no power to order a re-trial but if there was a procedural irregularity (such as an unqualified doctor) the court could issue a writ of *venire de novo* and order fresh proceedings.
- If an accused was mistakenly thought to be fit when they were not the Court can quash the conviction.
- There is a special category of jury verdict known as 'not guilty by reason of insanity'.
- In appropriate cases, it is worth considering making submissions to the CPS to apply their guidelines.
- If the Court overturns a verdict of insanity, they can substitute a verdict of guilt.
- If the Court finds that whilst not insane, that the defendant did the act under a disability, they may dispose of the case as they would on a finding of insanity – by way of a hospital order, a supervision order, or an absolute discharge.

Chapter 15

Special cases

15.1 Appeals against conviction and sentence in the Court of Appeal are determined in accordance with the relevant statutory tests and the principles which have developed at common law through the decisions of the Court. However, there have emerged in recent years certain categories of case which have involved repeated themes or issues. These are sometimes areas of professional speciality at first instance – protest cases being the clearest example, which often involve the provisions of the ECHR – but also cases which can engage difficult factual issues, namely, pregnant defendants and potential victims of modern slavery. What follows in this chapter is a summary of the issues which have emerged in these 'special cases' and an explanation of how the Court of Appeal approaches them. Children and young people deserve a category of their own.

The structure of this chapter is as follows:

1 Women, caring responsibilities and pregnancy;

2 Children and young people;

3 Modern slavery;

4 Protest.

1 WOMEN, CARING RESPONSIBILITIES AND PREGNANCY

INTRODUCTION

15.2

> 'It is now well recognised that a misplaced conception of equality has resulted in some very unequal treatment for the women and girls who appear before the criminal justice system. Simply put, a male-ordered world has applied to them its perceptions of the appropriate treatment for male offenders. The criminal justice system could … ask itself whether it is indeed unjust to women.'[1]

1 Baroness Hale DBE in 2005 Longford Trust Lecture.

15.3 *Special cases*

Particular issues can arise on appeal in respect of women who are imprisoned, including around caring responsibilities or pregnancy.[2] The case law, the principles that apply, the practical aspects of bringing an appeal in such cases and procedure are all considered below.

SENTENCING GUIDELINES

15.3 The principles applicable to such cases are now distilled in the Sentencing Guidelines. From 1 April 2024, the Sentencing Council included a new mitigating factor of 'Pregnancy, childbirth and post-natal care' in the General Guideline: overarching principles. This feature has also now been incorporated into the majority of offence-specific guidelines. 'Sole or primary carer for dependant relatives' has been listed as a mitigating factor in the General Guideline: overarching principles since October 2019 but was revised on 1 April 2024. The Imposition of Community and Custodial Sentences Guideline includes 'sentencing female offenders' and 'sentencing mothers with dependent children, pregnant and post-natal offenders' as specific issues to be considered by the sentencing court when looking at the 'effectiveness of sentencing'. Regard should be had to all of those Guidelines when preparing for appeal in such cases.

WOMEN AS OFFENDERS

Equal Treatment Bench Book

15.4 A useful summary of the particular issues and difficulties for women offenders, including those who are imprisoned is set out in the Equal Treatment Bench Book (ETBB).[3] In particular, the ETBB notes:

> 'The previous life experiences of women offenders, their reasons for offending, their offending patterns, the impact of custodial sentences on themselves and their dependants, and the long-term effect of prison sentences all tend to differ between men and women.'[4]

The ETBB notes that women's offending is commonly linked to underlying mental health needs, drug and alcohol problems, coercive relationships, financial difficulties, and debt and sets out the higher likelihood of mental health implications of incarceration on women as compared to men.[5]

2 See the Corston Report at https://prisonreformtrust.org.uk/wp-content/uploads/2022/08/The-Corston-Report.pdf.
3 July 2024, updated May 2025.
4 Equal Treatment Bench Book, at para 101.
5 ETBB, at para 106.

On appeal

15.5 It remains the case that, despite their presence in Sentencing Guidelines, such matters are still frequently not taken into account at first instance and will then have to be brought to the Court's attention upon appeal. Care should be taken to ensure that all factors relevant to a reduction in culpability or in mitigation are put before the Court on appeal. Factors that often arise for women in appeals against sentence are the role a relationship has played in their involvement in offending; their previous good character; their caring responsibilities or pregnancy. The last two are considered in more detail below.

CARING RESPONSIBILITIES

Relevant principles

15.6 In *R v Petherick*[6] the Court gave guidance on the interrelationship between Article 8 of the European Convention on Human Rights (ECHR) and the sentencing exercise. In summary, the following principles emerge:

(a) the sentencing of a defendant inevitably engaged not only their own Article 8 family life but also that of their family, including any dependent children;

(b) the correct approach in all Article 8 cases included asking whether the interference with family life was proportionate on a balance of the various factors;

(c) a criminal court should be informed about the defendant's domestic circumstances, and where the family life of others, especially children, would be affected, would take it into consideration. The Court would ask whether the sentence contemplated was a proportionate way of balancing such effect with the legitimate aims that sentencing had to serve;

(d) in a criminal sentencing exercise the legitimate aims which had to be balanced against the effect a sentence often had on the family life of others, included: society's need to punish serious crime; the interest of victims that punishment should constitute just deserts; society's need for appropriate deterrence; and the requirement that there should not be unjustified disparity between defendants convicted of similar crimes;

(e) the balance would be likely to be a fine one where the case stood on the cusp of custody. In that kind of case, the interference with the family life of one or more entirely innocent children can sometimes tip the scales and means that a custodial sentence otherwise proportionate may become disproportionate;

6 [2013] 1 Cr App R (S) 116.

(f) the likelihood of any interference with family life inherent in a sentence of imprisonment being disproportionate was inevitably progressively reduced the graver the offence;

(g) where custody could not proportionately be avoided, the effect on children or other family members might afford grounds for mitigating the sentence length but also might not. There could be no standard or conventional reduction; it was an infinitely variable factor to be trusted to the judgement of experienced judges.

Subsequent case law

15.7 Much of the case law set out in the section on pregnancy below is relevant also to those with dependants. Regard should be had to the cases set out there.

15.8 In *R v Foster*[7] the Court considered the proper sentence for the offence of administering poison with intent to procure a miscarriage. The Court drew particular attention to and cited at length two sections of the ETBB (updated since the judgment): 'Women as offenders; Who is in prison?' and 'Dependants and primary carers'. The judgment added two factors to those set out in *Petherick*:

(1) because there are comparatively few female prisons, women held in custody may often be a long distance from their families, which may add to the adverse consequences for them and for the children deprived of their care;

(2) in accordance with long established principles, the conditions in which prisoners are confined can properly be taken into account in sentencing, including in deciding whether to suspend a sentence.

15.9 The impact on children of a caregiver being imprisoned is of course not limited to women. *R v Secker*[8] is an example of the Court taking account of such impact when considering personal mitigation and the suspension of a sentence of imprisonment.

PREGNANCY

Relevant principles

15.10 The principles set out in *Petherick* apply of course to women who are pregnant at the point of sentence. However, additional considerations also

7 [2024] 1 Cr App R (S) 29.
8 [2021] 2 Cr App R (S) 32.

apply. There has been a sea-change in recent years in the Court's approach to pregnancy as a mitigating factor. This may in part be due to the tragic deaths of babies born in custody[9] and an understanding of the catastrophic effect on outcomes where a pregnant woman is incarcerated.

Case law

15.11 There have been a series of cases setting out the approach that should be taken. In *R v Cheeseman (Hollie)*[10] the Court referred to *Petherick* and stated that in cases involving young babies, the impact of a custodial sentence on family life might be considerably ameliorated by mother and child being accommodated together. By the time of the appeal, the appellant had given birth whilst in prison and was accommodated with her baby in the prison's mother and baby unit (MBU) but would continue to be incarcerated after the time at which her baby would have to leave the MBU. The Court had regard to the fact that separation when the child was aged two would come at a very sensitive time for the child. In the interests of proportionality and most particularly the interests of the child, the Court 'exceptionally' reduced the sentence so that there would be no separation.

15.12 In *R v Doyle (Sharnah)*[11] where the applicant was due to give birth in prison whilst serving a sentence of six months' imprisonment, the Court, relying on the principle that for offenders on the cusp of custody imprisonment should not be imposed where there would be an impact on dependants which would make a custodial sentence disproportionate to achieving the aims of sentencing, the Court quashed immediate imprisonment and imposed a suspended sentence.

15.13 In *Byron (Charlotte)*[12] Mrs Justice May stated that sentencing judges should not refer to how or why the defendant has become pregnant, 'whether a pregnancy is planned or not can be of no concern to a sentencing judge whose focus must be on the risks to mother and baby of pregnancy and birth in custody'. The Court was of the view that the judge had given no or no adequate consideration to the welfare of the appellant's 14-year old daughter or her unborn child. Having reduced the sentence to one that was capable of suspension, the Court considered suspension afresh. The Court had up to date reports on the effect of her mother's imprisonment on the 14-year old child

9 The inquest into Aisha Cleary's death at HMP Bronzefield concluded that serious operational and systemic failings contributed to her death – see https://www.inquest.org.uk/Handlers/Download.ashx?IDMF=a82f26f4-db5e-41d4-990c-307d6bb75e23.

10 [2020] EWCA Crim 794.

11 [2020] EWCA Crim 429.

12 [2024] EWCA Crim 818.

and to the appellant's medical notes and an expert midwifery report on the appellant's pregnancy and its risks.

15.14 The principles have recently been reiterated in *R v Saville*.[13] There the Court found that an otherwise appropriate immediate custodial sentence was not appropriate when the appellant's pregnancy and the significance of that for a woman in custody were considered. This was the case even for offences that would ordinarily attract immediate custody.

Minimum terms

15.15 In *R v Charlton (Claire Victoria)*[14] the applicant was subject to a 'third-strike' domestic burglary sentence. It was not known at sentence that the applicant was pregnant. On appeal the Court stated, 'We are satisfied that when the pregnancy is added to the other personal mitigation in the applicant's case, there are particular circumstances relating to the offender which would make it unjust to impose the minimum prison sentence which would otherwise be required.'[15]

15.16 In *R v Bassaragh (Maya Tiger)*[16] the Court held that in the particular circumstances of that case, the pregnancy of the applicant amounted to exceptional circumstances such as not only to disapply the minimum term of five years' imprisonment for possession of a prohibited firearm but to reduce the custodial term commensurate with the seriousness of the offence to one of two years. This enabled the Court to take 'the very exceptional course' of suspending the custodial term. The Court emphasised that it was not the case that every pregnancy would amount to exceptional circumstances. The Court also accepted that a separation of a baby from her mother at 18 months was significant but would not on its own necessarily amount to exceptional circumstances.[17]

PREPARATION FOR APPEAL

15.17 Appeals in such cases bring particular challenges. Speed is often of the essence, but it is also essential to ensure that relevant evidence particular to the appellant is obtained and is before the Court. There are, however, resources to assist. The Guidelines readily distil the relevant principles that apply. The Registrar will assist with expediting cases where necessary. Charities and

13 [2025] 2 Cr App R (S) 4.
14 [2022] 2 Cr App R (S) 18.
15 At para 15 of judgment.
16 [2024] 2 Cr App R (S) 11.
17 At para 22 of judgment.

pressure groups also provide helpful resources: Level Up provide a Legal Toolkit for those representing pregnant women and mothers in the criminal justice system which provides extremely helpful information and guidance for representatives.[18] Contact should also be made with the liaisons at MBUs and with probation.

Evidence gathering

15.18 It can be seen that in many of the cases referred to above, additional evidence was gathered between sentence and appeal. In *Bassaragh*[19] (where the appellant was not aware she was pregnant at the time of sentence) evidence as to the high risk of the applicant's *particular* pregnancy was gathered, as was more general information as to the relevant statistics around the risk to pregnant women in prison. In *Byron*[20] the Court had up to date information as to the effect of incarceration on the appellant's 14-year old child and also had medical information as to the risks in the appellant's pregnancy.

Risk in pregnancy

15.19 The National Health Service, the Prison Ombudsman and the Ministry of Justice categorise all pregnancies in prison as high risk. There is general recognition that the impact of custody on pregnant offenders can be harmful for both the offender and the child and it is acknowledged that there are likely to be difficulties in accessing medical assistance or specialist maternity services in custody.[21] This information should be placed before the Court and is set out in the Sentencing Guidelines.

Race

15.20 Risks in pregnancy are elevated for Black women, with a significantly increased risk of negative maternal outcomes for those from racialised backgrounds.[22] Evidence of the statistics on worsened outcomes for such applicants should be placed before the Court.

18 See https://static1.squarespace.com/static/679b8f0e7d497f64c646270a/t/679ce524fa56a2131a6b12e3/1738335556794/LU+x+DSC+Legal+Toolkit+14-Jan-25.pdf.

19 [2024] 2 Cr App R (S) 11.

20 [2024] EWCA Crim 818.

21 See *Bassaragh* judgment, para 26.

22 See https://www.npeu.ox.ac.uk/mbrrace-uk/data-brief/maternal-mortality-2020-2022.

Risks particular to the applicant

15.21 However, in addition to setting out in any grounds of appeal those general risks, enquiries should be made as to the *particular* medical position, both physical and mental, of the particular applicant. The medical records should be obtained if possible, within the time available and instructions taken as to any particular risk factors that pertain. If medical records are not forthcoming, the applicant's solicitor should gather information from the applicant and family members and reduce this into a signed affidavit placed before the Court. As the medical position can change as a pregnancy progresses, enquiries should continue to be made as close to the appeal date as possible. As well as the applicant herself, consideration should be given to the family history of pregnancy and birth.

Expert reports

15.22 It is likely that the Court will require an expert report as to the risk factors that pertain to that particular pregnancy or in respect of issues such as the impact of separation on a child. The relevant expert will depend on the particular issue(s) that are relied upon but may include: psychiatrists/psychologists; midwives/obstetricians; independent social workers; and GPs. If the funding in place is the Advice and Assistance scheme such reports can be funded as a disbursement. If a Representation Order from the Court is in place, whilst the Registrar cannot pre-agree that funding will be granted for a particular report, the representative should set out in writing what the reasoning is for obtaining such a report at the time the report is sought, making it more likely that funding will be allowed.

Mother and baby units

15.23 Those representing pregnant applicants or applicants with very young babies should ascertain whether there is a mother and baby unit (MBU) either at the prison to which the applicant has been sent or another prison to which the applicant could be transferred, to ascertain whether she would be eligible for the unit and, if so, until which age the baby would be permitted to stay. Contact should be made with those responsible for admissions to MBUs as to the criteria that would apply and the likelihood of the applicant getting a place.

15.24 Many MBUs allow babies to stay only until they are 18 months old but allow an extension application to be made until the baby is two years old. In *Bassaragh*,[23] the Court acknowledged that uncertainty about whether any

23 [2024] 2 Cr App R (S) 11.

extension would be allowed would in the meantime exacerbate the anxiety for the applicant in the early months of the baby's life in the prison setting.

It must be remembered that whilst a MBU is usually better than separation, it is not an ideal environment in which to bring up a baby. The availability of a MBU is not the end to arguments that a sentence of immediate imprisonment should not have been imposed.

Absence of an alternative carer/separation

15.25 Enquiries should be made with the wider family of the applicant as to what the alternative care provision would be in the event of incarceration. Consideration should also be given to the impact of separation on mother and child and relevant factors such as the age of the child, whether there has previously been separation, whether there is ongoing breast-feeding, should be ascertained and placed before the Court.

Procedure

15.26 Such cases give rise to particular pressures of time as very often an appeal will have to be brought quickly to minimise the risk of separation or to ensure the appeal is heard before the applicant's due date. Once the representatives become seized of such a case all preparation should be expedited. Once the appeal is ready to be lodged, application should be made to the Registrar for the appeal to be expedited.

15.27 An email should be sent to the Registrar setting out why the case needs to be expedited. Relevant factors to be set out include: the impact that separation is having on the child/children; particular difficulties caused by imprisonment; the risk to the pregnancy; and likelihood of birth taking place in prison.

15.28 Expedition is often achieved by the Registrar referring the case straight to the Full Court for consideration of both leave and the appeal itself. Representatives must ensure they are ready for an appeal to be listed at short notice.

Funding for a solicitor

15.29 Such cases are prime examples of where there is a need for a litigator as well as an advocate on appeal. An application for the Representation Order to be extended to a litigator should be made. See Chapter 8 as to applying for an extension.

SUMMARY OF KEY POINTS

- Particular considerations apply in sentence appeals concerning women, those with caring responsibilities and where the applicant/appellant is pregnant.
- The Sentencing Guidelines now incorporate many of the principles that have developed over the years.
- Representatives must ensure that these are before the Court on appeal.
- Where an applicant has dependent children the rights of the child must be taken into account when sentencing.
- Up to date evidence of the effect on dependants should be placed before the Court.
- When an offender is on the cusp of a custodial sentence, the effect on dependants may be the deciding factor.
- All pregnancies in custody are high risk. If a custodial sentence can be avoided in such cases it should be.
- Specific evidence relevant to the particular applicant as to risk should be gathered to be placed before the Court.
- The representative should liaise with the CAO to ensure such appeals are expedited.

2 CHILDREN AND YOUNG PEOPLE

INTRODUCTION

15.30 It is worth taking a historical perspective when considering appeal issues for children convicted or sentenced by the Crown Court. Progress has been slow in reforming the justice system for children and young people since the landmark decision in *Venables & Thompson v the UK*.[24] That decision exposed the failings of the trial process at the Crown Court when Jon Venables and Robert Thompson were convicted of the murder of Jamie Bulger. The relevant events happened when they were only ten years old.[25] Given that the case was decided by a European Court whose judges' member states had an average minimum age of criminal responsibility in the mid-teens, it was unsurprising that they were shocked by how these children were dealt with in an adult Crown Court. In concluding that the children had been subject to an unfair trial in breach of Article 6 of the ECHR they stated:

> 'The Court does, however, agree with the Commission that it is essential that a child charged with an offence is dealt with in a manner

24 Judgment given 16 December 1999 see https://hudoc.echr.coe.int/fre?i=001-58593; *R v T* [2009] UKHL 20.

25 Children and Young Persons Act 1933 (CYPA 1933), s 50.

> which takes full account of his age, level of maturity and intellectual and emotional capacities, and that steps are taken to promote his ability to understand and participate in the proceedings.'

These comments were the starting point in a slow process of reform.

CHILDREN AND YOUNG PEOPLE

15.31 The first distinction in dealing with those under 18 is the age group for 'children' (up to 14) and 'young persons' (14–17).[26] Apart from how they are referred to, those groupings mark a distinction in the powers to sentence and to remand them into detention. The Children and Young Persons Act 1933 (CYPA 1933) also requires that arrangements shall be made for preventing a child or young person while detained in a police station, or while being conveyed to or from any criminal court, or while awaiting before or after attendance in any criminal court, from associating with an adult (not being a relative) who is charged with any offence other than an offence with which the child or young person is jointly charged.[27] The CYPA 1933 also prohibits the use of the words 'sentence' or 'conviction' for matters dealt with in the Youth Court; these should be referred to as 'findings of guilt'.[28] Children and young people under 21 cannot receive a sentence of 'imprisonment', but instead detention, to mark their special status.[29] Finally, legal aid for those under 18 is not means tested so that is never a hurdle to representation – see Chapter 8.

KEY PRINCIPLES

15.32 The two key principles applying to children and young persons in the criminal justice system are:

(1) prevent offending; and

(2) the welfare principle.

The statutory aim of the youth justice system is to prevent offending:

> '... it shall be the principal aim of the youth justice system to prevent offending by children and young persons.'[30]

That sits alongside the welfare principle which was enacted as long ago as 1933:

> 'Every court in dealing with a child or young person who is brought before it, either as an offender or otherwise, shall have regard to

26 CYPA 1933, s 107(1) and Children and Young Persons' Act 1969, s 70(1).
27 CYPA 1933, s 31.
28 CYPA 1933, s 59.
29 Sentencing Act 2020, s 227.
30 Crime and Disorder Act 1998, s 37.

the welfare of the child or young person and shall in a proper case take steps for removing him from undesirable surroundings, and for securing that proper provision is made for his education and training.'[31]

DIFFICULTIES AFFECTING CHILDREN AND YOUNG PEOPLE

15.33 Despite that, for many years children and young people appearing in criminal courts have not been treated as children. There has been a failure to take account of their lack of maturity and the extreme way that children behave at times. In an adversarial system based on each side understanding the law and providing clear and careful instructions children are at a severe disadvantage. They lack the oral and written communication skills expected of adults. They often hide cognitive impairment or a lack of literacy. Slow processing speeds cannot be detected without expert assessment and their lack of maturity and vulnerability can be easily masked. Poor communication skills and other difficulties not only affect how they give evidence but also their lack of ability to absorb material and provide clear instructions. Without specialist representation these inadequacies can be missed and lead to miscarriages of justice or inappropriate sentences as appropriate experts are not instructed to highlight these issues.

15.34 Many studies have shown the disproportionate numbers of children who enter the criminal justice system from a background in care homes, who have poor literacy skills or are from certain ethnic minorities, especially young Black boys.[32] In the past they have been treated as mini-adults and in the case of some, 'adultified' by judges and other professionals.[33] Teenage boys who are physically developed are still very immature and often lack the ability to think consequentially. They are also highly susceptible to peer pressure.[34] This is especially a problem in conspiracy cases where they can be dragged along with group behaviour that can lead to terrible outcomes that they failed to foresee or understand. Children also are prone to extreme reactions in response to the strong emotions that they experience due to their immaturity. They struggle to

31 CYPA 1933, s 44.

32 See the Lammy Review at https://www.gov.uk/government/publications/lammy-review-final-report; The Charlie Taylor Review at https://assets.publishing.service.gov.uk/media/5a81513740f0b62302696a70/understanding-educational-background-of-young-offenders-full-report.pdf; 'Justice for children with SEND and neurodiversity 1025 at https://www.michaelsieff-foundation.org.uk/wp-content/uploads/2025/04/SEND-Neurodivergence-and-Youth-Justice-Report-Sieff-Foundation-2025.pdf.

33 Independent Office for Police Conduct guidance: see https://www.policeconduct.gov.uk/sites/default/files/documents/discrimination-toolkit-adultification-bitesize-july-2024.pdf and YJLC: see https://yjlc.uk/resources/legal-updates/adultification-bias-yjb-resources-raise-awareness-harmful-effects-treating.

34 See https://hmiprobation.justiceinspectorates.gov.uk/our-research/evidence-base-youth-justice/specific-areas-of-delivery/lifestyle-and-peer-relationships/

control themselves in the way adults can. Teenagers can catastrophise emotions and feelings that adults are much better at rationalising. In the courtroom, especially in multi-handed cases, bravado in front of peers can look like a lack of care as to the outcome of their actions or the case itself. Judges and juries need to be constantly reminded that perceptions with children and young people can be very misleading. Many parents see this with their own teenage children but fail to recognise it when it is displayed in a courtroom setting. There are also serious safeguarding issues with young people carrying knives because they are vulnerable and feel unprotected.[35]

15.35 Disparities of outcome due to race are now recognised in the Sentencing Guidelines and in the recent case of *Oni*[36] the Court of Appeal significantly reduced the sentences of detention after trial and in doing so acknowledged the disparity of sentencing certain groups, noting.

> 'As to the final point about disproportionality when sentencing Black defendants under the guideline for section 18 offences, the Sentencing Council guidelines specifically identify that sentencers should be aware that there is evidence of disparity in sentence outcomes that indicates that for Black and Asian offenders immediate custodial sentence lengths have on average been longer than for White, Mixed and Chinese or other ethnicity offenders. This is important guidance, and we have had regard to it in identifying the appropriate sentences for Mr Savi and Mr Okoya.'

Apart from the fair trial protection provisions guaranteed by Article 6 of the ECHR,[37] there is wider international protection for children appearing before courts in the 'best interests' principle:

> 'In all actions concerning children, whether undertaken by public or private social welfare institutions, courts of law, administrative authorities, legislative bodies, the best interests of the child shall be a primary consideration.'

THE SUCCESS OF THE CRIME AND DISORDER ACT 1998 (CDA 1998)

15.36 The CDA 1998 restructured the architecture of the youth justice system. It created the Youth Justice Board (YJB), Youth Offender Panels,

35 See Ofsted, 'Safeguarding children and young people in education from knife crime' at https://assets.publishing.service.gov.uk/media/5f5a269fe90e07207ac98082/Knife_crime_safeguarding_children_and_young_people.pdf, at para 13 'The common denominator of pupils who are found carrying bladed objects into school is their vulnerability'.

36 *R v Oni* (Justice intervening) [2025] EWCA Crim 12.

37 Human Rights Act 1998, s.1.

and local Youth Offending Teams (YOT – now known as the Youth Justice Service (YJS)) in each Local Authority to address the special needs of those arrested by police or appearing before the Youth Court. It was a huge change in culture. The intention was to have a 'joined up' system incorporating designated police officers, members of youth service teams within a local Youth Offender Panel to proactively intervene and engage with children who became entangled in the system. It aimed to divert children away from offending and attempt to rehabilitate those who could not be diverted. Whilst some were worried about the emasculation of the adversarial process as it encouraged acceptance of guilt and greater candour from the children, its success cannot be doubted. Over the past 20 years there has been a 50 per cent reduction in prosecutions of children and young people and there has been an equivalent reduction in those children being held on remand. This success shows how children's behaviour can be turned around at an early age and offending reduced. However, the CDA 1998 was aimed at the Youth Court, not the Crown Court, and the judges and advocates in that court are often unaware of how successful positive intervention can be. As a result, the Crown Court can seem a very different place. It has helped that the Youth Court is encouraged to retain as much work as it can.[38] However, the general lack of experience of solicitors, advocates and judges in the Crown Court in dealing with children and young people can lead to important issues on appeal.

CHRONOLOGICAL AGE AND IMMATURITY

15.37 The relevant age is the age at the time of the offending:

> 'The sentencer must consider the offender's level of maturity at the time of the offence, and assess the extent to which young age and lack of maturity reduced the offender's culpability in committing the murder.'[39]

The courts have long recognised that there are no cliff edges when dealing with children and young people. This is twofold: rates of change in maturity; and neurodevelopment. Both are exacerbated by other mental or cognitive disorders. Studies in neurodevelopment show that young peoples' brains continue to develop and mature beyond the age of 18. As a result, the courts have begun to acknowledge that the age range from 18 to 25 is relevant to issues of culpability and the capacity to change. Given the applicable sentencing principles these may well be relevant to whether to appeal a sentence that fails to take this into account adequately.

38 *Youth Court Bench Book: Jurisdiction and Grave Crimes* 'Trials in the Crown Court should be reserved for the most serious cases'.

39 *R v Popoola* [2021] EWCA Crim 842 at [36].

15.38 The maturity point was recognised in *R v Clarke* by the then LCJ, Lord Burnett of Maldon:[40]

> 'Reaching the age of 18 has many legal consequences, but it does not present a cliff edge for the purposes of sentencing. So much has long been clear. The discussion in *R v Peters* [2005] EWCA Crim 605, [2005] 2 Cr App R(S) 101 is an example of its application: See paras [10]–[12]. Full maturity and all the attributes of adulthood are not magically conferred on young people on their 18th birthdays. Experience of life reflected in scientific research (eg The Age of Adolescence: thelancet.com/child-adolescent; 17 January 2018) is that young people continue to mature, albeit at different rates, for some time beyond their 18th birthdays. The youth and maturity of an offender will be factors that inform any sentencing decision, even if an offender has passed his or her 18th birthday.'

15.39 The developmental point was raised by the then Youth Justice Lead Judge, May J In ZA:[41]

> 'It has been recognised for some time that the brains of young people are still developing up to the age of 25, particularly in the areas of the frontal cortex and hippocampus. These areas are the seat of emotional control, restraint, awareness of risk and the ability to appreciate the consequences of one's own and others' actions; in short, the processes of thought engaged in by, and the hallmark of, mature and responsible adults. It is also known that adverse childhood experiences, educational difficulties and mental health issues negatively affect the development of those adult thought processes.'

That case went on to emphasise:[42]

> 'In having regard to the welfare of the child or young person, a court should ensure that it is alert to:
>
> - any mental health problems or learning difficulties/disabilities;
> - any experiences of brain injury or traumatic life experience (including exposure to drug and alcohol abuse) and the developmental impact this may have had;
> - any speech and language difficulties and the effect this may have on the ability of the child or young person (or any accompanying adult) to communicate with the court, to understand the sanction imposed or to fulfil the obligations resulting from that sanction;

40 *R v Clarke* [2018] EWCA Crim 185, para 5.
41 *R v ZA* [2023] EWCA Crim 596 (*ZA*), at [52].
42 *ZA*, para 57.

- the vulnerability of children and young people to self-harm, particularly within a custodial environment; and
- the effect on children and young people of experiences of loss and neglect and/or abuse.'

SENTENCING GUIDANCE

15.40 The Sentencing Act distinguishes between the position of those **over 18** *at the time of conviction* and those who are under that age. For those over 18, the relevant principles of sentencing are:[43]

The court must have regard to the following purposes of sentencing:

(a) the punishment of offenders;

(b) the reduction of crime (including its reduction by deterrence);

(c) the reform and rehabilitation of offenders;

(d) the protection of the public; and

(e) the making of reparation by offenders to persons affected by their offences.

For those under 18 the purposes of sentencing are not stated but the Act reiterates that the two key principles are not affected.[44] It is arguable that deterrence is not relevant when sentencing a child or young person as their brains are incapable of factoring in deterrent sentences.[45] In any event it is another important distinction in sentencing under 18s.

SENTENCING COUNCIL GUIDE TO SENTENCING CHILDREN AND YOUNG PEOPLE

15.41 There is no better place to start than the 'Sentencing Guideline for Children and Young People'.[46] This provides a comprehensive set of special factors that apply when sentencing children and young people. The sentencing judge's sentencing remarks should be assessed against these factors. If the judge has not taken relevant ones into consideration, then it may well be grounds for appeal. It may be that the information that would have triggered that consideration was not before the court, so it is important to consider what

43 Sentencing Act 2020, s 57.

44 Sentencing Act 2020, s 58.

45 Section 142A of the Criminal Justice Act 2003 excluded the aim of deterrence for those under 18 but was never implemented for political reasons.

46 Sentencing Council, 'Sentencing children and young people' at https://sentencingcouncil.org.uk/guidelines/sentencing-children-and-young-people/.

assistance the prosecution and the defence provided to the sentencing judge. It should be a matter of routine for the defence to obtain a psychological assessment of a young client. If this was not done, it should be obtained immediately. Any assessment needs to be informed by background material that would include a full set of medical records, educational records, and any social services records. It may well be helpful to obtain details of previous offences that may aggravate sentence as prosecution summaries of these can be misleading.

MURDER AND THE RELEVANT STARTING POINTS

15.42 Revised starting points in murder cases are set out in the Sentencing Act 2020, Schedule 21, paragraph 5A,[47] and apply to any convictions on or after 28 June 2022. There is a sliding scale of statutory starting points as set out in the table below.

Age of offender when offence committed	Starting point supplied by para 3(1) had offender been 18	Starting point supplied by para 4(1) had offender been 18	Starting offender point by para 5 had been 18
17	27 years	23 years	14 years
15 or 16	20 years	17 years	10 years
14 or under	15 years	13 years	8 years

15.43 In the recent case of *R v Kamarra-Jarra*[48] the Court of Appeal agreed that an additional reduction should have been made given the age of the defendant:

> 'Cases involving the sentencing of young adults and children to very long terms of custody are always disturbing and anxious. It is not just age, but maturity and any other factors going to culpability, that matter when arriving at a final outcome that is just and proportionate in all the circumstances. That principle applies to the sentencing of young adults now, just as it did before the introduction of paragraph 5A in Schedule 21. Sentencing decisions cannot be prescribed by accidents of time.'

Whilst the recognition that young people must be afforded a greater reduction for those factors is welcome, it is still a concern that immature children and young people from particularly challenging backgrounds who have serious issues in addition to the usual vulnerabilities are receiving very long sentences

47 Introduced by the Police, Crime, Sentencing and Courts Act 2022, s 127.
48 [2024] EWCA Crim 198, para 54, per Carr LCJ.

indeed. That reflects the statutory framework that has been imposed but appeal lawyers should continue to identify for judges just how many factors apply in mitigation to allow then to move substantially away from the statutory starting points.

ASSESSING WHETHER TO APPEAL THE SENTENCE

15.44 When assessing an appeal against sentence involving someone under 18, you should consider what guidance and assistance was provided to the sentencing judge. A transcript of the mitigation should be considered. Read the judge's 'Sentencing Remarks' to identify what approach the sentencing judge took. This will indicate what material was, or was not, before the judge. There should have been a detailed sentencing note drawing attention to the relevant parts of the Guidelines and the material put in mitigation. Expert reports should have been obtained addressing any special psychological or psychiatric issues that may have been relevant. These experts should specialise in adolescent and child psychology or psychiatry as it is quite different to adult assessments. Social services and educational records should have been examined and referred to. The defence case papers should indicate from the proof of evidence and information from the parents or carers and other file enquiries whether the original solicitor did the necessary investigative work. If they did not, then you must get these records and consider obtaining these reports or other relevant material.

15.45 The Guidelines will only operate effectively if that material is obtained and considered. There are a lot of factors that can be deployed but they must be referenced with supporting material. The child or young person is unlikely to be a reliable historian, so the burden is on the solicitor. The payment of fixed fees has not incentivised solicitors to do this extra essential digging, but it must be done if a child or young person is to be treated in the holistic way the system is designed to achieve. It is always worth asking the child and their parents or carers for as much information as possible as this may lead you in the right direction. Interventions at school by educational psychologists or therapists and SEND assessments should be investigated. Check for any material that might point to a NRM referral.

FRESH EVIDENCE

15.46 The Court of Appeal will admit fresh evidence that is relevant to an issue of sentence. A recent example is a case where a diagnosis of ASD would have altered the judges' perception of the defendant:

> 'The judge did not have the benefit of Dr Yates and Dr Halsey's most recent reports as to the effect that ASD may have on a person's presentation, in particular the lack of emotion in that presentation and the effect that may have on any assessment of maturity. The judge regarded the applicant's inability to express emotion as a form of "cold" or "calculating" maturity. As convincingly explained by both Dr Yates and Dr Halsey, this may in fact be due to specific neurological deficits in how the applicant's brain processes social and emotional engagement. A "flat" or "cold" presentation may well not be an indication of being cold or calculating but instead reflect a difficulty with emotional recognition and expression, a core feature of the applicant's ASD.
>
> In our judgment, had this evidence been available the judge would have been bound to approach the reduction for the applicant's age more generously.'[49]

The Court reduced the sentence by one year and quashed the finding of dangerousness in light of signs of insight post sentence.

The important point to note is the expert material needs to address the specific grounds and be persuasive.

The Court will consider whether there are any issues relating to modern slavery.[50] Many children and young people enter the serious end of the criminal justice system as a result of adult exploitation.

REMAND TIME

15.47 A common appeal issue with children and young people is a failure to credit time whilst refused bail. In the case of a child or young person when an order is made to remand a child or young person to youth detention accommodation under section 91(4) of the Legal Aid Sentencing and Punishment of Offenders Act 2012 that time will automatically count towards any custodial sentence but not if they are simply remanded to Local Authority accommodation under section 91(3) when they may be subject to a qualifying curfew. In that case the court may allow for time depending on the circumstances and the restrictions on their liberty.[51] However, that will depend on the circumstances of the case and the court may refuse a downward reduction if they do not have sufficient evidence of the restrictions imposed whilst remanded.[52] So make sure you have sufficient material to persuade the Court.

49 *R v Malakai Wheeler* [2025] EWCA Crim 558.
50 *R v Daniel Kovalkov* [2023] EWCA Crim 1217, para 16–18.
51 *R v A* [2019] EWCA Crim 106.
52 *R v Sean Chibueze John* [2025] EWCA Crim 511.

ASSESSING WHETHER TO APPEAL A CONVICTION – ARTICLE 6 AND EFFECTIVE PARTICIPATION

15.48 The typical Crown Court was not designed to accommodate the needs of child defendants. The original Practice Direction for dealing with Children in the Crown Court that was issued in 2001 following *V&T v the UK* was seldom followed. Matters have improved in recent years and the Criminal Procedure Rules 2025 specify what measures should be considered to promote effective participation.[53] However, children are routinely seated behind screens in secure docks in the Crown Court when they should be sitting beside their parents and legal teams to promote better understanding of what is happening and communication with their lawyers.

Many advocates prefer not to have defendants in close proximity and are happy for them to remain in the dock. It is easier for the trial judge to allow them to stay in the secure dock on 'security grounds' even though there is little or no evidence of children trying to escape from courtrooms. In multi-handed cases where young people are grouped together behind a distant screen the dangers are far greater: often children act up and pretend to be unconcerned especially if they feel detached from the proceedings, they are also highly susceptible to peer pressure, and their behaviour can give a misleading appearance as they try to impress their peers and hide any fear.

15.49 The manner of cross-examination of children and young people who are defendants is often in stark contrast to that of vulnerable prosecution witnesses where ground rules hearings allow for extremely limited questioning in a very simple style. Common issues that arise with vulnerable defendants are addressed in the Advocates Gateway Toolkit and the Equal Treatment Bench Book. The use of an intermediary is an essential consideration and if missed when one was necessary, could give rise to a ground of appeal.

Although the case of *ZA*[54] dealt with a sentence appeal it did make strong statements as to the proper approach at trial and sentence generally when dealing with children and young people. May J concluded her judgment with a reminder of the importance of following the guidance for trying children and young people contained in the updated Practice Direction, the Youth Court Bench Book, and the Crown Court Compendium.[55]

15.50 The judgment in *Oni*[56] also recognised the need for greater clarity when the judge directs the jury on the facts it would be reasonable for a young defendant to mention in interview.[57] The Court suggested it would be a good

53 CrimPR(23)90(b), paras 6.4.3–6.4.6.
54 *R v ZA* [2023] EWCA Crim 596.
55 *ZA*, paras 85–88.
56 *R v Oni* (Justice intervening) [2025] EWCA Crim 12.
57 *R v Oni*, para 98.

idea for the prosecution to provide a list of such matters. The case also addressed the difficult issues of drill music and gang membership. It highlighted the importance of contextualising this evidence and warning juries 'not to convict any defendant largely upon the basis of this background evidence'.[58]

The Court of Appeal has been reluctant to find that difficulties the immature defendant experienced at trial have led to an unfair trial, but they have recognised the need for modification to the trial process for young people.[59] The Court will find it easier to dismiss appeals which make general criticisms, so it is vital that the expert evidence addresses the particular connection between the specific vulnerabilities of the defendant, the conduct of the trial and how that impacted upon the relevant issues that made the trial unfair.

SUMMARY OF KEY POINTS

- Expert evidence is key to understanding the client's vulnerabilities and how these impact on a fair trial and an appropriate sentence.
- Good background information is essential.
- Children are not 'mini-adults'.
- The Youth Court system has been built to address their needs, but the Crown Court has not.
- Many judges and lawyers are ignorant of the special considerations that apply to children and young people.
- The parallel overriding principles are the welfare of the young person and to prevent offending.
- The adversarial system is badly suited to serving these principles.
- The burden on solicitors and advocates is far greater.
- Many disadvantaged groups have poorer outcomes and appeal lawyers must identify and challenge the underlying reasons for this and educate the judiciary.

3 MODERN SLAVERY

INTRODUCTION

15.51 In recent years, practitioners will have encountered an increasing number of cases which engage the provisions of the Modern Slavery Act 2015 (MSA 2015). The MSA 2015 gave effect to a suite of international obligations

58 *R v Oni,* paras 108–111.
59 *R v Grant Murray* [2017] EWCA Crim 1228, para 110.

concerning the fight against compulsory labour and human trafficking, enacting criminal offences pertaining to slavery, servitude and human trafficking (sections 1 and 2) and also creating a statutory defence for victims of modern slavery or exploitation where certain criteria are met (section 45).

This chapter will not consider the criminal offences which have been created by the MSA 2015 in sections 1 and 2 but will focus on the operation of the statutory defence contained in section 45. The section 45 defence has now been examined by the Court of Appeal on several occasions – not just in relation to the ambit of the defence itself, but also in relation to the interaction between the defence, the CPS guidance, and the jurisdiction of abuse of process. Moreover, it is not uncommon for the CCRC to refer cases to the Court of Appeal on the basis that a defendant was not advised, or was advised incorrectly, about the availability of the section 45 defence at the time of their trial.

15.52 Preparation of a section 45 defence typically involves reference to various agencies and published guidance. It is therefore important for practitioners to familiarise themselves with the following matters when dealing with an appeal involving a client who is a potential victim of modern slavery:

- Modern Slavery Bill, Factsheet: Defence for victims (Clause 45) Home Office, November 2014;
- CPS Guidance: Modern Slavery and human trafficking: offences and defences, including the section 45 defence;
- CPS Guidance: County Lines Offending;
- Home Office statutory guidance: Modern Slavery: statutory guidance for England and Wales;
- The Law Society: Victims of modern slavery – guidance for solicitors.

At the time of writing, the key decisions of the Court of Appeal in relation to the section 45 defence are:

- *R v AFU*;[60]
- *R v AAD*;[61]
- *R v Brecani*.[62]

Background to the Modern Slavery Act 2015

15.53 Article 4 of the ECHR provides that no one shall be held in slavery or servitude, and no one shall be required to perform forced or compulsory

60 [2023] EWCA Crim 23.
61 [2022] EWCA Crim 106.
62 [2021] EWCA Crim 731.

labour. The protection afforded by Article 4 was transposed into domestic law by section 6 of the Human Rights Act 1998, which prohibits a public authority from acting in a manner incompatible with Article 4.

In addition, and of critical importance in the context of criminal appeals, Article 4 of the ECHR embraces a procedural obligation to investigate potential trafficking. The investigative requirement under Article 4 does not depend upon a potential victim making a complaint: once the matter has come to the attention of the relevant authorities 'they must act of their own motion. And, in order for the prosecution of an actual or potential victim of trafficking to respect the freedoms guaranteed by Article 4, their early identification is of paramount importance': *Rantsev v (1) Cyprus; (2) Russia*[63] at [288]; *VCL and AN v United Kingdom*[64] at [160]; *R v AFU*[65] at [81].

15.54 Article 4 of the ECHR operates in tandem with other international instruments which have been adopted by the UK. The UK is also a party to the UN Protocol to Prevent, Suppress and Punish Trafficking in Persons 2000 (the Palermo Protocol) and the 2005 Council of Europe Convention on Action against Trafficking in Human Beings (ECAT). Article 26 of ECAT provides:

> 'Each Party shall, in accordance with the basic principles of its legal system, provide for the possibility of not imposing penalties on victims for their involvement in unlawful activities, to the extent that they have been compelled to do so.'

On 6 April 2013, Directive 2011/36 of the European Parliament and of the Council of 5 April 2011 on preventing and combating trafficking in human beings and protecting its victims (the Directive) came into force in the UK. Article 8 of the Directive provides:

> 'Member States shall, in accordance with the basic principles of their legal systems, take the necessary measures to ensure that competent national authorities are entitled not to prosecute or impose penalties on victims of trafficking in human beings for their involvement in criminal activities which they have been compelled to commit as a direct consequence of being subjected to [trafficking] …'

15.55 To achieve the aim of the effective identification of victims of trafficking, the UK established the National Referral Mechanism (NRM) which provides a framework for referrals of potential victims by 'first responders'. First responders include police officers, immigration officers, local authorities, and the National Crime Agency. Referrals to the NRM are considered by the relevant competent authority within the Home Office.

63 (25965/04) (2010) 51 EHRR 1.
64 (2021) 73 EHRR 9, [2021] Crim LR 586.
65 [2023] EWCA Crim 23, [2023] 1 Cr App R 16.

It is important to note that referrals are not just made on behalf of foreign nationals but are often made on behalf of UK nationals. In the criminal justice context, many referrals are made in relation to British children who have been exploited by county lines drug gangs. The Government's Serious Violence Strategy (2018) defines county lines exploitation as follows:

> 'County lines is a term used to describe gangs and organised criminal networks involved in exporting illegal drugs into one or more importing areas within the UK, using dedicated mobile phone lines or other form of "deal line". They are likely to exploit children and vulnerable adults to move and store the drugs and money and they will often use coercion, intimidation, violence (including sexual violence) and weapons.'

15.56 Once a referral is made to the NRM, an intelligence gathering exercise will take place. The first stage is that the Competent Authority will issue a 'reasonable grounds' decision as to whether someone is or was a victim of modern slavery. If the decision is positive, the Competent Authority will move to the final stage and decide if there are 'conclusive grounds' that the individual is or was a victim of modern slavery.

Practitioners will need no reminder of the delay which has beset the NRM referral process and which, in turn – at least for a period – led to trials being delayed pending a defendant's resolution of the NRM process. Such delay was no doubt driven in significant part by an increase in the volume of referrals received by the NRM. By way of example, in 2016 the NRM received 3,805 referrals. By 2024, the number of referrals had increased to 19,125.

In both 2023 and 2024, the most common type of NRM referral for UK nationals was male children who reported criminal exploitation.

THE MODERN SLAVERY DEFENCE

15.57 The UK enacted protection for victims of modern slavery and exploitation through section 45 of the MSA 2015, which came into force on 31 July 2015 and applies to all relevant offences committed after that date. Schedule 4 to the MSA 2015 sets out the offences to which the section 45 defence does not apply – including the common law offences of kidnap, manslaughter and murder, and certain offences under the Offences Against the Person Act 1861, the Firearms Act 1968 and the Theft Act 1968.

Practitioners may find that it is commonly prosecutions for drug-related offences which will involve a defendant who may be a victim of modern slavery or exploitation and whose interests are met by raising the defence.

Section 45 provides:

> '(1) A person is not guilty of an offence if—

(a) the person is aged 18 or over when the person does the act which constitutes the offence.

(b) the person does that act because he is compelled to do it.

(c) the compulsion is attributable to slavery or to relevant exploitation, and

(d) a reasonable person in the same situation as the person and having the person's relevant characteristics would have no realistic alternative to doing that act.

(2) A person may be compelled to do something by another person or by the person's circumstances.

(3) Compulsion is attributable to slavery or to relevant exploitation only if—

(a) it is, or is part of, conduct which constitutes an offence under section 1 or conduct which constitutes relevant exploitation, or

(b) it is a direct consequence of a person being, or having been, a victim of slavery or a victim of relevant exploitation.

(4) A person is not guilty of an offence if—

(a) the person is under the age of 18 when the person does the act which constitutes the offence,

(b) the person does that act as a direct consequence of the person being, or having been, a victim of slavery or a victim of relevant exploitation, and

(c) a reasonable person in the same situation as the person and having the person's relevant characteristics would do that act.

(5) For the purposes of this section—

'relevant characteristics' means age, sex and any physical or mental illness or disability;

'relevant exploitation' is exploitation … that is attributable to the exploited person being, or having been, a victim of human trafficking.'

Procedure: are there indicators that the defendant was a victim of trafficking or exploitation?

15.58 It is for the defendant to raise evidence of each of the elements in section 45(1) and for the prosecution to disprove one or more of them to the criminal standard: *R v MK; R v Gega*[66] at [45]. Common indicators that a defendant was compelled to commit the offence because they were a victim of modern slavery (or, if a child, committed the offence as a direct consequence of it) include:

- *Lack of freedom/transient living arrangements* – a defendant may be reluctant to indicate where they live and may be restricted in when they can leave the property.
- *Poor living conditions* – a defendant may be living in overcrowded and poor conditions with limited facilities.
- *Personal belongings* – a defendant may have limited or no belongings including no identity documents.
- *Communication* – a defendant may have limited language skills and have third parties who speak on their behalf or 'manage' their lives for them.
- *Working hours* – a defendant may work unusually long hours including being directed to work very late at night and may be sent to different parts of the country.
- *County lines* – a defendant may persistently be missing from school, spend lengthy periods of time out of their local area, be unwilling to explain their whereabouts, carry weapons and have multiple phones and/or sim cards and clothing or belongings the cost of which is unaccounted for.

Whilst there is a clear overlap between the considerations which are relevant to the defence of duress and those relevant to the section 45 defence, the Court of Appeal has observed: 'The defence of duress and the statutory defence are not identical, and in some circumstances the latter may succeed even though the former fails'.[67]

15.59 The CPS guidance includes the following key principle:

> 'In all cases involving suspects/defendants who might be victims of modern slavery, prosecutors should adopt a four-stage approach, to ensure that their review of a case fully and properly applies relevant considerations set out in the Code for Crown Prosecutors.'

The four-stage test applied by the CPS is as follows:[68]

> '• Is there a reason to believe that the person is a victim of modern slavery?

66 [2018] EWCA Crim 667, [2018] 2 Cr App R 14.

67 *Lurdita Baniulyte* [2025] EWCA Crim 1205 at [79].

68 See CPS Guidance at https://www.cps.gov.uk/prosecution-guidance/modern-slavery-and-human-trafficking-offences-and-defences-including-section.

   - If yes, move to Question 2.
   - If not, you do not need to consider this assessment further.
- Is there clear evidence of a credible common law defence of duress?
   - If yes, then the case should not be charged or should be discontinued on evidential grounds.
   - If not, move to Question 3.
- Is there clear evidence of a statutory defence under section 45 of the 2015 Act?
   - If yes, then the case should not be charged or should be discontinued on evidential grounds
   - If not, move to Question 4.
- Is it in the public interest to prosecute? This must be considered even where there is no clear evidence of duress, or all the elements of the statutory defence under section 45, or where the offence is excluded under Schedule 4.'

Decisions of the Competent Authority

15.60 Where a defendant is in receipt of a positive decision of the Competent Authority by the time of their trial, it is no longer the case that such decisions are admissible before the jury: *R v Brecani*.[69] However, such decisions are admissible on appeal when it is contended that a defendant's trafficking status has been overlooked or inadequately considered by the prosecution.

Whilst the decisions of the Competent Authority are not binding upon a criminal court, its decisions will usually be respected unless there is good reason not to do so. However, there may be cases where it is necessary for an applicant's account to be tested independently for the purposes of safe resolution of the issues on appeal; for example, where a finding of trafficking is based on unsatisfactory evidence: *R v AAD*[70] at [108]; *R v AFU*[71] at [88]; *R v BRP*.[72]

The decision of the Competent Authority must be considered by the CPS. If the decision is taken to prosecute, even though there is a conclusive grounds decision that the suspect is a trafficked victim, clear reasons must be recorded, setting out the rationale for that decision.

69 [2021] EWCA Crim 731, [2021] 2 Cr App R 12.
70 [2022] EWCA Crim 106, [2022] 1 Cr App R 19.
71 [2023] EWCA Crim 23, [2023] 1 Cr App R 16.
72 [2023] EWCA Crim 40.

Decisions of other courts

15.61 A decision of a tribunal or court, where a finding of fact is made based on evidence, may be admissible to assess the prospects of a defence succeeding, or in the context of abuse of process proceedings for reviewing the decision of a prosecutor: see *R v Sadighpour*[73] at [35] to [36]; *R v Mateta*[74] at [23]; *AFU* (supra) at [89]. For example, a defendant may be in receipt of a decision from an immigration tribunal which contains findings of fact relevant to the question of whether they were a victim of modern slavery at the relevant time.

Expert evidence

15.62 The extent to which expert evidence can be of assistance when assessing an account of trafficking will likely depend on the extent to which it relies on the accuracy of an individual's untested account of events: see for example *R v N; R v L*[75] at [86(c)]; and *R v Joseph (Verna)*[76] at [67].

Abuse of process

15.63 The combined effect of the UK's implementation of the international instruments referred to above (Article 4 of the ECHR, ECAT and the Directive) meant that English law underwent a significant change in respect of the required approach of the CPS to victims of trafficking and modern slavery. This change has operated so as to engage the question of the criminal courts' jurisdiction of abuse of process, if identification of a person as a victim of trafficking is not made until after conviction.

In *R v AAD*, the Court of Appeal considered the question of whether it was still possible, following the arrival of the MSA 2015, to argue on appeal that prosecution of a victim of modern slavery was an abuse of process. At [142] to [143], the court held that the jurisdiction to stay for abuse of process on appeal had not been curtailed by section 45. The jurisdiction remains 'an additional safeguard, given appropriately exceptional facts … Cases of abuse of process will be (as they always should have been) very rare in this context and can arise in only very limited circumstances'.[77]

73 [2012] EWCA Crim 2669, [2013] 1 Cr App R 20.
74 [2013] EWCA Crim 1372, [2013] 2 Cr App R 35.
75 [2012] EWCA Crim 189, [2012] 1 Cr App R 35.
76 [2017] EWCA Crim 36, [2017] 1 Cr App R 33.
77 [2022] EWCA Crim 106, [2022] 1 Cr App R 19 at [143].

The operation of the jurisdiction of abuse of process in this context has been considered by the Court of Appeal in several significant decisions: *R v L(C)*;[78] *R v LM*[79] and *R v N/L*.[80]

15.64 There is no blanket immunity from prosecution for victims of modern slavery, even if they are in receipt of a positive decision from the Competent Authority: *R v S(G)*[81] at [76(i)]. When practitioners are dealing with a potential appeal against conviction for a potential or actual victim of modern slavery, the relevant enquiry is whether, had the prosecution known the true facts, the prosecution would not have (or might well not have) been maintained in the public interest. The Court of Appeal formulated the test in *R v S(G)* at [76(v)] as follows:[82]

> 'As always, the question for this court goes to the safety of the conviction. However, in the present context, that inquiry translates into a question of whether in the light of the law as it now is (this being a rare change in law case) and the facts now known as to the applicant (having regard to the admission of fresh evidence) the trial court should have stayed the proceedings as an abuse of process had an application been made. This question can be formulated indistinguishably in one of two ways which emerge from the authorities: was this a case where either: (1) the dominant force of compulsion, in the context of a very serious offence, was sufficient to reduce the applicant's criminality or culpability to or below a point where it was not in the public interest for her to be prosecuted? or (2) the applicant would or might well not have been prosecuted in the public interest? If yes, then the proper course would be to quash the conviction …'

In *R v BXR*[83] the Court of Appeal explained the necessary degree of 'nexus' between the trafficking and the commission of the offence as follows:

> 'Where there is no reasonable nexus, generally the conviction should not be set aside. At the other end of the scale, where the nexus is such that in reality culpability is extinguished, the conviction should normally be set aside. In between these examples at either end of the scale are cases in which there is a degree of causative connection between the trafficking and the offending. Whether it is sufficient to make it contrary to the public interest to prosecute will depend upon the extent to which it reduces the defendant's culpability for the offending.'

78 [2013] EWCA Crim 991, [2013] 2 Cr App R 23.
79 [2010] EWCA Crim 2327.
80 [2012] EWCA Crim 189.
81 [2018] EWCA Crim 1824, [2019] 1 Cr App R 7.
82 See also *R v BXR* [2022] EWCA Crim 1483 at [19] and *R v AGM* [2022] EWCA Crim 920 at [11].
83 [2022] EWCA Crim 1483.

15.65 The degree to which the prosecution has complied with CPS guidance will be relevant. Where the prosecution has applied its mind to the relevant questions in accordance with the guidance, it will not generally be an abuse of process to prosecute unless the decision to do so is 'clearly flawed': *R v AGM* at [12] and *R v BYA*[84] at [20].

However, if the CPS guidance has been disregarded, such that the question of whether to prosecute has not been properly considered (or considered at all), the court can intervene: *R v AGM* at [13] and [56]. It will then be open to the court to consider the question of the applicant's prosecution in the public interest.

Appeals

15.66 The Court of Appeal is now frequently called upon to consider appeals against conviction brought by defendants who were not advised about the availability of the section 45 defence at the time of their prosecution. In the context of modern slavery, such cases may well involve a defendant who entered a guilty plea to the index offence(s).

Often, such appeals will involve consideration of, first, whether the defendant's guilty plea was vitiated by inadequate legal advice, and/or second, whether the original proceedings were an abuse of process either because the prosecution was obviously inconsistent with the prosecution's duties in relation to victims of modern slavery or because, had the prosecution known of the true facts, the case may well have been brought to an end.

In respect of cases involving a guilty plea, the Court of Appeal has now considered several appeals against conviction on the ground that, through incorrect advice or a lack of advice, the statutory defence under section 45 was not advanced at trial. In *R v BTE*.[85] the Court of Appeal at [24] confirmed that an appellant must show he or she was: '… deprived of a defence that quite probably would have succeeded, such that a clear injustice has been done.'

15.67 The critical question for practitioners when faced with a potential appeal based on section 45 is: what was known by the parties before and during the trial? For that reason, it is likely that many appeals of this nature will require a waiver of privilege and will require an application to admit fresh evidence pursuant to section 23 of the Criminal Appeal Act 1968. It will also be critical to establish whether the defendant ever sought a referral to the NRM and if not, why not.

Practitioners should also consider obtaining the following, if relevant and available:

84 [2022] EWCA Crim 1326.
85 [2022] EWCA Crim 1597.

- decision(s) of the Competent Authority;
- psychological or psychiatric assessment of the defendant;
- any relevant decisions of the Home Office in relation to the defendant's status – such documents as being relevant to what account a defendant has given about the circumstances of their arrival and experience in the UK;
- any decision of the First-Tier Tribunal in respect of the defendant;
- a witness statement from the defendant explaining the circumstances under which they committed the index offence, what they told their solicitors and counsel before and during their prosecution, and what advice they were given about the availability of a defence.

Anonymity

15.68 The principles which apply to applicants seeking anonymity as victims of modern slavery on appeal were recently set out by the Court of Appeal in *R v Baniulyte*[86] *at* [111] and can be summarised as follows:

- no statutory provision imposes automatic reporting restrictions in favour of an adult accused who puts forward a defence under section 45 of the MSA 2015. An order derogating from open justice should therefore not be made on a routine basis. As in any other case, a person seeking anonymity bears the burden of demonstrating by cogent evidence why a derogation is strictly necessary;
- any application for anonymity must be made when the application for leave to appeal is lodged. The Criminal Appeal Office can then arrange for the applicant's name to be replaced by a cipher for listing and other purposes: that will be a convenient safeguard, but does not imply that the court will necessarily grant the application;
- the application must set out the order that is sought, the jurisdiction under which it can be made, and why it is strictly necessary for the order to be granted;
- any application for an anonymity order (and reporting restrictions) must be supported by evidence which establishes convincingly the need for the derogation(s) sought;
- if anonymity is sought on the grounds that the applicant has been anonymised in other proceedings, full details of those proceedings, and a copy of the order granting anonymity, must be provided. If it is contended that there is a risk of 'jigsaw identification' if an anonymity

86 [2025] EWCA Crim 1205.

order is not granted, the nature of that risk and how it arises must be explained and demonstrated;

- the evidence submitted in support of the application must explain the extent to which there has been reporting of the identity of the person seeking anonymity and reporting restrictions as a result of the proceedings at first instance;
- when the case comes before this court for hearing, it will generally be appropriate to address the issue of anonymisation at the outset;
- the court must make a fact-specific assessment of the competing rights which are in issue, and determine whether the applicant has established that it is strictly necessary to derogate from open justice;
- the court should ensure that any withholding order and/or reporting restrictions are clearly stated in the orders made and explained in the judgment.

SUMMARY OF KEY POINTS

- Section 45 of the MSA 2015 creates a statutory defence for adults and children where the defendant committed the offence as a result of being a victim of modern slavery or exploitation.
- The statutory defence does not apply to the offences listed in Schedule 4 to the MSA 2015.
- The defendant bears an evidential burden of raising a section 45 defence.
- Persons who may be victims of modern slavery can be referred to the NRM for a decision by the Competent Authority as to whether there are reasonable grounds to believe that they were a victim of modern slavery.
- If the Competent Authority concludes that there are reasonable grounds to so believe, the Competent Authority goes on to consider if there are conclusive grounds.
- The decision of the Competent Authority is generally not admissible at trial but is admissible on appeal to the Court of Appeal.
- A positive Conclusive Grounds decision does not confer blanket immunity from prosecution based on section 45 of the MSA 2015 nor does it provide an automatic basis on which an appeal against conviction will be allowed.
- If there are indicators that the defendant committed the offences as a result of being a victim of modern slavery, was that known at the time of the defendant's prosecution?
- If it was known, was the defendant advised of the availability of a section 45 defence?

- If they were not, and the prosecution had known of the true facts, might the CPS have declined to prosecute?
- A defendant is not entitled to anonymity on an appeal against conviction.

4 PROTEST

INTRODUCTION

15.69 In recent years, the Court of Appeal and Supreme Court have considered several prominent appeals against conviction and sentence which engage the right to protest. A number of these appeals have involved consideration of the compatibility of prosecutions with the provisions of the ECHR. A detailed examination of the appellate courts' development of the law relating to the ambit of certain legal defences and Convention-compatibility is beyond the scope of this chapter. This chapter will summarise the three main headlines which emerge from the recent case law and which practitioners may be asked to advise about on appeal:

- proportionality;
- the withdrawal of legal defences from the jury;
- sentencing.

At the time of writing, key cases in this area in recent years include:

- *R v Hallam*;[87]
- *R v Casserly*;[88]
- *Attorney General's Reference (No 1 of 2023)*;[89]
- *R v Trowland*;[90]
- *PWR v Director of Public Prosecutions*;[91]
- *Abortion Services*;[92]
- *Attorney General's Reference (No 1 of 2022)*;[93]
- *DPP v Cuciurean*;[94]

87 [2025] EWCA Crim 199, [2025] 2 Cr App R (S) 17.
88 [2024] EWCA Crim 25, [2024] 1 Cr App R 18.
89 [2024] EWCA Crim 243, [2024] 2 Cr App R 2.
90 [2023] EWCA Crim 919; [2024] 1 Cr App R (S) 13.
91 [2022] UKSC 2.
92 *Reference by the Attorney General for Northern Ireland – Abortion Services (Safe Access Zones) (Northern Ireland) Bill* [2022] UKSC 32.
93 [2022] EWCA Crim 1259, [2023] 1 Cr App R 1.
94 [2022] EWHC 736 (Admin), [2022] 2 Cr App R 8.

15.70 *Special cases*

- *R v Brown*;[95]
- *DPP v Ziegler*;[96]
- *R v Thacker*.[97]

Proportionality

15.70 Protest cases typically involve defendants who are charged with public order offences – most commonly: criminal damage; aggravated trespass; public nuisance at common law; public nuisance contrary to section 78(1) of the Police, Crime, Sentencing and Courts Act 2022; wilful obstruction of a highway without lawful authority or excuse contrary to section 137(1) of the Highways Act 1980; and conspiracies to commit the same.

Most protest cases do not involve allegations of violence against the person and will typically involve defendants who have engaged in peaceful protest/assembly in support or promotion of a cause. Many prosecutions may engage the ECHR and, in particular, Articles 10 and 11. In general terms, the ECHR is relevant to whether a conviction would be a proportionate interference with the defendant's rights.

It is increasingly common for trial judges to give pre-trial rulings on the question of proportionality. Practitioners will therefore want to review any such rulings when advising on appeal.

Case law

15.71 In a series of detailed decisions since 2021, the Court of Appeal and Supreme Court have examined the parameters within which a defendant can require a criminal court to assess whether a conviction would be a proportionate interference with their rights under the Convention. What follows below is a summary of the principles which have emerged from these decisions – in particular, the decisions of *Casserly*,[98] *Abortion Services*,[99] *Attorney General's Reference No 1 of 2023*[100] and *Attorney General's Reference No 1 of 2022*.[101]

95 [2022] EWCA Crim 6, [2022] 1 Cr App R 18.
96 [2021] UKSC 23, [2022] AC 408.
97 [2021] EWCA Crim 97.
98 [2024] EWCA Crim 25. Whilst *Casserly* is not a protest case, it is submitted that the Court's ruling in relation to proportionality is relevant to any prosecution which engages the right to free speech.
99 [2022] UKSC 32.
100 2024] EWCA Crim 243.
101 [2022] EWCA Crim 1259.

- Where the exercise of rights under Articles 9 to 11 ECHR is raised by the defendant in a criminal prosecution, there does not always have to be an assessment of the proportionality of any interference with those rights on the facts of the case: *Abortion Services* at [34], [42], [53].
- The case law which deals with the prosecution of speech or behaviour that is politically motivated has led to the identification of three broad categories of case (*Casserly* at [44]):
  - (i) those in which, on a proper analysis, the applicable criminal law does not interfere with fundamental rights at all, so that there is no need for any proportionality assessment;
  - (ii) those in which the criminal law does or may interfere with such rights but proof of the ingredients of the offence will, without more, be sufficient to render a conviction proportionate;
  - (iii) those in which the law does or may interfere with fundamental rights, but the ingredients of the offence do not of themselves meet the proportionality requirement, so that the court is required to address it.
- Criminal damage does not automatically fall within the category of offences whereby proof of the ingredients of the offence is sufficient to justify any criminal conviction as a proportionate interference with the Convention, without the need for a fact-specific proportionality assessment: *Attorney General's Reference No 1 of 2022*[102] at [116].
- Prosecution and conviction for causing *significant* damage to property during protest will fall outside the protection of the ECHR, either because the conduct in question is violent or not peaceful, or because prosecution and conviction would clearly be proportionate. The circumstances in which a proportionality assessment is needed will be very limited: *Attorney General's Reference No 1 of 2022* at [115].
- It is possible that cases involving minor or trivial damage to property will arise in the magistrates' court. In those circumstances, the Strasbourg case law suggests that conviction may not be a proportionate interference with the right to protest. The ECHR cannot be used to protect from prosecution and conviction those who damage private property to any degree other than trivial. *Attorney General's Reference No 1 of 2022* at [121].
- The third category identified in *Casserly* includes cases where 'the interpretative duty imposed by section 3 of the Human Rights Act may enable the court to construe the relevant provision in a way which renders it compatible with the Convention rights'. This may involve 'interpreting

102 [2022] EWCA Crim 1259.

it so as to allow for an assessment of the proportionality of a conviction in the circumstances of individual cases'; *Casserly* at [45]; *Abortion Services* at [57].

- It is essential that prosecutorial discretion on whether to proceed to trial should be exercised carefully, applying the Code for Crown Prosecutors in the context of the principles governing Articles 9, 10 and 11 with a clear eye on the proportionality of prosecution and conviction: *Attorney General's Reference No 1 of 2022* at [121].

Withdrawal of defences from the jury

15.72 Many protest cases now involve the question of whether a defendant is entitled to have certain legal defences left to the jury. This question most commonly arises where a defendant (typically, charged with criminal damage) raises the following:

- prevention of crime (Criminal Law Act 1967, section 3(1));
- belief in consent/protection of property (Criminal Damage Act 1971, section 5(2)(a)/(b));
- necessity/duress of circumstances at common law.

Practitioners may be asked to consider cases in which the prosecution applied successfully for any or all of these defences to be withdrawn from the jury. It is now increasingly common for such applications to be made and determined long before the trial begins. The following principles are relevant:

- an issue may be withdrawn from the jury if no reasonable jury properly directed could reach a particular conclusion: *Attorney General's Reference (No 1 of 2022)*[103] at [118]; *Attorney General's Reference (No 1 of 2023)*;[104] at [64];
- an issue should not be withdrawn from the jury for lack of evidence until the close of the case of the party who would be adversely affected by the withdrawal of the issue;
- if an issue is withdrawn at an earlier stage, exceptional care should be taken, bearing in mind that not all of the evidence will have been heard, and that it is for the jury to assess the evidence: *Attorney General's Reference (No 1 of 2023)* at [64].

103 [2023] EWCA Crim 243.
104 [2024] EWCA Crim 243.

SECTION 3 OF THE CRIMINAL LAW ACT 1967 (PREVENTION OF CRIME)

15.73 In *R (on application of DPP) v Stratford Magistrates Court*,[105] the Divisional Court considered the limits of the section 3 defence in the context of the right to protest and held as follows:

- the defence of prevention of crime involves a justification for the use of force, not an excuse to use it, and is linked to necessity;
- the defence requires an apprehension of a need to use force to prevent an imminent or immediate crime, with a clear nexus between the use of force and the prevention of crime. There is a clear difference between a protest against objectionable or even illegal conduct, and the use of force to prevent an imminent or immediate crime;
- where a defendant raises the section 3 defence, the court should consider whether the defence is available on the most favourable view of the facts; if there is no proper evidential basis on which it could be available, it should be withdrawn from consideration by the trier of fact.

SECTION 5(2)(A) AND (B) OF THE CRIMINAL DAMAGE ACT 1971

15.74 Section 5(2) of the Criminal Damage Act 1971 creates two statutory defences, commonly known as 'belief in consent' and 'protection of property'. In short, the former defence arises where a defendant believed that the person/persons whom they believed to be entitled to consent to the damage to the property in question had so consented, or would have so consented, if they had known of the damage 'and its circumstances'.[106]

The latter defence arises where a defendant damaged property and at the time of the act or acts alleged to constitute the offence they believed: (i) that the property, right or interest was in immediate need of protection; and (ii) that the means of protection adopted or proposed to be adopted were or would be reasonable having regard to all the circumstances.[107]

15.75 The Court of Appeal has recently examined the elements of the section 5(2)(a) defence in the context of protest cases. The following principles are relevant:

105 [2017] EWHC 1794 (Admin).
106 Criminal Damage Act 1971, s 5(2)(a).
107 Criminal Damage Act 1971, s 5(2)(b).

- The extent to which the exercise of the right to protest provides a defence to a criminal charge depends on the precise nature of the criminal offence and the available defences: *Attorney General's Reference (No 1 of 2023)* at [33]. The fact that a case was a protest case does not affect the proper construction of section 5(2)(a).
- In relation to the words of the provision 'at the time of the act or acts alleged to constitute the offence', the defendant's belief must be held at the time of the commission of the offence.
- The belief must be genuine in that it is honestly held; it does not need to be objectively justified: section 5(3). It follows that this element of the defence involves a subjective test.
- The defendant must believe that the owner of the property in question either had consented or would have consented to the damage if they had known of the damage 'and its circumstances'. The inclusion of the phrase 'would have' involved a certainty in the belief in the owner's consent, not merely that the owner might (or should) have consented. There was therefore a requirement that the defendant's honest belief must be that they were sure that the owner would have consented: *Attorney General's Reference (No 1 of 2023)* at [42].
- Only the circumstances of the damage are relevant. This can include the time, place and the extent of the damage caused. In protest cases, damage and 'its circumstances' includes the fact that the damage was caused as part of a protest against a particular cause.
- The need for a direct nexus between the circumstances of the damage and the anticipated giving of consent is implicit in the statutory language. The circumstances had to belong to the damage, not to the defendant. To that extent, there is an objective element to the defence: *Attorney General's Reference (No 1 of 2023)* at [46].

To establish the lawful excuse of protecting property under section 5(2)(b), the act of damage must be capable of conferring immediate protection on the property concerned. An act whose purpose was to pressure a public authority or official to act to protect property was not capable of immediate protection, as it required too many intermediate steps: *R v Ditchfield*.[108]

NECESSITY

15.76 The common law defence of necessity was considered by the Court of Appeal in *Re A (Children) (Conjoined Twins: Surgical Separation)*:[109]

108 [2021] EWHC 1090 Admin.
109 [2001] Fam 147 and defined at [240].

> 'According to Sir James Stephen there are three necessary requirements for the application of the doctrine of necessity: (i) the act is needed to avoid inevitable and irreparable evil; (ii) no more should be done than is reasonably necessary for the purpose to be achieved; (iii) the evil inflicted must not be disproportionate to the evil avoided.'

In *R v Martin (Colin)*,[110] the Court of Appeal described two limbs to the defence:

> '... assuming the defence to be open to the accused on his account of the facts, the issue should be left to the jury, who should be directed to determine these two questions: first, was the accused, or may he have been, impelled to act as he did because as a result of what he reasonably believed to be the situation he had good cause to fear that otherwise death or serious physical injury would result? Second, if so, may a sober person of reasonable firmness, sharing the characteristics of the accused, have responded to that situation by acting as the accused acted? If the answer to both those questions was yes, then the jury would acquit: the defence of necessity would have been established.'

Both formulations were applied in the case of *R v Thacker*[111] in which the Court of Appeal upheld the trial judge's withdrawal of the defence of necessity in relation to the 'Stansted 15' protesters.

Sentencing in protest cases

15.77 Sentencing for protest cases has undergone significant change in recent years. It is now more common for protesters to receive sentences of immediate imprisonment and for those sentences to be measured in years rather than months. At the time of writing, the case of *R* v *Trowland*[112] represents the longest sentence imposed for a non-violent protest offence in modern times, namely, a sentence of three years' imprisonment for an offence of causing a public nuisance contrary to section 78 of the Police, Crime, Sentencing and Courts Act 2022. In that case, the Court of Appeal set out general principles which arise in cases of non-violent protest:

- It was not part of the judicial function to evaluate the merit of the cause in support of which a protest was made. A conscientious motive on the part of protesters might be a relevant consideration, in particular where the offender was a law-abiding citizen apart from their protest activities and, in such cases, a lesser sanction might be appropriate.
- The more disproportionate or extreme the action taken by the protester, the less obvious the justification for reduced culpability and more lenient

110 (1989) 88 Cr App R 343, at p 346.
111 [2021] EWCA Crim 97.
112 [2023] EWCA Crim 919.

sentencing. Whether a sentence of immediate custody was warranted was highly fact-sensitive.[113]

- The judge's starting point does not have to be a non-custodial sentence.

15.78 In *R v Hallam*,[114] the Court of Appeal further considered the correct approach to sentencing in cases involving non-violent protests and set out the following 'central points of principle' in light of the decision in *R v Trowland*:[115]

- The correct approach to potential issues when sentencing in cases of non-violent protests, such as conscientious motivation and deterrence is set out in *R v Trowland.*
- The sentencing exercise should not be over-complicated because of engagement of the ECHR. Whether the Convention rights are engaged should be simple; if engaged, the court can carry out what should be a straightforward proportionality exercise.
- References to sentencing outcomes in different cases is unlikely to be helpful. The three-year custodial sentence imposed in *Trowland* was not a tariff. Although upheld on appeal, it was held to be severe and arguably manifestly excessive. An approach that treated a three-year term for offending as a benchmark risked undesirable and unwarranted sentence inflation.

15.79 The Court in addition held the following relevant principles:

- A defendant's conscientious motivation is a relevant factor. Conscientious motivation fell most logically to be factored into the culpability assessment, but did not preclude a finding that an appellant's culpability was high.
- A sentencing judge is not obliged to specify the amount by which a custodial term has been reduced to reflect a defendant's conscientious motivation.
- A trespassing protester does not automatically lose their Convention rights. However, the fact that a defendant's expressions of opinion involved criminal trespass significantly weakened the protections afforded by Articles 10 and 11 of the ECHR, and therefore the weight to be attached to those protections when considering proportionality of sentence.

113 Paragraphs 47 and 50–51.
114 [2025] EWCA Crim 199.
115 [2023] EWCA Crim 919.

SUMMARY OF KEY POINTS

- Prosecutions for criminal damage in the Crown Court, even in the context of non-violent protest, will ordinarily not require a proportionality assessment in order to determine Convention-compatibility. This is because the damage involved is unlikely to be trivial.
- Where a defendant in a protest case raises a defence under the Criminal Law Act 1967, section 3, the Criminal Damage Act 1971, section 5 and necessity at common law, it has become increasingly common for the Prosecution to invite the court to withdraw the defence before the evidence has been heard.
- Exceptional care should be taken by a judge when ruling on the availability of a defence before the evidence has been heard. When considering such an application, a judge should assess the availability of the defence by reference to the most favourable view of the facts.
- Sentencing in non-violent protest cases has hardened in recent years, with immediate custodial sentences becoming more common. However, a defendant's conscientious motivation is something which the court should take into account in their favour.

Appendix A

Guide to Proceedings in the Court of Appeal, Criminal Division

Current version March 2026

TABLE OF CONTENTS

INTRODUCTION

The purpose of this guide is to bring together the relevant Criminal Procedure Rules (CrimPR), Criminal Practice Directions 2023[1] (CPD), legislation and authorities[2] to provide guidance to practitioners on commencing proceedings (conviction, sentence and confiscation[3]) in the Court of Appeal, Criminal Division and the key stages of the appeal process including case management. The guidance is complemented by annex 1 which contains practical assistance on the presentation, format and submission of documents. The guide is updated periodically and users should access the most recent via The Court of Appeal, Criminal Division – Courts and Tribunals Judiciary.

The Registrar[4] has a duty of active case management (CrimPR 3.2 and 36.2 (2)) but there is also a duty on the parties to actively assist to progress cases[5] (CrimPR 36.2 (1)). Close contact between representatives, parties and the Criminal Appeal Office (CAO) is encouraged to facilitate the efficient preparation and listing of appeals, especially in complex cases and those involving witnesses.

It is important to note that practitioners **must** comply with the CrimPR and CPD which are the law and binding on the courts (CPD 1.1.3 – 1.1.5). The CPD also states that practitioners **must** comply with any additional guidance or direction set down by the Registrar in this guide (CPD 10.1.1, 10.8.15).

The Registrar is supported by a team of lawyers, summary writers, caseworkers and administrative staff. The CAO is paperless and uses two dedicated sections on the Digital Case System (DCS); CACD1 for relevant documents generated in preparation of the appeal. CACD2 contains private documentation for the judges. In non-DCS cases the CAO uses the eJudiciary Document Upload Centre (DUC).[6]

Users must not upload any documents to CACD1. Any appeal documentation such as transcripts must not be uploaded to DCS but lodged with the CAO.

1 As amended November 2025: Crimin\al Procedure Rules 2025 and Criminal Practice Directions 2023 – GOV.UK

2 Predominately CrimPR 36 & 39, CPD 10 and the Criminal Appeal Act 1968. Where possible information on funding is given at the relevant stage.

3 See notes to CrimPR 39.1 which contains a comprehensive list and annex 2 for other types of appeal.

4 The responsibilities and powers of Registrar of Criminal Appeals are contained in the Criminal Appeal Act 1968, CrimPR and CPD.

5 See CPD 10.3.5 for CAO/CACD target times. See also A Review of the Year in the Court of Appeal, Criminal Division (October 2023 – September 2024) – Courts and Tribunals Judiciary for annual statistic.

6 See annex 1.

On receipt of an appeal notice and accompanying documents, a file reference is generated, and the case is allocated to a lawyer and/or caseworker depending on the nature of the application (CrimPR 3.4 and 36.2 (3)).[7]

Terminology has evolved since the creation of the Court of Appeal, Criminal Division (CACD); for ease, this guide will use common terms which may not be the same as the source material. For example, 'applicant' is used until such time as leave is granted and 'appellant' when leave has been granted. 'Leave to appeal' is in place of 'permission to appeal'. 'Application' is used to encompass the 'appeal notice'/'notice of appeal' and 'form NG and grounds of appeal'. Occasionally terms are used interchangeably depending on the context.

A PRE APPLICATION PUBLIC FUNDING

A.1 Provision for advice and assistance on appeal is included in the Crown Court representation order.[8] Immediately following the conclusion of each stage of the case, legal representatives should give oral advice to their client as to the prospects of a successful appeal. If there are reasonable grounds, grounds of appeal should be drafted, signed[9] and sent to instructing solicitors as soon as possible so that the application is lodged within the time limits[10]. On receipt, solicitors should send a copy of the documents received from the advocate to the client.

A.2 Prior to the lodging of the application, the Registrar has no power to grant a representation order. The Crown Court can only amend a representation order in favour of fresh legal representatives if advice on appeal has not been given by trial representatives and it is necessary and reasonable for another legal representative to be instructed[11]. Where advice on appeal has been given by trial legal representatives, application for funding prior to the lodging of the application may only be made to the Legal Aid Authority (LAA) for example, if they wanted to instruct a fresh expert to support the appeal, as that would be "exceptional work" and fall outside the ambit of the Crown Court representation order.

7 HMCTS personal information charter. The CAO reference looks like 202301234 A1. Conviction cases are managed by B group (B1 to B5). Sentence cases are managed by A group (A1 – A4). All communications must contain the full CAO reference to avoid delay and sent to the correct email address

8 For fresh representatives see B.7 below

9 Can be an electronic signature

10 See here (CrimPR time limits) and lodging form NG B.2 below and annex 2 for other application types

11 For a discussion on funding see 7-165 – 166 in Archbold Criminal Pleading Evidence and Practice 2026 Ed.

A.3 Once the form NG has been lodged, the Registrar is the relevant authority for decisions about whether an individual qualifies for representation for the purposes of criminal proceedings before the CACD.[12]

A.4 Where work of an exceptional or expensive nature is contemplated to settle grounds, legal representatives can apply to the LAA for funding but an extension of time until grounds of appeal have been lodged cannot be given by the Registrar. Alternatively, a form NG and provisional grounds of appeal can be submitted with a note to the Registrar requesting a representation order to cover the specific work considered necessary to enable final grounds of appeal to be settled. The Registrar cannot grant prior authority for experts etc. but if she considers the work appropriate then a representation order will be granted for the work to be done/expert instructed. Practitioners can seek advice from our costs department as to whether the rates quoted are acceptable.

B APPLICATION STAGE

B.1.1 Leave to appeal is required in all cases except:

- Where exceptionally the trial or sentencing Judge has certified that the case is fit for appeal;
- Where the appeal has been referred by the Criminal Cases Review Commission (CCRC);
- Where the appeal is under s13 Administration of Justice Act 1960 (contempt proceedings)[13]
- Where there is no provision for the grant of leave by a single judge; for example an appeal against an order for trial without jury[14]

B.1.2 Where leave to appeal is not required, the Registrar will usually grant a representation order for the hearing of the appeal.

B.2 Lodging form NG and grounds of appeal

B.2.1 The form NG, signed grounds of appeal and any accompanying applications/ forms must be **lodged directly with the Registrar**[15] (CrimPR

12 ss.16(1) & 19(1) Legal Aid, Sentencing and Punishment of Offenders Act 2012 and Reg. 8 Criminal Legal Aid (Determinations by a Court and Choice of Representative) Regulations 2013).

13 Usually a finding of contempt, sentence for contempt or failing to appear

14 See annex 2

15 Direct lodgement with the Registrar applies to all applications to appeal conviction, sentence and confiscation falling within CrimPR's 39 and 42; for other types of appeal see annex 2.

39.2, s. 18 Criminal Appeal Act 1968) within 28 days[16]. There is a different form NG for conviction, sentence and confiscation order. Each must be lodged within the time limit as a stand-alone application.[17] There must be separate grounds of appeal for each accompanying Form NG.[18]

B.2.2 Applications must be sent via email to criminalappealoffice.applications@justice.gov.uk (CPD 10.4.6) or criminalappealoffice.applications@justice.gov.uk.cjsm.net. Representatives must not lodge the application or any documents in support by uploading directly onto DCS as this will not alert the CAO to the application and service will not be effected in accordance with CrimPR 4.6.

B.2.3 Please note the size limits when sending emails and follow the guidance in annex 1.

B.2.4 It is of assistance if, in the covering email, practitioners alert the Registrar to any features such as a short EDR, age or vulnerability of the applicant that might warrant consideration of expedition by the CAO casework team.

B.2.5 On receipt of an effective application, the CAO Registry will send an acknowledgment by letter to the applicant and by email to solicitors and counsel at the CJSM addresses provided on the Form NG. It is very important that correct CJSM addresses are provided on the Form NG[19]. In the event that no acknowledgment is received within 10 days, practitioners should make enquiries by email: criminalappealoffice.applications@justice.gov.uk with the full name of the applicant and the date of submission in the subject box. Please note that once the acknowledgment letter is received this email address **must not** be used for casework queries.

B.2.6 In a DCS case it is necessary to only email the form NG, grounds of appeal and ancillary applications. The grounds of appeal must contain electronic links of relevant documents to DCS (CrimPR 39.3 (1)(f)). In a non-DCS case representatives should email the core application documents and relevant documents to the CAO.[20]

16 See annex 2 for applications not covered by this guide. Time runs from the date of the verdict or finding that is being appealed, from the date that the sentence is passed (or varied; s.385 (6) Sentencing Act 2020) or, if against an order it is from the date of the making of that order and whether or not leave to appeal is required (e.g. where a trial Judge's certificate has been granted).

17 In practice this means that the time limits can start to run from different dates. Practitioners should not wait until the end of the proceedings to submit the applications.

18 i.e. the grounds of appeal for sentence and conviction **must not** be contained in one document.

19 Please inform the CAO casework team of any changes of contact details; chambers, addresses and CJSM addresses etc.

20 See annex 1 for practical guidance

B.3 Form NG and grounds of appeal

B.3.1 CrimPR 39.3 sets out in detail the information that must be contained in the appeal notice[21].

B.3.2 The correct form NG[22] must be fully completed (including ticking the box if an application is being made for a representation order) for each substantive application. The form contains prompts to attach the grounds of appeal and, if relevant, other forms, applications and documents that need to be lodged:

- Extension of time application(s) (CrimPR 39.3(1)(e), 36.4) (*see B.4 below*)
- Application for bail (Form B) (CrimPR 39.3(1)(e)) (*see B.9 below*)
- Application to introduce fresh evidence (s.23 CAA) (*see B.8 below*)
- Request for transcripts (section F) (CrimPR 39.3(1)(c), CPD 10.4.3)[23] (*see B.5 below*)

B.3.3 Advocates **should not settle or sign** grounds of appeal unless they consider that they are properly arguable. Grounds must be carefully drafted and properly set out and particularised pursuant to CrimPR 39.3 (CPD 10.4.1).

B.3.4 The grounds of appeal[24] must be concise and be contained within one document. In no more than the first two pages, they must contain a summary of the grounds so that what follows is easy to understand (CrimPR 39.3(2)(a)).

B.3.5 The grounds must specify what the applicant wants to appeal; the conviction, verdict or finding; the sentence; the order, or the failure to make an order (CrimPR 39.3(1)(a) & 39.3(2)(b) and **must**:

- be numbered consecutively where there is more than one ground (CrimPR 39.3(2)(e))
- identify each ground on which the applicant relies (CrimPR 39.3 (1)(b)) and
  - the event or decision to which that ground relates (CrimPR 39.3(2)(b))
  - contain a summary of the necessary facts relevant to that ground so that the issue is clear (CrimPR 39.3(2)(c))

21 In practice this is the form NG and grounds of appeal. See *R v James and Ors* [2018] EWCA Crim 285 para 21
22 Guidance notes on completing the form NG can be found here.
23 In a **privately funded** case the transcripts should be submitted with the application.
24 See annex 1 for practical guidance.

  - concisely outline each argument in relation to each ground (CrimPR 39.3(2)(d))

- in a sentence application, identify the relevant sentencing powers of the Crown Court (CrimPR 39.3(1)(d))
- identify any relevant document or thing and provide a hyperlink to it in DCS (CrimPR 39.3 (1)(f)). In addition, practitioners must identify with particularity the sections of any such material the court needs to consider (CPD 10.4.1 c.). In non-DCS cases it is acknowledged that total compliance might not be possible but there must be identification of the relevant document, sections that need to be considered and where and how that might be found.
- identify any relevant authority and –
  - state the proposition of law that the authority demonstrates, and
  - identify the parts of the authority that support that proposition; and
- attach an electronic copy of that authority, or if two or more such authorities are identified, provide them as a single pdf bookmarked document (CrimPR 39.3(1)(g) & 39.3(2)(f), CPD 10.8.13) subject to the paragraph B3.6 below.

B.3.6 Advocates are expected to provide[25] only the **essential authorities** to determine the issue(s) (CPD 10.8.9 – 10.9.12). The Vice-President, Court of Appeal, Criminal Division may, from time to time, publish[26] a list of 'frequently cited authorities' which practitioners need **not** supply within their bundles. Advocates may assume that the single judge/full Court will have a copy of these judgments and need only cite the case and the relevant paragraph number(s). For citation of Hansard, practitioners must comply with CPD 10.8.16 – 10.8.17.

B.3.7 Failure to comply with the requirements in CrimPR 39 and the CPD referred to above, may result in a direction from the Registrar that the defects be remedied within a directed period and prior to the case being allocated to a single judge. Failure to revise might lead to the single judge/court refusing leave (CPD 10.4.2).[27]

25 If the constitution hearing the case require a paper bundle, this will be communicated to the party by the CAO.

26 It will be incumbent on practitioners to check the website for the most recent version.

27 This applies equally to perfected grounds; see B.6 below

B.3.1 Criminal Cases Review Commission (CCRC)

B.3.2.1 On receipt, the Registrar will serve notice that the CCRC[28] has referred a conviction or sentence on the appellant's representatives. They must lodge[29] the form NG and grounds of appeal not more than 28 days after and explain how each ground of appeal relates (if it does) to the reasons given for the reference. If no form NG and grounds are lodged within the required period, then the reference shall be treated as the appeal notice (CrimPR 39.5 (2)). No extension of time is required as the effect of the referral is the same as the granting of leave.

B.3.2.2 The Registrar will serve the appeal notice on any party directly affected by the reference and will almost certainly direct that a form RN is lodged.

B.3.2 Insufficient weight given to assistance to prosecution authorities

B.3.2.1 Where a ground of appeal against sentence is that the judge has given insufficient weight to the assistance given to the prosecution authorities, grounds of appeal should be drafted in an anodyne form with a note to the Registrar alerting her to the existence of a "text" which will be obtained by the CAO[30]. The single judge will take it into account when considering leave, as will the full Court before the appeal hearing and it need not be alluded to in open Court.

B.3.2.2 If the representatives wish to make oral submissions in relation to any confidential material, any application to list the case anonymously or in camera must be made to the Registrar in advance of the appeal hearing to ensure the appropriate recording equipment is in place and the case is listed correctly.

B.3.3 Applications based on a change in law

B.3.3.1 If an application based on a change in law is lodged within time, the test to be applied by the full Court is whether the conviction is unsafe.[31]

B.3.3.2 If it is lodged outside of the time limits, **exceptional leave** will be required. Exceptional leave will only be granted if the applicant would

28 See Part II Criminal Appeal Act 1995 and s. 16C Criminal Appeal Act 1968
29 Via email to criminalappealoffice.applications@justice.gov.uk
30 *Royle* [2023] EWCA Crim 1311
31 *R v Johnson & Ors* [2016] EWCA Crim 1613

otherwise suffer "substantial injustice" due to the change in law. Grounds of appeal should therefore set out why the substantial injustice test is met.[32]

B.4 Extensions of time generally[33]

B.4.1 Time limits are intentionally strict[34] and an application for an extension of the 28-day period in which to make an application must be served with the form NG[35]. It is not enough to simply tick the relevant box and the application must always set out cogent reasons for the delay for the whole period (CrimPR 36.4[36]). A chronology can be useful to assist the narrative of the application where a long extension of time is being sought.[37]

B.4.2 If the Registrar/single judge or full Court on a renewed application, consider there are merits in the application for leave there is likely to be a referral to the full Court to determine the application to extend time and the application for leave[38].

B.5 Transcripts and notes of evidence

B.5.1 In **publicly funded** conviction cases, the Registrar will obtain the summing up and proceedings up to and including verdict as a matter of course. There is an obligation for advocates to identify any further transcript which they consider essential to the issues and to provide a note of dates and times to enable an order to be placed with the transcription company (CrimPR 39.3(1)(c)). Whether further transcript is required is a matter for the judgment of the Registrar or her staff. Transcripts of evidence are not usually ordered and, in some cases, it may be appropriate for the advocate to provide an agreed note of evidence.

32 *R v Johnson & Ors ibid*. For examples of how the Court of Appeal has applied these principles see: *R v Uthayakumar* [2014] EWCA Crim 123, *R v Jogee; Ruddock v The Queen* [2016] UKSC 8, [2016] UKPC 7, para 100.

33 The CrimPR refers to 'business days' and the Criminal Appeal Act 1968 refers to 'days'; the periods are the same.

34 *Gabbana* [2020] EWCA Crim1473.

35 S.31 (2)(b) and s.31A (2)(a) Criminal Appeal Act 1968 gives the power to extend time to the Court and the Registrar. In practice the Registrar/ single judge will not grant long extensions of time for leave to appeal or renew but will refer them to the single judge/full Court. However discretion may be exercised on very short extensions required.

36 *Wilson* [2016] EWCA Crim 65 and *R v James & Ors ibid* at [23] – [28] which provides a helpful summary of the authorities and Extensions of time for leave to appeal against a conviction or sentence in the Court of Appeal, Criminal Division; Sarah Bergstrom, Archbold Review Issue 3 28 April 2023.

37 See also fresh representatives see B.7 below

38 *Lurdita Baniulyte* [2025] EWCA Crim 1205 and other cases can be found here: Search results – Find Case Law – The National Archives

B.5.2 In sentence cases, the prosecution opening of facts[39] and the sentencing remarks are usually obtained. In other types of appeal, transcript relevant to the issue will be obtained by the Registrar unless it is a prosecution application in which case transcript is obtained by the prosecution authority.

B.5.3 If the Registrar and the advocate are unable to agree the extent of the transcript to be obtained, the Registrar may refer that matter to a judge or the full Court.

B.5.4 In certain circumstances the costs of unnecessary transcripts may be ordered to be paid by the applicant[40]. Where a transcript is obtained otherwise than through the Registrar, the cost may be disallowed on taxation.

B.5.5 If an applicant is **paying privately** for legal representation, the summing up to verdict and other relevant transcripts must be obtained and should be lodged at the same time as the notice of appeal.[41] If the Registrar directs that further transcripts are to be lodged then legal representatives must do so privately and must lodge with the CAO, via email, on receipt[42]. Where the Registrar has already obtained transcripts in a private case, the applicant's legal representatives will be required to pay the cost of the transcripts before they are released to them.

B.5.6 In all cases, where the trial/sentencing judge has provided a relevant written ruling or sentencing remarks these should be hyperlinked (or noted/ attached if a non-DCS case) within the grounds of appeal so that the Registrar may consider whether this avoids the necessity to obtain transcript[43].

B.6 Perfection of grounds of appeal

B.6.1 The purpose of perfection[44] is (a) to save valuable judicial time by enabling the Court to identify the relevant parts of the transcript easily and (b) to give the advocate the opportunity to reconsider the original grounds in the light of the transcript. Perfected grounds should consist of a fresh document which supersedes the original grounds of appeal and contains inter alia references by

39 Where there has been a guilty plea
40 S.29 Criminal Appeal Act 1968 and see *Kirk* [2015] EWCA Crim 1764
41 CrimPR 5.5 and CPD 2.6.10, 2.6.18-2.6.22 provides guidance and assistance. See *R v Lake* [2023] EWCA Crim 710 – [72] – [75]. Requests for transcripts must be made to the Crown Court using form EX107 and approved forms sent to the SHW.
42 No transcript is to be placed on DCS CACD1 or section Y.
43 It is of assistance if the advocate could indicate whether the transcript should be obtained and a note for the reasons why, i.e. the judge departed significantly from the written document.
44 And must be compliant with the CrimPR, CPD and guide.

page number and letter (or paragraph number) to all relevant passages in the transcript and hyperlinks to the relevant page.[45]

B.6.2 In conviction or confiscation appeals, the Registrar will almost certainly invite the advocate to perfect grounds to assist the single judge or full court. Generally, the advocate will not be invited to perfect the grounds of appeal in a sentence case. Where an advocate indicates a wish to do so, the Registrar will consider the request and will only invite perfection if it is considered necessary for the assistance of the single judge or full Court.

B.6.3 If perfection is appropriate, the advocate will be sent a link to the transcript and asked to perfect the grounds, usually within 14 days. In the absence of any response from the advocate, the existing grounds of appeal will be placed before the single judge or the full Court without further notice. If an advocate does not wish to perfect the grounds, an email to that effect will ensure that the case is not unnecessarily delayed.

B.6.4 If, having considered the transcript, the advocate is of the opinion that there are no valid grounds, the reasons should be set out in a further advice and sent to the instructing solicitors. The Registrar should be informed that this has been done, but the advocate should not send the Registrar a copy of that advice. Solicitors should send a copy to the applicant and obtain instructions, at the same time explaining that if s/he persists with the application the court may consider whether to make a loss of time order[46].

B.7 Applications by fresh legal representatives

B.7.1 Provision for advice and assistance for fresh representatives is limited and requires good reason and to apply for prior authority to exceed the initial limit will need to meet the sufficient benefit test.[47]

B.7.2 In all cases where fresh representatives are instructed, they must, before grounds of appeal are settled and lodged, make specific inquiries of the legal representative(s) who appeared and acted at the trial/plea hearing to ensure that the factual basis for each of the grounds of appeal (actual or prospective) is correct.

45 See annex 1 for instructions on how to hyperlink to a specific page. Non-DCS cases will not be expected to have hyperlinks and it will not be necessary for the transcript to be attached if already with the CAO.

46 See C.5 below

47 Clause 11.5 of the Standard Crime Contract Specification states: "If the Client has received an adverse opinion on appeal and wishes to obtain a further opinion, you must consider how long it was since the first opinion was given. If recent, and it appears that all issues have been considered, no further work may be undertaken." See also preventing audit issues section 15

Where necessary, further steps should be taken to obtain objective and independent evidence to substantiate the factual basis for those grounds[48].

B.7.3 To ensure compliance with this duty (CPD 10.4.4)[49]:

a. New legal representatives **must** confirm **within the grounds of appeal** that the duties set out in *McCook* and associated authorities[50] have been complied with.

b. If these queries result in privileged information being included within, or as an attachment, to the grounds of appeal (including but not limited to, explicit or implied complaints about the conduct of trial representatives), then a signed waiver of privilege **must** also be lodged with the grounds of appeal. Failure to lodge a signed waiver of privilege may mean that the single judge and/or the Court will not have sufficient information to determine whether the grounds of appeal are arguable. Grounds of appeal may be dismissed on that basis[51].

c. If trial representatives have failed to respond to these inquiries within a reasonable time, fresh representatives should instead seek other objective independent evidence to substantiate the factual basis for the grounds as far as they are able. A statement confirming that the trial representatives have failed to respond to their McCook inquiries should be lodged with the grounds of appeal, along with a signed waiver of privilege.

d. Fresh representatives must consider obtaining other objective independent evidence if the information provided by the trial representatives contradicts the applicant's instructions.

B.7.4 If there are exceptional circumstances and good and compelling reasons not to comply with this duty, these must be specified. Such exceptional circumstances would be very rare[52]. In cases where **fresh representatives** seek to adduce **fresh evidence**[53] that was not adduced at trial, not only will the fresh representatives be required to comply with their duties pursuant to McCook, but a signed waiver of privilege must also be lodged by new legal representatives in all fresh evidence cases, further to *R v Singh*[54] (CPD 10.4.4 e.).

48 Note *MT [2023] EWCA Crim 558* on the principles of an extension of time and the balance with due diligence

49 See also Criminal Appeals – Duties to the Court to Make Enquiries published by the Bar Council ethics committee

50 *R v McCook* [2014] EWCA Crim 734, *R v Grant-Murray & Others*, [2017] EWCA Crim 1228, *R v Lee* [2014] EWCA Crim 2928, and *R v Achogbuo* [2014] EWCA Crim 567.

51 *R v Frost-Helmsing* [2010] EWCA Crim 1200

52 *R v McCook* ibid

53 See applications to adduce fresh evidence B.8

54 [2017] EWCA Crim 466

B.7.5 The Court has confirmed that the duties of fresh representatives are not limited to conviction applications but also include sentence cases.[55]

B.7.6 The duties set out above apply at whatever stage the fresh representatives are instructed. Where instruction occurs post single judge, representatives should consider whether they are required to make an application to vary the notice of appeal (CrimPR 36.14(5) and CPD 10.4.5) and/or an application for an extension of time (CrimPR 36.4) to renew[56].

B.8 Applications to adduce fresh evidence

B.8.1 Where grounds of appeal rely upon fresh evidence that was not adduced at trial, an application pursuant to s.23 Criminal Appeals Act 1968 must be made. If the fresh evidence is provided by a witness, representatives should obtain a statement from the witness in the form prescribed by s9 Criminal Justice Act 1968. If the fresh evidence is documentary or real evidence, the representatives should obtain statements from all those involved in formally exhibiting the evidence. A form W should be lodged with respect to each witness dealing with the fresh evidence[57].

B.8.2 A supporting s.9 witness statement or an affidavit from the applicant's solicitor should accompany the fresh evidence setting out why the evidence was not available at trial and when and how it has come to light.[58] This will implicitly require fresh representatives to comply with *McCook*.[59]

B.8.3 The form W should indicate whether there is an application for a witness order. The Registrar or single judge may direct a witness order, but only the Court hearing the appeal may give leave for a witness to be called and only the full Court can formally receive the evidence[60].

B.8.4 Prior[61] to the full Court hearing, the practice of the Registrar is to seek the written views of the parties as to agreement or not on whether the

55 See *R v Roberts & Ors* [2016] EWCA Crim 71, at Para. 40 and *R v Lea* [2021] EWCA Crim 65, at Para. 43

56 See applications to renew D.6 below

57 In cases were there may be numerous documents or it might not be clear who should or can produce them, the CAO case lawyer should be contacted for advice.

58 Known as the Gogana statement; it must address the s.23 criteria; In *R v Gogana* The Times 12/07/1999 the Court said that provenance of the fresh evidence was extremely relevant to credibility. It can also have the dual purpose of supporting an application for extension of time.

59 See applications by fresh representatives B.7

60 *R v Cross* [2014] EWCA Crim 96

61 See D10.3 below for remote attendance applications

Court will be invited to receive the witness(es) evidence orally or in writing. The presiding judge's views are then sought, and directions may be given if appropriate. If the judge indicates that the court is likely to require a witness to give evidence or is unable to give an indication it is the responsibility of the solicitors for the party seeking to rely on the fresh evidence to ensure witness availability and attendance at court. If it is anticipated that an application for a witness to give evidence via CVP might be made, the application must be made as soon as practicable[62].

B.8.5 Solicitors are reminded that where a representation order has been granted for counsel[63], counsel should make an application to the Registrar for that to be extended for the purposes of this work.

B.8.6 The Registrar and single judge have power to make an order under s.23 (1)(a) Criminal Appeal Act 1968 for the production of evidence etc. necessary for the determination of the case.

B.9 Bail pending appeal[64] (CrimPR 39.8)

B.9.1 Bail may be granted (a) by a single judge or the full Court or (b) by a trial or sentencing judge who has certified the case fit for appeal. In the latter case, bail can only be granted within 28 days of the conviction or sentence which is the subject of the appeal and may not be granted if an application for bail has already been made to the Court of Appeal.[65]

B.9.2 An application for bail pending appeal must be supported by a completed form B. The application for bail must be served on the Registrar and the prosecution. An application cannot be decided without giving the prosecution the opportunity to make representations (CrimPR 39.8).

B.9.3 In practice, single judges will require the relevant transcripts to be available so they may consider the merits of the substantive application at the same time as the bail application. Where an application is urgent because of a short EDR[66], age of the applicant and/or vulnerability etc. practitioners should highlight this in the accompanying email to the CAO.

B.9.4 Where bail is granted pending appeal, the Court may attach any condition that must be met before the applicant is released and may direct

62 See remote hearings D.10 and D.11 below
63 Counsel also refers to solicitor advocates
64 S.19 Criminal Appeal Act 1968
65 s.81 (1D) & (1E) Senior Courts Act 1981
66 Earliest date of release

how such a condition must be met. The Registrar must serve a certificate recording any such condition on the applicant, the applicant's custodian and any other person directly affected by the condition (CrimPR 39.9). A condition of residence is always attached.

B.9.5 The Registrar can vary the conditions of bail only if the Respondent does not object to the variation (s.31A (2)(c) & (3)). It follows that in the absence of a clear indication from the prosecution that the variation is not opposed, the application must be considered by a single judge.

B.10 Respondent's Notice

B.10.1 In all cases, the Registrar will notify the relevant prosecuting authority of the case name, reference number and Crown Court (CPD 10.2.1). The appeal notice[67] will be served on any party directly affected by the appeal (usually the prosecution) if the Registrar or Court directs or invites a Respondent's Notice (RN) or on a party who wishes to do so[68] (CrimPR 39.6(1) – (2), CPD 10.2.2).

B.10.2 CrimPR 39.6(4)(a) states that the RN must be served within 14 days. However, the practice of the Registrar is to allow 21 days unless the case is urgent (in which case the Registrar may impose a deadline shorter than 14 days). The RN must be served on the Registrar and any other party on whom the Registrar served the appeal notice.

B.10.3 The RN must be in the specified form RN (CrimPR 39.6(5)) and must set out the grounds of opposition and include the information set out in CrimPR 39.6(6). It should be noted that hyperlinks must be included (CrimPR 39.6 (6)(g)). In non-DCS cases it is acknowledged that compliance may not be possible[69]. Authorities must be identified and an electronic copy of that authority provided. If two or more such authorities are identified, they are to be provided as a single pdf bookmarked document (CrimPR 39.6(6)(e) & (h)).[70]

B.10.4 In practice, this procedure primarily applies prior to consideration of leave by the single Judge. However, a RN may be sought at any time in the proceedings including at the direction of the single Judge.

67 In practice a link to CACD1 is provided. In non DCS cases the Form NG, grounds of appeal, ancillary applications and any available transcript will be securely emailed or link provided for secure download.

68 If a party wishes to submit a RN, they should contact the CAO and the necessary arrangements for service will be made.

69 See annex 1 for guidance on submission of documents

70 Note B.3.6 above regarding the 'frequently cited list of authorities'.

B.10.5 The Registrar will always direct a Respondent's Notice in all conviction and sentence applications involving a fatality including attempted murder.

B.10.6 Other examples of when the Registrar might direct a Respondent's Notice include:

- Where an assertion is made in the grounds of some irregularity that happened during the trial that cannot be fully reflected in the transcript.
- The grounds are legally complex, or the facts of the case are complicated and an RN might assist.
- There is a complaint about the prosecution and their conduct of the trial.
- Derogatory remarks are made about the credibility of a victim.
- There is fresh evidence not produced at trial.
- One of the grounds of appeal is that there were inconsistent verdicts.
- The grounds raise a juror irregularity or other conduct which might require investigation by the police.
- The grounds have not been considered by a single judge and there is an application to vary the notice of appeal before the full Court pursuant to *R v James and Ors* [2018] EWCA Crim 285.[71]
- The grounds raise points of public importance which require a co-ordinated approach from the prosecution.

The CPS will always be invited to lodge a Respondent's Notice in the following conviction cases:

- All those involving, a fatality, rape, attempted rape or a serious sexual offence.
- Where a CPS Complex Casework Unit dealt with the case, or the case was high profile
- Where the offence was perverting the course of justice, misconduct in public office and any conspiracy.

71 See applications to vary D.6 below.

B.10.1 a. Attorney General's reference of an unduly lenient sentence or reference of a point of law on an acquittal[72]

B.10.1.1 If the defendant wishes to make oral representations to the Court, a RN must be served within 14 days of the Registrar serving the application. There is no specific form available, but the document must be compliant with the CrimPR and CPD in terms of layout and hyperlinks etc. A representation order is usually granted to the offender for counsel to respond to the reference.

B.11 Case Management

B.11.1 Case management powers are exercisable by the Registrar and single judge[73]. They can and will make procedural directions for the efficient and effective preparation of an application or appeal[74].

B.11.2 Where the Registrar refuses an application to exercise case management powers in their favour, the party is entitled to have the application determined by a single judge. There is no provision for any appeal against a procedural direction given by a single judge and thus such decisions are final.

C THE S.31/LEAVE STAGE

C.1 Referral by the Registrar

C.1.1 Where leave to appeal is required, the Registrar, having obtained the necessary documents, will usually refer the application(s) to a single judge for a decision (on the papers).

C.1.2 The Registrar has power to refer an application[75] for leave directly to the full Court and will also refer an application for an extension of time, if one is required.[76]

C.2 Oral applications for leave to appeal

C.2.1 All applications for leave (together with any ancillary applications) are normally considered by a single judge on the papers, unless it can

72 See annex 2
73 See Criminal Appeal Act 1968 for the Registrar (s.31A) and for the single judge (s.31).
74 See s.31B Criminal Appeal Act 1968
75 See funding for grant of leave or reference to full court D.4 below
76 See time limits generally B.4 above

be demonstrated that there are exceptional reasons why an oral hearing is required. Representatives may request an oral hearing which must be supported by written reasons as to why the case is exceptional and any reasons why that hearing should be expedited[77]. The application should be copied to the prosecution. The single judge determining the substantive application will then decide whether an oral hearing should be arranged. An advocate may make an application for a representation order at the hearing itself. Oral applications for leave and bail are usually heard in Court, but in chambers at 9.30am before the normal Court sittings. Advocates appear unrobed. If the advocate considers that an application may take longer than 20 minutes, the Registrar must be notified. If the single judge declines to hear the application at an oral hearing, the application will then be considered on the papers by that judge.

C.3 Powers of the Single Judge

C.3.1 The single judge may grant the application for leave, grant limited leave, refuse leave or refer leave to the full Court[78]. The single judge may also grant, refuse or refer any ancillary applications.[79]

C.3.2 Where the single judge considers a fresh evidence application is potentially arguable, a referral to the full Court may be made rather than a grant of leave.[80]

C.4 Refusal by the Single Judge

C.4.1 Where the single judge refuses leave to appeal, the Registrar sends a notification of the refusal to the applicant and advises that any renewal[81] notice for the application(s) to be considered by the full court must be served on the Registrar within 14 days from the date the notice was served on the applicant (CrimPR 36.5). The application automatically lapses after 28 days from refusal if there is no renewal.

C.4.2 The single judge[82] may indicate that the full Court should consider loss of time or a costs order if the application is renewed. Where the applicant

77 Expedition will be a matter for the Registrar
78 This generally done on the papers.
79 See s.31 Criminal Appeal Act 1968; see time limits generally B.4 above for extensions of time
80 *R v Singh* [2017] EWCA Crim 466
81 A renewal form is provided to the applicant with the refusal notification
82 S.31 Criminal Appeal Act 1968. Absence of such an indication does not deprive the full court of the power

is not in custody the single judge has the option of considering whether to make any directions in respect of costs, which could include the prosecution costs (usually in providing a RN).[83]

C.5 Directions for loss of time

C.5.1 An appeal is not built into the trial process and must be justified on properly arguable grounds. To deter unmeritorious applications which waste precious time and resources the court will consider using their power[84] to direct that time spent in custody after lodging their application shall not count towards sentence or an order for costs (CPD 10.4.5 h., 10.5.1). In order not to deter litigants in person from lodging their own grounds of appeal, it is now the practice of the Court not to make loss or time orders at the single judge stage. However, where an application is wholly without merit and has been renewed to the full Court, the applicant is clearly at risk of such an order being made. Renewal on the advice of legal representatives is no protection on the use of these powers.[85] Where an applicant is not in custody an order for costs will be considered.[86]

C.5.2 Such an order may not be made where leave to appeal or a trial judge's certificate has been granted, on a reference by the CCRC or where an application has been abandoned.

C.6 Abandonment

C.6.1 An application or appeal which is abandoned is treated as being a final determination of the full Court (CrimPR 36.13(4)(c)).

C.6.2 An appeal or application may be abandoned without leave by lodging form A at any time before the hearing. An oral instruction or letter indicating a wish to abandon is insufficient. At the hearing, an application or appeal can only be abandoned with the permission of the Court (CrimPR 36.13(2)(b)).

C.6.3 A notice of abandonment cannot be withdrawn, nor can it be conditional. A person who wants to reinstate an application or appeal after abandonment must apply in writing to the Registrar with reasons (CrimPR 36.113(5)). The Court has power to allow reinstatement only where the

83 see *Kirk* [2015] EWCA Crim 1764
84 S.29 Criminal Appeal Act 1968
85 *R v Gray and Ors* [2014] EWCA Crim 2372.
86 s.18 Prosecution of Offences Act 1985

purported abandonment can be treated as a nullity and the applicant must provide the Court with the relevant information to determine the application (*R v Medway* (1976) 62 Cr App R 85 and *R v Zabotka* [2016] EWCA Crim 1771).

C.6.4 An application to treat the abandonment as a nullity is heard by the full Court. If the Court does agree to treat the abandonment as a nullity, the status of the application is restored as if there had been no interruption.

D PREPARATION FOR THE FULL COURT HEARING

D.1 Notice to the prosecution

D.1.1 The Registrar will notify the relevant authority when (CPD 10.2.3):

- leave to appeal against conviction or sentence is granted by the single judge; or
- the single judge or the Registrar refers an application for leave to appeal against conviction or sentence to the full Court for determination; or
- there is to be a renewed application for leave to appeal against sentence only.

D.1.2 If the prosecution authority had not previously been served with the appeal notice and transcript, these will be served with the notification and the comments of the single judge/Registrar (CPD 10.2.4). The prosecution may be directed to attend but if they are not, they should notify[87] the Registrar without delay if they wish to be represented at the hearing[88] and should be aware that the case may be listed at short notice (CPD 10.2.5).

D.1.3 In a conviction case, where the prosecuting authority is attending the full Court hearing (and no RN has previously been lodged), the Registrar will direct service of a RN or a skeleton argument.[89]

87 See Notice to the prosecution D.1 above. The advocate's details and a time estimate must also be provided (CPD 10.2.6)

88 Unless the application/appeal is to be heard on the papers; see attendance E.1 below

89 There is normally no need for both.

D.2 Limited leave

D.2.1 Where limited leave[90] has been granted advocates must notify the Registrar within 14 days whether any of the grounds upon which leave has been refused are to be renewed before the full Court (CrimPR 36.14[91]). If a representation order is granted, public funding will only cover grounds of appeal which the single judge or the full Court say are arguable.[92]

D.3 Renewal

D.3.1 The Crown Court representation order will not cover advice to the applicant on whether to renew. A late renewal notice must be accompanied by an extension of time application giving cogent reasons (CrimPR 36.4). An application for an extension of time to renew will normally be considered by the full Court at the same time as the renewed application for leave to appeal.

D.3.2 Where the applicant is to be represented at the renewed hearing, the CAO must be notified in writing as soon as practicable whether this is on a privately instructed or on a pro bono basis.

D.3.3 Whilst a representation order is not granted by the Registrar in respect of a renewed application for leave, the advocate may apply at the hearing to the Court for a representation order to cover that appearance and any further work done in preparation of the renewal retrospectively. In practice, this is only granted where the application for leave is successful.

D.3.4 The form SJ (renewal) includes a box for the applicant to give reasons why an order for loss of time or costs should not be made, whether or not an indication has been given by a single judge[93].

D.4 Public funding for grant of leave or reference[94] to full court

D.4.1 In the CACD only the interests of justice test is applied and there is no means testing[95]. Where leave is granted or the application referred to the

90 I.e. leave to argue some grounds but not others.

91 CrimPR 36.3 enables the court to extend the 14 day period (*R v James* ibid)

92 *R v Cox & Thomas* [1999] 2 Cr App Rep 6 and *R v Hyde and Ors* [2016] EWCA Crim 1031

93 See Refusal by a single judge C.4 above

94 On a referral, the applicant does not become an appellant until such time as the full Court grant leave to appeal. For ease appellant will be used.

95 Practitioners should note that the Court has the power in some circumstances to grant a recovery of defence costs order; The Criminal Legal Aid (Recovery of Defence Costs Orders) Regulations 2013 (SI 2013/511). The CAO summary will alert the court in relevant cases.

full Court, it is usual to grant a representation order[96] for the preparation and presentation of the appeal or the application and appeal if leave is granted. This is usually limited to named junior counsel only and will normally be the advocate who settled grounds of appeal. The single judge and/or Registrar will consider and determine an application for a representation order by virtue of the appropriate box being ticked on form NG.

D.4.2 If the appellant is a litigant in person, an advocate may be assigned by the Registrar. In such cases the Registrar will provide a brief but does not act as a solicitor.

D.4.3 The Registrar may assign one advocate to represent more than one appellant if appropriate. If it is considered that a representation order for two advocates is required, the advocate must apply[97] to the Registrar or single judge and provide written justification in accordance with Criminal Legal Aid (Determinations by a Court and Choice of Representative) Regulations 2013 (S.I. 2013/614).

D.4.4 An application for a solicitor's representation order can be made at any stage of the proceedings once an effective application has been lodged. There is no prescribed form for an application, but counsel should submit a note to the Registrar which outlines the work that is required to be done by the solicitor and why that work cannot be undertaken by counsel. Although the application could be for a general representation order for solicitors to assist with the preparation of the application/appeal, the Registrar is more likely to grant a representation order for a limited and specified purpose.

D.4.5 Common scenarios for granting representation orders to solicitors are:

- There are complex issues of disclosure, and the solicitor must liaise with the CPS/Prosecutor.
- In fresh evidence cases where the solicitor must take and lodge witness statements, instruct experts etc.
- Where the applicant is particularly vulnerable, young or has mental health issues.
- In other complex cases, such as special courts or where directions hearings are required.

D.4.6 If solicitors are assigned, it should be noted, that by virtue of regulation 12, a representation order can only be issued to a solicitor if they hold an LAA Standard Crime Contract. A solicitor not holding such a franchise

96 Practitioners should note work that a representation order can cover; *R v Tredget* [2022] EWCA Crim 1894

97 There is no prescribed form and a note to the Registrar will suffice.

may apply to the LAA for an individual case contract (ICC) by virtue of which the solicitor is employed on behalf of the LAA to represent an appellant in that case.

D.4.7 In cases where the Registrar refers an application to the full Court a representation order for junior counsel is usually granted. Where an application is referred because an unlawful sentence has been passed or other procedural error identified, a representation order will ordinarily be granted where the attendance of counsel is necessary. Where a technical issue can be resolved on the papers without oral argument, a representation order will not be granted.

D.4.8 A presiding Lord/Lady Justice giving directions on a case can grant a representation order.

D.4.9 A representation order can be retrospective to the date the application was lodged (regulation 8(2)) but cannot include work undertaken before the application was lodged[98].

D.4.10 A representation order can be revoked by the Registrar/full Court; where the individual does not agree to the terms of the funding; the individual asks that the order is withdrawn; the person/firm representing them under a representation order decline to act[99]. Where the order is withdrawn, the claim is to the date of withdrawal.

D.4.11 There is no right to a transfer of a representation order, but an application can be made to the Registrar/Court if the original advocate has had to withdraw under their rules of professional conduct or is unable to represent the applicant/appellant through circumstances out of their control which must be determined before a transfer can take place.[100] Practitioners should note that the test is a strict one.[101]

D.4.12 Mixed public and private funding is impermissible[102] but it is open to the Court to grant a retrospective representation order where there has been private funding. In *Gittins & Khan* [2007] EWCA Crim 806, the Court held that the principle that public and private funding could not co-exist only applied after the making of a representation order and where the Court made a retrospective representation order, advocates must forego and repay any fees

98 Tredget (Peter) [2022] EWCA Crim 1894

99 Regulation 9 The Criminal Legal Aid (Determinations by a Court and Choice of Representative) Regulations 2013 (legislation.gov.uk)

100 Regulation 14 Criminal Legal Aid (Determinations by a Court and Choice of Representative) Regulations 2013

101 See *R (on the application of Sharif Sanjari) v The Crown Court at Birmingham* [2015] EWHC 2037 (Admin)

102 *R v Banfield* [2014] EWCA Crim 1824, *Knaggs (Russell)* [2018] EWCA Crim 1152 at [149]-[153]

they have received under a private funding arrangement. The Court needs to be informed of such an arrangement, and the representation order should be on terms which ensure repayment of any sum paid privately (in that case counsel was also required to provide proof of repayment of fees received).

D.5 Referrals

D.5.1 Where an application or applications have been referred to the full Court by either the Registrar or a single judge, the application(s) for leave to appeal and, if required, for an extension of time will be considered by the full Court. In practice the CAO will prepare and list the applications in the same way as a full appeal hearing where leave has been granted and if the Court conclude that no directions are required, normally the application for leave and/or extension of time would be determined followed immediately by consideration of the appeal itself in a "rolled up" hearing.

D.6 Applications to vary the notice of appeal (fresh grounds) (CPD 10.4.5)

D.6.1 As a rule, all the grounds of appeal that an applicant wishes to advance should be lodged with the appeal notice, subject to perfection on receipt of transcripts. The application for leave is an important stage and it must not be treated lightly, or its determinations ignored.

- Where an appellant wants to rely on a ground of appeal not identified in the appeal notice after leave has been granted, an application for leave to vary must be made which identifies each new ground and reasons why it was not included in the appeal notice.[103] The application must be served on the Registrar and the respondent as soon as practicable (CrimPR 36.14 (5)).
- Where an applicant instructs (fresh) representatives to renew refused application(s) and introduce new/fresh grounds of appeal, an application for leave to vary must accompany the renewal within 14 days of refusal. Where an application to renew has been made after 14 days, an extension of time application will need to be made, and the hurdle will be higher if accompanied by an application to vary.

D.6.2 Fresh representatives will be required to comply with their duty of due diligence[104] and a waiver of privilege will almost certainly be required. On receipt of the trial representative's response, fresh representatives should again

103 There is no prescribed form but representatives should note their duties and that they must comply with CrimPR 39.3 and CPD 10.4.5.

104 *McCook* ibid and see fresh representatives B.7 above

consider with great care their duty to the court and whether the proposed fresh grounds should be advanced as reasonably arguable and particularly cogent.

D.6.3 Advocates must comply with CPD 10.4.5 and have regard to the criteria identified by the court in *R v James & Ors*[105] (ibid). It should be noted that fresh grounds must be particularly cogent and that the hurdle is a high one. If there is any doubt as to whether a ground is fresh, then an application to vary should be made. The court will consider the following (non-exhaustive) list of issues:

- The extent of the delay in advancing the new ground/s.
- The reason for the delay in advancing the new ground/s.
- Whether the issues / facts giving rise to the new grounds were known to the applicant's representative at the time he or she advised the applicant regarding any available grounds of appeal.
- The interests of justice and overriding objective in CrimPR part 1.

D.6.4 The Registrar will consider whether any further transcripts should be obtained and will direct a RN. An application to vary the notice of appeal will be considered by the full Court when considering the renewed application for leave to appeal.

D.7 CAO summaries, index and bundles

D.7.1 In preparation for the full Court hearing the CAO will write a summary[106]. It is important that the advocate considers the contents promptly and **must** notify the Registrar if any significant alterations are proposed (CPD 10.6.3). See also D.9.1 below in respect of the time estimates.

D.7.2 In most sentence cases the CAO summary will contain hyperlinks to DCS or the Document Upload Centre (DUC)[107] in non-DCS cases. An index is not provided in these cases.

D.7.3 In all other cases the CAO summary (CPD 10.6.2) will be hyperlinked from the index (CPD 10.7.1) or sent to the advocate if a non-DCS case. Where the Registrar directs, or the advocate on their own volition provides, a core bundle, practitioners should follow the guidance in annex 1. Bundles should only contain documents and material which are necessary for the proper understanding of, and determination of, the issues (CPD 10.7.4). The bundle

105 It should be noted that the Court refers to a previous version of this guide. A5 is now B.6
106 See CPD 10.6 for the makeup of the summary and restrictions on its use
107 See annex 1.

will be placed on CACD1 or DUC[108] **by CAO staff** and the index will contain a hyperlink to that bundle and any administrative documents that the court may need. Where no core bundle is lodged, the index will provide links to the procedural and relevant core documents.

D.7.4 It is important that the advocate considers the index/summary and checks the links on receipt. The caseworker should be notified as soon as practicable if there are amendments that need to be made (CPD 10.7.3).

D.7.5 Late papers[109] are discouraged. In the exceptional event that late papers are sent, the advocate must follow the instructions on the index and ensure any other party, if represented, is copied in (G.7 below).

D.7.6 The index will contain a link to any authority, and if more than one, the bundle of authorities lodged pre single judge. Advocates should consider lodging an amended bundle in furtherance of the principles in CrimPR 39.3(1)(f) & 39.3(2)(f), CPD 10.8.9 – 10.8.10 and having regard to the current list of frequently cited authorities.

D.8 Skeleton arguments

D.8.1 The grounds of appeal and/or RN should normally suffice in that all the points that are to be argued are already in the single document (CPD 10.8.1). On occasion the Registrar or the single judge will direct one or both parties to submit a skeleton argument. Where this has not happened an advocate must, in a conviction case, serve a skeleton argument when the grounds of appeal are not sufficiently outlined, particularly in complex or novel point of law cases and in sentence cases, it may be helpful where there is a complex issue (CPD 10.8.2).

D.8.2 Skeleton arguments must be concise, succinct and define the issues[110]. A numbered list of points in no more than one or two sentences should be grouped under each ground of appeal. Cross references should be made to relevant document(s) but should not contain extensive quotations from documents and/or authorities. Authorities, where necessary should be cited as per CPD 10.8.4 a., and state the proposition of law and identify, but not quote, the part in support of the proposition. Where there is more than one, the skeleton should briefly state why (CPD 10.8.4 – 10.8.5). A chronology of relevant events will be necessary in most cases (CPD 10.8.6). In the event of non-compliance with the CPD or unless requirements have been varied by the Court, the CAO can refuse to accept service and may return for amendment.

108 The CAO can provide any documents from a DUC index that the advocate does not have.
109 See annex 1
110 See annex 1 for the practical requirements.

At the hearing the Court may refuse to hear argument on the point. A request for variation must give reasons and accompany the non-compliant document (CPD 10.8.7 – 10.8.8).

D.9 Listing of appeals[111]

D.9.1 The CAO summary contains time estimates for the hearing (including the delivery of the judgment) and the judge's reading time of the core material which advocates must review. The hearing date will be fixed using those estimates unless the listing officer is notified within seven days of receipt of the summary. Likewise, it is incumbent on the advocate to notify the Registrar of any matter which affects the estimates (e.g. abandonment of a ground) after the date has been fixed so that time estimates can be reconsidered (CPD 10.3.4). The Court will expect advocates to comply with the time listed.

D.9.2 Where necessary the Registrar may give directions for the listing of cases. The arrangements for the fixing of dates lies with the CAO listing officer (CPD 10.3.1). The CACD retains precedence over the lower courts but where possible, regard will be had for advocates existing commitments and particularly if an advocate is acting pro bono, the list office will try and accommodate any reasonable listing request. In general, a commitment in a lower court will not be regarded as a good reason for failing to accept a proposed date. A lower court can and should contact the Registrar where there are difficulties in releasing the advocate (CPD 10.3.2).

D.10 Remote attendance requests (live-link direction): participants (s.51 Criminal Justice Act 2003[112]*)*

D.10.1 The default position is that hearings will be in person[113]. The Court has the power to require[114] or permit remote[115] attendance by giving a live-link direction which can be varied or rescinded at any time.

D.10.2 Crim PR 3.35 – 3.39 reflects the provisions contained in s.51 – s.56 CJA 2003[116] which practitioners will be familiar with as they apply to all criminal courts.

111 Appeal includes applications for leave to appeal (CPD 10.3.6) and directions hearings.

112 See Crim PR 3.35 – 3.39

113 It is acknowledged that this will not always be possible or reasonable in the circumstances of the case; see Review of the Year In the Court of Appeal, Criminal Division pp 7 – 8.

114 For applicants/appellants in custody, subject to their right to attend (see E1 below); the Court requires attendance via live-link unless the Court orders that they be 'bought up'. For a court approved interpreter for the hearing, the Registrar may give a live-link direction.

115 In practice it is the presiding Lady/Lord Justice who will consider and give any direction.

116 See also Guidance for criminal courts on live links (judiciary.uk)

D.10.3 To request a live-link direction, each advocate or other instructed legal representative, applicant/appellant not in custody and witness, including expert witness[117], must complete a separate application form[118] and send by email to criminalappealoffice.courtclerks@justice.gov.uk as soon as reasonably practicable[119] and where possible at least 7 days before the hearing to allow sufficient time for the request to be considered. Applications received after 4.00pm on the day before the hearing may not be granted.

D.10.4 In considering the written application[120], the Court will consider the interests of justice, any guidance issued by the Lady Chief Justice and all the circumstances of the case. For the purposes of the CACD, this includes the views of other represented parties. Any party making an application for remote attendance (i.e. a live-link direction) must confirm that that the parties have been given an opportunity to make representations[121]. Where the party making the application has been informed that there are no objections, this information should be included on the form.

D.10.5 In cases where witnesses may be called to give evidence, the form must be emailed to **the casework group with conduct of the case**[122] as soon as practicable after leave has been granted or referral made to the full Court. It is the practice of the Registrar to[123] obtain directions about the need for witnesses to attend either in person or via live-link from the presiding Lady/Lord Justice prior to the final hearing.

D.10.6 All participants must comply with the **general conditions and rules for remote participation** contained within the application form and advocates are additionally referred to the guidance issued by the LCJ on the 14th February 2022.

117 S.52 CJA 2003.

118 The forms can be downloaded from Procedure Rules and Practice Directions for the Court of Appeal – Courts and Tribunals Judiciary. Practitioners will be familiar with the Crim PR form "application for a live-link direction, Crim PR 3.36" whilst the CACD prefers the use of its own form, this form will be acceptable and it must be sent to criminalappealoffice.courtclerks@justice.gov.uk

119 Crim PR 3.36 (1)(a)

120 Crim PR 3.35 – 3.36 and s.51 (4) – (6).

121 See s.51 (4)(b). The Court does not require the application to have been served in accordance with Crim PR 3.36(1)(b)(ii).

122 criminalappealoffice.areference@justice.gov.uk (A Group) criminalappealoffice.breference@justice.gov.uk (B Group).

123 See B.8.4 above

D.11 Remote observation requests (transmission direction): professional, court users, public (s.85A Courts Act 2003)

D.11.1 Only the full Court has the power to grant permission. Anyone seeking a transmission direction[124], including practitioners who are not formally instructed in the proceedings must email the application[125] for remote observation to criminalappealoffice.courtclerks@justice.gov.uk as soon as reasonably practical and where possible at least 7 days before the hearing to allow sufficient time for the request to be considered. Applications received after 4.00pm on the day before the hearing may not be granted. The Registrar, through the CAO staff, will ensure that the constitution is consulted as soon as possible but, if necessary, the links can be arranged by the court staff on a provisional basis, subject to the full Court making a direction at the start of the hearing.

D 11.2 All observers must comply with the conditions and rules contained in the application form.

E FULL COURT HEARING

E.1 Attendance

E.1.1 Leave granted/referral.

E.1.1.1 An appellant in custody is entitled to be present at an appeal and to be represented by an advocate, if instructed. The full Court is likely to grant permission to attend a referral. Attendance by an applicant in custody is usually via video link.

E.1.1.2 However, if the single judge/Registrar deems that issue is a technical error and that the full Court can deal with the case without oral argument, then the application for leave and appeal will be determined on the papers.[126] If the matter is listed for directions then the appellant/applicant in custody will not be entitled to attend unless the Court give him leave. In practice the presiding judge will consider the application in advance of the hearing.

124 E.g. public observers or journalists. Note s.85A (5)(b) that a direction may give further provision that "the persons who are to be able to watch or listen to the transmission (including provision making that ability subject to conditions, or aimed at preventing persons who are not meant to watch or listen from being able to do so)"

125 The application form is on Procedure Rules and Practice Directions for the Court of Appeal – Courts and Tribunals Judiciary

126 S.22 Criminal Appeal Act 1968, CrimPR 39.11, *R v Hyde and Ors* [2016] EWCA Crim 1031).

E.1.2 Renewal

E.1.2.1 An applicant in custody is not entitled to be present[127] unless leave is given by the Court but may be represented by an advocate on a pro bono or privately paying basis. A litigant in person (LIP) is not entitled to address the Court unless permission is given by the Court.[128] If the prosecution advocate is present, for example, because there are linked applications which require the presence of the prosecution, the advocate must take care "not to stray into issues that are particular to an unrepresented applicant".[129]

E.1.2.2 In sentence cases involving a fatality, if leave is granted and the prosecution is not in attendance, the Court must consider adjourning the hearing so that the CPS may instruct an advocate and to give the victim's family notice and opportunity to attend[130] (CPD 10.2.7).

E.1.2.3 In all other sentence cases, if an advocate attends on behalf of the applicant, instructions should be obtained prior to the hearing should the Court grant leave and proceed in the applicant's absence and hear the appeal[131].

E.1.3 Evidence Presentation System (EPS)

E.1.3.1 The EPS has now replaced the Clickshare system which was previously used by practitioners to share digital evidence during court proceedings. This system no longer requires the use of dongles; instead, practitioners may connect their devices via a wired connection at the prosecution end of the bench or wireless adapters which can be used elsewhere in the court.

E.1.4 Funding

E.1.4.1 If a representation order is not already in place, the full Court on a directions or renewal hearing (if the full Court think there is merit in an application) can grant a representation order.

127 S.22 Criminal Appeal Act 1968, CrimPR 39.11; either in person or via CVP. An applicant not in custody can attend the hearing but leave is still required to address the Court.
128 The obligations on LIP's was addressed by the Court in *Zuman* [2023] EWCA Crim 79
129 *Zuman* ibid at [67]. It is of note that the CPD no longer contains the bar to prosecution attendance but the principles of *Nasteska v The former Yugoslav Republic of Macedonia (Application No.23152/05)* must still be observed per Zuman at [68].
130 This is to allow the prosecuting authority to comply with statutory obligations under the Victims Code.
131 *R v Spruce and Anwar* [2005] EWCA Crim 1090

E.2 Judgments

E.2.1 Where judgment is reserved, CPD 10.9 sets out the expectations in respect of the draft judgment, amendments, communication of it to the parties and timetabling. It is **extremely important** to read both the covering email and the judgment heading and to abide by the restrictions placed on the handling of the judgment[132].

E.2.2 Where there is to be an application for a retrial[133] or either party wishes to make any other application consequent on the judgment, the judge's clerk, copied to the caseworker and listing, should be informed with a time estimate by 12 noon on the day before the judgment is handed down. Where proposed directions are requested by the court, these should be sent to the judge's clerk, copied to the caseworker and listing.

E.2.3 No fee is payable to advocates attending a hand down if not required to do so by the Court (CPD 10.9.6).

E.3 Re-trials[134] ordered by the Court of Appeal

E.3.1 Practitioners should note the provisions in CPD 5.11.6 and 5.11.7; the Crown Court must comply with the directions of the Court of Appeal and cannot vary those directions without reference to the Court of Appeal. The custody time limit is 112 days starting from the date that the new indictment is preferred i.e., from the date that the indictment is delivered to the Crown Court.

E.3.2 Arraignment must take place within two months from the date of the order for a retrial[135].

E.3.3 Where an order has been made pursuant to s.4(2) Contempt of Court Act 1981 which postpones reporting of the appeal proceedings pending conclusion of the retrial, the prosecution must notify the Registrar as soon as the retrial proceedings have concluded.

132 R v Hussain [2013] EWCA Crim 990 and R v Counihan [2024] EWCA Crim 799

133 S.7 Criminal Appeal Act 1968

134 S.8 Criminal Appeal Act 1968; see also CrimPR 39.8, 39.9 and 39.14

135 *R v Layden* [2025] UKSC 12 The procedure set out in section 8 is mandatory and should be followed. Where there has been no arraignment within two months of the order for retrial this should be brought to the attention of the Crown Court and the prosecution should make an application to the Court of Appeal for leave to arraign out of time. Once such an application is made the Court of Appeal has jurisdiction to deal with it pursuant to section 8 *(overruling R v Llewellyn [2022] EWCA Crim 154).*

E.4 Certification of a point of appeal to the Supreme Court.

E.4.1 It is of assistance for the judge's clerk to be informed prior to hand down of any intention to request a certification but this is not obligatory, and the time limit is 28 days[136]

F USEFUL CONTACTS AND INFORMATION

Registrar of Criminal Appeals: Master Alexandra Beldam KC

Address:

Criminal Appeal Office
The Royal Courts of Justice
Strand
London
WC2A 2LL
Telephone: 020 7947 6011
General Email: criminalappealoffice.generaloffice@justice.gov.uk
Lodging new applications: criminalappealoffice.areference@justice.gov.uk

Enquiries/service after form NG lodged
All cases are assigned a CAO Reference number, and each case has a letter at the end which dictates where the relevant query should be directed:
Conviction (B Group): criminalappealoffice.breference@justice.gov.uk
Sentence (A Group) enquiries: criminalappealoffice.areference@justice.gov.uk

Hearing enquiries
Including matters relating to CVP/remote hearings and other practical issues:
Listing: criminalappealoffice.listoffice@justice.gov.uk
Court clerks: criminalappealoffice.courtclerks@justice.gov.uk
Opening hours and facilities
HMCTS Personal Information Charter

Useful Websites:
The Court of Appeal, Criminal Division – Courts and Tribunals Judiciary Judiciary
Criminal Procedure Rules (Appeal) and Criminal Practice Directions
Criminal Procedure Rules; forms: See part 34 onwards
Daily Cause Lists
Previous Court of Appeal decisions: Bailii, National Archives; Court of Appeal (Judiciary.uk)
Sentencing Council
Criminal Cases Review Commission

136 S.34 Criminal Appeal Act 1968

CPS; Appeals to the Court of Appeal
The Supreme Court
Court of Appeal Criminal Division – GOV.UK (www.gov.uk)

Legislation:
Administration of Justice Act 1960
Criminal Justice Act 1967
Criminal Appeal Act 1968
Criminal Justice Act 1972
Prosecution of Offences Act 1985
Criminal Justice Act 1987
Criminal Justice Act 1988
Criminal Procedure and Investigations Act 1996
Proceeds of Crime Act 2002
Criminal Justice Act 2003
Domestic Violence, Crime and Victims Act 2004
Serious Organised Crime and Police Act 2005
Serious Crime Act 2007
Legal Aid, Sentencing and Punishment of Offenders Act 2012
Sentencing Act 2020
Judicial Review and Courts Act 2022
Police, Crime, Sentencing and Courts Act 2022

SI's:
The Criminal Legal Aid (General) Regulations 2013
Criminal Procedure (Amendment) Rules 2021 (S.I. 2021/40)
Criminal Legal Aid (Determinations by Court and Choice of Representative) Regulations 2013 [SI 2013/614]

Recommended reading:
Court of Appeal Criminal Division; A Practitioners Guide – 2nd edition; edited by Alix Beldam & Susan Holdham, ISBN 9780414064737, published by Sweet & Maxwell.

G ANNEX 1 – PRACTICAL GUIDANCE ON PREPARATION OF DOCUMENTS, BUNDLES AND SUBMISSION TO THE CAO

G.1 Grounds of appeal/skeleton arguments/RN's

G.1.1 DCS

It is a requirement to create hyperlinks to relevant documents on DCS. Its purpose is to assist the practitioner and avoid the need for producing and lodging annexes. It assists the judiciary as the material will be more easily navigable.

To create a hyperlink:

- In the DCS review pane use the 'Copy Link' tab which takes the URL of the page and allows it to be pasted in a document.
- When pop-up window appears, select the text and press 'Ctrl+C' on your keyboard to copy the URL.
- Please note that this method allows the user to hyperlink to a specific page. For example, if the reader needs to be taken to page 6 of a particular document, then the link can be created by going to page 6 and following the steps above.
- On occasions the advocate might want to refer the reader to a sequence of documents and to hyperlink each would be unwieldy. In that case a particular section could be hyperlinked. To do this:
    - Select the sections pane and go to the section required.
    - Click on view documents and press 'Ctrl+C' on your keyboard to copy the URL from the address bar.

The reader can then download relevant documents in one bundle or individually.

To embed the link into a word or phrase:

- Highlight the word or phrase with the cursor.
- Press 'Ctrl+K'
- In the pop-up box, click 'existing file or web page' (usually opens as default)
- Paste link into box and click ok.
- The word or phrase should now be underlined and in blue text.

Note: it is only possible to put URL links (https://) such as DCS and other websites (e.g. sentencing council). Hyperlinks to documents on a desktop (C:/Users/jbloggs/Downloads/) will not work for other users.

There is guidance also available on the DCS training page.

Having created the word document and inserted the hyperlinks and the document is ready for submission; the word document needs to be saved as a PDF file; click 'save as' on the word document and then under the name of the document click 'save as type' and select PDF. Do not use the 'print PDF' option. The title should include the applicant's name and CAO case number.

G.1.2 Non-DCS cases

These cases are generally those that pre-date DCS (2015), some confiscation cases and non-CPS prosecutions. For these cases the CAO and CACD use eJudiciary Document Upload Centre (DUC). Only the CACD judges and the CAO can access documents on DUC albeit the CAO can provide a time limited link so that practitioners can upload documents in non-DCS cases.

It is recognised that practitioners may not be able to fully comply with the CrimPR by hyperlinking grounds of appeal/skeleton arguments/RN's to relevant material.

Practitioners are, therefore, encouraged to submit the form NG, grounds of appeal and any ancillary application or RN and a single bundle of relevant documents. The grounds must comply with the CrimPR and CPD as far as possible and instead of a hyperlink ensure that relevant documents are identified, the sections which need to be considered and an adequate description of where they can be found, for example at title, page and paragraph number (CPD 10.4.1 c.).

G.2 Document guidance

Where possible documents created, such as grounds of appeal, should be served in pdf format. They must be:

- presented in A4 page size and portrait orientation, in not less than 12-point font and in 1.5 line spacing (CPD 10.4.1).
- set out in consecutively numbered paragraphs.
- So that the document text can be 'copy and pasted' and is searchable. This is referred to as OCR in some guidance[137].
- Check that the hyperlinks work before submission.

G.2.1 Skeleton arguments (CPD 10.8)

- The beginning of the document must include CAO reference number, the appellant's surname and titled skeleton argument, the date on which the document was served and conclude with the advocates' names.
- Should be A4 and in portrait orientation, in no less than 12-point font and in 1.5-line spacing.
- Not normally exceed 15 pages and be self-contained

137 If a document is created in word and saved as a PDF it will contain editable text. If the document is scanned an OCR program needs to be used to convert the graphic into text. OCR technology reads text from PDFs and images, then converts them into actual text that you can interact and work with.

G.3 Bundles: authorities and core bundles for the full Court.

The most appropriate format for the core[138] and authorities[139] bundle will be a PDF file. To create bundles, it is necessary to have access to pdf bundling software. The 'how to' instructions will depend on the software but invariably it will be user friendly and/or have a simple guide/tutorial to assist the user.

- Core bundles should follow the CAO index template where possible (CPD 10.7.4). In more complex cases it might be necessary to order the bundle differently. The case lawyer can always advise if necessary.
- The filename should contain the CAO reference number, the appellant's surname and a short title for the bundle, i.e., "Bundle of Authorities" or "Appeal Bundle".
- All documents should be A4 and in portrait orientation. If an original document is in landscape, then it should be inserted so that it can be read with a 90-degree rotation clockwise. No document should appear upside down.
- The default view for all pages should be 100%
- Pages should be numbered. This can be done automatically from the 'Number Pages' tab but care should be taken to ensure that the number does not mask relevant detail on the original document.
- The PDF should be fully booked marked. The bookmark description should be clear, e.g., the name and citation of the authority or what the document is, e.g. witness statement of A Bloggs 10.2.23.

To create the bookmark:

- In the home tab click on the blue ribbon. This opens the navigation pane.
- Highlight some text on the page – it need not be the authority's name or document name

Click and a box with 'untitled' in it will appear; type the descriptive name of the authority or document in the box (or paste ('ctrl + v') if the copied text is the description)

- There must be an index at the start of the document; clickable links to the documents are useful – look for 'build a table of contents' tab; this will build an index from the bookmarks and the index will contain clickable links and page references.
- If amendments need to be made to the bundle, practitioners should liaise with the CAO and confirm whether a replacement bundle should be served or whether any additions can be lodged as a supplemental bundle.

138 CPD 10.7
139 CPD 10.8.13 – 10.8.14

The default position is that paper bundles will not be required unless in exceptional circumstances (CPD 10.7) and this will be communicated to the parties. In such cases, four copies should be supplied to the CAO in good time for the hearing (CPD 10.7.4)

G.4 Bundles and functionality of DCS in court

It might be helpful for judges and advocates alike to be aware that there can be limitations for viewing bundles within the DCS review pane. The two main issues are that, firstly, the number generated (in red) by DCS will not be the same as the bundle pagination and secondly, the document is not being viewed as a PDF and will not have the PDF functionality e.g., the bookmark navigation pane. To ensure consistently between judges and advocates it is recommended that bundles are downloaded to the users' desktop. This can be achieved in more than one way, but the easiest way is:

- From the review pane go to the 'PAGE' tab
- Click on 'download document'.
- A pop-up window will show the PDF in a list.
- Do not open file from the pop-up window (if you do, then click on 'save as' and save to desktop and open the file from there)
- Open file explorer on your desktop; go to downloads and select the file from there. This will open the file in a PDF.
- Click on the blue ribbon and this will open the navigation pane from which you can click to go directly to the document required.

G.5 Video material

It is helpful to the CAO if the grounds of appeal and/or RN indicate whether any footage is relevant to the grounds and issues to be determined by the Registrar/single judge and/or the full Court. Advocates are requested to provide guidance to the judges by identifying files/dates/times of the relevant footage, including providing a hyperlink to any footage already included on DCS and giving a short narrative in cases where it might not be obvious what the footage is showing, e.g., that a witness is not in the footage when the evidence suggests they should be (CPD 10.4.1).

It should be noted that CACD judges cannot view egress via links on DCS, however hyperlinking to that material does assist in identifying it. In cases where the parties have identified footage relevant to the application and/or appeal. CAO staff will liaise with the CPS for an egress link to be provided to the judges. This will not be accessible by anyone else, and the parties need to make arrangements with the CPS to ensure that they have an accessible link.

CACD judges and the CAO have no access to material on Evidence.com or similar platforms such as one drive. The CAO and judiciary are also unable to view material provided on removable media such as USBs. In these cases, which may include fresh evidence cases, it will be necessary for the parties to contact the CAO so that arrangements can be made with the CPS for the uploading of material onto egress.

G.6 Submission of documents to the CAO

- **Users must not upload any document to CACD1.** Any relevant document outside of CACD1 must be hyperlinked in the grounds. **Transcripts must be lodged with the CAO and not uploaded to DCS:Y.**
- The form NG, grounds of appeal and ancillary applications are likely to be within the email size limit (or can be emailed in more than one email – each email must be clearly marked) but if an authorities bundle (and/or core bundle) is too large to email, the CAO caseworker should be notified. A time limited link to the eJudiciary Document Upload Centre can be provided and CAO staff will transfer any bundle to DCS or in non-DCS cases to the case file in DUC.
- Before submission of any document or bundle containing hyperlinks, please check the links work.
- Documents should not be emailed to the case lawyer/caseworker as this will not be effective service. The correct email addresses are in G.7 below.

G.7 Late papers

The expectation is that bundles and material for the Court will be submitted in good time for the hearing (CPD 10.7.4). Any late papers for the judges must be identified with an URGENT – LATE PAPERS marking, the case reference number and the hearing date and emailed to:

- criminalappealoffice.areference@justice.gov.uk (sentence cases) or
- criminalappealoffice.breference@justice.gov.uk (conviction and confiscation cases) and
- The other party if represented at the hearing.

DO NOT email late papers to the case lawyer and/or worker as there is no guarantee that the papers will reach the judges in good time or before the hearing.

G.7.1 Index template (only include relevant documents; these are prompts and examples)

Part 1 APPEAL DOCUMENTS

- Grounds of Appeal or Perfected Grounds of Appeal
- Extension of time reasons.
- Form RN
- Waiver of Privilege Documents
- Signed Waiver
- Trial counsel's comments dated
- Trial solicitors' comments dated
- Applicant's response dated
- Fresh evidence
- Applicant's / Appellant's Skeleton Argument
- Respondent's Skeleton Argument

Part 2 TRIAL / CROWN COURT DOCUMENTS

- Indictment
- Committal for Sentence or Memorandum of Conviction
- Other Order e.g., SHPO, ASBO, SOPO, Restraining Order

Part 3 TRANSCRIPTS

- Rulings
- Evidence
- Summing Up
- Prosecution Facts
- Sentencing Remarks
- "Newton" Hearing (NB: important to distinguish this transcript)
- Oral Probation Report
- Other (specify)

Part 4 REPORTS

- Antecedents
- Antecedents (co-defendant e.g., in "disparity" cases)
- Pre-Sentence (in chronological order, earliest first, if more than one)

- Medical (Physical) (in chronological order, earliest first, if more than one)
- Medical (Psychiatric/Psychological) (in chronological order, earliest first, if more than one)
- Prison Report
- Victim Personal Statement
- Character References (applicant/appellant/co-defendants)
- Other (specify)

Part 5 OTHER (material from the Crown Court proceedings)

- Prosecution Case Summary/Opening Note
- Written Basis of Plea
- TICs
- Defence Statement
- Admissions / Agreed Facts
- Route to Verdict
- Record of Police Interview
- Photographs/video footage
- Judge's written rulings/orders

H ANNEX 2 – OTHER APPEAL TYPES

H.1.1 Interlocutory Appeals against rulings in Preparatory Hearings (CrimPR 37)

Where a judge has ordered a preparatory hearing, they may make a ruling as to the admissibility of evidence and any other question of law relating to the case.[140]

The defence or the prosecution may appeal to the CACD (and ultimately to the Supreme Court) against such a ruling, but only with the leave of the trial Judge, single judge or the full Court. As to the scope of a judge's powers in relation to a preparatory hearing and thus the extent of appeal rights, see *H* [2007] UKHL 7; *R v V.J.A* [2010] EWCA Crim 2742 and *BHQ* [2023] EWCA 1018.

If the trial date is imminent and the application is urgent, the Registrar should be notified so that consideration can be given to a referral to the full Court.

140 s.9 of the Criminal Justice Act 1987 or s.35 of the Criminal Procedure and Investigations Act 1996

An application for leave to appeal is made to the trial judge and should be made orally immediately after the ruling, or within two business days by serving a notice of an application on the appropriate officer of the Crown Court and all parties directly affected (CrimPR 37.4). Notice of an appeal[141] or application for leave to appeal (form NG (Prep)) must be served on the Registrar, the Crown Court and the parties within five business days of the ruling or the trial judge's decision whether to grant leave (CrimPR 37.2).

A Respondent's Notice (form RN (Prep)) must be lodged within five business days of service of the appeal notice (CrimPR 37.5).

Defence representatives are usually covered by the Crown Court representation order if one is in force (s.16 (3) (b) and para 5(3) Sched.3 Legal Aid, Sentencing and Punishment of Offenders Act 2012).

If the relevant time limits are not complied with, the Court has power to grant an extension of time. Where a single judge refuses leave to appeal or an extension of time within which to serve a notice, the application may be renewed for determination by the full Court by serving the notice of renewal, appropriately completed, upon the Registrar within five business days of the refusal being served (CrimPR 37.7).

H.1.2 Appeals by a prosecutor against a ruling adverse to the prosecution[142] (CrimPR 38)

The prosecution has a right of appeal in relation to some rulings in relation to a trial on indictment[143]. The right to appeal a ruling has been held to be wide enough to encompass a case-management decision[144].

There is no right of appeal in respect of a ruling that the jury be discharged or a ruling in respect of which there is a right of appeal to the Court of Appeal by virtue of another enactment[145]. The prosecution should therefore consider whether there is a right of appeal under s.9 CJA 1987 or s.35 CPIA 1996.

The prosecution must inform the Court that it intends to appeal immediately after becoming aware of the ruling[146] after the ruling or request an adjournment until the next business day to consider whether to appeal in which case the Court must be told on or before the expiry of the time limit (CrimPR 38.2(2), CrimPR 38.5). The judge has discretion to adjourn for longer if there is a real reason

141 See CrimPR 37.3 for the requirements and format of the applications and see annex 1

142 The CACD disapproved the use of "terminating" or "terminatory" ruling; R v AYP [2024] EWCA Crim 952 at [20]

143 S.58 Criminal Justice Act 2003

144 *R v Clarke* [2007] EWCA Crim 2532

145 s.57(2) Criminal Justice Act 2003

146 On the 7th April 2025, CrimPR 38.2 (1) (a) amended the rule to include "after becoming aware of the ruling"

for doing so.[147] Leave should be granted only where the Judge considers there is a real prospect of success and not to speed up the hearing of the appeal[148]. Whether or not leave is granted, the trial judge must decide if the appeal is to be expedited and if so, adjourn the case. If he decides that the appeal should not be expedited, then he can adjourn the case or discharge the jury.[149]

The application (form NG (Pros)) and grounds of appeal[150] must be served on the Crown Court, Registrar and every defendant affected by the ruling the next business day if the trial judge expedites the appeal or five business days if not (CrimPR 38.3). The prosecution must give the undertaking (as to the defendant's acquittal if the appeal is abandoned or leave to appeal is not obtained) at the time when it informs the Court of its intention to appeal. The failure to give it then is fatal to an application to the Court of Appeal for leave[151]

A RN (Form RN (Pros)) must be served the next business day if the trial judge expedites the appeal or within five business days of service if not (CrimPR 37.5).

Defence representatives are usually covered by the Crown Court representation order if one is in force (such proceedings being considered incidental; (s.16 (3) (b) and para 5(3) Sched.3 Legal Aid, Sentencing and Punishment of Offenders Act 2012), although the Registrar/Court can grant a representation order for two counsel or an application for a K.C even if not covered by the Crown Court representation order, if the Regulations are satisfied.

Expedition does not impose time limits on the Registrar or CACD. However, if leave has not been granted by the trial judge, the application may be referred to the full Court by the Registrar to ensure that the matter is dealt with quickly.

The Registrar endeavours to list prosecution appeals, as quickly as possible, where a jury has not been discharged. In such cases it is of great assistance if a phone call is made to the Registrar or CAO General Office (0207 947 6011) notifying the office even before the appeal notice is sent, so that preliminary views can be taken as to the constitution which may be able to hear the appeal. The listing of an urgent appeal invariably means that other cases have to be removed from the list.

147 *R v H* [2008] EWCA Crim 483
148 *R v G* [2006] EWCA Crim 3276
149 s.59 Criminal Justice Act 2003
150 See CrimPR 38.4 for the requirements and format of the applications and see annex 1
151 s.58(8) Criminal Justice Act 2003, *R v LSA* [2008] EWCA Crim 1034; *R v NT* [2010] EWCA Crim 711; *R v B* [2014] EWCA Crim 2078).

H.1.3 Other appeal types at a glance – For guidance see the requisite legislation and CrimPR.

Type of appeal	Legislation	CrimPR	Note	Respondent's Notice (RN)	Funding	Leave to appeal
Attorney General's reference of an unduly lenient sentence The Attorney General can refer sentences only in relation to specific offences or sentences (ss.35 & 36 Criminal Justice Act 1988 and Criminal Justice Act 1988 (Reviews of Sentencing) Order 2006)	S. 36 Criminal Justice Act 1988	CrimPR 41	Although CrimPR 41.3(1) implies there is a specific form to commence proceedings, in practice a standard letter with supporting documents is sent to the Registrar by the Attorney General's Office no more than 28 days after sentence	If the defendant wishes to make representations to the Court he **must** serve a Respondent's Notice within 14 days of the Registrar serving the application upon him. Again, there is no specific form available	Representation orders are granted by the Registrar to respond to an Attorney General's reference	Full court
Attorney General's reference of a point of law on an acquittal			There is no time limit			Leave not required

Type of appeal	Legislation	CrimPR	Note	Respondent's Notice (RN)	Funding	Leave to appeal
Prosecution appeal against the making of a **confiscation order** or where the Court declines to make one (save on reconsideration of benefit) Prosecution and third party appeal against a determination, under S.10A Proceeds of Crime Act 2002, of the extent of the defendant's interest in property	S.31(1) & (2) Proceeds of Crime Act 2002 S. 31(4) & (5) Proceeds of Crime Act 2002	CrimPR 42	Serve Form PoCA 1 on all affected parties and the Registrar within 28 days of the decision appealed against	Form PoCA 2 served on the Registrar and applicant not later than 14 days after receiving **Form PoCA 1**	An undischarged Crown Court representation order will cover advice and assistance on the merits of opposing the appeal and drafting the RN, otherwise an application for a representation order can be made to the Registrar. Where an application for a representation order is made on Form **PoCA 2**, the Registrar will consider a representation order for the hearing. For interested parties, civil legal aid may be available.	Single judge or the full court

Type of appeal	Legislation	CrimPR	Note	Respondent's Notice (RN)	Funding	Leave to appeal
Appeal in relation to a **restraint order** – The prosecution or an accredited financial investigator can appeal a refusal to make a restraint order. A person who applied for an order or who is affected by the order can apply to the Crown Court to vary or discharge the order and then appeal that decision to the CACD	S. 43 Proceeds of Crime Act 2002	CrimPR 42	Serve Form PoCA 3 on the Registrar within 28 days of the decision being appealed and must then be served on any respondent, any person who holds realisable property to which the appeal relates, or is affected by the appeal, not later than seven days after the form is lodged with the Registrar.	Form PoCA 4 served on the Registrar not later than 14 days from request and on applicant and any other respondent within 21 days of request	If a defendant has been charged with a criminal offence connected to the order, then the proceedings are regarded as incidental and treated as criminal proceedings for funding (s.14 LAPSO 2012). Before proceedings and for persons affected by the order civil legal aid may be available.	Single judge or the full court
Appeal in relation to a **receivership order** – The appointment, non-appointment or powers of a receiver can be appealed, as can an order giving a direction to a receiver and the variation or discharge of a receivership order. An appeal can be brought by the person who applied for the order, a person who is affected by the order or the receiver	S. 65 Proceeds of Crime Act 2002	CrimPR 42	Serve Form PoCA 3 on the Registrar within 28 days of the decision being appealed and must then be served on any respondent, any person who holds realisable property to which the appeal relates, or is affected by the appeal, not later than seven days after the form is lodged with the Registrar.	Form PoCA 4 served on the Registrar not later than 14 days from request and on applicant and any other respondent within 21 days of request	See restraint above	Single judge or the full court

Type of appeal	Legislation	CrimPR	Note	Respondent's Notice (RN)	Funding	Leave to appeal
Appeal in relation to a **receivership order** – The appointment, non-appointment or powers of a receiver can be appealed, as can an order giving a direction to a receiver and the variation or discharge of a receivership order. An appeal can be brought by the person who applied for the order, a person who is affected by the order or the receiver	S.65 Proceeds of Crime Act 2002	CrimPR 42	Serve Form PoCA 3 on the Registrar within 28 days of the decision being appealed and must then be served on any respondent, any person who holds realisable property to which the appeal relates, or is affected by the appeal, not later than seven days after the form is lodged with the Registrar	Form PoCA 4 served on the Registrar not later than 14 days from request and on applicant and any other respondent within 21 days of request	See restraint above	Single judge or the full court

Type of appeal	Legislation	CrimPR	Note	Respondent's Notice (RN)	Funding	Leave to appeal
Appeal against a **finding of unfitness to plead or a finding that the accused did the act or made the omission charged**	S. 15 Criminal Appeal Act 1968	CrimPR 39	See section A2. Lodging of Form NG and grounds of appeal, *R v Roberts* [2019] EWCA Crim 1270 and *Arion Kurtaj v R* [2025] EWCA Crim 1163	See B.10 Respondent's Notice	Payment is from central funds but is dependent on outcome, *Arion Kurtaj v R* [2025] EWCA Crim 1163	Crown Court judge, single judge or the full court
Appeal against the order **following a verdict of not guilty by reason of insanity or a finding of unfitness to plead**	S. 16A Criminal Appeal Act 1968		An accused who, as a result of a verdict of not guilty by reason of insanity or a finding of fitness to plead has a hospital order, interim hospital order or supervision order made against him may appeal against the order	See B.10 Respondent's Notice		
Appeal against a **verdict of not guilty by reason of insanity**	S. 12 Criminal Appeal Act 1968	CrimPR 39	See section A2. Lodging of Form NG and grounds of appeal	See B.10 Respondent's Notice	Payment is from central funds but is dependent on outcome. *Arion Kurtaj v R* [2025] EWCA Crim 1163	Crown Court judge, single judge or the full court

Type of appeal	Legislation	CrimPR	Note	Respondent's Notice (RN)	Funding	Leave to appeal
Appeal against **review of sentence** A defendant or specified prosecutor may appeal	S. 74(8) Serious Organised Crime and Police Act 2005	CrimPR 39	Serve Form NG (RD) on the Registrar not more than 28 days after the review	See B.10 Respondent's Notice	An application for a representation order can be made to the Registrar	Single judge or the full court
Appeal against an order for **trial by jury of sample counts** Appeal against an order relating to a **trial to be conducted without a jury where there is a *danger* of jury tampering** Appeal against an order that a **trial should continue without a jury or a new trial take place without a jury *after* jury tampering** All Prosecution or defence	S. 18 Domestic Violence, Crime and Victims Act 2004 S. 45(5) and (9) Criminal Justice Act 2003 S. 47 Criminal Justice Act 2003	CrimPR 37	Form NG (Prep) must be served on the Crown Court, the Registrar and any party directly affected not more than five business days after the order or the Crown Court Judge granting or refusing leave	Form RN (Prep) should be served if the court directs or the prosecution (or any party affected) wants to make representations to the court	Representatives are usually covered by the Crown Court representation order if one is in force; (s.16 (3)(b) and para 5(3) Sched.3 Legal Aid, Sentencing and Punishment of Offenders Act 2012).	Crown Court judge, single judge or the full court

Type of appeal	Legislation	CrimPR	Note	Respondent's Notice (RN)	Funding	Leave to appeal
Appeal against a **wasted costs order** by third party against a third party costs order made against them by legal or other representative against the making of a wasted costs order against them	Regulation 3C Costs in Criminal Cases (General) Regulations 1986		There is no specific form. Notice of appeal should be served on the Registrar and any interested party within 21 days of the order being made.	Any interested party can make representations orally or in writing		Leave is not required (s. 19A Prosecution of Offences Act 1985)
Appeal relating to **Serious Crime Prevention Orders** A person subject to the order, an applicant authority or anyone given the opportunity to make representations at the Crown Court about the making, variation or non variation of an order	S. 24 Serious Crime Act 2007	CrimPR 39	Serve of Form NG (SCPO) on the Registrar not more than 28 days after the order			

Type of appeal	Legislation	CrimPR	Note	Respondent's Notice (RN)	Funding	Leave to appeal
Appeal against orders **restricting or preventing reports or restricting public access** Applications for leave to appeal and appeals in relation to reporting restrictions may be heard in private (CrimPR 36.6(1)). Applications for leave to appeal and appeals relating to restricting public access may be decided without a hearing but the decision must be announced at a hearing in public (CrimPR 36.6(3)). In either case, if the hearing relates to public interest immunity, it must be in private unless the Court otherwise directs (CrimPR 36.6(2)).	S. 159 Criminal Justice Act 1988	CrimPR 40	Serve Form NG (159) on the Registrar, the Crown Court, the prosecutor and defendant and any other affected person. Applications against orders **restricting reporting** shall be made within 10 business days after the date on which the order was made. Applications against orders to **restrict public access** must be made the next business day after the order was made. If advance notice of an order restricting public access is given, then advance notice of an intention to appeal may be made not more than five business days after the advance notice is displayed	Form RN (159) if he wishes to make representations to the court or the court so directs within three business days	The court may make such order as to costs as it thinks fit (s.159(5)(c) Criminal Justice Act 1988), but not out of central funds (*Steele Ford & Newton v. CPS No.2* [1994] 1 AC 22	Single judge or the full court

H.1.4 Application for a Retrial for a Serious Offence

H.1.4.1 Application by a prosecutor to quash an acquittal and seek a retrial of a qualifying offence[152] *(CrimPR 27)*

There must be new and compelling evidence and it must be in the interests of justice for the acquitted person to be re-tried. Evidence was "new" if it had not been adduced at trial and for the purposes of s.78 (2), evidence was "adduced" if it had been put forward in evidence.[153]

Proceedings can begin in one of two ways:

1. By serving notice of the application on the Registrar and the acquitted person within two days of the decision having been made. This notice charges the acquitted person with the offence. It requires the personal written consent of the Director of Public Prosecutions (DPP)

   If the acquitted person is not in custody the prosecution can ask the Crown Court to issue:

   (i) A summons for the acquitted person to appear before the Court of Appeal for the hearing of the application

   (ii) A warrant for his arrest

   Once arrested on the warrant the acquitted person must be brought before the Crown Court within 48 hours.

2. An acquitted person may be charged with the offence before an application has been made. This may be after an arrest in an investigation authorised by the DPP or where no authorisation has been given, after arrest under a warrant issued by a justice of the peace. Having been charged, the acquitted person must be brought before the Crown Court to consider bail within 24 hours and can be remanded in custody or on bail for 42 days whilst an application is prepared. Once a notice of application has been made, stating that the acquitted person has previously been charged with the offence, the acquitted person must be brought before the Crown Court to consider bail within 48 hours of the notice being given to the Registrar, if the acquitted person is already in custody under s.88 (above) (s.89(2) CJA 2003).

In either case, bail is dealt with largely by the Crown Court. The CACD only considers bail on the adjournment of the hearing of the application under s.76[154].

152 S.76 (1) Criminal Justice Act 2003; see also ss.78, 79, s.80, s.87, s.88, s.89

153 Criminal Justice Act 2003 and *MH* [2015] EWCA Crim 585 for a review of the authorities

154 s.90(1) Criminal Justice Act 2003

The notice should where practicable be accompanied by the witness statements which are relied on as the new and compelling evidence, the original witness statements, unused statements, indictment, paper exhibits from the original trial, any relevant transcripts from the original trial and any other documents relied on (Crim PR 27.2(2)).

An acquitted person who wants to oppose a s.76 application must serve a response not more than 28 days after receiving the notice (Crim PR 27.5(2)).

H.1.4.2 Application by a prosecutor for a determination whether a foreign acquittal is a bar to a trial and if so, an order that it not be a bar

The prosecution can apply, with the personal written consent of the DPP for a determination whether an acquittal outside the UK is a bar to the acquitted person being tried in England and Wales and if it is found to be so, an order that the acquittal not be a bar. Proceedings can begin in the same way as for an application under s.76 (1) Criminal Justice Act 2003, *see section E1 above.*

H.1.5 Application for restrictions on publication relating to an application under s.76 Criminal Justice Act 2003

An application can be made by the DPP for reporting restrictions[155]. This can be made after a notice of an application for a re-trial has been made and may also be made by the Court of its own motion. An application can also be made by the DPP for reporting restrictions **before** a notice of an application for a retrial if an investigation has been commenced. The application for reporting restrictions must be served on the Registrar and (usually) the acquitted person (CrimPR 27.3(2)).

A party who wants to vary or revoke an order for restrictions on publication may apply to the Court of Appeal in writing at any time after the order was made (CrimPR 27.3(3)).

The Registrar will grant a representation order to the acquitted person for solicitors and counsel to respond to any of the above applications.

155 S.82 Criminal Justice Act 2003

Appendix B

Sample pleadings

1 SAMPLE GROUNDS OF APPEAL AGAINST CONVICTION AND APPLICATION TO EXTEND THE TIME LIMITS

The following is a sample that has been drafted in order to indicate a possible approach to a straightforward application for leave to appeal against conviction and an application for extension of the time limit within which to give notice of application for leave to appeal. It is not intended as a rigid blueprint.

IN THE COURT OF APPEAL

CRIMINAL DIVISION

REGINA
-v-
NED KELLY

GROUNDS OF APPEAL AGAINST CONVICTION AND APPLICATION FOR EXTENSION OF TIME WITHIN WHICH TO APPLY LEAVE TO APPEAL

Introduction

1. The Applicant appeals against his conviction for possessing an offensive weapon. He does so on the grounds of a material misdirection at his trial, whereby the Judge failed to tell the jury what, in law, they would have to find proved to be sure the petrol bomb was an 'offensive weapon'. Had the jury been directed that it was for the prosecution to make them sure that the bomb was made to injure a person, they may well have doubted whether the prosecution had proved its case.

2. The Applicant also apples for an extension of time within which to apply for leave, given these *Grounds* are submitted approximately 18 months after conviction. That application is dealt with as a discrete topic at the end of these *Grounds*.

Facts

3. The allegations concerned an incident that took place on 11 August 2011. Police in the London Borough of Tower Hamlets were patrolling the local area in a police carrier as violent disturbances took place across London. At around 1:20 am, the carrier was travelling along Mile End Road, E1 the location of the rear entrance to Stepney Police Station. Officers saw four to six males standing near to the rear gates of the police station. On seeing the carrier, the males ran and entered a parked Ford Escort car. The Applicant, who had been part of that group, did not enter the car but ran off. It later transpired that the car belonged to him.

4. The carrier attempted to stop the car but was unable to do so. One of the officers chased and caught up with the Applicant. He stopped, turned towards the officer and raised his hands above his head. He was detained. An officer found a pair of gloves on the route that the Applicant had run. While speaking to the Applicant it was noted that he smelt of petrol.

5. A search of the area around the rear of the police station revealed four petrol bombs. The Applicant was arrested for possession of an offensive weapon. He was taken back to the police stationed and interviewed. In interview, the Applicant denied the offence saying that he had been walking towards his girlfriend's house when he had been confronted by a group of young men wearing gloves and masks. He denied that it was his vehicle that the men had fled into and that he had ever seen the petrol bombs before.

6. Further enquiries by the police demonstrated that much of what the Applicant had said in interview was untrue. At trial, he accepted that he had travelled to the police station in his car. He claimed that he had been kidnapped and taken there by drug dealers to whom he owed money. Once at the scene he had been forced to assist in making petrol bombs by pouring petrol into beer bottles. He had no involvement with the bombs thereafter and had just been standing alongside the group when the police carrier had turned the corner.

The trial

7. The Applicant stood trial before His Honour Judge Jones at Inner London Crown Court in February 2012 charged with the following two counts:

   (1) Count 1. Possessing petrol bombs with intent to destroy or damage property, contrary to section 3(a) of the Criminal Damage Act 1971.

(2) Count 2. Possessing an offensive weapon, the petrol bombs, contrary to section 1 of the Prevention of Crime Act 1953.

8. The two counts were in the alternative. In opening the case Prosecution Counsel said in terms:[1]

> 'You will see there are two counts on the indictment and these counts are in the alternative … If [count 1] is proved … then you don't need to consider count 2.'

9. In summing up the Judge:

(1) Made clear the two counts were in the alternative.[2]

(2) Directed the jury that petrol bombs were offensive weapons and 'no-one has suggested" otherwise, given "there is no lawful or peaceful reason to put petrol in a bottle with a paper wick that anyone can think of. It is designed specifically for use as a weapon, as a missile, to cause fire and damage'.[3]

(3) Explored the issues the jury would need to consider on count 1, including 'did he share the intention in count 1 to destroy or damage property, whether the police station or some other building or a car or whatever, by the use of those items?'[4]

10. After lengthy deliberations and following a majority direction, the jury acquitted the Applicant of count 1, but convicted him of count 2 by a majority of 10 to 2 on 20 February 2012.

Events after trial

11. After the Applicant was convicted and imprisoned he and his family sought fresh advice. After some delay those now acting for the Applicant were supplied with the papers in the case and have settled these *Grounds*. The history of the new representation is dealt with in more detail in the final section below, seeking an extension of the normal leave period.

12. Pursuant to the Court's guidance in *R v McCook* [2014] EWCA Crim 734, those now representing the Applicant, who did not act at trial, have sent these *Grounds* in draft form to the trial advocate; his reply is attached to this document. In essence he accepts that it would have been preferable had he raised the point taken in these *Grounds* with the trial judge before the summing up. The Applicant is grateful for that concession and would note that the judge and prosecuting advocate fell into what is submitted to be the same error.

1 Transcript 1, 5B then 6B.
2 Transcript 2, 6B and 27D.
3 Transcript 2, 6E to H.
4 Transcript 2, 9A.

Submissions

13. Section 1 of the Prevention of Crime Act 1953 [as amended], insofar as relevant to this appeal, states:

> '(1) Any person who without lawful authority or reasonable excuse, the proof whereof shall lie on him, has with him in any public place any offensive weapon shall be guilty of an offence …
>
> …
>
> (4) In this section … "offensive weapon" means any article made or adapted for use for causing injury to the person, or intended by the person having it with him for such use by him or by some other person.'

14. In *R v Simpson* (1984) 78 Cr App R 115, Lord Lane CJ identified three categories of offensive weapon: those made for use for causing injury to the person (offensive per se), those adapted for such a purpose, and those not so made or adapted, but carried with the intention of causing injury to the person. In the first two categories, the prosecution do not have to prove that the defendant had the weapon with him for the purpose of inflicting injury. Once a jury are sure that the weapon is offensive per se, the defendant will only be acquitted if he establishes lawful authority or reasonable excuse.

15. The jury at the Applicant's trial were told that petrol bombs were offensive weapons and 'no-one has suggested' otherwise, given 'there is no lawful or peaceful reason to put petrol in a bottle with a paper wick that anyone can think of. It is designed specifically for use as a weapon, as a missile, to cause fire and damage'.[5]

16. It is submitted this is wrong. An incendiary device can be made either to injure people or damage property. Indeed, it was the prosecution case that the latter was probably what was intended here; see the nature of count 1 and the summing up in respect of that count:

> 'did he share the intention in count 1 to destroy or damage property, whether the police station or some other building or a car or whatever, by the use of those items?'[6]

17. There may be many cases in which the circumstances of the possession of a petrol bomb may provide an irresistible basis for an inference that it was made with the intent of injuring a person or persons. However, on the facts of this case there was an alternative possibility, that the Applicant was in possession of the bomb with the intention of causing damage to property; indeed that alternative was the main thrust of the prosecution case.

5 Transcript 2, 6E to H.

6 Transcript 2, 9A.

18. It follows that had the issue been left to the jury they may have entertained at the very least a doubt, and consequently the conviction for count 2 is unsafe and this appeal should be allowed.

Application for an extension of leave period

19. The Solicitor who now acts for the Applicant has made a witness statement, attached to these *Grounds*, setting out the history of the passage of time between the Applicant's conviction and these *Grounds* being lodged. In essence the time was taken up as follows:

    (1) Trial Counsel advised that there were no grounds of appeal; given the concession now made by Counsel, it is submitted that that advice may not have been correct.

    (2) Thereafter the Applicant and his family made numerous efforts to seek fresh advice. Those efforts were handicapped both by their lack of wealth and the fact that, perhaps unsurprisingly, they did not spot the technical legal point now pursued.

    (3) Some months later they made contact with the Solicitor now acting who agreed to consider whether there were grounds for an appeal. There was then a very considerable delay while the trial papers were obtained from the previous solicitors. Those papers were 'chased' on numerous and regular occasions.

    (4) Once the papers were located and passed on, Counsel was instructed and she advised that a transcript of the summing up was required. The Legal Aid Authority then refused the application for funding and that refusal had to be appealed to the area Committee.

    (5) Once the transcript was finally obtained and supplied to Counsel along with all the trial papers, these *Grounds* were drafted and lodged within three weeks.

Conclusion

20. In conclusion, it is submitted that this Applicant has always protested his innocence and he and his family have done all that was practically possible to get fresh advice. Once new lawyers were in place it is submitted that they acted properly and efficiently in getting these *Grounds* in a fit state to be lodged. For all these reasons it is submitted that the Court should allow the extension now sought.

[Signed by the advocate drafting]

Quality Street Chambers

25 September 2014

2 SAMPLE GROUNDS OF APPEAL AGAINST SENTENCE

This is a sample that has been drafted in order to indicate a possible approach to a straightforward application for leave to appeal against sentence. It is not intended as a rigid blueprint.

IN THE COURT OF APPEAL

CRIMINAL DIVISION

REGINA
-V-
KARON JOSEPH

GROUNDS OF APPEAL AGAINST SENTENCE

Introduction

1. The Applicant applies for leave to appeal against her sentence of seven years' imprisonment, passed by HHJ Jolly at Acton Crown Court on 13 February 2014. In summary the grounds advanced are:

    (1) The Judge was wrong to reject the basis of plea without at least warning that he was minded to do so. Such a warning would have allowed the Applicant's advocate to make submissions and inform the Judge of unused material of which he was unaware.

    (2) The Judge was wrong to only allow a reduction of 12.5 per cent for the Applicant's guilty plea at the pleas and case management hearing.

Facts

2. The Applicant was arrested on 23 September 2013 after police officers entered and searched the address where she lived. They found a knotted carrier bag under the Applicant's bed that contained some 25 wraps of crack cocaine. Each wrap was made from cling film, with a total weight of 120 grams. They also found electronic scales with two pans that a scientist was later to say had 'very probably' been used to make crack cocaine from the powered form of the drug, 14 rolls of cling film [all in the kitchen] and three mobile phones in the sitting room that rang on numerous occasions during the search. A police officer attempted to answer these calls but when he did so the calls were immediately terminated. These facts were all evident from the prosecution papers that were supplied to the Judge.

3. The unused material contained the following material [as attached to these *Grounds*] that was not served on the Court and consequently was not known to the Judge:

   (1) Various documents that suggested at least three other people lived in the same house, including Martin Jones and Ken Owen.

   (2) Jones had a number of previous convictions for supplying cannabis and heroin, and a recent conviction for possession of a small amount of cocaine.

   (3) Owen had two previous convictions for possessing cocaine and cannabis and seven for offences of violence, mainly of a low level but he had served a six-year sentence for wounding with intent some eight years before the time of the search.

4. The Applicant did not speak at all when the house was being searched or when she was arrested on suspicion of possession with intent to supply the crack cocaine. She was later interviewed under caution and answered 'no comment' to all the questions asked of her. She had one previous conviction for assault police some five years previously for which she had received a community order. She was aged 27 at the time of sentence and worked part time as a carer.

5. In preparing the case her solicitor had taken a number of statements from her mother, father and elder sister who between them suggested that she had little money and would often borrow small sums of money from them or allow them to buy her drinks on social occasions.

6. The Applicant was committed to the Crown Court. At a preliminary hearing no plea was entered despite HHJ Dour QC reminding her and her advocate that under the authority of *Caley*, maximum credit for any guilty plea could only be guaranteed by a plea indicated or entered at that hearing.

7. At the PCMH the Applicant pleaded guilty to the single count she faced, that of possessing cocaine with intent to supply. She did so on the basis of a written basis of plea [copy attached] that included the passage:

   > 'The defendant was not a drug dealer in the sense that she did not sell to drug users or anybody else, but she admits by her plea that she possessed the drugs intending to supply them; another person had given her the drugs to look after. While she does not claim to have been acting under duress, she did feel obliged to help out another who lived in the same house from time to time, so she put the drugs under her bed until that other person would ask for them back.'

8. The Prosecution opened the facts of the case to HHJ Jolly, but made clear they 'could not gainsay' the basis of plea and did not seek a *Newton* hearing. The mitigation advanced on behalf of the Applicant included:

(1) Reliance on the basis of plea and the submission that this placed the Applicant in the category of 'lesser role' in the sentencing guidelines. Given the Prosecution's stance and the very heavy list that HHJ Jolly was dealing with, no further time was taken up rehearsing the items of unused material or familial evidence, as set out above, such as supported the basis.

(2) A submission that the Applicant, as a woman of almost good character, could be forgiven for being too scared of the inevitable custodial sentence that would follow to plead at the preliminary hearing, and that therefore the Court should grant her maximum, or close to maximum, credit for her timely plea at the PCMH.

9. In passing sentence HHJ Jolly said:

(1) He did not believe a word of the basis of plea. The Defendant was a grown woman. It was all too easy for any major drug dealer to claim, when caught red handed, that they were only minding the drugs for no profit. Yet here was a defendant arrested in her own house, surrounded by all the accoutrements of a busy commercial drug dealer. She had not said a word about any lesser role either upon arrest or in her interviews under caution. Therefore he would take her role to be a 'leading role' under the sentencing guidelines. Given that the drugs were clearly being packaged and prepared for sale to street level users [which was not in dispute] this was a category 3 case. He therefore adopted a starting point of eight years six months.

(2) *Caley* makes clear the sentencing judge is not deprived of all flexibility; this was a defendant who had chosen to stay silent at interview, had not indicated a plea at the preliminary hearing despite being specifically warned, and now entered a guilty plea when confronted with overwhelming evidence of guilt; the drugs, the wrappings, the scales, the pans and the 'dealer phones'. As such while he would of course make a reduction for the guilty plea, it would be a moderate one.

10. The judge then took the above starting point, eight years six months, deducted six months for the defendant's lack of relevant previous convictions and deducted one year (thus an eighth or 12.5 per cent) for the guilty plea. The Judge consequently passed a sentence of seven years imprisonment.

Submissions

11. It is submitted the Judge was wrong to disregard the basis of plea without at least warning the Applicant that he was minded to do so, see *R v Smith (Patrick)* (1988) 87 Cr App R 393 and *R v Dudley* [2012] 2 Cr App R (S)

15. Similarly, paragraph B10, *Criminal Practice Directions (Sentencing)* [2013] 1 WLR 3164 states in terms that, 'A Judge is not entitled to reject a defendant's basis of plea absent a Newton hearing unless it is determined by the court that it is manifestly false'. It is submitted that the basis advanced was not manifestly false and, in any event, if the Judge were of that belief he was still obliged to warn the Applicant of that view.

12. This was not merely a technical failing. The unused and defence material, as set out above, would have allowed submissions to be made that:

   (1) There was an obvious better candidate for the person with the senior position in the drugs supply from that house, Martin Jones.

   (2) Another person who was a perfectly sensible candidate for playing a role in the supply of drugs, also linked to the house was Ken Owen. His history of violence provided a perfectly credible explanation for why the Applicant might not have been keen to set out the history of her limited involvement with the drugs either on arrest or in interview.

   (3) The evidence from the Applicant's family would have gone beyond merely providing other possible candidates for the main drug dealing, and would have been positive evidence that she was not engaged in what is obviously a highly lucrative trade.

13. It is therefore submitted that the Judge was wrong not to warn of his view of the facts. Had he done he may well have been persuaded that he should accept the Applicant's basis of plea was the proper basis for sentence.

14. As such, it is submitted, the proper starting point in the Applicant's case, from the sentencing guidelines, for a defendant with a lesser role in category 3, one of three years' custody.

15. This Court will be very familiar with the case of *Caley* [2013] Cr App R (S) 47 and the Sentencing Guidelines Council guidelines on credit for guilty pleas. To summarise the relevant parts for the purposes of this appeal [with paragraph numbers from *Caley*]:

   (1) Whilst the sentencing judge does have flexibility as to the first reasonable time for a guilty plea to be indicated or entered, the criminal justice system should aim to be consistent between defendants, thus allowing those who act for them to advise properly [9].

   (2) The Court specifically rejected using the police interview as the first opportunity [12]

   (3) The reduction for a plea at the PCMH will be about a quarter [19]

(4) The Courts need to be very slow and cautious before concluding a case is overwhelming and withholding the normal reduction. Even in a truly overwhelming case where the sentencing court was entitled to reduce the credit, it would still not go below 20 per cent for a plea at the first opportunity [23 and 24].

16. Applying the above to the facts of the instant application, it is submitted:

(1) The Judge was quite entitled to reject the defence application for full, 33 per cent, credit as there had been no plea at the preliminary hearing.

(2) The Judge was wrong to attach significance to the Applicant remaining silent in interview and at the scene, given the views of this Court in *Caley*.

(3) This was not an overwhelming case. Although it was obvious that the house was being used as a centre for drug dealing, the existence of other candidates who were identified as users of the house, including a man who had been convicted of serious offences of violence and the Applicant's very limited criminal history may have lead some defendants in her position to seek to advance the defence of duress. As such the Applicant should have received the usual 25 per cent reduction. If this Court accepts that argument, the final sentence should have been in the region of 23 months [in other words three years as above, reduced by 25 per cent] plus any allowance such as the Judge made for the lack of any relevant convictions.

(4) Even if the case were overwhelming, it is submitted the reduction the Judge allowed, of 12.5 per cent, was simply insufficient for a plea at the PCMH.

17. For all these reason it is submitted this Applicant should be granted leave and her sentence should be very significantly reduced.

Anthony Advocate

Criminal Solicitors

Date

3 DRAFT STATEMENT OF FACTS AND STATEMENT OF ALLEGED VIOLATION AND LEGAL ARGUMENTS FOR AN APPLICATION TO THE EUROPEAN COURT OF HUMAN RIGHTS

An application to the European Court of Human Rights must be made using the Court's own application form. However, the substance of the application will be contained in the statement of facts and the statement of alleged violation(s) and relevant legal arguments that will accompany the form itself. This is a sample that is intended to indicate a possible approach to both drafting exercises. It is not intended to be a blueprint.

Statement of the facts

1. On 10 September 2010, Alfred Jones was the victim of various offences. He gave police an account of being parked outside his home waiting for his friend Ralph to join him when he was kidnapped and placed into a van. Thereafter he was driven around, assaulted, robbed and demands were made to his friends via his own mobile phone to bring large amounts of cash to a meeting place. His car was also stolen. He was able to escape some hours later. He supposedly identified the Applicant Davies as the man who first approached him as part of the kidnap and identified a blue Suzuki van as the vehicle used in the kidnap, false imprisonment and blackmail. There were a series of links between the Applicant Dawes and that van.

2. The purported identification of Davies was, at its highest, qualified. In essence, Mr Jones stated at the identification procedure that he could not be sure ['Out of all of them number 3 gave me an inkling … Can't be 100 per cent sure but I'd say number 3', number 3 being the position in the video line up at which the Applicant Davies was shown] but by stages ended up claiming in a later witness statement that he was sure of his identification of Davies as the man who had first approached him.

3. There were various alleged links between the Applicant Dawes and a blue Suzuki van. After describing the van used by his abductors in terms no more than, at best, consistent with the blue Suzuki van ['a Rascal … a little Nissan van … a little blue thing … that royal kind of blue … a transit'], six months later he was shown photographs of that van and said, 'This is the type of van I was kidnapped in … I can say that this is exactly the van that it was'.

4. In the course of the kidnap Mr Jones was asked to tell the kidnappers where his cocaine was to be found and the abductors clearly assumed that his friends would have ready access to large amounts of cash. Peter Huseyin, a friend of Jones who became a prosecution witness, first became aware of these events when the friend Ralph drove up and said that 'someone's tried to rob me and Alf outside his flat. I saw some guys near Alf's car but I don't know where he is'. Huseyin then drove for a few minutes to the area of Jones' flat. Ralph did not assist the police and was not a witness. Neither Ralph nor Huseyin called the police. Jones' girlfriend eventually called the police and the call was logged as being received at 00:20.

5. In addition to the identifying evidence from Jones, the prosecution relied on phone calls between the three defendants' mobile phones, and all three phones being cell sited in the same general area where the offences were taking place. It is noted in passing that the Applicant Davies was acquitted of counts 2 and 3 [false imprisonment and blackmail] and the

co-defendant Phipps acquitted of all counts. Thus the jury did not regard the cell site alone evidence as sufficient proof of guilt on any count.

6. Counts 4 and 5 on the trial indictment alleged that the Applicant Dawes and the co-defendant Phipps had committed an aggravated burglary on 24 September. That allegation was based on phone evidence, the use of the car stolen from Jones in the course of counts 1 to 3, and the possession of a blackberry mobile phone, stolen in the aggravated burglary, by Phipps shortly afterwards. Both men were acquitted.

7. Count 6 alleged a robbery of a lorry delivering cigarettes on 24 November 2010. A camera in that lorry showed that the Suzuki van to which Dawes had the links was used by the robbers and a photograph from the same source was said to be him; he was found guilty of that count.

8. The trial was fixed for 7 June 2012. In the days before trial Mr Jones notified the police that he would not attend Court to give evidence. He alleged that on Monday 30 May his mother received a call on her landline number asking to speak to him. He then received a phone call on his mobile phone. According to Mr. Jones' statement 'It was from a private number on my mobile phone number ending 138. A male voice said, "I would advise you not to go to trial. There are a lot of people upset, they are on standby waiting for the word". I did not recognise this voice. It sounded black. I hung up the phone. Straightaway the phone rang back with private number. I answered the call but did not say anything. I did not listen to the phone and hung up. The phone rang again and my girlfriend Simone answered the call. They told her the same things and said they were in ********. She told them not to ring again and hung up the phone. During the first phone call the person told me details about the case such as what I said in my statement and details about the identity parade. I do not know if I want to go to court now. I am scared for my family. I am worried that they know details about the case.'

9. Mr Jones was visited by Detective Constable Stewart who offered him various forms of witness protection and told him he might be witness summonsed; he replied that in that case he would not say anything in Court and would not give his evidence.

10. The prosecution did not seek a summons or warrant but applied to read Mr Jones' evidence under section 116 of the Criminal Justice Act 2003.

11. The application was opposed and the arguments advanced encompassed the conditional or mixed nature of the identifying claims made by the witness. Further, as regards the potential for the defendants to have been responsible for the threats, it was known that at the time that the Appellant Davies was in custody and in solitary confinement and the Appellant Dawes, being under 21, was in a Young Offenders Institution, separate from both his co-defendants.

12. In addition, there was submitted to be another candidate for having made the threats; Darren Davies was a cousin of both Applicants. He was, at

the time leading up to the trial, wanted as a suspect with regard to all the counts on the indictment and was indeed named as another offender on count 6 of the trial indictment. He was arrested a few days prior to trial and found to have the trial committal bundle stored on his laptop, with the statements by Alfred Jones highlighted. He was charged, but at a later stage the Prosecution dropped all charges against him.

13. The trial Judge ruled that the evidence could be adduced. His decision was based on his finding that the Appellants had played some part in the threats being made. The terms of that finding were:

    '(1) On basis of material available to me at the moment, I conclude as a matter of fact, so that I am sure about it, that Mr. Jones was put in a state of extreme fear by these defendants or by somebody associated with them and with their knowledge and/or approval. In other words, these defendants are associated with those threats. I find that as a fact to the criminal standard.

    (2) I have found as a fact it is through deliberate actions attributable to these defendants or with their approval that Mr. Jones is absent.'

14. The Judge also accepted that Mr Jones' evidence was 'sole or decisive' in one sense, though there was supporting evidence in the phone evidence. This ruling also, in effect, admitted the partial identifications, as it considered that aspect and made reference to section 78 of the Police and Criminal Evidence Act 1984. The Judge also referred to both *Horncastle* and *Al-Khawaja*.

15. In terms of whether the evidence was reliable, the Judge did not deal with the later recognition of the van, but dealt with the identification of the Appellant Davies; he held that the stages of the move from the uncertain terms of the identification procedure to the later witness statements were all documented and provided a 'clear line of reasoning' for his doing so, concluding that in his judgment, 'the evidence of Mr Jones is reliable in the senses that I have described. It is documented, it is reasoned, it can be tested and it can be fully commented upon'.

16. The trial proceeded. The defendants all gave evidence and proffered various reasons for their phone contact and the presence of their phones in or around the general area of the kidnap. In summary, Dawes spoke of being in the area driving around selling cannabis. Davies testified that he had left his phone at the home of his cousin Darren Davies and it was being returned to him. The co-defendant Phipps spoke of being in the area and calling Dawes to try to buy some cannabis from him.

17. The Judge summed up and gave warnings as to the difficulties faced by the defence through the absence of the witness. He also gave a traditional Turnbull direction, to warn the jury of the dangers of identification evidence, namely that an honest witness can nonetheless be mistaken. In dealing with Mr Jones' 'identification' of the blue Suzuki van, the Judge

again warned the jury of the disadvantage the defence said they faced, but went on to suggest that the other links between the Appellant Dawes and the van could support the identification [whereas, it is submitted they were the distinct next link in the evidential chain, which only became relevant once the jury accepted that first identification]:

> 'The question for you, I would suggest, is that the van, that particular blue van, linked to the crimes? I have reminded you, I think though, on Mr Jones' evidence he gives a general description of the van for you to consider. He is then shown photographs and I have reminded you about those and what he has said about it, and how the defence say they have been disadvantaged by him not having him here to question him. But you also have, have you not, other evidence, if you accept it, which links Mr. Dawes to that particular van, where police observations of him in the street going to it are on two occasions at least.'

18. After their retirement the jury posed a question about the identification of the van by Alfred Jones, namely:

> 'In reference to admission 5, do the defence say that Alfred Stevens positively identified the Suzuki van with the registration X493LBJ? We feel there is a contradiction between paragraph 5 of the admissions and Mr Dunn's [defence Counsel at trial for Dawes] closing statement regarding the positive identification of the particular van.'

19. The Judge answered the question, pointing out that the admissions merely gave the date, 18 March 2011, when Alfred Jones 'wrote a statement concerning the Suzuki Supercarry panel van X493LBJ'. He added a reminder of the disadvantage that the defendant faced given the inability to question Mr Jones about that identification.

20. Amongst the varied verdicts, the jury acquitted of a number of counts that were founded on phone use and cell site evidence placing phones connected to the three defendants in the area of the false imprisonment, namely counts 2 and 3 against the Appellant Davies, and counts 1 to 3 against the defendant Phipps.

21. All the convictions that are the subject of these appeals were by way of majority verdicts.

22. The Applicant's appealed against their convictions. Both were given leave to appeal against their convictions on the basis of the trial Judge's admission of Alfred Stephen's evidence. In summary, their grounds of appeal submitted:

    (1) There was no evidential basis such as allowed for the conclusion reached by the trial Judge that the Defendants were behind threats made to the complainant Alfred Jones such as prevented him from attending to give evidence at trial.

(2) Further, it is submitted that the combined effect of *Horncastle* in the Supreme Court and *Al-Khawaja and Tahery* in the Grand Chamber of the European Court of Human Rights was such that in the absence of an individual defendant threatening a witness away from trial, 'sole or decisive' evidence should not be admitted as hearsay unless there is exceptional and compelling support such as to suggest it is truthful and accurate.

23. The Applicants were granted leave to appeal. The Court of Appeal heard their case on 7 September 2012. The Court dismissed their appeal, finding:

(1) The trial Judge should have required the prosecution to make attempts to get Mr Jones to come to court, but that failing was not fatal to the conviction.

(2) The trial Judge's finding that the Applicants could be blamed for the fear of Mr Jones was impeccable. The Court did not identify what, if any, evidence could possibly be the basis for such a finding.

(3) The Court held that the evidence was admissible under the test expounded in *R v Riat* [see below].

24. On the same day, the Applicants applied to the Court of Appeal for the following question to be certified as a point of law of general public importance [thus allowing the Applicants to apply for permission to appeal to the UK Supreme Court]:

> 'Should the sole or decisive evidence of an absent witness be admitted as hearsay if it is not demonstrably reliable?'

25. Later that day the Court of Appeal indicated, by way of phone calls between Lady Justice Thorne's clerk and defence Counsel's clerks that the Court would not certify the question.

26. In the light of the refusal to certify, there was no further avenue of appeal open to the Applicant's in the domestic Courts.

Statement of alleged violation(s) of the convention and relevant arguments

The law

RELEVANT STATUTORY PROVISIONS

1. Section 116 of the *Criminal Justice Act* 2003 states as follows:

'116. Cases where a witness is unavailable

(1) In criminal proceedings a statement not made in oral evidence in the proceedings is admissible as evidence of any matter stated if–

(a) oral evidence given in the proceedings by the person who made the statement would be admissible as evidence of that matter,

(b) the person who made the statement (the relevant person) is identified to the court's satisfaction, and

(c) any of the five conditions mentioned in subsection (2) is satisfied.

(2) The conditions are–

(a) that the relevant person is dead;

(b) that the relevant person is unfit to be a witness because of his bodily or mental condition;

(c) that the relevant person is outside the United Kingdom and it is not reasonably practicable to secure his attendance;

(d) that the relevant person cannot be found although such steps as it is reasonably practicable to take to find him have been taken;

(e) that through fear the relevant person does not give (or does not continue to give) oral evidence in the proceedings, either at all or in connection with the subject matter of the statement, and the court gives leave for the statement to be given in evidence.

(3) For the purposes of subsection (2)(e) "fear" is to be widely construed and (for example) includes fear of the death or injury of another person or of financial loss.

(4) Leave may be given under subsection (2)(e) only if the court considers that the statement ought to be admitted in the interests of justice, having regard–

(a) to the statement's contents,

(b) to any risk that its admission or exclusion will result in unfairness to any party to the proceedings (and in particular to how difficult it will be to challenge the statement if the relevant person does not give oral evidence),

(c) in appropriate cases, to the fact that a direction under section 19 of the Youth Justice and Criminal Evidence Act 1999 (special measures for the giving of evidence by fearful witnesses etc) could be made in relation to the relevant person, and

(d) to any other relevant circumstances.

(5) A condition set out in any paragraph of subsection (2) which is in fact satisfied is to be treated as not satisfied if it is shown that the circumstances described in that paragraph are caused–

(a) by the person in support of whose case it is sought to give the statement in evidence, or

(b) by a person acting on his behalf,

in order to prevent the relevant person giving oral evidence in the proceedings (whether at all or in connection with the subject matter of the statement).'

RELEVANT ARTICLE OF THE CONVENTION

1. Article 6 states:

'(1) In the determination of his civil rights and obligations or of any criminal charge against him, everyone is entitled to a fair and public hearing within a reasonable time by an independent and impartial tribunal established by law. Judgment shall be pronounced publicly but the press and public may be excluded from all or part of the trial in the interest of morals, public order or national security in a democratic society, where the interests of juveniles or the protection of the private lives of the parties so require, or to the extent strictly necessary in the opinion of the court in special circumstances where publicity would prejudice the interests of justice.

(2) Everyone charged with a criminal offence shall be presumed innocent until proved guilty according to law.

(3) Everyone charged with a criminal offence has the following minimum rights:

(a) to be informed promptly, in a language which he understands and in detail, of the nature and cause of the accusation against him;

(b) to have adequate time and facilities for the preparation of his defence;

(c) to defend himself in person or through legal assistance of his own choosing or, if he has not sufficient means to pay for legal assistance, to be given it free when the interests of justice so require;

(d) to examine or have examined witnesses against him and to obtain the attendance and examination of witnesses on his behalf under the same conditions as witnesses against him;

(e) to have the free assistance of an interpreter if he cannot understand or speak the language used in court.'

Case law

1. A series of cases in the European Court of Human Rights considered the meaning of the Article 6(3)(d) right to 'examine or have examined witnesses against him'. In *Luca v Italy* (2003) 36 EHRR 46 at paragraph 40, the Court stated as follows:

> 'If the defendant has been given an adequate and proper opportunity to challenge the depositions, either when made or at a later stage, their admission in evidence will not in itself contravene Article 6.1 and 3(d). The corollary of that, however, is that where the conviction is both solely or to a decisive degree based on depositions that had been made by a person whom the accused has had no opportunity to examine or to have examined, whether during the investigation or at the trial, the rights of the defence are restricted to an extent that is incompatible with the guarantees provided by Article 6.'

2. This line of authority was ultimately considered by the Supreme Court in *R v Horncastle* [2010] 1 Cr App R 17. The Court rejected the 'sole or decisive' test, Lord Phillips holding at paragraph 108:

> 'In these circumstances I have decided that it would not be right for this court to hold that the sole or decisive test should have been applied rather than the provisions of the 2003 Act, interpreted in accordance with their natural meaning.'

3. The Court declined to follow the earlier ECHR section judgment in *Al-Khawaja and Tahery*, in the following terms [paragraph 11]:

> 'There will, however, be rare occasions where this court has concerns as to whether a decision of the Strasbourg Court sufficiently appreciates or accommodates particular aspects of our domestic process. In such circumstances it is open to this court to decline to follow the Strasbourg decision, giving reasons for adopting this course. This is likely to give the Strasbourg Court the opportunity to reconsider the particular aspect of the decision that is in issue, so that there takes place what may prove to be a valuable dialogue between this court and the Strasbourg Court. This is such a case.'

4. That reconsideration duly occurred when the Grand Chamber gave judgment in the UK government's appeal, *Al-Khawaja and Tahery* [2012] 54 EHRR 53. In essence, the Grand Chamber reaffirmed the 'sole or decisive' rule but modified the rigidity with which it should be applied. Thus at paragraph 147:

> 'The Court therefore concludes that, where a hearsay statement is the sole or decisive evidence against a defendant, its admission as evidence will not automatically result in a breach of Article 6 § 1. At the same time where a conviction is based solely or decisively on the evidence of absent witnesses, the Court must subject the proceedings to the most searching scrutiny'

5. Neither of the absent witnesses in *Al-Khwaja and Tahery* had been kept from court by the acts of the accused, but in discussing that situation the Grand Chamber stated [at paragraph 123]:

> 'When a witness's fear is attributable to the defendant or those acting on his behalf, it is appropriate to allow the evidence of that witness

to be introduced at trial without the need for the witness to give live evidence or be examined by the defendant or his representatives – even if such evidence was the sole or decisive evidence against the defendant. To allow the defendant to benefit from the fear he has engendered in witnesses would be incompatible with the rights of victims and witnesses. No court could be expected to allow the integrity of its proceedings to be subverted in this way. Consequently, a defendant who has acted in this manner must be taken to have waived his rights to question such witnesses under art. 6(3)(d). The same conclusion must apply when the threats or actions which lead to the witness being afraid to testify come from those who act on behalf of the defendant or with his knowledge and approval.'

6. In applying the modified test as to when 'sole or decisive' hearsay might be admitted, the Grand Chamber discussed the facts of the two cases. In *Al-Khawaja* the Court allowed the UK's appeal, finding that it 'would be difficult to conceive of stronger corroborative evidence' [paragraph 156] for the accuracy and truthfulness of the absent witness. In contrast, in *Tahery* the finding of a violation was upheld; in that case the victim had been stabbed but was unable to say which of the various men in the vicinity had stabbed him. The only witness who claimed that Tahery was the stabber made a statement to police within two days, then refused to attend court through a fear of being seen as an informer, which fear could not be shown to be brought about by Tahery. The Grand Chamber spoke of his evidence in these terms: 'Even though the testimony may have been coherent and convincing on its face it cannot be said to belong to the category of evidence that can be described as "demonstrably reliable"' [paragraph 160].

7. In *R v Ibrahim* [2012] EWCA Crim 837, the Court of Appeal considered the differing conclusions of *Horncastle* and the Grand Chamber judgment and suggested [at paragraph 89]:

> 'This difference may be more one of form than substance, however. Thus, the Court of Appeal talked of a conviction being based "solely or to a decisive degree on hearsay evidence admitted under the CJA" and the Supreme Court talked of the hearsay evidence being "critical evidence". That may not be very different from the Grand Chamber's concept of "sole or decisive". Next, the Court of Appeal and the Supreme Court both emphasise that when the untested hearsay evidence is "critical", the question of whether the trial is fair will depend on three principal factors. First, the English courts accept that there has to be good reason to admit the untested hearsay evidence. To decide this under English law there must be compliance with the statutory code. The Grand Chamber necessarily puts this requirement on a more general basis, but it emphasised the need for "justification". Secondly, and we think most importantly, all three courts stipulate that

there must be an enquiry as to whether that evidence can be shown to be reliable. Thirdly, all three courts are concerned with the extent to which there are "counterbalancing measures" and if so whether they have been properly applied in deciding whether to admit the "critical" untested hearsay evidence or to allow the case to proceed. In the case of England and Wales those "counterbalancing measures" must include all the statutory safeguards in the "code", as well as a proper application of common law safeguards, such as proper directions in the summing up. The Grand Chamber emphasised the same thing at paragraph 144 and particularly in its "general conclusion on the sole or decisive rule" at paragraph 147'

8. In the subsequent case of *R v Riat* [2012] EWCA Crim 1509, the Court of Appeal considered a number of appeals in the light of the Supreme Court judgment in *Horncastle*, the Grand Chamber decision in *Al-Khawaja and Tahery*, and the Court of Appeal's judgment in *Ibrahim*. At paragraphs 4–6 and 17, the Court explained that if *Horncastle*, *Al-Khawaja* and *Ibrahim* had been understood to suggest that evidence that was central or sole and decisive should only be admitted if it was clearly or manifestly reliable, that is to say accurate, then that was a misunderstanding. In fact, the position is that evidence can be admitted either if it is manifestly reliable or if any possible unreliability is such as can be tested by the jury.

Submissions: alleged violations of Article 6 of the Convention

1. The Grand Chamber in *Al Khawaja and Tahery* constructed a delicate accommodation so as to guard the rights of those within signatory states and yet to concede a degree of sovereignty to national courts as to the manner in which such rights are protected. It is submitted, with regret, that the decision in this case show that the English Court of Appeal has disregarded that delicate balance and that the current state of law now propounded by the UK Court of Appeal permits flagrant breaches of the right to a fair trial. It is further submitted that the response of the UK perhaps, with respect, confirms the fears of honourable dissenting Judges in the Grand Chamber decision, that:

   'The sole or decisive rule that has been followed so far was intended to protect human rights against the "fruit of the poisonous tree" … The adoption of the counterbalancing approach means that a rule that was intended to safeguard human rights is replaced with the uncertainties of counterbalancing.'

2. It is submitted that the Applicants rights under Article 6(3)(d) to 'examine witnesses against him' were violated at their trial. The witness Jones was central to the cases against both men. Without his account the prosecution could not have even begun their case. The evidence adduced was such as to identify the Applicant Davies and to identify the vehicle

closely associated with the Applicant Dawes. It is submitted to be telling that the other counts that were not supported by such identifications, both against these Applicants and against their co-defendant at trial, led to acquittals.

3. In the Grand Chamber of *Al-Khawaja and Tahery* this honourable Court adopted the modified test of not absolutely barring 'sole or decisive' hearsay evidence, but subjecting such evidence to 'the most searching scrutiny'. That level of scrutiny was illustrated in the outcome of those cases, whereby the 'demonstrably reliable' evidence against the Applicant Al-Khawaja led to the UK's appeal being allowed, whereas the lack of such evidence led to the decision in *Tahery* being unchanged. To apply a similar test, the evidence of the absent witness in the Applicants' case, his identification of the Applicant Davies was a flawed example of a form of evidence, identification evidence, that is considered dangerous even when given by a 'live' witness. In the Applicant Dawes's case, a bland statement describing a very common type of van in the most general terms was then followed much later by an assertion that the vehicle linked to the Applicant was the very same van.

4. In addition to the obvious weaknesses and potential for error in the nature of the evidence the missing witness gave, there was what could be seen as a 'drugs' background, in that his friends declined to call the police and the demands made of Mr Jones were, according to him, for cash and cocaine. Without expecting this honourable Court to make any finding adverse to that absent witness, that background of possible criminal activity by the complainant and his associates is such as to make his account even more in need of the most careful testing under cross examination.

5. If there were any evidential basis for the trial Judge's finding that the Applicants were both responsible for the absent witness being placed in fear, then it is accepted that this case would be outside the judgment in *Al-Kahwaja and Tahery*. It is submitted that there was simply no evidence of the Applicants being those responsible. It is submitted to be telling that neither the trial Judge nor the Court of Appeal even purported to identify any evidence such as could justify such a finding. Whilst this Court will very often defer to the facts found by the trial tribunal, if the Court is to guarantee rights that are practical and effective, it must be prepared not to allow a national court to shield its breaches of Convention rights by completely indefensible findings of fact.

6. The decision of the Court of Appeal in *Ibrahim* had the potential to resolve the dispute between this Court and the UK domestic courts by an accommodation that seemed to allow for the use of sole or decisive hearsay only it was manifestly reliable. The later judgment in *Riat* specifically 'explained away' that approach such that no such limit is now in place in the English law.

7. This Court will notice that the 'valuable dialogue' that Lord Phillips spoke of in the Supreme Court judgment in *Horncastle* has not taken place. This is because the English Court of Appeal has refused to certify a point of law of public important, thus cutting off the possibility of a further appeal within the English system, as section 33(2) of the Criminal Appeal Act 1968 states, inter alia, that an 'appeal lies only with the leave of the Court of Appeal or the Supreme Court; and leave shall not be granted unless it is certified by the Court of Appeal that a point of law of general public importance is involved in the decision'.

8. The Applicants therefore submit that they have suffered a violation of their right to a fair trial in that the trial judge's admitted sole or decisive evidence that they had no chance to challenge.

4 GOGANA STATEMENT

STATEMENT OF WITNESS

(Criminal Procedure Rules, r 27.2;
Criminal Justice Act 1967, s 9, Magistrates' Courts Act 1980, s 5B)

STATEMENT OF [Insert full name]

Age of witness (if over 18, enter 'over 18'): over 18

This statement consisting of [Insert number] pages is true to the best of my knowledge and belief and I make it knowing that, if it is tendered in evidence, I shall be liable to prosecution if I have wilfully stated in it anything which I know to be false, or do not believe to be true.

1. I am [Insert job description and role in the case] at [Insert employer/company]. [Insert brief overview of what you do] in the case of [Insert case name]. This statement is made in accordance with the guidance in *R v Gogana* and the Criminal Procedure Rules 2025. For ease of reference, I will refer to [Insert name of client] as 'the Applicant/Appellant [Delete]'.

   Any references to privileged documents which form part of the Applicant/Appellant's [Delete] file will not be exhibited with this statement.

   This statement deals with following proposed fresh evidence: [Insert list of new material] In accordance with section 23(1) of the Criminal Appeals Act 1968, I can confirm to the best of my knowledge that none of this material was adduced in evidence at the Applicant/Appellant's [Delete] trial.

2. <u>Medical reports contained in the medical records of [Insert name]</u>

   (a) During the course of our investigation into a potential appeal we discovered these medical records in [Describe how new material came to light and efforts made to obtain it]. The Applicant/Appellant [Delete] waived legal privilege with his previous representatives on [Insert date], and in accordance with our McCook duty to the court, we asked each of the original trial representatives about their knowledge of, and [potential failure to deploy], these records in letters dated [Insert summary of requests/responses]

   (b) [Provide details of all relevant exchanges]

3. <u>The witness statement of [Insert details of any witness evidence]</u>

   (a) [Summarise McCook exchanges] the defence advocate was asked in requests dated [Insert dates] whether the evidence of [Insert witness name] was put before the jury in any form, and if so, whether s/he was cross examined on the [Describe relevant issues].

   (b) [Describe all related steps/actions]

4. <u>The criminal convictions of [Insert name]</u>

   (a) Enquiries regarding bad character were put to the defence representatives in further McCook letters dated [Insert date(s)]. [All representatives responded/did not respond [Amend] to confirm the bad character applications were refused.]

   (b) On the [Insert date], we requested disclosure from the Crown of the particulars of further matters regarding [Insert name] that were outstanding at the time of his/her [Amend] conviction.

   (c) On the [Insert date], the Crown emailed this information to us.

   [Add any additional paragraphs covering other new information/ material in similar format to the above]

   [Add or refer to an attached chronology]

5. I believe the facts in this statement are true.

Signed: ....

Date:

Appendix C

Court of Appeal Bill of Costs

COURT OF APPEAL (CRIMINAL DIVISION)

BILL OF COSTS
FOR TAXATION BY REGISTRAR

If you require a version of this form to use with a screen reader (such as JAWS), or if you have a question about the form, please contact the Cost Office.

CRIMINAL APPEAL REFERENCE NO: ....

Regina v		Representation Order granted by lower Court	☐
Messrs	....	Representation Order granted by Court of Appeal dated	☐
of	....		
		Prosecution costs against Appellant	☐
Ref	....		
V.A.T. No	....	Appellant/Prosecution costs from central funds	☐

PLEASE READ NOTES ON PAGE 4 IMMEDIATELY

Solicitors should send with the Bill of Costs:- (a) The Brief and any instructions to and advice from Counsel: (b) The file of correspondence and record of attendances: (c) Details of all Disbursements and Accounts where appropriate.

DO NOT ENCLOSE COPY STATEMENTS OR EXHIBITS

In Representation Order cases no item in this Bill should relate to work undertaken prior to the date of conviction or sentence in the Crown Court, or prior to the date from which a Representation Order was granted in the Court of Appeal.

THIS BILL MUST BE COMPLETED IN BLACK INK OR BE TYPEWRITTEN FOR PHOTOGRAPHIC PURPOSES

1. PREPARATION OF APPLICATION FOR LEAVE TO APPEAL AND/OR APPEAL – PREPARATION AND CONSIDERATION OF DOCUMENTS.

Documents/Prepared considered (state nature and specify)	Status of Fee Earner ie Sen Sol, Sol Sen L Ex, Sen Clk, L Ex, or Art Clk	Date Work Undertaken	Time Taken Hrs Mins	Claimed £ p	Allowed £ p
			C.F.	£	

The Criminal Defence Services (Funding) Order 2001.

2. PREPARATION OF APPLICATION FOR LEAVE TO APPEAL AND/OR APPEAL – ATTENDANCES

PERSON INTERVIEWED [State name and whether client (c) or witness (w) and if alibi, factual, expert etc] and reasons for interview	**Status of Fee Earner ie Sen Sol, Sol Sen L Ex, Sen Clk, L Ex, or Art Clk**	**Date Work Undertaken**	**Time Taken Hrs Mins**	**Claimed £ p**	**Allowed £ p**
Brought forward from page 1				£	
The necessity for an interview with the client, in the prison or other place must depend upon the difficulty of the case.					
Travelling time to be shown separately.					
Show location of interviews.					
CONFERENCES [State purpose, Conferences held at Court should not be included here].					
LETTERS/EMAILS (Routine)					
TELEPHONE CALLS (Routine)					
NOTE Petty disbursements such as telephone charges, postage, etc form part of the overheads and should NOT be claimed.					
	Totals carried forward to Summary on page 3			£	

State below any unusual features of the case or any particular problems that were experienced in preparation which contributed materially to weight or difficulty.

3. CONDUCT OF APPLICATION FOR LEAVE TO APPEAL AND/OR APPEAL AT COURT – ATTENDANCES

PURPOSE [Specify as appn for bail, hearing etc. conferences at Court are normally included in the daily fee unless they represent material progress: please specify]	Status of Fee Earner ie Sen Sol, Sol Sen L Ex, Sen Clk, L Ex, or Art Clk	Date Work Undertaken	Time Taken Hrs Mins	Claimed £ p	Allowed £ p
	Totals carried down to Summary below:			£ 0.00	

SUMMARY		CLAIMED £ p	ALLOWED £ p
B/f from page 2 –	PREPARATION OF APPLICATION FOR LEAVE TO APPEAL AND/OR APPEAL	£	
B/d from above	CONDUCT OF APPLICATION FOR LEAVE TO APPEAL AND/OR APPEAL AT COURT	£0.00	
DISBURSEMENTS LIABLE TO V.A.T. [please specify]			
(a) Travelling expenses [identified by reference to parts 1 and 3]			
	Miles @		
	TOTAL for V.A.T. purposes	£	
	V.A.T.	£	
DISBURSEMENTS NOT LIABLE TO V.A.T. [eg agency work] Please specify and include vouchers			
	TOTAL CLAIMED AND ALLOWED	£	

Determining Officer: DATE:

COURT OF APPEAL – CRIMINAL DIVISION

IMPORTANT – PLEASE READ IMMEDIATELY

1. Where work of an exceptional nature is contemplated, or where the expenses will be heavy eg in travelling a long distance for a conference, it will be wise to consult the Registrar beforehand as to whether the work or the expense is likely to be regarded as reasonable.

   IF IN ANY DOUBT, DO PLEASE CHECK FIRST.

2. Appeals against Sentence: It is very rare that the Court grants Representation Order to solicitors – it is normally confined to Counsel only.

3. Appeals against Conviction: Although Representation Order to Solicitors is granted more frequently than in appeals against Sentence, it is still only granted in a small minority of cases: see note 2 above.

4. If Representation Order is granted to solicitors to cover attendance at the appeal hearing, consideration should be given to the instruction of solicitor agents if the cost of travel will be heavy.

5. Typing and Photocopying: these items are not normally allowed on taxation – if copies of Committal documents, transcripts etc are considered necessary, you should consult the Registrar before undertaking any expense.

6. A claim must be submitted within 3 months of the conclusion of the proceedings to which the Representation Order relates (Para 11, Schedule 1). No claim can be considered after this unless an extension of time is granted (Para 23, Schedule 1).

7. Reminders: Where

   (a) there are special circumstances, which should be drawn to the attention of the appropriate authority, the solicitor must specify them;

   (b) the solicitor claims that paragraph 4 of schedule 2, part 1 (ie enhanced rates) should be applied in relation to an item of work, he must give full particulars in support of the claim (Para 11, Schedule 1).

Index

All references are to paragraph numbers

– *contd*

G

S

T

DOUGHTY STREET CHAMBERS

doughty street chambers

Criminal Appeals

Since its foundation in 1990, Doughty Street Chambers and its barristers have taken as their guiding principle the use of the law for the advancement of the protection of human rights and civil liberties. It is now amongst the very largest and most wide-ranging civil liberties practices in the world, providing specialist advice, advocacy and training in the UK and around the world. Their practice areas include crime and criminal appeals, international crime (such as war crimes), fraud and financial services regulation, extradition, prisoners' rights, actions against the police, immigration, media law, professional regulation, children's rights, social welfare and housing, clinical negligence and more.

The Criminal Team is the largest practice group at Doughty Street Chambers. Its members have long-standing experience of defending in many of the most serious and complex criminal trials, appeals and extradition cases to come before the UK Supreme Court, Privy Council, Court of Appeal and High Court, as well as their daily work in the Crown and Magistrates' Courts. Abroad they appear in the courts of Northern Ireland, Hong Kong, Singapore, the Caribbean, South America, the International Criminal Court and the European Court of Human Rights.

The Criminal Appeals Unit at Doughty Street Chambers spans all this criminal work, and is widely regarded as home to several of the best appellate lawyers in the UK. Members of the team regularly appear as fresh counsel in appeal matters and have appeared in many of the most important appeal cases rectifying miscarriages of justice. A wrongful conviction or sentence at any level can have a devastating impact on an appellant and their family, and the appeal specialists at Doughty Street Chambers advise across the full range of cases, from the relatively minor, challenging decisions of magistrates, right up to appeals in cases of homicide and terrorism, and appearing at all levels up to the Supreme Court and the European Court of Human Rights. Their work includes appeals to the Court of Appeal on sentencing (including whole life tariffs and indeterminate sentences), and on appeals against conviction, including issues such as jury irregularities, psychiatric issues (eg automatism, loss of control and diminished responsibility), anonymous witnesses, fresh evidence and deficient trial representation. Their work also includes fraud and confiscation appeals, appeals by way of Case Stated and Judicial Review and applications to the Criminal Cases Review Commission.

Doughty Street Chambers also offers its solicitor clients use of a Criminal Appeals Advice Line, which provides free preliminary advice and guidance for those considering potential appeals and CCRC matters. More information on this, and the criminal appeals and other barristers at Doughty Street Chambers, can be found at www.doughtystreet.co.uk or by e-mailing crime@doughtystreet.co.uk.